GEIR LUNDESTAD

INTERNATIONAL RELATIONS SINCE 1945

Sara Miller McCune founded SAGE Publishing in 1965 to support the dissemination of usable knowledge and educate a global community. SAGE publishes more than 1000 journals and over 800 new books each year, spanning a wide range of subject areas. Our growing selection of library products includes archives, data, case studies and video. SAGE remains majority owned by our founder and after her lifetime will become owned by a charitable trust that secures the company's continued independence.

Los Angeles | London | New Delhi | Singapore | Washington DC | Melbourne

GEIR LUNDESTAD

INTERNATIONAL RELATIONS SINCE 1945

EAST, WEST, NORTH, SOUTH
8TH EDITION

Los Angeles | London | New Delhi
Singapore | Washington DC | Melbourne

Los Angeles | London | New Delhi
Singapore | Washington DC | Melbourne

SAGE Publications Ltd
1 Oliver's Yard
55 City Road
London EC1Y 1SP

SAGE Publications Inc.
2455 Teller Road
Thousand Oaks, California 91320

SAGE Publications India Pvt Ltd
B 1/I 1 Mohan Cooperative Industrial Area
Mathura Road
New Delhi 110 044

SAGE Publications Asia-Pacific Pte Ltd
3 Church Street
#10-04 Samsung Hub
Singapore 049483

© Geir Lundestad 2018

Fifth edition published 2005. Reprinted 2007, 2008, 2009.
Sixth edition published 2011.
Seventh edition published 2014.
This edition first published 2018.

Editor: Natalie Aguilera
Assistant editor: Delayna Spencer
Production editor: Katie Forsythe
Copyeditor: Mary Dalton
Proofreader: Clare Weaver
Indexer: Adam Pozner
Marketing manager: Susheel Gokarakonda
Cover design: Stephanie Guyaz
Typeset by: C&M Digitals (P) Ltd, Chennai, India
Printed by CPI Group (UK) Ltd, Croydon, CR0 4YY

Library of Congress Control Number: 2017940489

British Library Cataloguing in Publication data

A catalogue record for this book is available from
the British Library

ISBN 978-1-4739-7345-9
ISBN 978-1-4739-7346-6 (pbk)

At SAGE we take sustainability seriously. Most of our products are printed in the UK using FSC papers and boards.
When we print overseas we ensure sustainable papers are used as measured by the PREPS grading system.
We undertake an annual audit to monitor our sustainability.

CONTENTS

CONTENTS

ABOUT THE AUTHOR

Geir Lundestad was born in 1945. He was professor of history and American Civilization at the University of Tromsø from 1974 to 1990. He has held fellowships at Harvard University (1978–79, 1983) and the Woodrow Wilson Center in Washington, DC (1988–89).

From 1990 to 2014 Lundestad was the director of the Norwegian Nobel Institute and permanent secretary of the Norwegian Nobel Committee. The Committe awards the Nobel Peace Prize. From 1991 to 2014 he was also adjunct professor of international history at the University of Oslo.

Lundestad has written numerous books and articles on the Cold War and on transatlantic relations. His most recent books are *The Rise & Decline of the American 'Empire'. Power and its Limits in Comparative Perspective* (Oxford: Oxford University Press, 2012) and, edited, *International Relations Since the End of the Cold War. New & Old Dimensions* (Oxford: Oxford University Press, 2013). He has also written books in Norwegian about the history of the Nobel Peace Prize.

FROM THE PREFACE TO THE FIRST EDITION

Books that deal with international politics after 1945 are not exactly scarce. Why, then, one more? My response to that question is threefold.

In the first place, very few such surveys have been published in the Scandinavian languages. By far the greatest number are in English. This book attempts to present extensive international research to Scandinavian readers. At the same time, it is my hope that the English translation will fulfill a need outside Scandinavia.

In the second place, nearly all the existing works, also among the English literature on the subject, are limited to one or at most a few main aspects of international politics after 1945. There are many works on relations between East and West, fewer on relations between North and South, and even fewer on relations between the United States and Western Europe. Of course it has been necessary to make a selection of themes even in this book. However, there can be no doubt that the breadth of selection is great. Perhaps some readers will feel that it is too great.

In the third place, during my many years of teaching I have experienced that the existing works are unsatisfactory. To some extent their choice of themes is too limited. To some extent they are either so historically detailed that the main lines of development disappear, at least for many readers, or they are so theoretical that they do not provide the minimum of factual and chronological information that even such theoretical generalizations ought to be based on.

This book deals with relations between East and West in general, and between the United States and the Soviet Union in particular; with the arms race, relations within the Western and the Communist camps, and North–South relations (decolonization and economic issues).

It is obvious that so many themes cannot be dealt with in depth in a little over 300 pages. The book is in many ways intended as an introduction to the subject. Even so, I believe that the method of presentation is highly significant for the insight the reader is able to acquire into international politics after 1945. This book places less emphasis on describing concrete events than is normally the case in historical presentations. Such descriptions are readily available elsewhere.

On the other hand, correspondingly greater emphasis has been placed on presenting long-term trends and on analyzing motivating forces and cause–effect relationships. It is my hope that this method of presentation will be of benefit not only to students, but to the so-called general reader as well, whoever that may be. I believe it is important to create as much understanding as possible of historical interrelatedness, of the major development trends.

The method of presentation I have chosen probably makes the book more subjective than many others. It is easier, and less controversial, to describe than to explain. I have tried to compensate for this in three ways. First, with regard to particularly controversial issues I try to give the reader a summary of various interpretations of the historical topic. Moreover, I state my own view relatively openly, so that the reader will be able to identify it and react to it. In East–West issues I consider myself one of the so-called post-revisionists; in North–South questions I am more skeptical of structuralist than of liberalist theories. (These will be encountered later in the book.) In general I have an ingrained skepticism of single-factor explanations. Finally, despite my personal viewpoints, I have tried to leave some of my most subjective hobby-horses in the stable.

This book deals with international politics, or in other words with relations between nations. Although it covers many themes and tries to be relatively global in its perspective, it is not a comprehensive world history. Domestic affairs are only discussed to the extent that they can shed light on nations' foreign policies. The book is also mainly concerned with top-level politics. This is due in part to the fact that it is at this level that decisions are most often made, in part to the fact that there is not sufficient space to take up a discussion of decision-making processes in the various countries. Formulations that depict nations as units, such as 'the United States acted thus' or 'Britain believed thus and so', can likewise be attributed to considerations of simplification.

The two superpowers, the United States and the Soviet Union, have been accorded the most attention because they have been the two most central actors during the post-war period. The United States has probably been granted more space than the Soviet Union, partly because it has been the more dominant of the two superpowers, and not least because our knowledge is so much greater about the open United States than about the more closed Soviet Union.

The method of presentation I have chosen does not entail only advantages. I should like to mention some of the disadvantages. The historian keeps separate from one another events that make up an organic whole in real life. This infringement on reality is probably greater in a thematic arrangement than in a chronological one. For instance, relations between East and West, between the United States and Western Europe and the arms race are closely intertwined. Here they are analyzed in separate chapters. Certain repetitions from one chapter to another have thus become necessary. However, I have used cross-references more than repetition.

Of course not all the chapters are based on the same degree of research and reflection. Certain sections are relatively analytical, others more descriptive. This is virtually inevitable in a work of this type. I hope that the book will be well received nonetheless, and that it will satisfy a true need. If that proves to be so, advice and comments from my readers may make future editions even more satisfactory. In any case, history is never written once and for all. It must be written over and over again.

PREFACE TO THE EIGHTH EDITION

Over the years *East, West, North, South* has become available in Norwegian, Swedish, English, Chinese (Mandarin, first Taiwan, then Beijing), Russian and Turkish. While the first three editions were published first in Norwegian, the last five have been presented first in English.

In the eighth edition the changes are comprehensive. First, the story has been updated to January 2017. Second, I have also taken the opportunity to go through the entire manuscript again and make changes reflecting the most recent literature on the many topics dealt with in this book. The sections on the environment and on regionalism have been substantially strengthened. More theory has been included to make the book even more relevant not only for future historians, but also for political scientists. Needless to say, the relevant literature is vast and not always easy to fit into a framework first developed in 1985. Yet, I have been pleased to see that so many of my early interpretations have held up rather well over the years.

I am very grateful to Senior Commissioning Editor Natalie Aguilera and Commissioning Editor Amy Jarrold at Sage for taking the initiative on the Eighth Edition and for soliciting responses from English-language users of the book. These responses have been very helpful in making the changes in this edition.

I am also grateful for responses from other readers of the book. Their letters have reduced the number of mistakes in the book. For the remaining ones I am solely responsible.

G.L.
January 2017

ONLINE RESOURCES

CHAPTER 1

- Wikipedia has provided a valuable resource throughout the present work. Many different items have been consulted in virtually all chapters. http://en.wikipedia. org/wiki/mainpage

CHAPTERS 2-7

- There are many useful online resources relevant to the study of the Cold War. The US Department of State through the Office of the Historian has provided much useful material, also in the Foreign Relations of the United States (FRUS) series available on the net, http://history.state.gov/historicaldocuments
- H-Diplo, Diplomatic and International History Discussion Network, regularly publishes valuable debates about the most important new books being published, www.h-net.org/~diplo
- Declassified Documents Reference Services (DDRS) has published more than 500,000 previously published documents, http://gdc.gale.com/products/declassi fied-documents-reference-system. In an unofficial way, WikiLeaks has done the same, http://wikileaks.org

CHAPTER 8

- SIPRI Yearbook Online presents the resources of the yearbooks in a convenient form. http://www.sipriyearbook.org

CHAPTERS 13-14

- The yearly World Development Report provides the most useful statistical infor- mation about economic and social developments in most of the world's countries, http://wdronline.worldbank.org
- The World Bank eAtlases are also useful, http://data.worldbank.org/about/country- classifications/world-bank-atlas-method

THE NEW WORLD

THE RISE AND FALL OF GREAT POWERS

Whether we call them superpowers, Great Powers, empires or hegemons, one thing seems certain: they come and go, they rise and fall. No state has managed to remain permanently Number One; although few, if any, historical laws exist, it is most unlikely that any state will in the future be able to remain permanently on top. As we learned from our Eurocentric history books, the Roman Empire rose and fell; so did the Carolingian Empire (732–814), the Habsburg Empire, and, allegedly, three German Reichs; so did the British and the French colonial empires; and by 1991 the Soviet empire had not only collapsed, but the Soviet Union itself was dissolved into its 15 constituent parts.

In a wider geographical context, after the fall of the Roman Empire the vast Muslim expansion started with Mohammed in the 620s, and ended with the fall of Baghdad to the Mongols in 1258. The conquered territory stretched from the initial base in Saudi Arabia, to Spain in the west, and Uzbekistan in the east. The Mongols under Genghis Khan (1162–1227) and Tamerlane (1336–1405) established one of the biggest empires ever, combining ruthlessness with surprising ethnic and religious tolerance. As John Darwin has argued, Tamerlane's 'empire was the last attempt to challenge the partition of Eurasia between the states of the Far West, Islamic Middle Eurasia and Confucian East Asia.' Yet that vast empire was soon divided into several different parts. Empires in Byzantium (395–1453), and various versions in different centuries in Iran, rose and fell. In the sixteenth and seventeenth centuries the Ottoman Empire (1299–1922) threatened even Vienna, until it started its protracted decline that ended with modern Turkey.

The Mogul Empire in India flourished for a few centuries until even its last formal remnants were abolished in 1857. China remained dominant much longer. Centuries earlier its position had been quite similar to that of the Roman Empire. The two empires were broadly comparable in terms of size and population, and for a certain period even somewhat alike in chronological terms, although the Chinese empire lasted well beyond the fall of Rome in 395.

It has been estimated that as late as 1800 China's share of world manufacturing output was still 33.3 per cent, and India's 19.7, while Europe as a whole produced

28.1 per cent. With the exception of Britain, even at this late stage production was still primarily a reflection of population. The greater the population, the greater was generally the production. As a matter of course China viewed itself as the leader of the world, as could be witnessed in Emperor Qianlong's reply to Lord Macartney in 1793 when the latter, on behalf of King George III, asked for the establishment of trade and diplomatic relations between Britain and China:

> We have never valued ingenious articles, nor do we have the slightest need for your country's manufactures. Therefore, O king, as regards your request to send someone to remain at the capital, while it is not in harmony with the regulations of the Celestial Empire we also feel very much that it is of no advantage to your country.

With the financial and industrial revolutions throughout the nineteenth century, this situation changed rapidly, so that in 1900 China's and India's percentages had been reduced to 6.2 and 1.7 per cent respectively, while Britain's share alone was 18.5 and that of the United States 23.6 (see Table 1.1).

Thus, the Eastern expansion was replaced by a huge Western wave that, to simplify matters vastly, could be said to have started in 1492 when Columbus discovered America and the *Reconquista* in Spain was completed with the fall of Granada, reversing the wave of Muslim expansion. First Spain and Portugal, then Britain and France, and even smaller European countries, established their vast colonial empires. From its small base, Britain came to control about 20–25 per cent of the world's territory and population. North and South America, Australia, much of Asia, and even more of Africa, came under European control. Colonial control appeared to last forever, but of course it did not. The United States was the first colony to establish its independence.

Europe's supremacy rested on several pillars. European powers took the lead in technology and finance. Weapons technology was certainly an important part of this. Small Western forces could defeat large non-European ones. The development of relatively effective nation states was also important. They were able to use the available resources more effectively than other units. Finally, most non-European systems of government were in various stages of decline from the sixteenth–seventeenth century onwards. This was the case in China, in India and in several parts of Africa.

In many ways Europe still dominated the world during the years between the two world wars. The European empires still ruled much of the world, with the British Empire reaching its maximum extent in the interwar years. International politics to a large extent still focused on relations between the European Great Powers. Many of the dominant issues were resolved by the leading European powers. Thus, in the summit at Munich in September 1938, Germany, Britain, France and Italy participated to decide the future of Czechoslovakia – and about war and peace, at least in Europe. In Asia, Japan had become the preeminent power.

After its intervention in the First World War, the United States had chosen to revert to 'isolationism' in security matters vis-à-vis Europe. After the revolution in 1917 that turned Russia into the Soviet Union it too had become largely an outsider in international politics. The Kremlin concentrated on building 'socialism in one country.'

Table 1.1 Relative Shares of World Manufacturing Output, 1750–1900

	1750	1800	1830	1860	1880	1900
(Europe as a whole)	23.2	28.1	34.2	53.2	61.3	62.0
United Kingdom	1.9	4.3	9.5	19.9	22.9	18.5
Habsburg Empire	2.9	3.2	3.2	4.2	4.4	4.7
France	4.0	4.2	5.2	7.9	7.8	6.8
German States/Germany	2.9	3.5	3.5	4.9	8.5	13.2
Italian States/Italy	2.4	2.5	2.3	2.5	2.5	2.5
Russia	5.0	5.6	5.6	7.0	7.6	8.8
United States	0.1	0.8	2.4	7.2	14.7	23.6
Japan	3.8	3.5	2.8	2.6	2.4	2.4
Third World	73.0	67.7	60.5	36.6	20.9	11.0
China	32.8	33.3	29.8	19.7	12.5	6.2
India/Pakistan	24.5	19.7	17.6	8.6	2.8	1.7

Source: Kennedy, 1987, *The Rise and Fall of the Great Powers*

THE WORLD IN 1945

The world that emerged after the destruction of the Second World War was rather different from this previously Euro-centric one. The United States and the Soviet Union now emerged as the two leading powers. For more than a century observers had speculated that inevitably this was bound to happen. Only the United States and Russia, it was argued, had the resources and the population required to dominate great parts of the world. So powerful were these two powers that they now dominated even Europe itself. The United States came to take overall charge in Western Europe while the Soviet Union ruled with a firmer hand in the East. Outside Europe, the Second World War led to huge changes in the colonies, particularly in Asia. With India in the lead, the colonies were to become independent, although it took time before the world understood how truly momentous these changes were to be.

The most striking new feature of the world following the Second World War was the role of the United States. Even during 'isolationism,' US influence had been great in certain geographic areas, such as Latin America and the Pacific. Economically in terms of production, trade, and investments, the United States had long been a superpower. Economic relations with other countries increased after the Second World War, but not more than the overall growth of the national product.

What was new was first and foremost the military and political role the United States would play, not only in certain parts of the world, but virtually throughout the globe. In 1938 the US defense budget totaled slightly more than one billion dollars. The United States was not a part of any military alliance and had no troops stationed outside US-controlled areas. During the first years after the war the defense budget stabilized at around 12–13 billion dollars. The Rio Treaty and NATO were established, with the

United States as the dominant member in each of them. US forces participated in the occupation of Germany, Japan, Italy, and Austria. Bases were established in many different parts of the world.

The next major development in the role of the United States evolved from 1950 onwards, primarily due to the outbreak of the Korean War. The defense budget was tripled. Numerous treaties were established with countries around the world, especially in Asia. The United States took the initiative for the establishment of the South-East Asia Treaty Organization (SEATO) and was more loosely associated with the Baghdad Pact. In 1955 the United States had approximately 450 bases in 36 countries. Complementing these military commitments was its cultural influence, which was not easily quantifiable, but which was nevertheless highly significant.

The spread of US influence was due to the fact that it was the strongest country in the world. While all the other major powers had suffered heavy material losses during the war, the US economy had prospered. The gross national product increased (in 1958 prices) from 209.4 billion dollars in 1939 to 355.2 billion dollars in 1945, representing almost half of the total world production of goods and services. With 6 per cent of the world's population, the United States had 46 per cent of the world's electricity supply, 48 per cent of the radios, and 54 per cent of the telephones, and US companies controlled 59 per cent of the world's known oil reserves.

Until 1949 the United States had a monopoly on nuclear weapons, and after 1949 the country continued to have a considerable technological lead over the Soviet Union in both the military and nonmilitary spheres. The United States had the world's strongest air force and the world's leading navy. The United States and the Soviet Union each had about 12 million men under arms at the end of the Second World War.

Although US interests were not equally great in all parts of the world, and although remnants of isolationism persisted after 1945, the United States became a global power during this period. The United States had influence in more and larger parts of the world than the Soviet Union did. This influence often went deeper in the societies affected, economically and culturally as well as politically. The US expansion was thus more comprehensive than that of the Soviet Union. Several decades would pass before the Soviet Union was able to play a global role.

The power base of the Soviet Union was not comparable to that of the United States. The USSR had suffered enormous losses during the war. Its population was reduced by approximately 25 million. Whereas steel production in the United States had increased by 50 per cent during the war, Soviet steel production had been cut in half. Similar conditions existed in agriculture. In some areas they were two different worlds. The Soviet Union produced 65,000 cars a year, the United States seven million. According to extremely rough estimates, the Soviet national product in 1950 was less than one-fourth as large as that of the United States.

Nevertheless, the fact that the Soviet Union was now second-ranking among world powers represented something new. It was a superpower primarily in terms of military strength, especially the number of men under arms. After demobilization the Soviet Union had more troops than the United States, although Soviet demobilization was more extensive than was assumed at the time. Soviet strength was also ideological. The leaders in the Kremlin were convinced that history worked in their favor and that 'the contradictions among the capitalist powers' would greatly benefit the Communist cause. In most countries in the world significant groups supported the Soviet Union and communism. Yet, whereas the United States could choose from a broad arsenal of instruments, economic and cultural as well as political and military, the Soviet Union had to depend primarily on its military and, less so, ideological strength.

Soviet expansion was geographically less comprehensive than US expansion. On the other hand, it was more firmly established in the areas which were most important for the Soviet Union. The country increased its territory considerably: the Baltic countries, Eastern Karelia and Petsamo, the eastern parts of prewar Poland and the northern part of East Prussia, Carpathian Ukraine, Bessarabia and northern Bukovina, southern Sakhalin, and the Kurile Islands.

The Soviet role in countries beyond its neighboring areas was limited. But with its size and geographical location, this still meant that several central areas of the world almost automatically became significant for the leaders in Moscow. Moscow insisted on virtually complete control over large parts of Eastern Europe. Europe was most important for the Kremlin, as it was for the White House, but the position of the Soviet Union was strengthened in Asia as well, where it was dominant in North Korea and would gain significant influence in North Vietnam.

In 1948–49 the Communists, under the leadership of Mao Tse-tung, were victorious in China, the most populous country in the world. This was a victory won with little support from Moscow. However, Mao's assertion in 1958 that 'the Chinese revolution was victorious against the wishes of Stalin,' was an exaggeration. In 1950 China and the Soviet Union entered into a 30-year alliance. The leadership of Stalin and the Soviet Union within the Communist movement was indisputable, although the first cracks appeared with the break between Stalin and the Yugoslavian leader Tito in 1948.

After 1945, world politics was characterized by the conflict between the two new superpowers. Of course, unfriendly relations between the United States and the Soviet Union were nothing new. The rapport between these two countries had not been good after 1917. Diplomatic relations were not established until 1933. Previously, however, the temperature of such relations between the United States and the Soviet Union had had little significance for the overall international climate. Both the United States and the Soviet Union were outsiders in international politics. Both countries isolated themselves, and the Soviet Union was also isolated by the other major powers.

After the Second World War, the United States and the Soviet Union faced each other directly in various parts of the world. They were the two main actors in the international arena; the geographic distance separating them was gone, but the political distance would soon be greater than it had ever been. During the first years after the war, the Cold War between these two countries and their allies, between East and West, was concentrated on Europe, where both sides had their most important interests. The front lines froze quickly here. Outside Europe major changes could still take place without the superpowers being involved to any great extent. The civil war in China was the most obvious example of this. The Soviet Union gave some support to the Communists; the United States gave more support to its side, but compared with later events the restraint of the superpowers is striking.

The war had weakened the old major powers. Much of Germany and Japan lay in ruins. Germany was divided into zones controlled by the United States, the Soviet Union, the United Kingdom, and France, respectively. The intention was that these four should cooperate in governing the country until the Germans at some time in the future were capable of doing so themselves. However, the split between East and West resulted in a division into a large Western part and a smaller Eastern part. This division helped solve the traditional German problem in European politics, a problem which had been an important factor in the outbreak of both the First and Second World Wars. Germany should never again be allowed to become strong enough to dominate Europe. For some time it was accepted that Germany should remain demilitarized. But with the rapid escalation in superpower rivalry, East and West began to compete for German support. Thus even this aspect of occupation policy was subject to pressure.

In Japan the United States had things its own way, despite the formal apparatus that was established to give the other allies a certain degree of influence. The war in the East had been ended with the two atomic bombs over Hiroshima and Nagasaki. A new era had begun. Here, too, occupation policy was based on the premise that the occupied country should never again be given the opportunity to start a war. The United States was so firmly decided in this matter that a provision prohibiting military forces was included in the constitution. The war, and not least the two atomic bombs, had also caused fundamental changes in the attitudes of the Japanese.

In 1945 the United Kingdom was considered the third major power. Britain's contribution to the war had been considerable; no other country had so persistently fought against Hitler's Germany. Prime Minister Winston Churchill played an important role in wartime diplomacy. The United Kingdom was the head of a global empire, of the Commonwealth, as it was now called. The country also held a leading role among the other Western European countries and had the advantage of close relations with the United States.

However, in July 1945 Prime Minister Churchill was replaced by Clement Attlee, the leader of the Labour party. This change symbolized a new direction, with less emphasis on world politics and a greater focus on domestic affairs. Britain's position was clearly weakened compared to the period between the wars. A major reason for this decline was the cost of the war. War destruction totalled about £3 billion. Assets worth more than £1 billion had been sold overseas to finance the war. Revenue from investments abroad was halved. In 1945 the UK spent more than £2 billion abroad, while revenues were only £350 million. In order to rectify this imbalance, London had to ask other governments for help. In practice that meant Washington.

The United Kingdom was not the only country in Western Europe to pursue such policies. Almost without exception, they all asked the United States for support, both economic and political. In 1948–49 the European countries also exerted pressure on the United States to play a more active role in the military sphere.

Western Europe feared that the United States would return to isolationism. A new isolationism would be extremely harmful, most Europeans felt, much more so now than after the First World War. Destruction had been great in many areas. The need for economic assistance was correspondingly great. It became increasingly evident that Europe needed a counterpart to the local Soviet dominance. Only the United States could provide such a counterweight.

France had suffered a humiliating defeat in 1940. Despite the efforts of General Charles de Gaulle, the country could never regain the position it had formerly enjoyed. If Paris were to play a central role in international politics once more, it would have to do so as a spokesman for a concordant Western Europe. But despite the foundation the war had laid for such cooperation, there were many barriers: France itself was divided in its attitudes; the role of Germany was problematic; Britain was only mildly interested when all was said and done.

In one area the old European major powers could apparently still bask in the glory of the past. They had their colonies. The war was bound to mean changes for the better for the colonial subjects. But with the exception of India, where Britain had promised independence when the war was over, the colonial powers did not have the intention of freeing their colonies – at least not in the near future. Reforms were one thing, independence something quite different. In 1942 Churchill had pronounced the memorable words, 'I have not become the King's First Minister to preside over the liquidation of the British Empire.' Many British politicians and people were willing to go further than Churchill in terms of reforms. On the other hand, the other colonial powers were even more determined to regain control over their colonies than the United Kingdom was. In fact, France and Portugal claimed that the ties were to last forever. Colonies and mother country should merge and become one.

Surprisingly quickly, however, all this was to prove an illusion. The war had destroyed the old colonial magic, both for those ruling and for those ruled. What happened in India was soon to have dramatic consequences in Africa too. How Britain responded to her colonies was bound to affect the other colonial powers as well. The Euro-centric world of previous centuries was about to disintegrate.

THE NEW WORLD: THE LITERATURE

The bibliography and recommended literature supplied at the end of the various chapters has a limited objective. In the first place, it shows what works have been most important for this book, chapter by chapter. An exhaustive list of all the literature that has been used would have been much longer than the present one. In the second place, the aim is to give the interested reader ideas for further reading. Experience has told me that if the number of titles recommended or supplied is too great, it merely tends to discourage the reader. Those who may desire further suggestions will find many more in the books mentioned in the individual chapter bibliographies.

GENERAL SURVEYS

For the most recent example of the broad sweep of history, see John Darwin, *After Tamerlane – The Global History of Empire Since 1405* (London, 2007).

For a stimulating survey of the 'short' twentieth century, see Eric Hobsbawm, *Age of Extremes: The Short Twentieth Century 1914–1991* (London, 1994). Peter Calvocoressi, *World Politics Since 1945* (London, 2009) contains a wealth of information. More focused on the Cold War is P. M. H. Bell, *The World Since 1945: An International History* (London, 2001).

Among the abundance of surveys on US foreign policy after 1945, I recommend: Seyom Brown, *The Faces of Power: Constancy and Change in United States Foreign*

(Continued)

(Continued)

Policy from Truman to Clinton (New York, 1995). For many years the standard work on Soviet foreign policy was Adam B. Ulam, *Expansion and Coexistence: Soviet Foreign Policy, 1917–73* (New York, 1974). A useful version of history from the perspective that long prevailed in Moscow is *Soviet Foreign Policy: Volume II: 1945–1980* (Moscow, 1981). We lack an updated standard work on Soviet foreign policy from 1945 until the present based on all the new material that has been made accessible in recent years. Vladislav M. Zubok, *A Failed Empire: The Soviet Union in the Cold War from Stalin to Gorbachev* (Chapel Hill, NC, 2007) comes the closest.

Joan Edelman Spero, *The Politics of International Economic Relations* (New York, 1981 and subsequent editions) has been most useful, as it deals with economic relations between East and West, within the West and between North and South.

Paul Kennedy, *The Rise and Fall of the Great Powers: Economic Change and Military Conflict from 1500 to 2000* (New York, 1987) aroused debate in the late 1980s. A response to Kennedy may be found in Joseph S. Nye, *Bound to Lead: The Changing Nature of American Power* (New York, 1990). My own interpretation of the US role after 1945 in a comparative perspective has been presented in *The American 'Empire' and Other Studies of U.S. Foreign Policy in a Comparative Perspective* (Oxford–Oslo, 1990). The debate on the rise and fall of Great Powers is pursued further in Geir Lundestad (ed.), *The Fall of Great Powers: Peace, Stability, and Legitimacy* (Oslo–Oxford, 1994) and in Charles S. Maier, *Among Empires: American Ascendancy and its Predecessors* (Cambridge, MA, 2006); Stephen G. Brooks and William C. Wohlforth, *World Out of Balance. International Relations and the Challenge of American Primacy* (Princeton, NJ, 2008); Fareed Zakaria, *The Post-American World* (London, 2008) and in my own *The Rise and Decline of the American 'Empire': Power and its Limits in Comparative Perspective* (Oxford, 2012).

Much of the statistical material in this book has been derived from the World Bank, *World Development Report* (New York, 1983 and subsequent annual editions); the US Department of Commerce, *Historical Statistics of the United States: Colonial Times to 1970* (Washington, DC, 1975); the annual *Statistical Abstract of the United States* (Washington, DC, 1985 and subsequent editions), and from Herbert Block, *The Planetary Product in 1980: A Creative Pause?* (Washington, DC, 1981).

THE COLD WAR IN EUROPE, 1945-1949

POLITICAL SCIENCE AND HISTORY

In political science the study of international relations has been dominated by two basic general approaches, realism and liberalism. Realism was long the dominant approach. Its starting point was the anarchic nature of the international system, in the sense that the predominant consideration of each state was to protect its own security. You could never be certain what other states would do in the future. Therefore you had to prepare for the worst contingencies. In a world of sovereign states, international institutions mattered only on the margins. The international community differs from the domestic situation within individual nations in that there is no effective central power having more or less a monopoly of the use of force.

No state was really willing to leave its primary security requirement to an international authority. The United Nations could perform some useful functions, but the Great Powers all insisted on having a veto to stop the new organization from undertaking actions contrary to their interests. The Soviet Union came to use its veto quite frequently. Since the Western powers dominated the UN, they long had less of a need to use their vetos.

Conflicts are therefore inevitable in the international system. The normal state is rivalry rather than cooperation. Of course major powers can cooperate, but when they do so it is most often to face a joint threat. When the threat no longer exists, cooperation normally dissipates. In this perspective the antagonism between East and West is a new variation on a familiar theme. The coalition between the United States, the Soviet Union, and the United Kingdom was dissolved after Germany and Japan were defeated in 1945. A similar situation pertained after the Napoleonic wars and after the First World War. But the objection can be raised that the tension between East and West after the Second World War reached a higher level than after earlier, corresponding conflicts.

There is a lot to be said for this general theory, but it should be remembered that in the course of history there have been long periods in which the tension was kept at a relatively low level. The years from 1815 to 1914 may serve as an example of this. Liberalists argue that basic security requirements are tempered by many different considerations. Trade and numerous other forms of contact are growing among states. Environmental concerns represent a challenge to the entire planet. The result is increasing economic interdependence and the gradual emergence of a transnational global society. Some states are also more peaceful than others and liberalists argue that democracies tend to be more peaceful than authoritarian states, at least in relations with other democracies. As democracy spreads throughout the world the prospects for peace should improve.

The debate between realists and liberals has really gone on for centuries. Realists date their history back to the Greek historian Thucydides (c. 460–400 BC) and philosopher Thomas Hobbes (1588–1679); liberals go back to eighteenth-century philosophers Immanuel Kant, Baron de Montesquieu and John Stuart Mill. Realists point out that time and again our hopes for peace have been frustrated. Every major war leads to expectations of peace that are not fulfilled. Liberals argue that realists focus only on extreme situations. There is not only conflict in international relations, but also growing cooperation in many important fields.

Historians tend to be skeptical towards single theories that try to explain most if not all aspects of human behavior. Wars do not all have the same explanations. Except in certain rather abstract ways, the causes of the First and Second World Wars and of the Cold War were all different. With growing globalization cooperation has also been strengthened among many different states. Historians therefore focus on explanations more specific for the conflict or the cooperation at hand. Grand theories also have a tendency to underestimate the importance of the many different local actors in the many conflicts of the world. The outcomes of the conflicts in Korea, Vietnam, in the Middle East and elsewhere were thus determined by a complex interplay of Great Power, regional and local factors.

SOME OLD AND NEW THEORIES ABOUT THE COLD WAR

Why did antagonism develop between East and West after the Second World War? There are nearly as many answers to that question as there are historians who have researched the subject. Nonetheless, their answers could long be grouped into three rather loose schools of thought. Representatives of these main schools are often called traditionalists (Herbert Feis, William McNeill, Arthur M. Schlesinger, Jr.), revisionists (William Appleman Williams, Gabriel Kolko, Lloyd Gardner), and post-revisionists (John Lewis Gaddis, Daniel Yergin). All three schools are represented among scholars today, although they have dominated during different periods. The traditionalists held sway almost alone until the mid-1960s. Then a strong revisionist wave took hold, to be succeeded by post-revisionism in the course of the 1970s. Later a number of leading revisionists came to be drawn towards post-revisionism (Thomas Paterson and Melvyn Leffler).

The scholarly debate on the origins of the Cold War was long dominated by Americans. Soviet writings tended to reflect official attitudes. In Western Europe, the number of generalized accounts long greatly exceeded the number of specialized studies. Most of these accounts were clearly traditionalist in tone (André Fontaine, Raymond Aron, Desmond Donnelly, Wilfrid Knapp), although a few showed revisionist inclinations (Claude Julien). A variety of post-revisionist ideas emerged during the 1970s and 1980s (Wilfried Loth, Geir Lundestad), but post-revisionism was an even more complex phenomenon in Western Europe than in the United States. The present account is written in a post-revisionist spirit.

Many factors distinguish the three schools. Three questions are particularly pertinent in defining them: Who was responsible for the Cold War? Who was most active in the years immediately following the Second World War? What are the primary motivating forces, particularly for US foreign policy?

Few people, if any, maintain that all the blame can be placed solely on one side. After all, this is a question of interplay among several actors. However, the traditionalists hold the Soviet Union primarily accountable for the Cold War. The revisionists place the responsibility on the United States, whereas the post-revisionists either do not say much about this question, or they stress the mutual accountability of the two countries more than the other two schools do.

The question of blame is closely linked to an analysis of which side was most active in the years immediately following the Second World War. According to the traditionalists, US policy was characterized by passivity. Washington emphasized international cooperation within bodies such as the UN and attempted to a certain extent to negotiate between the two major antagonists, Britain and the Soviet Union. Demobilization of the armed forces was effected at a rapid pace. Not until 1947 did Washington change its course, and then as a response to Soviet expansion in Eastern Europe. The Truman Doctrine and the Marshall Plan were the turning points.

The revisionists present an entirely different picture. Even before the war had ended, the United States had tried to limit the influence of the Soviet Union and of leftist forces throughout the world. The United States had such wide-ranging goals that it came into conflict even with the United Kingdom. In order to attain their goals, the Americans employed a number of different instruments, from atomic bombs to loans and other forms of economic support. The Soviet Union is considered defensive in orientation. Soviet policies in Eastern Europe were to a great extent a response to American ambitions in the area.

The post-revisionists agree with the revisionists that important elements in US policy had fallen into place before the Truman Doctrine and the Marshall Plan. They also agree that the United States implemented a number of different measures to promote its interests. But they maintain that the revisionists are too eager to perceive the use of these measures as motivated only by anti-Soviet considerations. They also reject the idea that Soviet policy in Eastern Europe can be considered a result of US ambitions.

With regard to the motivating forces behind US policies, the traditionalists emphasize the US need to defend its own and Western Europe's legitimate security interests in the face of an expansive Soviet Union. These security interests coincide with the defense of democratic rights. The revisionists, however, perceive US policy as determined primarily by the needs of capitalism and a fundamental anti-communism. The post-revisionists claim that all these motivating forces played a part. They also include a number of additional factors, such as the role played by public opinion, the Congress, and various pressure groups. The relative significance attributed to the different factors varies from author to author, but the post-revisionists consider economic conditions less significant than the revisionists do. On the other hand, they disagree with the traditionalists' almost total dismissal of such motivating forces for US policy.

Perception of the motivating forces behind Soviet policies does not distinguish the schools to the same degree as attitudes towards the United States do. There is, however, a tendency for traditionalists to perceive Soviet policy as motivated by considerations of ideology and expansionism, whereas the revisionists place greater emphasis on the security needs of the Soviet Union. Once more the post-revisionists stress plurality, emphasizing that one type of explanation need not exclude the other.

In recent years the debate on the origins of the Cold War has become increasingly complex. While the three main schools of interpretation are still very much alive, certain new trends are noticeable. First, the emphasis has shifted from a post-revisionist towards a more traditionalist direction again. Post-revisionism was felt to be too vague; it contained both left- and right-of-center elements. The material more lately made available by the Russian side served to underline the links between domestic and foreign policy. The surprise for many was the extent to which Stalin and other Russian leaders saw almost everything in ideological terms, including in their own internal debates and presentations. This renewed emphasis on ideology, and particularly on a Soviet 'revolutionary–imperial' paradigm, has moved the debate to the right again and was seen both with well-established scholars (John Lewis Gaddis, Vojtech Mastny) and with some scholars of Russian origins (Vladislav Zubok, Constantine Pleshakov, Vladimir Pechatnov).

Second, a whole series of new perspectives has been developed. The role of Britain has emerged again after an extended period of emphasis on the two superpowers (David Reynolds). Historians from a range of other countries have also added their respective national perspectives. Non-European actors have been analyzed more in general as well (Odd Arne Westad). The local scene was often of greater importance than earlier analyses suggested. This multilingual and multinational new Cold War history liked to see itself as transcending the old historiographical schools, although it was often not particularly difficult to fit the new wine into the old bottles.

SOME STRUCTURAL EXPLANATIONS FOR THE COLD WAR

Historians can describe what happened and suggest explanations as to why certain events occurred. Causal explanations, in particular, often contain an element of attributing blame or responsibility. But any discussion of blame and responsibility is also influenced by the author's appraisal of how advantageous the outcome of a situation was. Whether the outcome was good or bad is, however, a political conclusion. In such appraisals the judgment of historians is no better than anyone else's. In line with that reasoning, this post-revisionist presentation will describe US and Soviet policies and attempt to say something about the motivating forces behind those policies. The question of blame will not be explicitly considered, despite the place it has been granted in historians' writings.

The outbreak of the Cold War can be analyzed on several different levels. A number of features were determined by the international system as such, while others were linked to ideologies, nations, and individuals. The more general explanations will be considered here; the more specific ones will be dealt with in the section on motivating forces behind the superpowers' policies.

The changes that resulted from the Second World War were enormous. The most important change was the vacuum created by the defeat of Germany and Japan. This theory is most clearly presented by Louis Halle in his book *The Cold War as History*:

> the decision to eliminate German power from Europe rather than make ... peace was the basic cause of the Cold War. ... It is evident that such a vacuum can hardly persist, even for a week. It had to be filled by something.

Both the United States and the Soviet Union were capable of filling the vacuums in Europe and Asia, and the two new superpowers were both drawn into them. Since there was no mutually acceptable way of filling them, conflict was the inevitable result.

Ever new vacuums would arise during the postwar period. Conditions in Central Europe and Eastern Asia were scarcely stabilized before the colonial empires began to crumble. As the new nations of Asia and Africa suffered from a lack of domestic stability and as the former colonial powers were often unable to fill the vacuums which arose, the stage was set once more for a conflict between the two superpowers, the United States and the Soviet Union. To an increasing degree, the most important conflicts between East and West took place in Asia and Africa.

The tension between the United States and the Soviet Union was naturally also affected by the fact that the two countries had differing political and economic systems. The systems were not only different; the two countries mutually denounced each other's system. The ideological gap made cooperation difficult and a sober analysis of the adversary nearly impossible. This had been evident even before the Second World War. Relations between the United States and the Soviet Union were poor then, too. The new element was that the two powers now confronted each other face to face in several parts of the world.

The assertion has even been made that these were different types of people confronting each other: on the one side the Russians, who have often been described as insecure, fearful of the outside world, and with a clear inferiority complex towards the West; on the other side the Americans, who supposedly represented the opposite qualities – optimistic, superior, and expansive.

This factor cannot be discounted, although many historians are skeptical about explanations based on distinctive national characteristics. The picture was certainly not uncomplicated. The Americans may well have felt that they were God's chosen people, but the fear of evil was also present, as the Communist witch hunt showed. The isolationism of the period between the wars did not indicate a strong feeling of confidence towards the rest of the world. However, the political climate was far different from that of the Soviet Union. 'Enemies' of the United States lost their reputations; 'enemies' of the Soviet state lost their lives.

The differing political and economic systems are a more concrete factor than the various personality types. The fact that the United States was capitalist and the Soviet Union communist was highly significant. A few comments are needed, however, to shed light on the fact that there were certain complications involved in even this apparently obvious explanation of the antagonism between the United States and the Soviet Union.

In the first place, social democracy did not necessarily represent a sort of middle course that could tone down the conflict, even though many people were convinced

well, manifest destiny was a big part of W. expansion towards CA etc.

that this was so. Relations between Britain and the Soviet Union were no better than between the United States and the Soviet Union. Until the spring of 1946, the Labour government in London was more sharply criticized by Moscow than the Truman administration in Washington was. On several vital issues regarding Germany and Poland, antagonism was even greater between Britain and the Soviet Union than between the United States and the Soviet Union, although the two Western powers had relatively close ties. And, as we shall see, many of the new initiatives in US policy – such as the Truman Doctrine, the Marshall Plan, and NATO – were measures that were eagerly applauded by the British government. In fact, they were not only endorsed, but even to a certain degree initiated or at least encouraged by the British.

In the second place, the alliance during the war had created an atmosphere which influenced the climate in the postwar years. The Soviet attitude towards the United States – as expressed during the war in Stalin's declarations, in his correspondence with Roosevelt, and in the Soviet press – mellowed somewhat. Even so, this shift was quite insignificant compared to the change in the United States. A minority continued to be extremely suspicious of the Soviet Union, but the vast majority changed their minds dramatically. The American press regularly printed articles praising the Soviet Union. The conservative weekly *Life* magazine proclaimed that Lenin was 'perhaps the greatest man of modern times.' Nor was there any reason to fear the Soviet Union, because the Russians 'look like Americans, dress like Americans, and think like Americans.'

In 1943 and early in 1944, nearly all the experts on the Soviet Union who had been skeptical of Moscow before the war felt that it should be possible to cooperate after the war. Gallup polls showed that as late as August 1945, 54 per cent of the American population believed that the Soviet Union was to be trusted and felt that the USSR would cooperate with the United States. This was only 1 per cent less than the highest level during the entire war, which was registered in February 1945. Thirty per cent said that the Soviet Union could not be trusted, while 16 per cent had no opinion.

Thus a majority believed that it would be possible to continue to cooperate after the war. Even more, no doubt, hoped to avoid conflict. The transition from war to Cold War is sometimes made too automatic. It was politically impossible to go directly from one to the other. Only gradually did leaders and public opinion lose this optimism and prepare themselves for a new conflict.

The past bound East and West together, but only parts of the past. For there were also other experiences, which in the short term had limited influence but which would soon become more important. For the Soviet Union, in a long-term perspective these included all the invasions from the West, from the Vikings to Hitler, and in a more short-term perspective all the unfulfilled promises of the Second Front in 1942, as well as what Stalin considered suspicious contacts between the Western powers and Hitler's Germany. Moscow's conclusion was that in order to ensure its own security the Soviet Union would have to rely solely on itself.

The Americans were equally interested in what they could learn from the war. An important lesson was that aggression had to be contained as early as possible; encouraged by previous successes, Hitler's ambitions had grown continually. Feelings of guilt in the United States about their former isolationism reinforced this way of thinking.

The war had definitively ended American isolationism. Pearl Harbor had shown that the United States was vulnerable to attack. The Pacific and Atlantic oceans did

[handwritten margin notes: There was appreciation, I think, for their advances in space tech like Sputnik although that was a bit later]

[handwritten margin notes: in this particular situation or in general?]

[handwritten margin notes: which is why his nse to power is easier to understand — it was gradual and people didn't realize what was happening]

not make an attack on the United States impossible. New long-distance bombers and new weapons, not least the atomic bomb, made the world even smaller. The United States had to play an active part in order to prevent new wars and to create a world in accordance with American interests.

WHO ACTED WHERE?

The United States would come to play a part in politics throughout the world, although American influence was not equally pervasive in all parts of the globe. Soviet policy was less ambitious geographically, but the desire to dominate was even stronger in the areas which were most important to Moscow. The clash was between two different views. The United States and the Soviet Union, East and West, quite simply had conflicting interests in several countries and regions.

US Policy

The Americans had always considered themselves something special. In their own opinion, they represented principles that were not primarily in the interest of the United States, but rather in the interest of the entire world. These principles had been proclaimed by President Wilson in his Fourteen Points during the First World War. Even isolationism was a way of emphasizing the unique nature of the United States. The issues of European strife had no bearing on the country. The main dividing line in international politics was between the United States and all other major powers, not between groups of major powers. There was a constant fear that American ideals would be defiled by foreign influence. The strength of the United States was underestimated.

The war had shown that it did make a difference to the United States who controlled Europe. The country had closer ties with some powers than with others. But the belief that the United States had a special mission persisted. Wilson's Fourteen Points were reiterated in modified versions in the Atlantic Charter of August 1941 and in the Declaration on Liberated Europe from the Yalta Conference in February 1945. They also formed part of the background for the new international organizations.

With the enthusiasm that new converts often have, the United States was going to create a new foundation for peace and cooperation between nations. America was going to protect the world against the power politics of the old major powers – politics that had drawn the world into so many conflicts. The key phrases were international cooperation, self-government by the people, anti-colonialism and freer trade between nations. In the political sphere the United Nations was to be the central body. It was to be supplemented by others, such as regular meetings between the foreign ministers of the major powers. The United States would participate in international politics in an entirely different way than previously. No issue would be foreign to Washington any more. The so-called Bretton Woods institutions, the World Bank and the International Monetary Fund, were to be central actors in the economic sphere. Through an active lending policy and stable exchange rates they were to increase international trade, promote economic growth, and in so doing ostensibly contribute to ensuring world peace.

Although many leading Americans understood that the major powers would have unequal influence in various parts of the world, the overall ideology represented a sharp break with anything resembling the outdated policy of spheres of interest. As President Franklin D. Roosevelt expressed it in reference to the Yalta Conference: 'It spells the end of the system of unilateral action, exclusive alliances, and spheres of influence, and the balance of power and all the other expedients which have been tried for centuries and have failed.'

Under this ideal surface, concrete policies were adapted to US interests and other practical realities. The UN system would be strongly dominated by the United States and its friends. Free trade intrinsically favors the country with the strongest economy. Despite its high ideals, the United States would both have its cake and eat it. There were not to be spheres of interest, but the United States would continue to have a high degree of control over Latin America. Colonies and mandates were to be placed under international supervision, with the exception of the areas the United States was to have command over. The Rhine and the Danube were to be internationalized, but not the Panama Canal. Free trade was to be combined with protectionism where this best suited the United States. The Soviet Union was to have little say in the occupation of Italy and Japan, but the United States tried to have more of a say in the former enemy countries of Eastern Europe.

The war had undoubtedly suppressed most of the skepticism about the Soviet Union. But there were always 20 per cent or more who maintained that the United States could not trust the Soviets. As early as in the autumn of 1944 there were obvious signs that the climate was changing. In the State Department, the experts on the Soviet Union recovered their old skepticism. The lack of Soviet support – and sympathy – for the Polish uprising against the Germans in Warsaw during the summer and autumn of 1944 was particularly important in this context. According to expert opinions, the Kremlin now seemed determined to gain control of Poland, Romania, and Bulgaria. The war had not after all altered the policies of the Soviet leaders. The experts on the Soviet Union were supported by the Secretary of the Navy, James Forrestal, although the military establishment was not at all among the most staunch critics of the USSR. During the course of 1945, the signs of tough Soviet policies in Eastern Europe became clearer. Skepticism of the Soviet Union was strengthened and spread to ever new parts of the administration.

President Roosevelt was one among many who hoped to achieve cooperation with the Soviet Union. He was also one of the few who understood that it would be necessary to make considerable concessions to the Soviet Union in Eastern Europe in order to continue this cooperation. However, he did little to prepare public opinion for this type of concession. The general public wanted good relations with Moscow, but there were few indications that they were willing to sacrifice American ideals in Eastern Europe. In private, Roosevelt could accept the system of spheres of interest that Stalin and Churchill agreed on in October 1944, but it would have been political suicide to have publicly advocated this course of policy.

Just before his death in April 1945, Roosevelt was in the process of changing his view of the possibilities of continued cooperation with the Soviet Union. The new President, Harry Truman, intensified this skepticism, although during the first few months of his administration he was understandably uncertain as to exactly what policy to pursue.

From the time of the meeting of foreign ministers in London in September–October 1945 there was an open split between the United States and Britain, on the one hand, and the Soviet Union on the other. Now public opinion and attitudes in Congress began to change in earnest. The hopes for cooperation had been high. The disappointment at not having succeeded was thus even greater. From having believed that the Soviet Union was perhaps not so unlike the United States, a large part of public opinion swung to believing that Stalin was a new Hitler. Not much time was required to move from one extreme to the other.

The United States could not achieve the comprehensive policy goals it had laid out. Although the Americans may have underestimated their own strength before the Second World War, there were indications that they overestimated it after the war. These indications would become stronger as the postwar period progressed. This was probably mainly due to the ambitious nature of their goals, for the means which were available were considerable. The United States had a monopoly on nuclear weapons. There was a definite expectation in Washington that the atomic bomb, by its mere existence, would have a moderating effect on the Soviet Union. For instance, it would have a deterrent effect with regard to possible Soviet plans for an attack on Western Europe. However, there were few people in Eastern Europe who could see any positive effect of the new weapon. (The atomic bomb will be discussed in more detail on pp. 126–9.)

The United States had a wide-reaching network of bases throughout the world. The Pacific was considered an enormous US-dominated lake by many. In Europe, the United States had forces in the occupied countries and set up important bases on Greenland and the Azores and in Iceland. These were established primarily on the basis of US commitments in the occupied areas and on considerations of their significance for the defense of the American continent, but their purpose changed with the international situation. When Secretary of State James Byrnes announced in September 1946 that US troops would participate in the occupation of Germany as long as the occupation persisted, this was not directed primarily at Germany, but at the Soviet Union. His declaration put an end to the uncertainty as to how long the United States would have troops in Europe, an uncertainty due in part to Roosevelt's statement at Yalta that the US troops would have to be recalled within two years. Roosevelt had assumed that American public opinion would not tolerate this type of commitment in Europe for a longer period of time.

Roosevelt himself had advocated that postwar economic support to the Soviet Union ought to be linked to the policies pursued. Washington attempted to influence Moscow's policies through economic measures. First, Lend-Lease aid was reduced abruptly in May 1945 and then again in August. This was partly to express dissatisfaction with Soviet policies, particularly in Eastern Europe. Then the preliminaries for loan negotiations were prolonged, and when the negotiations were finally initiated at the beginning of 1946, the conditions were stringent. Agreement could not be reached. Loan policy was also used actively in relation to the countries of Eastern Europe in the hope of attaining political influence, but to little avail once more.

The distribution of economic support gives a good picture of Washington's involvement and priorities. During the period from July 1945 to July 1947, the countries which would later participate in the Marshall Plan received various American loans and credits amounting to 7.4 billion dollars. The corresponding figure for Eastern Europe was 546 million, including 106 million to Finland. Britain received 4.4 billion, the Soviet Union 242 million in so-called Lend-Lease pipeline deliveries. Stopping them would have damaged US interests almost as much as Soviet interests. France received 1.9 billion, Poland 90 million. Italy received 330 million, Czechoslovakia 73 million, the Benelux countries 430 million, Bulgaria and Romania nothing. *why?*

Loan policy was closely linked to Washington's evaluation of what was a politically acceptable government. The most Moscow-oriented regimes received little or nothing. In the autumn of 1946 US aid to Czechoslovakia, the bridge-builder among the Eastern countries, was abruptly cut off. Prague's foreign policy had become unacceptable to Washington. In the autumn of 1947 complaints about the bridge-builders among the Western countries, the Scandinavian countries, became ever stronger, although there was no question of cutting off economic aid to countries participating in the Marshall Plan.

what are these?
→ Belgium Netherlands Luxembourg (oh, I see)

The decisive factor was a country's foreign policy stance. Governments which were far from perfect in terms of democracy could increasingly count on support if they opposed the Soviet Union and communism. This was evident in US policy towards Greece and Turkey: in 1946 Washington was willing to increase economic assistance to these two countries, the Sixth Fleet was built up in the Mediterranean, the firm stand towards the Soviet Union in Iran was a signal for Greece and Turkey as well, and the United States was prepared to give the British the weapons they might need to fight the left-wing guerillas in Greece. In the autumn of 1946, the Truman administration decided to do whatever was necessary to prevent the guerillas from winning and to get the Turkish government to resist Soviet wishes with regard to boundary changes and a stronger position in the Bosporus–Dardanelles.

When the British economic situation in February 1947 was such that they had to withdraw from the area almost entirely, the Truman administration was ready to take over. The administration did not need to be convinced, as Congress and public opinion did, that major outlays were necessary. The striking new element was that assistance was linked to a general principle that US policy would support 'free peoples who are resisting attempted subjugation by armed minorities or by outside pressures.' This was the Truman Doctrine. *Would US meddling count as outside pressure ??*

Nor did the Marshall Plan represent anything dramatically new in Washington's relations with Western Europe. The economic assistance given during the years 1945–47 was, in fact, greater per year on average than it was during the Marshall Plan from 1948 to 1951. But the Marshall Plan was innovative in its organizational form, and it was given in a few large portions, not in many smaller installments (see pp. 153–6).

The establishment of NATO in April 1949 was a more wide-reaching change. As we have seen, the ties to Europe were considerable before 1949, so even the changes in US military involvement in Western Europe can easily be exaggerated. Nonetheless, for the first time in peacetime the United States entered into a military alliance with countries outside the Western hemisphere.

In March 1947, Britain and France had signed the Dunkirk treaty, which was formally directed against Germany – a situation that was realistic enough, particularly for France. The Soviet Union was not mentioned, but lurked in the background, particularly for Britain.

As early as the turn of the year 1947–48, Britain, with various forms of often uncoordinated support from France, Belgium, and the Netherlands, began to campaign for a more direct US contribution to the defense of Western Europe. As had been the case with the Truman Doctrine and the Marshall Plan, the Europeans' eagerness to link the United States more closely to Europe was an important precondition for the US stance.

According to the British, the defense of Europe could not be effective without US participation, preferably in the form of membership in a joint organization. At this time Washington was not prepared to make any commitment regarding participation. A vicious circle was in the making. The United States wanted to see what the Western Europeans established before deciding how strongly to support it. Western Europe would perhaps not be able to accomplish anything of substance if the US did not in advance guarantee comprehensive assistance.

A number of events in February–March 1948 contributed to a change of course by the United States, resulting in US participation in negotiations on the establishment of an Atlantic defense system: the coup in Czechoslovakia, the Finnish–Soviet cooperation pact, and the fear of a Communist victory in elections in Italy. From Germany came an alarming report by US commander General Lucius Clay that a conflict could erupt there. What seems to have had the most immediate effect, however, were rumors that the Soviet Union might suggest a type of Finnish pact with Norway. (Nothing came of this. For that reason, these rumors were long given little emphasis in analyses of the background for NATO.)

Even after US–British–Canadian negotiations had resulted in an agreement to establish some form of Atlantic security system, a year passed before NATO was established. The Americans disagreed among themselves as to what course to pursue. Such leading members of the Truman administration as George F. Kennan and Charles Bohlen were skeptical about an Atlantic treaty and wanted a more loose-knit association between North America and Western Europe. The military were unenthusiastic because they feared that Western Europe would attain too much influence on US strategy and make excessive demands on what were after all the limited resources of the United States. The Congress had to be consulted. The Democrats were uncertain as to what the outcome of the presidential election in the autumn of 1948 would be. In addition, time would show that although all the countries of Western Europe wanted to tie the United States more closely to Europe, they disagreed on just how this should be done. (Relations between the United States and Western Europe are discussed in more depth on pp. 153–6.)

There were definite limitations to both Washington's use of instruments to promote its aims and its foreign policy commitments. The atomic bomb was used primarily to end the war with Japan. There could never be any question of using it to threaten the Soviet Union directly. No one was prepared for such a rapid change from wartime cooperation to Cold War. Lend-Lease was not stopped primarily to frighten the Soviet Union. It was a program of assistance for all the allies, and the President had promised Congress that he would dismantle it as soon as the war was over. Loan negotiations were carried out with little confidence that anything of significance could be accomplished. The conditions attached were not unique to the Soviet Union and Eastern Europe; the many countries of Western Europe that received assistance from the United States were also expected to render return services of various kinds.

The limitations of US foreign policy involvement were made evident by demobilization and through attitudes towards the defense budget. Rapid demobilization undermined the US position, but there was no way of stopping it. It had to be carried out. Anything else was considered political suicide. The army was reduced from 8 million men at the end of the war to 1.5 million in the summer of 1946. The corresponding figures for the navy were 3.5 and 0.7 million. A large part of the remaining troops were merely waiting to come home. The defense budget sank drastically. The political leaders, following Truman's lead, felt that the upper limit to what the United States could bear in defense

Table 2.1 The Percentage Agreement between Churchill and Stalin

We alighted at Moscow on the afternoon of October 9, and were received very heartily and with full ceremonial by Molotov and many high Russian personages.

At ten o'clock that night we held our first important meeting in the Kremlin. There were only Stalin, Molotov, Eden, and I, with Major Birse and Pavlov as interpreters.

The moment was apt for business, so I said, 'Let us settle about our affairs in the Balkans. Your armies are in Roumania and Bulgaria. We have interests, missions, and agents there. Don't let us get at cross-purposes in small ways. So far as Britain and Russia are concerned, how would it do for you to have ninety per cent predominance in Roumania, for us to have ninety per cent of the say in Greece, and go fifty-fifty about Yugoslavia?' While this was being translated I wrote out on a half-sheet of paper:

Romania

Russia	90%
The others	10%

Greece

Great Britain (in accord with USA)	90%
Russia	10%

Yugoslavia	50–50%
*Hungary	50–50%
*Bulgaria	

Russia	75%
The others	25%

I pushed this across to Stalin, who had by then heard the translation. There was a slight pause. Then he took his blue pencil and made a large tick on it, and passed it back to us. It was all settled in no more time than it takes to set down.

Of course we had long and anxiously considered our point, and were only dealing with immediate war-time arrangements. All larger questions were reserved on both sides for what we then hoped would be a peace table when the war was won.

After this there was a long silence. The pencilled paper lay in the centre of the table. At length I said, 'Might it not be thought rather cynical if it seemed we had disposed of these issues, so fateful to millions of people, in such an off-hand manner? Let us burn the paper.'

'No, you keep it,' said Stalin.

Source: Winston S. Churchill, *The Second World War*, vi. *Triumph and Tragedy* (London, 1954), 197–8.
*Revised by Foreign Ministers Eden and Molotov on 11 October:
Hungary: 80% (USSR)–20% (UK)
Bulgaria: 80% (USSR)–20% (UK)

expenditure was 12–13 billion dollars. This was a high figure compared with the prewar period. But considering the extent of US occupation commitments, and not least compared with later defense expenditure, this was a small sum.

Although US involvement was global in principle and although it was far more comprehensive than Soviet involvement, the depth of US commitments varied considerably from place to place. As we shall soon see, Washington was willing to limit its role in Eastern Europe to the advantage of the Soviet Union. The surprising thing about US policy towards China was how little was done to prevent a Communist victory in the civil war (see pp. 37–41). To some extent, the United States tried to limit its involvement even in Western Europe. Washington encouraged European integration, in part to reduce Western European dependence on US assistance (see pp. 159–61). The United States also wanted to limit the number of members in NATO and consequently opposed membership by Greece and Turkey in 1948–49. why? more members = more opportunity for disagreement & discord?

Soviet Policy

The Soviet Union, too, represented a global ideology. For Marxists it was almost a law of nature that the world would become Communist one day. But from a Soviet point of view in 1945 that goal would inevitably seem a long way off. The Soviet Union faced the task of widespread reconstruction, and the country far from equalled the United States in terms of strength.

This did not mean that the Soviet Union lacked ambitions. There was an expansive pressure inherent in its ideology. Yet some areas were more important than others, and the possibilities of increased influence were greater in some places than in others. America, Africa, and even most of Asia were of little significance for the Soviet leaders. Few attempts, if any, were made to establish Communist regimes there. Africa illustrated this situation most clearly. There was only one Communist party in all of Africa, and that was in South Africa. The shaping of colonial policy was for the most part left to the mother countries' Communist parties. Stalin's interest in Latin America was also minimal. In Japan, Moscow was willing to accept the US-supported occupation regime without much protest. Support for the Communists in China was lukewarm. Revolutionary attempts were made in Southeast Asia, but there is still no definitive assessment as to the Soviet stance regarding the revolts there in 1948.

The alternative to Communist control was to support nationalist leaders. But after a brief period of a few years, these leaders were denounced as lackeys of the colonial powers. This was the case with Gandhi and Nehru in India and to a lesser extent with Sukarno in Indonesia (see pp. 41–3).

At first the Soviet Union seemed inclined towards cooperation in Western Europe. The Kremlin only half-heartedly tried to change the occupation regime in Italy in order to increase its influence there. The large Italian and French Communist parties were advised to take part in broad coalition governments, partly in order to meet the enormous tasks of reconstruction. The Communists became constitutional and moderate.

In contrast, the Soviet position was strong in North Korea and in Outer Mongolia. Attempts were made to increase influence in other border areas. The Soviet Union was interested in acquiring the provinces of Kars and Ardahan in Turkey, as well as in attaining as much control as possible over the Dardanelles. Moscow tried to use Soviet troops in northern Iran to build up a loyal regime there. In China, Stalin wanted to regain the rights Russia had lost after being defeated by Japan in 1904–5.

Roosevelt thought the changes in China were a reasonable price to pay for Soviet participation in the war against Japan. Thus agreement on this point was reached during negotiations at Yalta. In return, Moscow recognized Chiang Kai-shek as the legitimate ruler of China. Churchill was kept out of these discussions, a fact which illustrated the weakened position of the United Kingdom. In March–April 1946, a firm Western reaction combined with tactical Iranian concessions resulted in a Soviet withdrawal from Iran. The demands with regard to Turkey were toned down. The same was true of more tentative wishes that had been expressed concerning joint bases with Norway on Spitsbergen and acquisition of the Italian colony Tripolitania (Libya).

However, all these 'concessions' had a price. Restraint in areas which were important to the West was to be reciprocated by similar restraint by the West in Eastern Europe. Stalin was relatively clear on this point. The most important objectives were established as early as December 1941, in talks with British Foreign Minister Anthony Eden. The Baltic countries were to be reincorporated in the USSR, the Polish border was to follow the Curzon line, and the Soviet Union wanted bases in Romania and Finland. In return, Stalin expressed his willingness to support British demands for bases in Western Europe, e.g. in France, Belgium, the Netherlands, Norway, and Denmark.

This was not the last time Stalin himself clearly expounded on Soviet policy. The gist of the percentage agreement with Churchill in October 1944 was that the Soviet Union was willing to grant the British a free hand in Greece if the Kremlin was granted the same freedom in Romania, Bulgaria, and to a lesser extent Hungary. Stalin's message to Churchill on 24 April 1945 illustrated the same line of thought, this time with regard to Poland:

> Poland is to the security of the Soviet Union what Belgium and Greece are to the security of Great Britain ... I do not know whether a genuinely representative Government has been established in Greece, or whether the Belgian Government is a genuinely democratic one. The Soviet Union was not consulted when these Governments were being formed, nor did it claim the right to interfere in those matters, because it realises how important Belgium and Greece are to the security of Great Britain. I cannot understand why in discussing Poland no attempt is made to consider the interests of the Soviet Union in terms of security as well.

Stalin did not waver when it came to the border changes mentioned in his conversation with Eden. Even when the existence of the Soviet regime was at stake, these were minimum demands.

Poland was the most important Eastern European country both for the Soviet Union and for the Western powers. For the Soviet Union it was a buffer towards Germany and the West. An attack from the West would have to go through Poland. Britain had gone to war to defend Poland. That made it difficult to accept complete Soviet dominance. Both in London and in Washington, Poland was considered a test of whether and to what extent the Soviet Union would accept independent regimes in Eastern Europe.

From the summer of 1944 it seemed obvious that Moscow was determined that Soviet sympathizers, in other words the Lublin group, should be in control in Poland. Criticism of the exiled government in London, recognized by the Western powers, became harsher. The London government's forces in Poland were pushed aside and partly suppressed by the advancing Red Army. Local administration in the liberated areas was left in the hands of those who were loyal to the Soviet Union. In January 1945 Lublin was formally recognized by Moscow as the government of Poland. When it became evident that Stalin's Poles would not stand much of a chance of winning free elections, the elections which were presupposed both at Yalta and at the Potsdam Conference were postponed indefinitely.

why was Romania excluded from Lend-Lease benefits then?

Developments in Poland were an indication of how things would develop in Romania. In March 1945 Moscow imposed a change of government to the advantage of the circles that were loyal to the USSR. The Soviet Union enjoyed more support in Bulgaria than in Poland and Romania, which were traditionally anti-Russian. For this reason the Kremlin's methods were more indirect in Bulgaria, but the tendency was unmistakable: purging of the political opposition and increased control by Soviet sympathizers.

Even in the three countries mentioned, the Soviet Union was willing to make minor concessions to the Western powers. For instance, it appears that Stalin was prepared to accept the Eastern Neisse as the border between Poland and Germany. The Poles insisted on the Western Neisse. The United States and Britain accepted the western border without Stalin really being tested on this point. The Soviet Union was also willing to accept Western-oriented politicians in the governments of all three countries, although in a minority. When Washington and London protested against the biased elections that were planned for Bulgaria in August 1945, Moscow agreed to postpone them. Monarchy persisted in Bulgaria until the autumn of 1946 and in Romania yet another year.

Moscow's flexibility was greater in Hungary and especially in Czechoslovakia, although limits were set for the freedom of action of these countries, too. In Hungary there were free elections. They were held in the autumn of 1945 and represented a victory for the Smallholders' Party, whereas the Communists made a poor showing. During the first year after liberation, at least, the broad coalition government enjoyed considerable freedom of action, although it was gradually limited by the Soviet occupying power. From early in 1947 it was evident that Moscow would take complete control of Hungary. In Czechoslovakia there was widespread support for a course that meant close military and political cooperation with the Soviet Union. Economically and culturally, on the other hand, Czechoslovakia was oriented towards the West. Soviet forces were withdrawn in December 1945. Free elections were held in May 1946. In contrast to most of the countries of Eastern Europe, the Communist party enjoyed a strong position in Czechoslovakia, receiving 38 per cent of the votes. The extent of Soviet intervention was limited until the summer of 1947.

There were Soviet troops in Austria as well, and in Finland the Soviets dominated the allied control commission. But in these countries developments took an entirely different course than in Eastern Europe. In its foreign policy, Finland emphasized close cooperation with the Soviet Union. The Communists were represented in the Finnish government until 1948, although they were in a minority. In terms of domestic policy Finland functioned like a Western democracy. After the peace treaty was signed in 1947, the Russians retained a base in Porkkala until 1955. Part of Austria was under Soviet occupation, but in contrast to Germany the country was administered as a single unit. In the elections of November 1945 the Communists received only 5 per cent of the votes. The country even participated in the Marshall Plan.

Soviet dominance in Eastern Europe was mainly based on the presence of the Red Army in the area. The widespread impression in the West was that Soviet demobilization was quite limited. For various reasons Stalin found it advantageous to exaggerate Soviet strength willfully. The number of Soviet troops had probably declined to 2.8 million by 1948. This figure was still higher than the corresponding figure for the United States, but much lower than was thought at the time. Even so, it was more than enough to retain control over Eastern Europe. Developments there cast long shadows into Western Europe.

As we have seen, the Soviet Union was willing to make certain concessions to the Western powers, who in turn were prepared to limit their influence in Eastern Europe, and agreements were entered into which reinforced Moscow's position in the region. They ranged from ceasefire agreements and the percentage agreement in 1944 to the agreement on the governments of Bulgaria and Romania in December 1945 and the peace treaties in 1947. Both Washington and London were aware that Western control over Italy and Japan had to be paid for to a certain extent with return favors in Eastern Europe, although of course both sides tried to have their bread buttered on both sides.

The United States and Britain admitted that Eastern Europe was more important to the Soviet Union than to themselves. It was reasonable that the Soviets had considerable influence there. The border changes did not represent major problems. Nor was a certain orientation towards Moscow in foreign policy, such as in Czechoslovakia, particularly problematic during the very first phase of the Cold War.

Despite such concessions on both sides, the distance between them was considerable. Conflict over Eastern Europe would destroy the cooperation established during the war. Neither Washington nor London was willing to relinquish fully their influence in the area. The Soviet Union, on the other hand, had limited geographic objectives in Europe, but in at least the inner ring of countries the Kremlin was firmly set on establishing quite complete control.

Free elections were the largest obstacle. The problem was that in the countries which were of most importance to the Soviet Union the Communists were weakest. There was little doubt that the peasant parties would win free elections in both Poland and Romania. Moscow would not accept this type of result, while the Western powers could not allow the opposition to be simply pushed aside. In Poland and Romania it was impossible to combine free elections with a government friendly to the Soviet Union, at least if the Western powers were to define what were free elections and the USSR what was a government friendly to the Soviet Union. There was no basis in domestic policy for a 'Czech' or 'Finnish' pattern in anti-Russian Poland and Romania. Soviet interests were also greater in these two countries than in Czechoslovakia and Finland.

US requirements as to what could be considered 'friendly' governments rose continually. The same thing happened on the Soviet side, although with the difference that the consequences of not fulfilling these requirements could be even more dramatic. During the initial period after the war, non-Communists were represented in

Germany in 1939
Iron curtain
Soviet conquests
Countries where communist regimes were established in 1945–8
Italian territory transferred to Yugoslavia

Figure 2.1 Territorial changes in Europe after the Second World War

all the governments of Eastern Europe and were even in the majority in several of them. They gradually lost influence. The pace varied from country to country, but by the autumn of 1947 most non-Communists were out of the picture. Of the prominent peasant leaders, Petkov in Bulgaria had been hanged, Maniu in Romania sentenced to prison for life, and Mikolajczyk in Poland and Nagy in Hungary had to flee from their native countries. From the summer of 1947 Moscow began to pursue a more active policy in Czechoslovakia as well. The coup in Prague in February 1948 arose partly from local conditions but undoubtedly enjoyed Soviet support. In 1948–49, comprehensive purges were initiated within the various Communist parties, purges which even ended with death even for a number of leading party members (see pp. 184–6).

From the autumn of 1947, Moscow's attitude towards Western Europe changed as well. The French and Italian Communist parties were severely criticized for the passive policies they had pursued, although they had done so with the Kremlin's support. Now comprehensive strikes and demonstrations were launched, even though they were probably intended more to weaken the effect of the Marshall Plan than to take power in these two countries.

The Problem of Germany

The antagonism between East and West spread from Eastern Europe to Germany. The war against Hitler's Germany had drawn the two sides together. After the country was defeated, they agreed on important principles as to the course of development for Germany. It was taken for granted that Germany would remain demilitarized. Even though the three major powers had discussed dismembering the country into several small states as late as at Yalta, in the following months all three would commit themselves to keeping Germany as one unit. Dismemberment would entail the danger of a new nationalistic movement being created by a rally call for unity. The three also agreed that clear limitations had to be placed on the German economy. The United States promoted the Morgenthau Plan for a short time, to the effect that all heavy industry was to be closed down. Even after this plan was abandoned towards the end of 1944, their mutual point of departure was that Germany should not have a higher standard of living than the average in the European countries.

At Yalta the United States, Britain, and the Soviet Union had grudgingly agreed to allow France to administer one of the zones of occupation, but it was to be carved out from the US and British zones. This rather humble start did not prevent France from pursuing a distinctive course. None of the other powers so strongly emphasized the importance of keeping Germany weak. Paris was opposed to a possible German central government attaining anything more than purely symbolic functions. The best solution would be to dismember the country, but France had entered into the discussion at such a late stage and had so little influence that this goal was unattainable. Instead the Saar province was to be annexed to France, whereas the Ruhr and the Rhineland regions were to be partitioned off from the rest of Germany and placed under international control in a manner that allowed France to play a central role.

Unlike France, the Soviet Union wanted a strong central government in Germany. As the US desire for a federal Germany reflected the American way of thinking, centralism reflected the Soviet model. A strong central government could be an instrument for procuring larger reparations from Germany. Moreover, the Soviet Union controlled a much smaller part of the country than the three Western powers combined. Through a strong central government Moscow could attain a certain influence even in the other zones.

The Soviet Union naturally had a particular interest in the payment of reparations. The Germans were to pay for the tremendous destruction they had caused. At Yalta Roosevelt and Stalin accepted the sum of 10 billion dollars as a basis for discussion concerning reparations to the Soviet Union. Moscow would return to this question again and again. The United States – and to an even greater extent Britain – was afraid that it would be impossible for the Germans to pay such large reparations as the Soviet Union wanted, and that in the end it would be American and British taxpayers who would be called on to keep the Germans alive while they in turn had to transfer large sums to the Soviet Union. London and Washington could recall unpleasant lessons from the First World War to this effect. At the Potsdam Conference in July and August this difficulty was partially, but only partially, resolved by agreeing that most of the reparations were to be taken from one's own zone of occupation.

It is difficult to find clear patterns in the policies of the major powers with regard to Germany immediately after the war. Several courses competed with one another. This was perhaps most evident on the part of the Soviet Union. Moscow advocated German unity and even a strong central government. At the same time, the Soviets pursued policies which were bound to undermine both the desire for unity and the possibilities of attaining political influence. Rape and pillage were widespread. Their hard line in terms of reparations was poorly received by the Germans. The merging of the Communist party and the Socialist party in April 1946 was a sign that the Soviet Union was beginning to organize its zone according to the Eastern European pattern.

Churchill did not want to agree to the 10 billion dollars in reparations to the Soviet Union, even as a basis of discussion. The British were skeptical, too, about the conditions of the Potsdam agreement regarding reparations. In the discussions as to how high industrial production should be in Germany, the British pressed for the highest figures. This was mostly because the Ruhr, the major industrial area, was in the British zone, and the British were afraid their weak economy would suffer because of outlays in Germany. The object of not weakening Germany too much in relation to the Soviet Union was another contributory factor.

On 3 May 1946, General Clay stopped payment of reparations from the US zone. The background for this action was the fact that it had proved impossible to administer Germany as a political and economic unit. France was the country which was most strongly opposed to any coordination, and Clay's halt in the payment of reparations was aimed not only at the Soviet Union, but just as much at France. Gradually, however, the United States and Britain began to accept that the Saar region be linked to France. They still opposed partitioning the Ruhr and the Rhineland from the rest of Germany.

On the part of the United States there were obvious differences between the local authorities in Germany who, in order to facilitate their tasks then and there, advocated a more lenient policy, and the State Department in Washington, which was concerned about the reactions this course would evoke in other countries. For instance, these differences had manifested themselves in the negotiations regarding the level of industrial production: the US local authorities advocated a level slightly lower than the British proposal, whereas the State Department originally pressed for a level which was lower than that suggested by both the Soviet Union and France. (The stance taken by these two countries was partially determined by the fact that they themselves wanted to reap some of the benefits of increased production.)

Nevertheless, the tendencies in allied policies towards Germany were clear. The United States would follow an ever more lenient course. In July 1946 Washington proposed that those who wanted to could merge their zones with the US zone. Britain soon accepted, but both France and the Soviet Union declined. The establishment of the so-called Bi-zone illustrated two things: in the first place, that consensus as to Germany was in the process of disintegrating entirely and, in the second place, that the United States had assumed leadership in the West, here as elsewhere.

The major breakthrough for a new policy towards Germany was Secretary of State Byrnes's speech in Stuttgart on 6 September 1946. Byrnes not only made it clear that US troops would participate in the occupation as long as it lasted; in addition, the German economy had to be made self-sufficient so that the country would not be dependent on supplies from abroad. The Germans would also have to be granted self-government to an increasing extent.

At the Potsdam Conference it had been decided that Poland was to administer the territory as far west as Oder-Neisse, but a final decision regarding the Polish–German border was to be made in connection with a German peace treaty. The Western powers had seemed to reconcile themselves to the fact that the temporary border would become the final border, but in Stuttgart Byrnes stated that it was not at all certain this would be the case. This initiative strengthened the US position in Germany, while the Soviet Union, which had tried to secure a foothold in relation to both Germany and Poland, now gave its full support to the Poles.

Germany was no longer an adversary. Increasingly, it became a prize the major powers competed for. The colder the Cold War became, the greater was the interest in granting new concessions to the Germans. Moreover, it became increasingly evident that Europe could not be rebuilt economically without the reconstruction of Germany. The Western zones thus played an important role in the establishment of the Marshall Plan in 1947.

The Cold War made it more difficult for France to continue its independent course in Germany. In April–May 1948, Paris assented in principle to merging the French zone with the US–British zone. A constitutional assembly was to be convened and a federal German government to be established for the three Western zones. French policy regarding the Ruhr and Rhineland regions was abandoned. In return, agreement was reached that the Ruhr should have an international controlling authority, although a relatively weak one.

Seen from Moscow, these developments were ominous. The Soviet Union was excluded from the Ruhr and from most of Germany. The tremendous economic potential of the Western zones was about to be released. US assistance was being poured in. In June the Western powers implemented a monetary reform, which made it unmistakably evident that Germany was no longer an economic unit. The new West Germany would be integrated into Western European cooperation, but that did not improve the situation, as the country could easily become the dominant member.

how does economic assisstance from the US work re: reparations? oh jk assisstance for firmerly soviet holdings

28

The Berlin blockade was Moscow's response to these events. The first obstructions of traffic to West Berlin were introduced in April 1948. From 25 July the blockade was complete except for air connections. This was Moscow's most dramatic action after the war. For the first time force was used to promote changes in an area where Western troops were stationed. However, Moscow allowed itself a certain scope for maneuvering by arguing that the measures were due to repairs. Thus the blockade could be lifted when the repairs were completed. The Soviet objectives were not at all clear. A maximum objective may have been to prevent the creation of West Germany and to achieve control of all of Germany by the four powers. A minimum objective may have been to isolate West Berlin in order to bring the city under Soviet influence.

The Western powers improvised by establishing an airlift, a measure which was expected to be temporary but which proved to be protracted. The airlift exceeded everyone's expectations. The Soviet Union could not stop the traffic without resorting to more direct use of force. Nor could Moscow prevent the developments leading

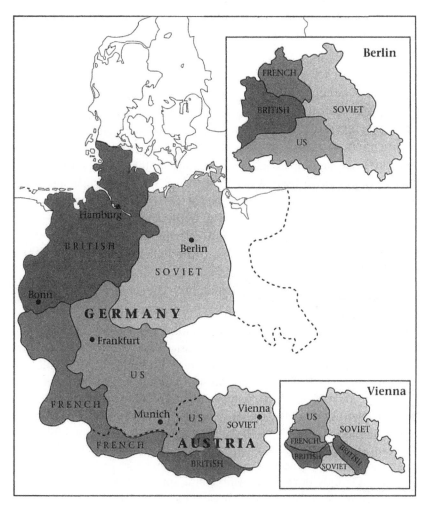

Figure 2.2 Allied zones in Germany and Austria

to the creation of a West German state. The blockade of West Berlin hastened the establishment of NATO and weakened the Soviet position in Western Europe. The Western blockade of East Germany in response to the Berlin blockade had a certain effect as well.

In May 1949 Moscow agreed to end the blockade without having achieved anything except minor concessions. The day after the blockade was ended, the three Western military governors approved the new West German constitution. Ten days later the new state was formally established. In October East Germany followed suit.

But the Berlin wall didn't fall until the 90s?

MOTIVATING FORCES BEHIND US AND SOVIET POLICIES

It is almost always easier to describe a course of events than to explain why something happened. The difficulties are especially great in relation to the motivating forces behind Soviet policies because for decades little material was available from the Soviet Union. With regard to the United States, the problem has been the opposite: an overabundance of sources.

The United States

A number of different factors were of significance for the Americans. The question of national security was one of them. This could be observed even in US policy towards Eastern Europe. The region in itself was not of particular strategic importance to the United States. However, two circumstances diminished the distinction between important and less important regions. In the first place, many leading politicians in the Roosevelt and Truman administrations asked themselves whether 'relinquishing' Eastern Europe to the Soviet Union would not merely result in the pressure being transmitted to the next layer of countries. Then the strategically important Western Europe would be threatened. This layer-by-layer theory was accepted by more and more policy-makers in Washington during 1944–45. In the second place, and this may explain why the theory so easily gained ground, the lesson of the Second World War was that aggression developed gradually. Hitler had not been stopped in time; this mistake should not be made a second time.

In 1945–46 the conflict concerned Eastern Europe and to some extent Germany. In 1947–48 Washington began to fear Soviet expansion into Western Europe. The main threat was not direct aggression. The chances of a direct attack were small, although they could not be disregarded entirely. Most politicians believed that an exhausted Soviet Union wanted to avoid a destructive conflict with the West. However, considering the long shadows Soviet control of Eastern Europe cast over Western Europe, the chances were greater of Moscow succeeding in less dramatic ways, as a result of political pressure, economic chaos, and active local Communist parties. Czechoslovakia was an example of this type of expansion.

A number of events during the winter and spring of 1948 contributed to the impression that Western Europe was threatened. The attitude of Western Europe itself was important; as we have seen (pp. 18–20), there was fairly constant pressure on the United States to play a more active role in European politics. This involved first economic assistance, then political and moral support, and finally direct military guarantees.

The influence of Britain was especially important. This country had the best relations with the United States and worked most actively to draw the United States closer to Western Europe. Another important consideration was the fact that it was less necessary for the United States to play a new role in foreign policy as long as others could represent US interests. Washington and London did not see eye to eye on all matters. They disagreed as to colonial policy, international trade, the question of Palestine, and a number of other issues. Nevertheless, they had an important mutual interest in containing Soviet influence. As long as Britain was able to fulfill this function, there was less need for the United States to do so.

However, the position of the United Kingdom changed dramatically in the years immediately after the war. The British had to retreat on a number of fronts. In India, the colonial system began to collapse. The British withdrew from Palestine when the political problems piled up and their economy did not allow them to be actively present. Even more important in terms of the Cold War was the reduced presence of the British in Greece and Turkey and in Germany. The economic problems of the United Kingdom were the immediate cause of the proclamation of the Truman Doctrine in March 1947. When the British could no longer hold back the leftist guerillas in Greece nor support the Turkish government against Soviet pressure, the Truman administration saw that it had to take over.

In Germany, too, the weak British economy was an important reason for their close cooperation with the United States, as evidenced for instance by the merging of the two countries' zones in 1946. In more comprehensive terms, it could be argued that both the Marshall Plan and NATO were measures that were established because the Western Europeans could not solve their economic, political, and military problems by themselves.

A number of different domestic conditions also influenced US policy. There was a strong ideological desire to spread the American gospel to other countries. America was God's own country, with a duty to proclaim her values to others. Everyone wanted democracy and freer trade, or at least would have wanted them if they could have expressed their wishes. The more subdued version of this message was the emphasis on US responsibility to defend democracy against an expansive communism.

There was widespread political agreement in the United States as to the main course the country pursued after the Second World War. However, some groups were more active than others, depending on which issue was most pressing. Ethnic considerations played a part. The many Polish-Americans were especially active with regard to Eastern Europe in 1944–45. The Italian-Americans played a corresponding role with regard to Western Europe. These groups in turn enjoyed support in wider circles, such as the Catholic Church.

After the 1946 election, Congress was controlled by the Republicans, and even though they were often even more anti-communist than the Truman administration, they were skeptical of most things that cost money. Anti-communism was to be inexpensive. Thus considerations of party politics influenced US policy. In order to compensate for the lack of enthusiasm with which the request for 400 million dollars for Greece and Turkey was met by a Congress bent on saving, the Truman Doctrine was presented in extra dramatic terms. Other concessions had to be made to the Republicans in general and the chairman of the Senate Foreign Relations Committee, Arthur Vandenberg, in particular. The Marshall Plan was pruned here and there; Western Europe had to promise to do more on its own both economically and militarily; the United States avoided automatic military commitments towards Europe.

After such concessions the Truman administration managed to get its most important measures passed in Congress, usually by a large majority. The opposition which existed came from both the left and the right. On the left it was centered around former Vice President (1941–45) and Secretary of Commerce (1945–46) Henry Wallace and his supporters. Wallace was dismissed in the autumn of 1946 because of his more conciliatory attitude towards the Soviet Union. However, most of the opposition came from the right and was linked to Senator Robert Taft. The right wing was even more anti-communist than the majority, even more nationalistic, but also even more cost-conscious. The Marshall Plan cost the American taxpayer far too much. NATO limited US military freedom of action. Taft and his supporters represented the mild postwar variant of American isolationism.

Economic considerations, too, influenced US policy. A recurrent question was whether the US economy would slide into a new depression when the war was over. Many people believed that this type of setback was likely, even more believed that it was possible. It could be avoided or possibly softened by foreign policy measures. Exports could be increased, and possible surplus capital used for investments abroad. Important raw materials the United States lacked could be imported from abroad. The motives of pure self-interest behind these policies were reinforced by the ideology they were a part of. The dominant circles were convinced that tariffs and regional trade blocs were detrimental not only to the United States but to all countries, and that they were also an important explanation as to why war and conflict arise between nations.

Several factors moderated these economic considerations. In the first place, most people quite soon became more optimistic with regard to the possibilities of avoiding a new depression. In the second place, the United States was one of the countries in the world which was least dependent on its foreign trade. In absolute figures, the United States had by far the largest volume of foreign trade in the world, but in relation to total production, export and import each represented less than 5 per cent. This figure was much lower than for the countries of Western Europe. The United States was also more self-sufficient in terms of raw materials than almost any other country.

US dependence on other countries did not increase significantly until the 1970s. Nor was the business world more skeptical of the Soviet Union than other people were. Many branches, such as the aviation industry, obviously profited from international tension and large defense budgets, but most of the business world was more interested in keeping taxes down than in increasing the defense budget.

The vast majority of exporters were interested in increasing trade with the Soviet Union: here was a market that could really amount to something. Thus these circles advocated both increased trade with and large credits to the Soviet Union. The many restrictions imposed on trade with the Soviet Union from the end of 1947 did not represent the attitude of big business in the United States.

The most important basis for US policy seems to have a tendency to be forgotten, namely the tremendous power of the United States at the end of the war. History affords few examples of overwhelming power that does not express itself in active policies.

Considering US strength in 1945, it was almost inevitable that the country should try to shape the international environment in its own image to a considerable degree.

The Soviet Union

Stalin and the other Soviet leaders often stressed the fact that Soviet policy in Eastern Europe was motivated by considerations of national security. There is little reason to doubt that this was the case. During the preceding 30 years alone, Russia/the Soviet Union had been attacked by Germany twice. Besides this, there had been Western intervention in the civil war and war with Poland. The First World War had caused the fall of the Czar's regime. The Second World War had nearly resulted in a collapse of Stalin's rule.

National security considerations would necessarily carry a lot of weight with any leader in the Kremlin. But Stalin made higher demands than most leaders. This had become evident in his domestic policy through the many extensive purges. Now the position of the Soviet Union in terms of foreign policy was to be secured. The only problem was that what was security for one country tended to be insecurity for another. This was true both in relation to the neighbors who were no longer to be given the opportunity to represent a threat and in relation to the Western powers.

On rare occasions Stalin could give credit to the Western powers. After the Second Front was finally established at Normandy in June 1944, he proclaimed that 'one cannot but recognize that the history of warfare knows of no other similar undertaking in the breadth of its conception, in its giant dimensions, and in the mastery of its performance.' *Pravda* went to the unheard of step of publishing the figures for the help the Soviet Union had received from the West during the war.

But these were rare exceptions. Stalin's skepticism of the Western powers was considerable. It did not diminish as the war drew to a close. In March–April 1945, Stalin accused the Western powers of having made a separate peace in Italy, which would give the Germans the opportunity to transfer troops from Italy to the Eastern front. At the end of April, the Red Army in Austria built up large defense installations. At that time the Germans were nearly defeated. It actually appears as though the Soviet leaders were now afraid that the Western powers would make a separate peace with Germany which applied throughout Europe, rather than just for Italy.

In August 1945 the leaders in the Kremlin began openly to emphasize their conviction that even though the danger of fascism was over, the Soviet Union could not reduce its vigilance on that account. The attacks on capitalism were increased. References to the mutual interests of the three major powers ceased. Stalin's so-called election speech in February 1946 was an expression of this new orientation. (The Western leaders were cautious in their public descriptions of the Soviet Union, with few exceptions. Their private opinions were another matter. Thus the Truman administration tried to create the impression of a greater distance to opposition leader Churchill's attack on the Soviet Union in March 1946 than the actual attitude of the administration would indicate.)

Soviet control in Eastern Europe was not only a military cordon sanitaire in relation to the West, but also an ideological barrier. The Soviet Union would no doubt be capable of closing its borders to undesired influences, but adding an extra margin here could not hurt. Consideration of the many Soviet soldiers in Eastern Europe played a part as well.

In addition, the risk that Moscow's policy in Eastern Europe involved was very small. It is quite possible the Soviet leaders had the impression that the Western powers were prepared to 'relinquish' the region to them if a number of more or less cosmetic concessions were made. Little in the actions of the Western powers indicated otherwise, at least before the Yalta Conference. After Yalta it must have been evident to the Kremlin that both the United States and Britain intended to pursue an active policy, particularly with regard to Poland, but also in other countries. Former Foreign Minister Litvinov probably expressed genuine confusion when he said to an American journalist in June 1945: 'Why did you Americans wait until now to begin opposing us in the Balkans and Eastern Europe? … You should have done this three years ago. Now it's too late and your complaints only arouse suspicion here.'

Economic considerations played a role in Soviet as well as in US policy. The Soviet Union acquired substantial benefits in Eastern Europe and in other border areas, such as in China. Often the local economies were brutally exploited. Through trade agreements, joint companies, reparation payments, and war spoils, considerable resources were transferred to the Soviet Union.

Soviet expansion was certainly also in accordance with communist ideology. Stalin's 'socialism in one country' had been an admission that, in direct opposition to Lenin's expectations, the Communist revolution had been limited to the Soviet Union. Now, at last, history had begun to take its proper course. But expansion in Eastern Europe was much less a historical necessity than it was an expression of the possibilities created by the advance of the Red Army. Power was an important condition for the policy pursued, even though the Soviet Union's power was considerably less and geographically more limited than that of the United States.

THE COLD WAR IN EUROPE 1945-1949: THE LITERATURE

A fine source collection of the entire Cold War period is Jussi M. Hanhimäki and Odd Arne Westad (eds), *The Cold War: A History in Documents and Eyewitness Accounts* (Oxford, 2003). A good anthology is Melvyn P. Leffler and David S. Painter (eds), *Origins of the Cold War: An International History* (New York, 2005). A good collection of different approaches is found in Odd Arne Westad (ed.), *Reviewing the Cold War: Approaches, Interpretations, Theory* (London, 2000).

Herbert Feis, *From Trust to Terror: The Onset of the Cold War, 1945–1950* (New York, 1970) is a key traditionalist presentation, whereas Gabriel and Joyce Kolko, *The Limits of Power: The World and United States Foreign Policy, 1945–1954* (New York, 1972) presents an unequivocal revisionist version. The best post-revisionist book is still John Lewis Gaddis, *The United States and the Origins of the Cold War, 1941–1947* (New York, 1972). My own analyses of this period are to be found in *The American Non-Policy Towards Eastern Europe 1943–1947* (Oslo–New York, 1975) and *America, Scandinavia and the Cold War 1945–1949* (New York–Oslo, 1980). Vojtech Mastny, *Russia's Road to the Cold War: Diplomacy, Warfare and the Politics of Communism, 1941–1945* (New York, 1979) is the best analysis of Soviet policy during the period in question.

Among more recent books on key aspects of the Cold War, two are particularly noteworthy: Melvyn Leffler, *A Preponderance of Power: National Security, the Truman Administration, and the Cold War* (Stanford, CA, 1992), and David Reynolds (ed.), *The Origins of the Cold War in Europe: International Perspectives* (New Haven, CT, 1994).

The leading new interpretations of the origins of the Cold War are found in John Lewis Gaddis, *We Now Know: Rethinking Cold War History* (Oxford, 1997) and his *Cold War* (London, 2005); Vojtech Mastny, *The Stalin Years: The Cold War and Soviet Insecurity* (Oxford, 1996); and Vladislav Zubok and Constantine Pleshakov, *Inside the Kremlin's Cold War: From Stalin to Khrushchev* (Cambridge, MA, 1996). For a lively and fascinating account, see Frank Costagliola, *Roosevelt's Lost Alliances: How Personal Politics Helped Start the Cold War* (Princeton, NJ, 2012).

THE COLD WAR BECOMES GLOBAL, 1945-1962

During the years 1945–49, the Cold War was concentrated mainly on Europe and the areas bordering on Europe, such as Turkey and Iran. This chapter will first show that the superpowers' involvement in other parts of the world in the years immediately following the war was relatively limited. This was particularly true for the Soviet Union. The argument then proceeds to analyze how the Cold War later spread to ever new areas, first to Asia, then to the Middle East and Africa, and finally to Latin America as well. In the 1960s the Cold War had become global.

THE UNITED STATES, THE SOVIET UNION, AND ASIA, 1945-1950

The Civil War in China

Although Japan and the European powers had controlled parts of China, they had never managed to dominate it to the same degree as they did most of the remainder of Asia. China was a vast country and the most populous in the world. The Chinese could play off the various great powers against each other. During the postwar period, China would illustrate the limitations even of the superpowers' influence.

Many Americans had had a certain fondness for China for a long time. Europe was the Old World; like America, Asia belonged to the New World. Businessmen, missionaries, and teachers had flocked from the United States to China in their thousands to spread American ideals.

This sentiment towards China had also been evident during the war. Washington had insisted that China should be one of the major powers, thus becoming a permanent member of the UN Security Council. Although despair as to the ineffectiveness of Chiang Kai-shek's war against the Japanese could reach considerable levels, the Americans always remained determined that he should be the future leader of this major power. China suited Washington's plans for the postwar period perfectly. In relations between East and West, China, under the leadership of Chiang, would support the United States against the Soviet Union. In colonial questions, too, China would undoubtedly side with the United States, primarily in opposition to Britain.

How much opposition?

China represented an important market which could become even more important in the future. Parts of American opinion still sympathized more with fledgling Asia than with aging Europe.

Chiang's Kuomintang regime was authoritarian, corrupt, and ineffective. Even so, there was no alternative. Leading circles in Washington considered Mao Tse-tung a Communist who did have an independent streak, but who nonetheless cooperated with Moscow.

The United States gave considerable support to the Kuomintang. From 1945 to 1947 total economic assistance amounted to 1.4 billion dollars. Even so, it was not enough to keep the regime functioning. From 1947–48 Chiang was on the defensive. The Truman administration and the Congress responded with the China Act of 1948. In the rhetorical language of Washington, it declared that the US objective was to 'maintain the genuine independence and the administrative integrity of China, and to sustain and strengthen principles of individual liberty and free institutions in China through a program based on self-help and cooperation.' An additional 275 million dollars were given as economic assistance and 125 million for military supplies.

Nevertheless, there were clear limitations to this assistance. The US troops that were in China at the end of the war were withdrawn, and only indirectly and to a diminishing extent were they used to support the Kuomintang army. New troops were not sent in to prevent a Communist victory in the civil war. In 1948 the Truman administration only half-heartedly granted further assistance to Chiang. The administration was particularly skeptical about the military part of the program of assistance, but it was also in doubt as to whether there was any purpose in sending further economic assistance.

The new assistance was in part a concession to the military and to rightist circles in Congress. Again and again Taft and other conservative Republicans had asked why one policy was to be pursued in Europe and a different one in Asia. If it was right to curb communism in Europe, it must be right to do the same in Asia. Although public opinion had long been opposed to escalating the US involvement in Asia, in 1948 there were unmistakable signals that this attitude was in the process of changing.

The opposition wanted more forceful rhetoric and an increase in Washington's economic and military assistance. They were also in favor of sending American military advisers to China, suggesting a figure of about 10,000. But even the strongest pro-Chiang circles denied that they wanted to send US combat forces to fight on the side of the Kuomintang.

The sizeable, yet limited, support by the United States may seem surprising in the light of the comprehensive US involvement in Europe and not least in comparison with the US interventions that would later follow in Asia.

A primary reason was that China was certainly important, but it was far from equal to Europe in importance. Within the Truman administration, both the State Department and the military establishment agreed that efforts to stop the Communists in China had to be subordinate to the policy of containment in Europe. Europe was primary in terms of both strategic and economic significance. During the Second World War, Germany had to be defeated before Japan. The same priority was evident now. Even those who in theory felt that Asia ought to be at least equal to Europe in importance supported the 'Europe first' policy in practice, although this course was less pronounced for them than it was for the administration.

A second reason was that US resources were limited, especially when Europe was to be granted top priority. Demobilization had reduced the US armed forces to a bare minimum. They were not even sufficient to fully realize US commitments in the occupied countries. There was no desire, least of all among those who opposed the administration's China policies, to induct extraordinary forces or to increase the defense budget in order to procure resources for a more active policy in China.

In the third place, China was a vast country, and the tasks involved could easily become equally vast. The 10,000 'advisers' there was talk of sending were intended to be just that. Few people, if any, wanted the United States to become involved in another war such a short time after the Second World War. In a sense, the tasks in China were more comprehensive than in Europe, where the objective was primarily to deter Soviet expansion, not to support troops in combat. Moreover, no one could know how many 'advisers' could be needed to prevent a Communist victory in China.

In the fourth place, there was uncertainty as to what the Soviet response would be if the United States began to send in troops. A US intervention could easily result in a corresponding Soviet reaction. Since the Soviet Union had not yet given military support to the Communists, the United States would be left with the responsibility for having let a local conflict develop into something that could threaten world peace.

Finally, Washington was dissatisfied with Chiang Kai-shek and his policies. Rightist regimes could receive, and did receive, support from the United States to an increasing extent, but in China there were few indications that this assistance had much effect. Chiang was already getting considerably more assistance from abroad than Mao was. The problems of the Kuomintang were internal. Popular support seemed to decline, but that did not increase the willingness to implement reforms that could strengthen the basis for popular support for the regime. Aid could not compensate for political disintegration. This had long been the conclusion among most of the US experts on China. To an ever-increasing degree it was also shared by Truman and his leading advisers.

If US support to Chiang was limited, Soviet support to Mao Tse-tung was even more limited. The Soviet Union provided some military support, particularly in the form of Japanese weapons that had been left behind in Manchuria when the Red Army withdrew in 1946. It is likely that Moscow also gave a certain amount of economic assistance, but it must have been much less than the amounts the Americans gave to their side. (In return, the Soviet Union took spoils worth considerable sums during their withdrawal from Manchuria.)

There is little reason to doubt that the Soviet Union preferred Mao to Chiang, but this ideologically based involvement was kept at a modest level. In the Sino-Soviet pact of 14 August 1945, Moscow recognized Chiang as China's legitimate leader. This recognition was formally sustained until 30 September 1949. Despite the party contacts the Kremlin had with the Chinese Communists, there was little mention of the war in China in the Soviet press. Not until 3 October 1949 were the Chinese Communists praised on the first page of *Pravda*.

In October 1949, former Secretary of State Marshall, who had recently left the cabinet, stressed that with regard to Soviet assistance to the Communists:

I never could see any trace of it ... Well, as far as I could see, what they were preparing themselves for was a case before the United Nations, where they could appear clean as driven snow and we would have our hands muddied by every bit of propaganda they could manufacture.

Mao Tse-tung would later express a similar view, although he was at the time still a great admirer of Stalin.

An important reason for this lukewarm attitude was that like the Americans, but to a much greater extent, the Soviets had to admit that they had limited resources. Moscow wished to concentrate the resources that were available on Europe – again even more clearly than Washington – particularly in Eastern Europe and Germany. China came further down on the list of priorities.

It is true that Moscow hoped to strengthen its position in parts of China. In many ways a relatively weak China could serve Soviet interests. Only then could Moscow secure the influence in the Sino-Soviet border areas it openly hoped to obtain. The first step was to regain what Russia had lost in the war with Japan in 1904–5. This was achieved at Yalta and confirmed in the Sino-Soviet pact of August 1945. The southern part of Sakhalin was returned to the Soviet Union and the Kurile Islands were ceded to the Soviets, including the southernmost islands, which had not previously belonged to Russia. More directly in relation to China, Port Arthur was again to become a Soviet navy base. Dairen was internationalized under Soviet leadership, and the railroad in Manchuria came under Soviet influence. In addition, Moscow's supremacy over Outer Mongolia was recognized.

In 1944, Islamic rebels had established an independent republic in East Turkestan. The Soviet Union was obviously in contact with them, and not until 1949 was the republic reintegrated into China. As late as July 1949, Moscow made a separate trade agreement with Manchuria. Since it was evident that all of China would soon be under the Chinese Communists' control, this could be interpreted as a threat against Chinese unity. The local Communist leader, Kao Kang, was later sharply denounced by Mao. In Sinkiang, too, Moscow emphasized the expansion of Soviet regional interests.

Moreover, it is likely that in the years immediately following the Second World War Stalin expected Chiang to be victorious in the conflict with Mao, which may have been conducive to moderation, in part to retain the privileges mentioned. The US stance was probably significant as well. The Soviet Union wanted to avoid a direct conflict with the United States. How Washington would react to Soviet interference in China was unknown. Moderation there could mitigate the consequences of the conflict over Eastern Europe to some extent. When the Communists showed dramatic progress during the civil war, the need to provide assistance disappeared. Developments were moving in the right direction anyway. Why strain relations with the West under these circumstances?

Finally, it is likely that the conflict with Tito (see pp. 185–6) came to influence Moscow's evaluation of the Chinese Communists. At a time when Stalin had become extremely suspicious of anything that could appear to be national communist dissent, there was much in China that could give rise to worry. There were evident signs of independence in the ideology of the Chinese Communists. Like Tito, Mao rose to power mostly on his own. Both of them had little to thank Moscow for on that account. Mao had

But wasn't Mao a stalin supporter?

oh, Stalin wanted someone less independent over such a large landmass

had even less contact with Moscow than Tito had, and he would govern a much larger country than the Yugoslavian leader did. On the other hand, Mao too emphasized the leading position of the Soviet Union and Stalin within the communist movement.

It was not the international but the local factors that led to the Communists' victory in the civil war. Support for Mao increased rapidly. The majority of the peasant population had long been on his side, and corruption, incompetence, and a lack of willingness to institute reforms gradually limited Chiang's support, even among the urban bourgeoisie. Or as Mao summed up the principles of the guerilla war: 'The people are the sea – we are the fish.'

Because on paper communism helps the poor?

Other Countries in Asia

Both Washington and Moscow obviously placed greater emphasis on events in Europe than in Asia. This was evident not only in China, but in other parts of Asia as well.

For the Truman administration, what mattered was supporting the regimes in Western Europe, as Washington's attitude towards the European colonial powers showed. On the one hand, the US stance was clearly anti-colonial: the colonial empires had to be dissolved. On the other hand, the United States wanted to contain communism and stabilize conditions in Western Europe. This often required a cautious course with regard to decolonization.

During the first phase of the war, the Roosevelt administration had spoken out in favor of hastening India's independence, but even during the war Washington increasingly left the initiative to London. Churchill did not want any American interference. Relations improved as the British made a clear commitment that India would become independent after the war. When the Labour government took over in 1945, it further accelerated the process. That diminished the differences between Washington and London even more. The United States supported Britain's plans to keep Hindus and Muslims together. When this proved impossible, both countries were in favor of partition into two states, India and Pakistan.

The priority given to stability in Europe became even more evident in relation to France and the Netherlands. The United States had fewer mutual interests with these two countries than with Britain. Roosevelt had favored the establishment of an international trusteeship in Indochina. He felt that France, through its exploitation of the region, had proven itself unworthy of ruling the region again. This idea died with Roosevelt. France regained control over Indochina.

Washington's insistence during the first years after the war that military assistance to France should not be used in Indochina was reduced. It soon became evident that support to France also assisted the French in their colonial war in Indochina. Washington still maintained that France ought to pursue a far more liberal colonial policy, but found it increasingly difficult to build up the country in Western Europe and at the same time pressure it to make concessions in Asia. The latter objective had to yield. This conclusion was strengthened as it became more evident that the independence movement in Vietnam was controlled by Communists.

If anti-colonial considerations should have shown themselves anywhere in their purest form, that would have to have been in Indonesia. The Netherlands were not a major power in a European context. The Indonesian independence movement was clearly non-communist. Even so, US policy until 1948 was primarily aimed at attempting to negotiate between the two sides. Only when violence escalated and both the UN and Congress began to take an interest in the conflict in earnest did the Truman administration change its course. Then Washington threatened to halt all economic and military assistance to the Dutch. This was an important factor behind their decision to grant Indonesia independence. (Decolonization will be dealt with more thoroughly in Chapter 12.)

During the first few years after the Second World War, Moscow showed a certain degree of openness towards nationalist movements in Asia and the Middle East. Even in Andrei Zhdanov's so-called two-camp speech in September 1947 there were certain non-camp exceptions. Vietnam and Indonesia were perceived as 'associated' with the socialist camp. India, Egypt, and Syria had sympathies with the Eastern bloc, but were obviously not a part of it. However, for the most part the world was divided into two blocs: 'the imperialist and anti-democratic camp, on the one hand, and the anti-imperialist and democratic camp, on the other.'

Verbal attacks on the new nationalist leaders soon increased in intensity. Moscow expressed the view that it made little difference whether the British administered India or whether they did so indirectly through their lackeys, Gandhi and Nehru. From 1949 Indonesia's Sukarno, who had previously been treated more warmly, was denounced in strong terms. Those who did not show complete support for the East belonged to the West. At the same time, Stalin and the other Soviet leaders increasingly lost interest in what was happening in the new nations of Asia. Expression of official attitudes in these matters was left to lower levels in the hierarchy, such as the press and scholars.

It was difficult to count on Communist takeovers, as the local Communist parties other than in Vietnam and Korea were rather weak. Even so, Communist revolts broke out in Burma, Malaya, Indonesia, and the Philippines in 1948. A similar occurrence had taken place earlier in Hyderabad in India.

The role of the Soviet Union is not at all clear. It is uncertain whether the Soviet leaders had inspired the revolts. The conference in Calcutta in 1948, where Moscow's directives were supposedly given, was not a very suitable forum, as participation far exceeded the ranks of the Communists. It seems more likely that the overall international climate, and the resulting division into two camps, stimulated both the Soviet Union and the local movements to strike out on a more radical course. The progress of the Communists in China may also have been of great significance. Moscow did little or nothing to quell revolts once they had broken out, and aside from speeches and articles in the press they did not give any active support either. In the press, interest seems to have been greater for a broad front against the colonial powers, such as in Malaya, than for revolts against established independent governments, such as in Burma and to some extent in the Philippines. Sympathy for the revolt in Indonesia was something in between.

Even for Moscow, France was more important than Vietnam. At least this must have seemed to be the case for the Vietnamese Communists. Nothing was to be done that could possibly weaken the position of the French Communists. To a great extent, policy was left to the French comrades themselves, who wanted to attain a compromise, particularly while they were members of the French cabinet. After war had broken out between France and the Vietminh in December 1946, Moscow declared that: 'The further development of Vietnam depends to a significant degree on its ties with democratic France, whose progressive forces have always spoken forth in support of colonial liberation.' Until 1950, the Soviet Union gave little or no material assistance to the Vietnamese Communists.

SIGNS OF RE-EVALUATION IN THE SUPERPOWERS' ASIAN POLICIES

The Communist victory in China led to a re-evaluation of Moscow's Asian policies. It was one thing to have been lukewarm towards Mao and his forces during the civil war. When victory had been achieved, the best had to be made of the possibilities which undoubtedly presented themselves. In 1948, China had not been mentioned in the main speech during Moscow's celebration of the October Revolution. In the following year, Malenkov declared that Mao's victory would lead to a new and higher stage in the people's struggle for independence in Asia and other parts of the world.

The Chinese for their part stressed that in the Cold War no nation could choose a middle position between the imperialist bloc led by the United States and the anti-imperialist bloc led by the Soviet Union. Mao proclaimed that neutrality was only camouflage. In February 1950 the two countries signed a 30-year alliance and friendship pact. Among other things, they promised each other mutual assistance in the event of attack by Japan or a country allied with Japan.

The Soviet Union would give up its territorial privileges no later than in 1952. Moscow also granted a 300-million-dollar loan on reasonable terms. But tensions were noticeable even at this stage. It was strange that Mao had to spend three months in Moscow at a time when he was urgently needed in his own country. Nor was 300 million dollars a very large amount. Poland had just been granted a 450-million-dollar loan on even better terms. It cannot have been absolutely necessary to retain Soviet privileges for a few more years, either. The economic partnerships that were to be established cannot have been perceived as a boon by the Chinese if they were to follow the pattern established in Eastern Europe.

On 18 January 1950, Peking recognized the Vietminh as the government of Vietnam. Moscow soon followed suit. The Kremlin had formerly explained to their Chinese comrades that recognition was to be given only after they had won control of the country. Now, all at once, this established practice could be broken.

In 1949–50, there were clear signs of changes on the part of the United States as well, but until the outbreak of the Korean War this re-evaluation was less comprehensive than that of the Soviet Union. After the Communist victory on the Chinese mainland, the Truman administration planned to let events take their course as far as Taiwan was concerned. Washington expected the island to be conquered and did not intend to use military intervention to prevent such a result. Some policy-makers even felt that it might then be appropriate to recognize the new leaders in Peking.

That was not the course events would take. Attitudes in Congress and in large parts of public opinion made diplomatic recognition difficult. Economic assistance to Taiwan continued. From the spring of 1950, military supplies were sent as well. Leading Republicans spoke in favor of sending troops to the island; the US navy was to halt any attempt at invasion. However, on this issue the administration held firmly to its original stand. The 'fall of China' made it necessary for the Truman administration to pursue a more active policy in Asia. Further communist expansion would represent a foreign policy defeat for the United States and a domestic setback for the Democrats. In December 1949, Truman approved *National Security Council (NSC) 48/2*. This document aimed at creating a basis for escalation of economic and military assistance to Asia. It established that special attention was to be paid to the situation in Vietnam.

For a long time, Washington had tried to get Paris to make concessions to non-communist nationalists. France finally agreed to grant Vietnam formal independence. In practice this did not mean major changes, for French control remained about the same as previously. Nevertheless, in February 1950 the United States recognized the new government under the weak, French-oriented Bao Dai. Washington was now prepared to increase assistance, and in May the first military assistance was given directly to France in Vietnam.

Japan was the most important country in Asia from an American perspective. Japan's significance increased even more after the Communist victory in China. US occupation policy had gradually changed because of the importance of Japanese resources for the West in the Cold War (Japanese–US relations will be discussed further on pp. 214–15).

The changes in US Asian policies were, however, relatively small until the outbreak of the Korean War. Europe was still far more important than Asia. In Asia the main emphasis was on Japan, the Philippines, and other strategically important islands off the Asian mainland.

US strategic interests in Asia were clearly defined in 1949–50. Secretary of State Dean Acheson stated in January 1950 that the US defense perimeter went from the Aleutians to Japan and continued to the Ryukyu Islands and the Philippines. Several important areas were thus outside this line: Taiwan, Indochina, and South Korea. There was a considerable amount of debate about US policy in regard to Taiwan, but as far as the Asian mainland was concerned Acheson had broad support at the time. Disagreement as to the content of his speech would become much stronger at a later date. General Douglas MacArthur, supreme commander in Japan and highly active during the Korean War, declared as late as two days after the outbreak of the war that whoever thought US troops ought to combat communism on the Asian mainland 'ought to have his head examined.'

This did not mean that the countries which were beyond the defense perimeter were not of interest to Washington. Economic and military assistance was given to them as well. The increase in assistance to Taiwan and Indochina has already been mentioned.

US commitments were even more direct in South Korea. With the collapse of Japan, Korea was divided into two zones of occupation at the thirty-eighth parallel. The Red Army advanced in the North, the US army into the South. The Soviets molded their zone in their own image. They were supported by large groups of Communists and radicals in the relatively industrialized North. The political situation was much more chaotic in the South, with as many as 200 political parties and groups. The Americans would support the reactionary Syngman Rhee, and the favoring of the right became more evident as Rhee was faced with ever-increasing problems. In January 1950, Acheson stressed that although South Korea lay beyond the US defense perimeter, an attack on the country would be a matter for the UN.

When the Red Army was withdrawn from North Korea in 1948, the Pentagon felt that South Korea was a place where money could be saved on a tight defense budget. The last US troops were withdrawn in June 1949. In January 1950 the Congress voted down a proposal by the Truman administration for economic assistance to South Korea, but by promising a little extra support for Taiwan the administration persuaded Congress to reverse this decision.

There were many reasons for Washington's restraint in South Korea. The most important US interests were undoubtedly linked to the islands off the Asian mainland. Moreover, intervening in Korea seemed illogical when the United States had not intervened in China. In a sense, the statements of Acheson and others were rationalizations which arose from the policy that had already been pursued, particularly in regard to China.

Evaluations of the relative local strengths varied, but many Americans expected South Korea to be able to withstand North Korean attacks. It was considered unlikely that the Soviet Union or China would be directly involved in an attack on South Korea. Finally, Syngman Rhee, despite the increasing support he gradually enjoyed, was viewed with skepticism in Washington. He was far from democratic, but there was no other strong anti-communist alternative. The United States even feared that South Korea might attack North Korea, and to prevent this the Americans withheld deliveries of heavy military equipment such as planes and tanks.

US policy also rested on a specific analysis of the relationship between nationalism and communism. Nationalism was a growing force on the Asian mainland. It was important that the United States should not become antagonistic to nationalistic forces but should be able to use them against communism. In this context, and partly to soften the consequences of China's fall for US domestic politics, the Truman administration developed the theory that in the course of time there might be a breach between the Soviet Union and China. Acheson claimed that the most important interference in Asia was Soviet attempts to win control over parts of China. Thus 'we must not undertake to deflect from the Russians to ourselves the righteous anger and the wrath and the hatred of the Chinese people which must develop.' In the long term, nationalism would be victorious in China. US policy showed – despite many general statements that could indicate otherwise – that Washington still distinguished between important and less important regions, and that the United States was capable of perceiving differences within the Communist bloc.

The Korean War

Many clashes had taken place between troops from the two parts of Korea. However, the North Korean attack on 25 June 1950 was of a completely different magnitude than these minor skirmishes. It is now clear that Moscow not only knew about, but had also given its consent to the attack. Even though the Red Army had been withdrawn, many Soviet military and civilian advisers remained, and they were to be found both centrally and locally. North Korea was dependent on the Soviet Union for weapons, receiving substantial supplies in April–May 1950. The North Korean leader Kim Il Sung could show signs of independence, but to a great extent he was dependent on Moscow.

Kim Il Sung had contacted Stalin numerous times to request his consent to an invasion in the South, a consent that was finally given in the spring of 1950. Thus Khrushchev is right when he claims in his memoirs that the initiative was taken by the North Koreans. There were strong wishes in both North and South for a reunification of Korea. The North Korean leaders hoped that an attack could lead to a revolt in the south that would make the war short-lived. Mao had consented to the Korean plans. The time was ripe for the revolution to be victorious in Korea as well. But with the enormous tasks facing China at home, the Chinese role was modest during this early phase. Perhaps Stalin wanted to demonstrate to the Chinese that he, too, could actively support national liberation movements.

In terms of great power politics, there was little reason to believe that the United States would intervene directly. The country had kept out of the civil war in China and, as we have seen, there were numerous declarations that Korea was beyond the US defense perimeter. A successful drive would not only result in a unified communist Korea, it might also stop the ever-stronger integration of Japan into US military strategy.

Although the risk involved in an attack was considered small, such a conflict meant a clear increase in Soviet involvement in Asia. The situation in Europe was stabilized somewhat, and Moscow could devote more attention to what was happening in Asia.

The United States responded to the North Korean attack with air and naval forces. When this proved insufficient, ground troops were also sent in. Thus the United States was at war on the Asian mainland after all. The American commander was Douglas MacArthur. With the Soviet Union boycotting UN Security Council meetings because Taiwan held the Chinese seat, the Council could condemn North Korea's military offensive. Britain and the Commonwealth countries were foremost among those who sent troops to participate in the US-led action under the auspices of the UN.

What can explain this change on the part of the United States? There is often a difference between theory and practice. It was one thing to say that there would be no direct military response. It was another matter to keep to that policy in practice. Washington's declaration that South Korea was beyond the US defense perimeter was to a certain extent based on the expectation that the South Koreans themselves would be able to withstand an attack from the north. This proved not to be the case.

Even before the war broke out, US involvement in Asia was growing. The domestic political situation in the United States further undermined the original stance of the Truman administration. Verbal assaults for having 'lost China' to the Communists became steadily harsher. In February, Senator Joseph McCarthy had begun his attacks on communist influence within the administration. If South Korea now fell, too, that would undoubtedly sharpen the tone even further, just a few months before Congressional elections. Moreover, Truman liked to consider himself a man who could act swiftly and decisively, a characteristic he could now demonstrate. He received overwhelming support from the Congress and public opinion.

It was more or less assumed that Moscow was behind the North Korean attack. In Western capitals, the usual analysis had been that the Soviet Union would probably try to gain control of new areas, but that this would happen by indirect means. Now, however, the Kremlin had resorted to very direct methods nonetheless.

The policy of containment required a Western response. A large-scale attack across a clearly defined, even though temporary, border revived the memories of the 1930s.

The lessons from those years were unambiguous. Aggression had to be stopped as early as possible. If not answered in Korea, it would only result in new advances in more central areas. Japan and Western Europe might be new goals, and confidence in the United States would be weakened in these areas if the country did not oppose communist aggression in Korea. Thus the experience of Hitler lent support to the domino theory: that if one domino fell, the next one would also fall. Such thoughts were a central element in the decision to send US troops into Korea.

During the first two to three months, the Americans had their hands full just making sure they were not thrown into the sea. But after MacArthur's amphibious landing at Inchon on 15 September, their luck turned full circle. The Americans were soon crossing the thirty-eighth parallel. This violated the statement issued just after the war broke out that the US objective was to return to the situation that had existed before the war.

This change was to a certain extent a result of pressure by MacArthur and highly conservative circles in the United States, but for the most part the administration agreed with the new policy. The objective had always been to unify Korea. Now the opportunity presented itself. The Communists had actually created this opportunity themselves, according to Washington. The United States would not have crossed the dividing line without provocation, but once the North Koreans had done so, it was only reasonable that they had to take the consequences of their actions. Korea was to be united as a non-communist nation.

The goal was the Yalu, the river bordering on China. That showed how the nature of the US involvement had changed. US troops had first been withdrawn from the Asian mainland. Now they were back. Not only were they back; for the first time Americans were fighting directly against communist forces. This was taking place in Asia, not in Europe. After 1 October, it took place on communist territory.

Washington had received signals that China might intervene if the United States crossed the thirty-eighth parallel. The US position was quite confusing. Troops were not to cross the dividing line if that would result in Chinese intervention. But certainty as to whether or not they would intervene could only be achieved by crossing the line. China was considered weak in military terms and preoccupied with internal problems. A second reason why the Truman administration placed little emphasis on the signals it received was that the State Department in particular still clung to the earlier analysis that Peking would understand that it was Moscow, and not Washington, that was the true antagonist.

The Chinese response was hesitant in October but harsh in November in the form of massive forces. Seen from Peking, the worst possible scenario must have been that MacArthur would not stop at the Yalu, but advance into China. This was not inconceivable in the light of new demands for support to Chiang Kai-shek. But even a united non-communist Korea was probably unacceptable to Mao. Such a country would cooperate not only with the United States, but probably with Japan and Taiwan as well. After his victory in the Chinese Civil War, there was also an element of 'revolutionary romanticism' in Mao's policies. He had defeated the United States in China; now he was ready to take on the Americans in Korea.

The Soviet Union was not interested in armed conflict with the United States. Moscow did not need to intervene as long as the Chinese could prevent a North Korean defeat. But it must have irritated the Chinese that they had to fight with poorer equipment than even the Koreans had. When new weapons came from the Soviet Union, it appears that Peking had to pay a relatively high price for them.

The Chinese intervention put an end to any hopes that Washington, and the State Department in particular, had had of a possible breach between the Soviet Union and China. Now their evaluations swung to the opposite extreme. With a slight exception for Tito's Yugoslavia, communism was considered a monolithic entity. A victory for a communist movement anywhere in the world thus necessarily entailed a loss for the West.

There were still a few who felt that a breach between the Soviet Union and China would come at some time in the future. Surprisingly enough, Secretary of State John Foster Dulles was among them when he assumed office in 1953. But the conclusion was still the same: China was to be kept isolated. By China becoming even more dependent on the Soviet Union, the possibilities for a breach would increase.

US policy towards China became even harsher than towards the Soviet Union. Any mention of diplomatic recognition was taboo. Trade (and virtually all contact) was severed. As early as from the outbreak of the war, the US navy was to prevent a communist takeover in Taiwan, but Washington's assistance to Chiang now increased rapidly.

Figure 3.1   Development in the Korean War

It consisted not only of economic and military assistance, but of subversive operations on the Chinese mainland as well. Support for reconquering the mainland, however, was out of the question.

There were still clear limitations on US anti-communist involvement in Asia. Nuclear weapons would not be used in Korea. General MacArthur was dismissed in April 1951, partly because the Truman administration had decided that the war should not be escalated further. The Yalu River was not to be crossed. The supply lines in China would not be bombed. Military assistance from Chiang was not to be accepted in Korea, and the support Chiang was to receive would be quite limited.

In the spring of 1951, the war in Korea stabilized itself at approximately the thirty-eighth parallel. Neither side went in for new major offensives. Nevertheless, it took two years and political shifts in several capitals before a ceasefire was reached.

CHANGES IN US POLICY IN ASIA

The war would cause major changes in US and Soviet policies. The changes were greatest on the part of the United States. (Changes in relation to strategy, rearmament in Western Europe, and the size of the defense budget will be described in more detail on pp. 129–31.)

For the most part, the Truman administration continued to concentrate its attention on Europe. The US military response in Korea became as comprehensive as it was only after it had become evident that Korea was not a diversionary maneuver for an attack in Europe. In the course of two to three years, the US defense budget was tripled, but only a small portion of these resources went to the war in Korea. The largest share was used for a build-up of forces in the United States for the purpose of preventing and, if that did not succeed, fighting a war in Europe. The US troops in Europe were reinforced with four new divisions. Europe was still far more important to Washington than Asia was.

Although the main emphasis was still on Europe, US military involvement increased considerably in most parts of the world. The increase was even greater in certain areas after the Korean War than it had been after the Second World War. Before the Korean War, the United States was only bound by one military treaty outside the Western hemisphere and that was NATO. After the outbreak of the war, the United States entered into treaties and made commitments in a number of different regions. The number of bases rose sharply.

As early as during the Second World War, it had become evident that Australia and New Zealand would orient themselves towards Washington, and away from London, in security matters. Australia in particular showed a strong interest in a separate security system in the Pacific. In 1951 the Truman administration was ready to consider an agreement between the United States, Japan, the Philippines, Australia, New Zealand, and perhaps Britain and Indonesia as well. The US army was still skeptical about commitments on the Asian mainland. That was the reason that Thailand, for instance, was not included.

It proved impossible to achieve such a comprehensive system. The situation in Asia was considerably more complex than in Europe. Asia was much bigger and more populous than Europe. The sense of cohesiveness was also more limited, with very few forms of pan-Asian cooperation, unlike the situation in Europe. Many forms of regional rivalries existed. There was widespread opposition to including Japan. After the peace treaty with Japan was signed in 1951, the United States and Japan made a separate defense agreement which gave the United States the right to have bases in Japan. A second agreement was made with the Philippines. The United States, Australia, and New Zealand entered into the ANZUS pact, all this in August–September 1951. Britain was not included. This emphasized the power shift to the advantage of the United States that had taken place in this part of the world as well as elsewhere.

The Eisenhower administration would place even greater emphasis than its predecessor on building up a bulwark against communism in Asia. Although the alliances and agreements here were considerably less stringent in their composition and commitments than NATO, the idea behind them was basically the same. Definite lines had to be drawn up. If the Soviet Union or one of its allies overstepped these lines, the West, led by the United States, would respond in military terms. The more countries that were included in these agreements, the stronger the West would become and the smaller the chances of communist aggression would be.

As early as in the report on the first 90 days of the administration, Secretary of State Dulles could declare that:

> the Far East has received a higher priority. Furthermore, it has been made clear that we think our friends in the Far East, from Japan, Korea and Formosa to Indochina and Malaya face a united enemy front, which has to be met by a common attitude and greater cooperation among the separate links of freedom.

In August 1953, the United States entered into a defense agreement with South Korea. This agreement was to guarantee the security of South Korea, and was necessary in order to get the South Koreans to agree to a ceasefire in the Korean War. Taiwan, too, had long been eager to attain closer contact with the United States.

The Eisenhower administration stepped up its verbal support of Chiang Kai-shek. The US fleet was withdrawn from the Formosa Strait. This would supposedly make it easier for Chiang to carry out operations on the mainland. But Washington was still not willing to support an attempted invasion, and without US assistance an invasion was impossible. In September 1954, the Communists began to bombard the island of Quemoy, which was located just off the mainland and far from Taiwan, which controlled it. Despite initial reservations on the part of President Eisenhower, Washington entered into a security agreement with Taiwan in December. The agreement was unclear as to Quemoy and Matsu, but even these islands could at least partially be said to fall within the scope of US defense commitments.

The Korean War and the setbacks France experienced in battle against the Vietminh troops resulted in a rapid escalation in US military assistance to the French in Indochina. In 1954 Washington paid about 80 per cent of the French war expenses. US advisers were also brought in.

Despite this assistance, the war went badly for France. In the spring of 1954, the French position was about to collapse, partly because of the battles around Dien Bien Phu and partly because of the domestic political situation in France. Paris would have liked a military victory but became increasingly interested in finding an alternative that could end the war. Washington still placed greatest emphasis on avoiding a communist victory. In order to prevent a French defeat, the question of US intervention was raised. Vice President Nixon, the navy, and the air force supported this option. However, Eisenhower was skeptical, as were the leaders of the US army, who felt that the Korean War had only emphasized the difficulties of fighting a war on the Asian mainland. As Britain and the Democratic leadership in the Senate were also opposed to US intervention, Eisenhower dropped the idea.

At the subsequent conference in Geneva, both sides had to make concessions. France granted complete independence to North and South Vietnam, Laos, and Cambodia. The Communist regime persevered in North Vietnam, and the chances were high that the elections which were to be held in Vietnam within two years might result in communist dominance over the entire country. For the time being, however, the North Vietnamese had to be content to control a smaller area than they had expected and less than the area developments in the war had given a basis for. Both the Soviet Union and China were interested in an end to the war and contributed to getting North Vietnam to accept the agreement.

After the Geneva meeting, the United States remained intent on saving what could be saved from communism. The most important step in that context was the establishment of SEATO, the South–East Asia Treaty Organization. SEATO had fewer members than Washington had hoped for. India and Indonesia had no desire to belong. The British protested against including Taiwan. France would not accept South Vietnam, Laos, and Cambodia. According to the Geneva agreement, they were to be neutral in any case. Nonetheless, they were partially covered by the SEATO pact. The members were the United States, the United Kingdom, France, Australia, New Zealand, the Philippines, Thailand, and Pakistan. In the United States there was widespread support for this new addition to the pact system. The treaty was ratified in the Senate by a vote of 82 to 1.

In Europe, too, the pact system was expanded. In 1948–49 the United States had opposed including countries in NATO that did not border on the Atlantic Ocean. Italy was the only exception, although many members of the Truman administration were skeptical even of Italian full membership in NATO. In 1952, the links to the Atlantic Ocean were weakened even more by the inclusion of Greece and Turkey. In 1955, after the French national assembly had rejected the plans for a European army with German participation, West Germany became a member of NATO (see p. 162).

There was considerable continuity from the Truman to the Eisenhower administration both in Europe and in Asia. The expansion of NATO and transference of the pact model from Europe to Asia had begun under Truman. The Korean War was the major breakthrough. It made evaluations of Soviet intentions even more negative than previously. Through an accelerated pace of rearmament, the United States also acquired an instrument to pursue an even more ambitious course, with more and more comprehensive commitments in new regions.

In principle, the Republicans were not quite as oriented towards Europe as the Democratic Truman administration had been. This was particularly true of the Republican right wing, which had roots back to the isolationism of the period between the wars and to the 'Asia first' policy during the Second World War. Eisenhower and

Dulles belonged to the more international and Europe-oriented group, but they showed some consideration for the minority in the party.

The change in administration meant that a larger share of Washington's program of assistance went to Asia, although a reduction in Europe at this stage was natural for many reasons. Asia's share under the Mutual Assistance Act increased from 12.6 per cent in 1953 to 54.5 per cent in 1954. During the Dien Bien Phu crisis it had also become evident that leading persons in the Eisenhower administration were more willing to intervene than the Democrats in the Senate were. But these differences can easily be exaggerated. As mentioned earlier, Senate support for SEATO was overwhelming.

After the establishment of SEATO, the largest gap in the alliance system was in the Middle East and western Asia, between Turkey in NATO and Pakistan in SEATO. Both Washington and London were eager to create a pact in this region. The first plans had been launched as early as 1952, during the Truman administration. For the Americans, the objective was primarily to create a front against communism. Britain was still the dominant major power in the Middle East and had considerable strategic, political, and economic interests in the area, even after the withdrawal from Palestine in 1948. To some extent, the United States perceived the British presence as a factor that contributed to making the countries there more radical, thus making the establishment of a front against communism more difficult. A weakening of the British role could also lead to a strengthening of the US position. These different perspectives, combined with the complex local conditions, made progress difficult, but in 1955 the Baghdad Pact was established with the United Kingdom, Turkey, Pakistan, Iran, and Iraq as members.

The United States was only indirectly linked to the new system. The main reason was that the pact resulted in a polarization in the Middle East. Those that were not included, and that meant the vast majority of the Arab countries, tended to be in a position of rivalry in relation to those that were members. Washington wanted to maintain relations with the countries that at least partially considered the Baghdad Pact the extended arm of British colonialism. When it came right down to it, Dulles actually felt that it would be best if even Iran waited to join. A certain amount of time ought to pass from the US–British coup in the autumn of 1953 against Prime Minister Mohammed Mossadeq until Iran joined the Western side directly. But the Shah of Iran saw things differently, and he had his way.

The new organization was not a great success. The British felt betrayed by the Americans. Iran and Iraq were the only countries that did not already belong to a pact. In July 1958, General Abdul Karim Kassem seized power in Iraq and withdrew the country's membership. The Baghdad Pact was reorganized as CENTO, the Central Treaty Organization, although it did not become more central even with its new name.

The US bloc build-up was accompanied by denunciations of neutrality. Dulles issued some harsh statements. In his opinion, neutrality was not only 'old-fashioned' and 'shortsighted,' but also 'immoral.' It was everyone's duty to cooperate in the struggle against the forces of evil in the world. At first sight this resembled the two-camp theory that Zhdanov had proclaimed on the Soviet side as early as 1947. However, Dulles made his statements at a time when, as we shall see, the Soviet Union was in the process of abandoning the theory, although it must be said that even Dulles could be more pragmatic than is often believed.

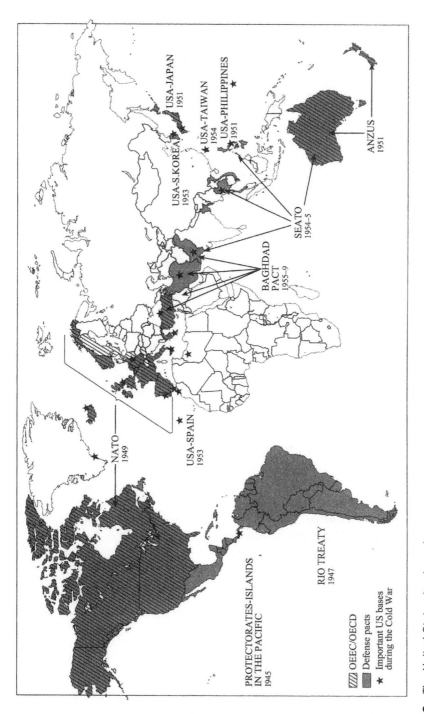

Figure 3.2 The United States treaty system

USA-JAPAN
1951

USA-TAIWAN
1954

USA-PHILIPPINES
1951

USA-S.KOREA
1953

ANZUS
1951

SEATO
1954-5

BAGHDAD
PACT
1955-9

NATO
1949

USA-SPAIN
1953

PROTECTORATES-ISLANDS
IN THE PACIFIC
1945

RIO TREATY
1947

OEEC/OECD

Defense pacts

★ Important US bases
during the Cold War

India was the most important of the nonaligned countries. The United States and India had differing views on several issues during the Korean War; they disagreed as to the peace treaty for Japan, and not least about the establishment of SEATO, which brought the United States into a close relationship with India's rival, Pakistan. Many US policy-makers felt that Nehru was naive in thinking that he could practice neutrality.

However, the US attitude was not as literal as Dulles's diatribes might seem to indicate. The United States gave considerable economic assistance to countries such as India, Indonesia, Egypt, and Yugoslavia as well. As we have seen, Washington was interested in establishing some type of relations even with the more radical Arab countries in the Middle East. On the whole, the US attitude towards neutrality became more conciliatory as the 1950s progressed.

In Africa, the United States was content for quite some time to leave the responsibility to its allies, the colonial powers of the United Kingdom, France, Belgium, and Portugal. The Eisenhower administration showed little interest in hastening the process of independence in Africa. For the most part it emphasized the need for moderation on both sides. After the countries had become independent, the administration stressed the advantages of continued cooperation with the former colonial powers.

The Kennedy administration would place more emphasis on having good relations with the countries of both Asia and Africa than its predecessor had done. The attacks on neutrality ceased. Interest in the new nations grew. Economic assistance increased, as did pressure on the colonial powers to complete the process of independence. Portugal's policies in Africa were of particular interest in this context. Even so, there was no question of a decisive break with the past. For instance, Portugal was still an important ally because the United States was dependent on continued base rights on the Azores.

THE SOVIET UNION TRIES TO PLAY A GLOBAL ROLE

The other superpower, too, tried to press complex local conditions into an East–West pattern. Gradually, however, Moscow began to pursue a friendlier, more active policy towards the many countries that had entered the international arena. This became evident first in Asia and the Middle East, then in Africa. The Kremlin would try to get a foothold in Latin America as well. However, the overall conclusion must be that in the 1950s and 1960s, Soviet influence in the Third World could not equal US influence by any means.

A New Policy in Asia and the Middle East

As early as 1949–50, Moscow had become less exclusively oriented towards Europe in its policies. As we have seen, the Communist victory in the civil war in China, the outbreak of the Korean War, and the conflict in Indochina were significant in this context. However, all of these events could be accounted for within the two-camp theory. It was a question of helping one's 'socialist brethren' in the fight against imperialism.

To some extent, the Soviet Union was drawn into new regions by events which were beyond Soviet control. But it was also a question of a conscious change in Moscow's policies. The first sign of movement away from a pure East–West division could be noticed while Stalin was still alive. In his *Economic Problems of Socialism in the U.S.S.R.* of October 1952, the Soviet leader had even cautiously suggested that peaceful coexistence between East and West might be possible. Moreover, the split in the imperialist bloc could become so great that the countries which came into the greatest opposition with the United States would seek to improve relations with the Soviet Union. This theme was made even more explicit by Malenkov at the Nineteenth Party Congress that same year.

Stalin's death in March 1953 gave a strong impetus to this cautious re-evaluation. The new leaders were much freer to make a break with a policy that had unquestionably had negative aspects. There could be no doubt that the two-camp theory had barred the Soviet Union from contacts with and influence in the new nations. The number of new nations was growing rapidly, and the vast majority of them chose to remain neutral in East–West matters. At worst, a negative Soviet attitude could press them into the comprehensive alliance systems the United States was in the process of building up. At best, a re-evaluation could result in closer cooperation against 'imperialism and colonialism.' The Chinese, too, were interested in pursuing a more active policy towards the new nations.

Moreover, the material basis for a new course of policy was more favorable. The wartime destruction had meant that at first resources had to be channeled into the enormous tasks of reconstruction. In 1950, at the close of the fourth five-year plan, the 1940 production level had been exceeded for almost all types of goods. Production continued to increase at a rapid pace throughout the 1950s. The Soviet Union could finally begin to use economic assistance and trade as policy instruments in Asia and Africa. The country was also much stronger in military terms now that it had developed the atomic and hydrogen bombs.

Moscow stopped describing Nehru and Sukarno as lackeys of imperialism. Terms of abuse that had previously been common in descriptions of these nationalist leaders were now reserved for reactionary leaders, such as Chiang Kai-shek and Syngman Rhee. The Kremlin began to show interest in entering into trade and cultural agreements with the leaders who had previously been so harshly denounced. In 1954, Afghanistan became the first non-communist country to receive economic assistance from the Soviet Union.

These new signals coalesced in 1955. In that year, Nehru visited the Soviet Union, and then both Khrushchev and Prime Minister Nikolaj Bulganin toured India, Burma, and Afghanistan. Substantial economic assistance was given. Moscow expressed its support for the Bandung conference, which was held by Asian and African countries (see p. 244).

The Kremlin's attitude towards the Arab countries in the Middle East was the best example of how hesitant this change of course was. At first, Stalin had tried to compete with Truman in being most strongly pro-Israeli. In the UN, the Soviet Union voted in favor of partitioning Palestine, and barely lost the race with the United States to be first to recognize the Jewish state. During the subsequent Israeli–Arab war, Moscow pronounced the Arabs the aggressors, and weapons were sent from Eastern Europe to Israel. The point of departure for Soviet policy seems to have been the desire to get Britain out of the Middle East as quickly as possible.

Soviet–Israeli relations soon cooled, however. Israel followed a clearly Western-oriented course, despite its socialist domestic policies. The Kremlin's suspicious attitude towards the Soviet Jews also made good relations difficult. At the end of his life, Stalin expressed unmistakably anti-Semitic views.

Even so, Moscow hesitated to improve relations with the Arab countries. The fact that many of them pursued reactionary policies is one explanation. But when King Farouk of Egypt was overthrown in 1952 and replaced by progressive military leaders, the Kremlin was skeptical even of them. The large Soviet *Encyclopedia* from 1952–53 described the coup as organized by 'US–British imperialists' and the new leaders as 'a group of reactionary officers.' The most important consequence of the overthrow seemed to be that it foreshadowed increasing 'clashes of interest' between the United States and the United Kingdom. Soviet relations with Syria and with Iraq in particular were even poorer than with Egypt.

Nevertheless, the domestic radicalization of several of the Arab countries, the polarization in the wake of the Western attempts to build up a system of alliances, and, most important of all, the Arab–Israeli conflict opened up unique opportunities for Moscow in the Middle East.

In 1954, Moscow used its veto in the UN Security Council for the first time to support the Arab countries in opposition to Israel. However, the red-letter year in the Middle East, as in Asia, was 1955. Gamal Abdel Nasser, who proved to be the dominant member of the group of military leaders that took over after Farouk, tried to buy new weapons. The Western powers showed little interest in selling, in part because they wanted to limit the sale of weapons to an area as full of conflict as the Middle East was, but also because they were dissatisfied with Nasser's negative attitude towards the build-up of a Western pact system. Thus Nasser turned to the East. Moscow was now prepared to pursue a more active policy. A 200-million-dollar weapons deal was camouflaged as a Czech–Egyptian agreement. When the turnabout did come, it was dramatic. The Egyptian Communists who did not support Nasser were denounced in the Soviet press as 'provocateurs who call themselves communists.'

However, the Soviet role was still modest. Although its influence was increasing, it was still far from equal to that of the West in the Middle East. Its limitations were evident during the Suez conflict in 1956 and again during the Middle East crisis of 1958.

In July 1956, Nasser nationalized the Suez Canal. This was mainly a reaction to US and British statements that they were going to withdraw their promised support for building the Aswan Dam. The United States in particular reacted to Nasser's overtures towards the East as evidenced in the weapons deal and in Egypt's recognition of China.

The attempts to achieve a peaceful solution to the dispute over the Suez Canal were unsuccessful. In October, Britain and France, in cooperation with Israel, went to war against Egypt. Britain had substantial interests in the canal, both in its operation and in the canal as a link between Europe and Asia. The British government was also highly irritated by Nasser's attempts to reduce British influence in the Middle East. Disapproval of the Egyptian leader was at least equally strong in Paris. The French government was convinced that the rebel forces in Algeria received a substantial share of their supplies from Egypt.

The Soviet Union kept a low profile during the first phase of the conflict. Later on, Moscow threatened to use nuclear missiles against the two Western powers and to send

Soviet volunteers to support Egypt. However, these threats came so late that there was probably little danger of them being implemented. The US stance seems to have had more significance for the French–British decision to call off their military action even though they had not achieved the victory they had hoped for. Eisenhower blocked Britain's application to the International Monetary Fund for a loan and threatened to deny both Britain and France the American oil they would need now that the Suez Canal was closed. The invasion of Egypt also produced strong reactions within many other countries, including Britain and France themselves.

The British–French fiasco undermined Britain's position in the Middle East. Moscow's threats represented a considerable propaganda victory in the Arab countries, and the Kremlin's influence was on the increase. In response to this situation, Eisenhower proclaimed the so-called Eisenhower Doctrine in January 1957. In a message to Congress, the President maintained that US troops would be used to protect nations in the region from countries that were 'controlled by international communism.' The Eisenhower Doctrine was to do in the Middle East what the Truman Doctrine had done in Greece and Turkey ten years earlier. The United States was to fill the vacuum the British–French defeat had created.

When Washington and London sent troops to Lebanon and Jordan respectively during the following year to support the conservative governments there against the after-effects of Kassem's seizure of power in Iraq, Moscow could only protest. The interventions of the two countries were as much an attempt to keep pro-Nasser circles from power as they were aimed against international communism. But the Soviet Union had neither the will nor the ability to neutralize such a direct intervention.

Quite contrary to what the Western powers had expected, hefty disagreements soon broke out between Kassem and Nasser. The Kremlin would have liked to have stayed on good terms with both sides but could hardly keep out of the bitter dispute. The choice fell on Iraq. One reason seems to have been Kassem's more radical domestic policies, emphasizing major economic reforms and cooperation with the Communists. Moscow could not entirely ignore domestic policies in its evaluations of the various countries of the Third World.

Nonetheless, there was never a question of a break with Nasser. The Soviet Union still gave substantial economic assistance to Egypt, for instance for the completion of the Aswan Dam. After the Iraqi Communists made an unsuccessful takeover attempt in 1960, their influence dwindled rapidly. Then Moscow turned back to Egypt, or the United Arab Republic, as the union between Egypt and Syria was named. The Union lasted from 1958 until Syria broke out in 1961. Changes took place quickly in the Middle East. No one was able to control events there.

A New Policy in Africa

The Soviet attitude towards the struggle for liberation in Algeria (1954–62) illustrated some of the problems the country had to face in relation to the Third World. On the one hand, the Soviet leaders wanted to support 'wars of national liberation.' This was ideologically correct and could lead to considerable political gains not only in Algeria, but elsewhere in Africa and Asia as well. These considerations must have been strengthened by the fact that China in 1958 officially recognized the National Liberation Front (FLN) as the legitimate government of Algeria. On the other hand France, and to a certain extent the United States as well, had to be taken into consideration. Even though General de Gaulle had an anti-communist stance on many questions, he was a nationalist in relation to the United States. Moscow could not have been interested in doing anything that would bring Paris and Washington closer together. Both countries would have reacted sharply to Soviet support for the FLN. The result was that here, as so often before, least emphasis was placed on ideological considerations. The Kremlin kept a low profile in the Algerian question. The FLN was not officially recognized until Algeria received its independence in 1962.

If US interest in Africa south of the Sahara was modest for a long time, that of the Soviet Union was even smaller. This was particularly the case during the colonial era, but even after independence the Soviet Union acted hesitantly, although Moscow had good cards to play in its fundamental opposition to the Western colonial system.

In 1956–57, Ghana was the first colony south of the Sahara to be granted independence (p. 234). However, it took two years before a Soviet ambassador came to Accra. The country's leader, Kwame Nkrumah, was considered a collaborator with the Western powers and a petty bourgeois politician. The re-evaluation which had taken place with regard to nationalist leaders in many Asian countries and in the Middle East seems to have been delayed here. In addition, Moscow had little expertise on this region. An African division was not established in the Soviet foreign ministry until 1958. The first trade contracts of any size were signed in 1959–60.

Guinea under Sekou Touré was a more promising partner for cooperation than Ghana under Nkrumah. Ghana maintained close contact with its former colonial ruler, the United Kingdom, but Guinea, as the only country in Africa to refuse the proposed constitution, broke with France in 1958. Ethnic rivalry was not as strong in Guinea as in Ghana, and Touré was the African politician Moscow knew and liked best, despite certain disagreements with him as well. The new nation was soon recognized. President Voroshilov described it as 'an important step on the path of the liberation of Africa from the colonialist yoke.'

Whereas the Soviet Union showed understanding for France's position in Algeria, which was highly significant to Paris, there was less need for caution in regard to a Guinea which had broken with France. But Touré had no plans to trade French dominance for Soviet dominance. Because of the break with France, he probably became economically more dependent on the Soviet Union than he liked. However, he did not tolerate any meddling in the domestic affairs of his country, and during the Cuban crisis in 1962 he refused to allow Soviet planes to refuel in Guinea on their way to Cuba. The progressive regimes in Africa were seldom as progressive as Moscow had hoped for. As compensation for a certain degree of disappointment in Touré, the Soviet leaders could be pleased that Nkrumah after 1960 pursued more radical policies than previously. Good relations were also established with Mali and Algeria after they became independent.

The Congo crisis in 1960 was the first clear signal that the Cold War had spread to Africa south of the Sahara. The crisis would confirm a pattern that had already shown itself in Asia and the Middle East: although Moscow was in the process of becoming an important actor in ever new parts of the world, Soviet influence was seldom equal to that of the Western capitals, particularly Washington.

Before the Congo became independent in 1960 it had had little contact with the Soviet Union and Eastern Europe. As so often elsewhere, Moscow mainly left the formulation of colonial policy to the Communists in the mother country, in this case Belgium. Following independence, the Soviet Union considered Prime Minister Patrice Lumumba a possible 'progressive' politician. But after the administration of the country had collapsed and Belgium intervened, Moscow chose at first to leave further initiatives to the UN.

However, relations between Lumumba and the UN deteriorated rapidly. That increased both the temptation and the possibilities for the Soviet leaders to play a more active role. They decided to help Lumumba, thus coming into conflict with the policy of the UN under the active leadership of Secretary General Dag Hammarskjöld. Transport planes, trucks and other supplies were sent, and several hundred advisers from Eastern bloc countries turned up in the Congo.

Once more, events would prove that Moscow had little luck. In September 1960, Colonel Sese Seko Mobutu seized control, with support from the United States and Belgium. Lumumba was imprisoned and the advisers from the Eastern bloc sent home. There was little the Russians could do to prevent this. In February 1961, Lumumba was killed. This contributed to the Kremlin increasing its support for a separatist government in Stanleyville under Antoine Gizenga. Assistance arrived in the form of political declarations and military assistance given through Egypt and Ghana.

The local situation was extremely complex. Many supplies never reached the intended groups. For a while, Moscow seems to have been afraid of being outmaneuvered by China in terms of relations to progressive forces. However, most of the countries of the Third World supported the role the UN tried to play.

In contrast to the Soviet Union, the United States would enjoy ever-increasing influence. Several years of unrest went by before Mobutu carried out his second coup in 1965 and declared himself president with complete control, to the extent that complete control was possible in such a vast, divided country as the Congo, or Zaire, as the name was changed to in 1971.

THE COLD WAR REACHES LATIN AMERICA

If the Soviet Union had been slow in establishing itself as a serious actor in Asia and Africa, it took even longer in Latin America. Since the Monroe Doctrine of 1823, Washington had considered the Western hemisphere its backyard. Through the establishment of regional systems, such as the Rio Treaty in 1947 and the Organization of American States in 1948, the United States had formalized its role as the only major power in this part of the world. Not only was the Soviet Union barred from entrance, but even Britain sometimes reacted to what it considered a US double standard of morality. The United States was opposed to other countries' spheres of interest, but retained the right to have its own. The fact that the United States was in favor of such regional arrangements did not necessarily mean that the Latin American countries opposed them. On the contrary, most of them showed active support.

The Soviet Union may have shown little interest in Latin America, but the countries in this part of the world were also skeptical of Moscow and of communism. In 1953, the

Soviet Union had diplomatic relations with only three countries: Mexico, Argentina, and Uruguay. In the same year, Moscow made its first trade agreement with such an important country as Argentina.

From a Soviet perspective, Guatemala was the most interesting country at this juncture. After Colonel Arbenz had taken over as president in 1950, Guatemala moved to the left. In terms of foreign policy, the country took a stand in opposition to Washington on several occasions. Land reforms were initiated, at the expense of the United Fruit Company, which had excellent contacts within the Eisenhower administration. However, the Communist party was weak, and the increasing criticism of the United States had not resulted in the establishment of diplomatic relations with the Soviet Union.

Arbenz wanted to acquire weapons, in part to prevent attempts to overthrow his government. The United States would not sell him weapons and he turned to Moscow. The Kremlin responded in the affirmative and tried to send supplies to Guatemala in complete secrecy. Washington had probably already decided to get rid of Arbenz by that time. The Central Intelligence Agency (CIA) was to carry out a coup in cooperation with opposition groups in Guatemala.

The coup was successful, mainly due to the fact that those responsible for it had the support of the army and the traditional upper class in the country. Guatemala's new military regime was one among many throughout Latin America. The Soviet Union could do little but protest against US intervention in a foreign country.

Washington considered Latin America a safe area in terms of the Cold War: so safe that Latin America received only very limited economic support. From 1945 to 1960, the United States gave three times as much assistance to the Benelux countries alone as to all of Latin America.

Yet by the end of the 1950s it was obvious that changes were underway. Granted, the situation was 'normal' in Guatemala, and the Soviet Union had not given military help to any country in the Western hemisphere since then. On the other hand, Soviet trade and other forms of contact increased rapidly. However, the anti-American sentiment that could now be perceived arose for the most part from local conditions. When Vice President Nixon toured some Latin American countries in 1958, he was met by protests and riots in several of them.

Washington realized that a more active policy had to be implemented. Latin America could no longer be taken for granted. The Inter-American Development Bank was established. Economic assistance was increased. There were also hints that Washington was less interested in supporting reactionary military dictatorships. The attitude towards Batista's government on Cuba was one example. When Fidel Castro assumed power in January 1959, he was considered an improvement compared to the previous regime. However, that would not last for long.

At first, the Soviet Union made no firm commitments towards Castro. Relations between him and the Cuban Communists were not very good. However, the policy of nationalization and comprehensive land reforms soon resulted in a deterioration of relations with the United States. The Communists gained more influence. From the turn of the year 1959–60, it was obvious that Moscow was beginning to have high expectations for Castro.

Anastas Mikojan's visit to Cuba in February 1960 was the first unmistakable sign that Moscow was prepared to take on far-reaching commitments. An agreement was reached that the Soviet Union would buy Cuban sugar. Havana received a loan amounting to 100 million dollars to purchase industrial equipment from the USSR. In May, the two countries established diplomatic relations. When the United States began drastic cutbacks in its imports of sugar from Cuba, the Soviet Union promised to buy what the United States no longer wanted. Cuba received more and more Soviet weapons. In late 1961, the first references cropped up in Moscow that Cuba could become a 'socialist' country, but not until 1963 was the establishment of socialism perceived as accomplished.

The Kennedy administration accelerated the re-evaluation of Latin America policies that had begun during the final years of the Eisenhower administration. Economic assistance was increased, and Washington stressed the need for social and economic reforms. These elements were bound together in the Alliance for Progress. However, the break with the past proved not as great as it first appeared.

As far as Cuba was concerned, Kennedy continued Eisenhower's policies for the most part. The plans for a US-backed invasion were taken over by the new administration. The invasion took place in the Bay of Pigs in April 1961. Kennedy expected the Cuban population to turn against Castro, somewhat like Guatemala seven years earlier. That did not happen. Castro's support was far more solid than Arbenz's had been. Naturally, the invasion served to strengthen further the bonds between Cuba and the Soviet Union.

In the spring of 1962, the Soviet Union must have decided to install the intermediate-range missiles on Cuba that in October would result in what was perhaps the most serious crisis of the entire postwar era. The Soviet decision was probably made on the basis of strategic considerations. The primary objective was to achieve parity with the United States in a simple manner. (This will be dealt with in more detail on pp. 135–6.) Castro probably saw the entire situation in a more local perspective, with emphasis on preventing new attempted invasions and on strengthening Cuba in relation to the United States in general.

Washington responded by establishing a blockade around the island to prevent new supplies, and threatened to invade if the missiles that were already on Cuba were not withdrawn. It later became known that nuclear warheads were already on the island for the intermediate-range missiles as well as for tactical weapons in the event of a US invasion. The Soviet Union backed down, despite strong resistance on the part of Castro. The retreat was made easier by the American promise not to invade the island in the future and by private assurances that US intermediate-range missiles would be withdrawn from Turkey.

The Cuban crisis illustrated in two ways that the Cold War involved the entire world. In the first place, a conflict between the United States and the Soviet Union could result in a catastrophe for humanity. In the second place, Cuba, which traditionally had been the best example of a country dominated by the United States, had now become closely linked to the Soviet Union. The Cold War had also reached Latin America. It had become global.

THE UNITED STATES, THE SOVIET UNION, AND THE THIRD WORLD: A COMPARISON

US involvement around the world had been considerable as far back as the first years after the Second World War. It had increased greatly during the postwar period, but US expansion gradually became less striking than Soviet expansion. The Soviet Union was far from a global power in 1945, but it had become one by the beginning of the 1960s.

The Soviet Union undoubtedly had greater influence in more geographic areas in the mid-1960s than had been the case 20 years earlier. Khrushchev had become a central actor in Asia, in the Middle East, in Africa, and even in Latin America. Stalin's possibilities of influencing developments in most of these regions had been small.

Even so, there was little doubt that in most areas the United States was still superior to the Soviet Union. The United States had a large lead in terms of strategic weapons. The same was true of their ability to exercise power in various parts of the world. Only after the defeat on Cuba did the Soviet Union concentrate in earnest on becoming equal to the United States strategically and on acquiring more resources for so-called power projection in remote areas.

In the economic sphere it was even less possible for the Soviet Union to compete with the United States. The Soviet Union had experienced substantial economic growth in the 1950s. The material basis for a more global policy had improved, but in 1960 the Soviet gross national product was still less than half that of the United States. The United States had a much wider range of instruments to implement its policies in relation to the Third World.

From 1945 to 1965, Moscow gave 7.9 billion dollars in economic and military assistance to the Third World (at least agreements were made to give this amount). This was a dramatic change in relation to the complete lack of such assistance under Stalin. The priority the various countries were given was evident by the fact that five or six countries received two-thirds of this entire amount; they were Afghanistan, India, Indonesia, Iran, and the United Arab Republic. India and the United Arab Republic alone received about 40 per cent. Compared with US assistance, this was still modest, for the United States gave more just to India and Pakistan than the Soviet Union gave to the entire Third World.

Many of Moscow's greatest successes had been transformed to disappointments in a somewhat longer perspective. This was particularly true in relation to China, but also in relation to countries outside 'the Communist bloc'. Even progressive regimes had an unfortunate tendency to suppress the local Communist parties. Even more important was the fact that during a period of some three years the Soviet Union's best friends disappeared in four important countries: Ben Bella in Algeria was deposed in 1965; Sukarno in Indonesia gradually lost his grip in the years 1965–68, and in 1965 one of the leading Communist parties in the non-communist world was crushed and several hundred thousand persons killed; Nkrumah in Ghana was deposed in 1966; Keita in Mali met the same fate in 1968.

The United States had to tolerate Cuba as a constant thorn in the flesh. This was a new experience. Power and impotence were intermingled in a complex mixture. The US capacity to influence events in various places around the world was limited, but was still much greater than that of the Soviet Union. Even Britain and France intervened to protect their friends in Africa and Asia (Britain in Oman, Jordan, Kuwait, Malaysia, and East Africa; France in several former African colonies). The Soviet Union had to sit and watch while radical regimes in the Third World were deposed.

There was a long way to go yet before the Soviet Union was the United States' equal in power and influence. But equality was undoubtedly what Moscow wanted.

THE COLD WAR BECOMES GLOBAL, 1945-1962: THE LITERATURE

The main book on the spread of the Cold War is now Odd Arne Westad, *The Global Cold War: Third World Interventions and the Making of Our Times* (Cambridge, 2005), although it deals primarily with the 1970s and 1980s.

Russell D. Buhite, *Soviet–American Relations in Asia, 1945–1954* (Norman, OK, 1981) is a useful survey of the two superpowers' Asian policies. William Whitney Stueck, Jr., *The Road to Confrontation: American Policy Toward China and Korea, 1947–1950* (Chapel Hill, NC, 1981) also contains interesting observations. Stueck's updated analysis of the Korean War is to be found in *The Korean War: An International History* (Princeton, NJ, 1995).

Central works on the Eisenhower period are still Robert A. Divine, *Eisenhower and the Cold War* (Oxford, 1981); Townsend Hoopes, *The Devil and John Foster Dulles* (Boston, 1973); and Stephen E. Ambrose, *Eisenhower: The President* (New York, 1984). An epoch-making work on the Cuban crisis was Graham Allison, *Essence of Decision: Explaining the Cuban Missile Crisis* (Boston, 1971 and New York, 1999). Sheldon M. Stern gives a more recent account in *The Week the World Stood Still: Inside the Secret Cuban Missile Crisis* (Stanford, CA, 2005). For the Soviet side, see Aleksandr Fursenko and Timothy Naftali, *'One Hell of a Gamble': Khrushchev, Castro and Kennedy, 1958–64* (New York, 1997).

Valuable surveys of Soviet policy in the Third World are to be found in Roger E. Kanet (ed.), *The Soviet Union and Developing Nations* (Baltimore, MD, 1974); Christopher Stevens, *The Soviet Union and Black Africa* (New York, 1976); Robert H. Donaldson (ed.), *The Soviet Union in the Third World: Successes and Failures* (Boulder, CO, 1981); Jerry F. Hough, *The Struggle for the Third World* (Washington, DC, 1986); and Galia Golan, *The Soviet Union and National Liberation Movements in the Third World* (Boston, 1988). William Curti Wohlforth, *The Elusive Balance: Power and Perceptions during the Cold War* (Ithaca, NY, 1993) is a fascinating analysis of how perceptions of strength influenced developments in the Cold War. The Congo crisis is well described in Lise Namikas, *Battleground Africa: The Cold War in the Congo 1960–1965* (Washington, DC, 2013).

Stimulating treatments of Chinese foreign policy immediately after 1949 are found in Chen Jian, *China's Road to the Korean War: The Making of the Sino-American Confrontation* (New York, 1994) and Shu Guang Zhang, *Deterrence and Strategic Culture: Chinese-American Confrontations, 1949–1958* (Ithaca, NY, 1992).

DÉTENTE BETWEEN EAST AND WEST, 1962-1975

The first 15 to 20 years after the Second World War were characterized by the spread of the Cold War to ever new parts of the globe. Until 1948–49 the situation in Europe was the focal point. Most of the conflicts after this time took place outside Europe. The most important ones, as we have seen, were the Korean War, the Vietnam War, the Congo crisis, the Cuban crisis, and the conflicts in the Middle East.

This geographic expansion did not necessarily mean a steady increase in the temperature between East and West. The period from 1945 to 1962 did not represent a constant rise in the level of tension between the power blocs; there were interim periods with signs of an easing of tensions. This is not easily quantifiable, but it can roughly be said that tension increased from 1945 to 1953, although there were fluctuations during this period as well. The following years, until 1956, showed improved relations between East and West. Although the temperature then rose somewhat, the tension level of the first postwar years was not reached again until the Cuban crisis of 1962.

After the Cuban crisis, the world entered an extended period of détente until the mid-1970s. Contact between the power blocs increased, and several important sources of conflict found at least a temporary solution. Most importantly, the situation in the central region, Europe, was normalized in a manner that was acceptable to both sides. In a sense, détente in Europe overshadowed the continuing conflicts in other parts of the world.

SIGNS OF DÉTENTE DURING THE 1950S

Improved relations were evident in several areas. In July 1953 a cease-fire was declared in Korea. In the following year the peace agreement for Indochina was concluded. In 1955 the Austrian question was resolved. The Soviet Union agreed to withdraw its troops, and Austria became a neutral country. The Soviet Union also withdrew from Porkkala in Finland. There were signs of rapprochement between the USSR and West Germany. The German Chancellor and 'arch-revanchist' Konrad Adenauer was invited to Moscow, diplomatic relations were established, and the German war prisoners sent home. In the following year diplomatic relations were established between the Soviet Union and Japan. Moscow even hinted at the possibility of a solution for the disputed Kurile Islands, although nothing came of it.

The last summit between the leaders of the Great Powers had taken place in Potsdam in 1945. In 1955 they met again, in Geneva: Eisenhower, Bulganin, Khrushchev, Anthony Eden, and Edgar Faure. No concrete results were reached, but the meeting demonstrated the altered climate between East and West, the 'spirit of Geneva.' Four years would pass before Eisenhower and Khrushchev would meet again, to generate the 'spirit of Camp David.'

Trade between East and West increased, the Soviet Union joined the Olympic summer games in 1952 and the winter games in 1956, and tourists began to make holes in the renowned 'Iron Curtain' which divided Europe. Negotiations on arms control were carried out with greater enthusiasm and realism than formerly. The central issue was a ban on the testing of nuclear weapons. Considerable progress was made at the end of the 1950s, although a final agreement was not reached until 1963.

There were many reasons for the improved climate. One important factor was the fact that the major powers began to accept the existing situation in Europe for the most part. Europe was still by far the most important region for both the Soviet Union and the United States, although conflicts outside Europe naturally influenced these relations as well. The Western powers still advocated unification of Germany, but it became increasingly evident that they were actually satisfied with a divided Germany of which the largest part was incorporated in NATO, as West Germany was in 1955. From the same year the Soviet Union openly supported the policy of a divided Germany.

The situation in Western Europe became more stable. There was no longer any danger of communism being victorious. The establishment of NATO and the high rate of economic growth had provided an increased feeling of security. US talk of 'liberation' and 'rollback' contributed to new uncertainty in relation to Eastern Europe, especially in the first years after Eisenhower assumed office in 1953. However, it soon became clear that this policy was mostly rhetoric. Neither during the revolt in East Berlin in 1953 nor in Hungary in 1956 did the Eisenhower administration have plans for intervening (see pp. 187–8). After Hungary, US propaganda was altered so that the inhabitants of Eastern Europe would not have unrealistic expectations as to what policy the United States actually pursued.

The death of Stalin in March 1953 led to comprehensive changes in Soviet policy. None of the new leaders could expect to attain Stalin's authority. The grip had to be relaxed somewhat. These new signals could be registered in a number of areas in addition to those already mentioned. The boundary claims in relation to Turkey were abandoned; relations were normalized with Greece, with Yugoslavia, and with Israel – once more. The Soviet attitude towards the nonaligned countries of the Third World became more positive.

Ideologically, the new tone was most clearly expressed at the Twentieth Party Congress in 1956. Stalin was denounced. The possibilities of peaceful coexistence between capitalist and communist nations that had been suggested previously were now emphasized. In the eyes of the Kremlin, the forces for peace under Soviet leadership had become so strong that no new conflict between East and West need arise. The transition from capitalism to socialism could also take place by parliamentary means. Revolution was no longer necessary. Communism would still conquer the world, but through peaceful competition.

On the part of the United States, the Eisenhower administration represented a mixture of desire for détente combined with a powerful anti-communist rhetoric, both at home and abroad. The rhetoric gradually weakened and the desire for détente grew stronger. For various reasons, primarily economic ones, Eisenhower advocated a reduction in the defense budget. On several occasions he expressed a strong desire to limit the level of armaments in the world. With his desire to keep the United States out of major armed conflicts, he contributed to decreasing the level of tension in the Cold War. However, the President had no strong desire to break with previous policies. He helped extend the pact system to new parts of the world, and there were strong anti-communist forces at work within the administration. The most central figure was Secretary of State John Foster Dulles. Dulles and Adenauer were the two Western leaders who were most skeptical about increased contact between East and West.

Yet the world witnessed only the first signs of an easing of tensions during the 1950s. Much of the impetus for détente had disappeared already in 1956 with the uprising in Hungary and the manner in which the Soviet Union quelled it, and through the Suez conflict (see pp. 56–7), although this was as much a conflict within the Western bloc as between East and West.

Tension in Europe increased once more. Except for the status of Austria, none of the central conflicts had actually been resolved. The question of Germany, and of Berlin in particular, was the most crucial in this context.

In November 1958, Khrushchev insisted that the situation in Berlin had to be changed. Moscow undoubtedly favored the integration of West Berlin into East Germany, but was willing to accept so-called free city status. The ties to West Germany were to be loosened in any case. An agreement to this effect would have to be reached within six months. If this was not achieved, the Soviet Union would transfer its occupation rights in East Berlin to the East Germans. Control of the traffic to West Berlin would also be their responsibility. As it had not proven possible to attain a peace treaty for a unified Germany, Khrushchev soon threatened to sign a separate peace treaty with East Germany.

The deadline was postponed, but tension in Europe increased. In a sense, it culminated with the erection of the Berlin Wall in August 1961. The flow of refugees from the East had been steadily growing. In 1959, 140,000 persons had left East Germany, in 1960 almost 200,000 and during the first half of 1961 over 100,000 persons. Tanks were driven up on both sides of the dividing line, but the Western powers made no attempt to stop the building of the wall.

The new conflicts outside Europe, such as the Congo crisis in 1960, also contributed to sustaining the level of tension. The Cuban crisis in the autumn of 1962 was in many ways the most dangerous of the entire postwar period. The world seemed even closer to a major war then than during the Berlin conflict in 1948 and the outbreak of the Korean War in 1950.

THE POLICY OF DÉTENTE, 1962-1975

The resolution of the Cuban crisis would have great significance for the international political climate. It resulted in a long period of relative détente, a détente that would culminate 10 to 13 years later. Once more it must be emphasized that there was not a constant evolution of steadily improving relations between East and West. There were many interruptions along this path. However, the main tendency was clear.

It was paradoxical that the most serious crisis of the postwar period should result in a period of détente. However, the background was simple enough. Moscow and Washington, and the rest of the world for that matter, had looked into the abyss a war would represent. As Khrushchev expressed it, 'the smell of fire hung in the air.' Both sides were interested in preventing a similar crisis in the future.

The interest in arms limitation and confidence-building measures between East and West increased. As Kennedy observed, with reference to this type of measure: 'Perhaps now, as we step back from danger, we can together make real progress in this vital field.'

Agreements and Contact between East and West

The Cuban crisis had demonstrated the need for the possibility of swift contact between the leaders in Washington and Moscow. A special hot line was installed to make this possible. It would have a useful function in crises when time was of the essence.

An important new agreement was the test ban treaty of 1963. Negotiations had been carried out ever since 1955. Considerable progress was made, but the new climate after Cuba caused the final breakthrough. The treaty banned all tests in the atmosphere, in outer space, and under water. It proved impossible to attain agreement as to a control system for underground testing. Thus ever, new weapons could be developed, even though there was an end to the radioactive fallout from the US, British, and Soviet tests.

Arms control continued to be both a result of and a part of further easing of tensions. An agreement that the Antarctic was to be used for peaceful purposes only had been signed as early as 1959. In 1967, the superpowers agreed to ban nuclear weapons in space. A separate agreement that same year prohibited nuclear weapons in Latin America. The non-proliferation treaty was signed in 1968. The nuclear nations promised to refrain from transferring nuclear weapons to countries not having them, and they in turn promised not to accept or develop such weapons. However, here as on previous occasions, many of the countries which would be most affected by the treaties refused to agree to them. Thus France and China signed neither the test ban treaty nor the non-proliferation treaty.

The most important of the arms limiting measures was SALT I, the Strategic Arms Limitation Treaty of 1972. SALT consisted of two parts. One of them was a treaty on anti-ballistic missiles (ABM) which restricted the United States and the Soviet Union to two such deployments each. By this agreement, the two superpowers refrained from developing real defenses against such weapons. The ABM treaty was of unlimited duration. The other part was a five-year agreement that placed a ceiling on the number of strategic weapon launchers the two powers could have. The Soviet Union was granted a larger number than the United States, 2,400 as compared to 1,700. This was to compensate both for the US lead in terms of multiple independently targetable re-entry vehicles (MIRVs) and for the fact that bombers, which the United States had many more of than the Soviet Union did, were not included.

In 1974, Washington and Moscow agreed to limit the number of ABM deployments to one apiece. (In practice, the United States did not develop its system.) That same year, agreement was reached on the guidelines for a new SALT treaty, SALT II. Both countries agreed to a ceiling of 2,400 weapon launchers, of which not more than 1,320 could be equipped with more than one warhead. Bombers were now included. The disparity in the number of launchers in favor of the Soviet Union, which had been sharply criticized in the Senate, had now been amended. On the other hand, the US lead in MIRV technology was in the process of being reduced.

The central element in the policy of détente was normalization in Europe. As we shall see, the geographic expansion of the Cold War did not cease in the early 1960s. It continued, not least during the 1970s. However, for a few years at the end of the 1960s and the beginning of the 1970s this expansion was overshadowed by the easing of tension in the area which was still most important, in Europe.

The question of Germany and Berlin was decisive. The breakthrough came in West Germany with the broad coalition between Kiesinger's Christian Democrats (CDU) and Brandt's Social Democrats (SPD) from 1966 to 1969 and especially with the Social Democratic–Free Democratic government under the leadership of Willy Brandt after 1969. The German *Ostpolitik* could not be pursued without a certain amount of support from the Western allies, but Washington and several other Western capitals were in doubt about some aspects of this policy. They feared that West Germany could become too independent and move too close to Moscow. The initiative for *Ostpolitik* definitely came from the West German government itself.

At first, Bonn tried to extend relations with the countries of Eastern Europe. However, with the exception of Romania, their success was limited, and the Soviet invasion of Czechoslovakia in 1968 served to emphasize the fact that an Eastern policy could not be pursued without the cooperation of Moscow. Priorities were changed. Relations with the Soviet Union became primary in importance.

On 12 August 1970, the Soviet Union and West Germany signed the Moscow treaty. Each side promised not to use violence to alter the existing boundaries in Europe, including the boundaries between Poland and East Germany and between East and West Germany. This was a major concession on the part of the West Germans, as Bonn had consistently maintained that these boundaries were temporary. In theory, they could still be changed, but in practice the agreement meant acceptance of the division of Europe and of Germany. On the other hand, this was merely an acknowledgement of the situation that had in fact existed throughout the entire postwar period.

This agreement with the Soviet Union laid the foundation for similar agreements with Poland and East Germany. Through the subsequent recognition of East Germany, one of the basic principles of West German postwar policy was abandoned.

However, West Germany achieved return favors for these concessions. The most important one was the Four Power agreement on Berlin in 1971. Although neither East nor West abandoned its formal position with regard to Berlin, this agreement meant that many questions that previously had caused conflict were now regulated. Access to West Berlin from West Germany was approved and West Berlin's ties to West Germany recognized, with certain limitations that were to preserve the city's special status. The access of the inhabitants of West Berlin to East Berlin and East Germany was improved. The wall between East and West Berlin remained. This was probably politically necessary if the question of Berlin was to be resolved. It consolidated East Germany's position and created more stable relations in the area at least in the long run.

West Germany also achieved other advantages by means of its *Ostpolitik*. Although there were slight variations from year to year, all in all West Germany became the Soviet

Union's largest Western trade partner. The same was true for most of the countries of Eastern Europe. Trade between East and West Germany was particularly important. The human gains were substantial: the emigration of Germans from Poland and the Soviet Union increased and contact over the border between East and West was facilitated considerably with regard to both personal visits and telephone calls. No other Western country experienced such great benefits from détente as West Germany did. That contributed to the gradual demise of Christian Democratic opposition to *Ostpolitik*. In the longer run Brandt seems even to have hoped that *Ostpolitik* could help transcend the East–West division and make the unification of Germany possible.

During the period of détente, summits between East and West became increasingly common. Kennedy and Khrushchev met only once, in Vienna in 1961. The same was true of Johnson and Kosygin, in Glassboro in 1967. In the 1970s summits became annual events. The greatest success was Nixon's visit to Moscow in 1972, where SALT I and a number of other agreements were signed, among them one called 'The basic principles of mutual relations between the United States of America and the Union of Soviet Socialist Republics.' That agreement, and a similar one the following year, 'The agreement on the prevention of nuclear war,' were to draw up the rules for mutual contact and prevent future conflicts between the two superpowers. Nixon and Brezhnev met again in both 1973 and 1974, Ford and Brezhnev in Vladivostok in November 1974. That would prove to be the last meeting for some years, except for the important summit in Helsinki in 1975.

Brezhnev and Kosygin's meetings with the leaders of France and West Germany were almost equally frequent. However, Moscow's relations with Britain were more strained, partly because the British expelled 105 Soviet citizens in 1971 for espionage. After Labour had assumed power again in 1974, Britain was more on the same terms as the other Western countries.

Détente in Europe culminated symbolically with the Conference on Security and Cooperation in Europe (CSCE) in Helsinki in August 1975. The final act from the conference represented a superstructure for the agreements West Germany had made. From a Soviet perspective, confirming the status quo in this manner was of primary importance. This goal was largely achieved, although borders could still be changed peacefully. The act also established certain principles for economic and cultural cooperation, principles which were generally acceptable to the United States, Canada, and all 34 European countries which participated at the conference. The participants also promised to promote basic human rights, and contact across national borders was to be made easier. Here the Soviet Union and the Eastern European countries had made promises they could hardly keep. In some years, however, these promises were to influence political developments more than virtually anyone had foreseen at the time.

Reasons for Détente

There were many reasons why détente went as far as it did. Several factors have already been touched upon. In the first place, the Cuban crisis disclosed the need to prevent a direct conflict between the two superpowers. No one could be interested in doing anything that would result in war between them. In the second place, the situation in Europe during the postwar period had become solidified to such a degree that all parties were finally ready to let the status quo be the basis for a formalization of conditions there.

The policy of détente also had many other explanations. It gave the Soviet Union a number of advantages. Not only did Moscow manage to establish the inviolability of the boundaries in Eastern Europe and at least indirectly attain acceptance of its sphere of interest there, the Soviet Union was also directly granted superpower status on a level with the United States for the first time. This was evident through the many summits and the agreements between the United States and the Soviet Union, especially the SALT treaty, and was also expressed openly by the Americans. For the Soviet leaders it followed naturally that the two superpowers should refrain from interfering in each other's domestic affairs. Nixon and Ford acknowledged this principle for the most part. When the Soviet author Alexander Solzhenitsyn was expelled from the Soviet Union, he was not received in the White House even though many in Congress wanted him to be.

Superpower status meant a lot. What greater honor could be imagined than the capitalist leaders themselves admitting that the Soviet Union was the equal of the United States? That meant legitimacy within the Soviet Union and in Soviet-controlled areas, and could give strength abroad, not only in relation to the Western countries, but throughout the world.

In fact, the Soviet Union could measure up to the United States in one sphere only – in military terms. Of course the hope was to attain the level of the capitalist superpower economically as well. Khrushchev had had high hopes of this. In 1959, for instance, he had promised that Soviet living standards should reach the US level within 12 years. They did not. The Soviet gross national product remained less than half the size of the US GNP. The difference in productivity was greatest in the field where Khrushchev had promised the most: within agriculture.

The growth in Soviet production was declining. In the 1950s it had been approximately 6 per cent annually. In 1962–63 it was probably around 3 per cent. Later it rose again somewhat, but the Soviet Union was facing serious problems. Economically, too, the policy of détente could be highly advantageous for the USSR.

In the first place, trade in general, and imports of Western technology in particular, would bring in important impulses for growth. As other methods for stimulating the economy, such as Prime Minister Kosygin's proposal for greater decentralization, were not carried out, this type of import became even more significant. In addition, Soviet crops often failed. Grain imports, from the United States in particular, were necessary. At the Twenty-third Party Congress in 1966, the importance of greater international trade was stressed by many participants. It was 'discovered' that Lenin had touched on the law of comparative advantage as a guideline for such trade.

In the second place, it was advantageous to get some control over defense expenditures. Khrushchev had introduced substantial reductions in the armed forces several times in order to meet the lack of money and labor in other sectors. Just before his fall in 1964, the Soviet leader suggested that Soviet defense was then at a 'suitable level.' By then the trend had already been reversed. Greater emphasis was to be placed on defense (see pp. 138–41). Brezhnev–Kosygin continued this policy, but that did not reduce the need to place certain limitations on armaments. With arms limitations, the

Kremlin could more easily realize the demand for equality with the United States at the same time as it was to maintain nonmilitary investments and consumption.

In the United States, Kennedy had increased defense expenditures considerably, and the US lead over the Soviet Union was great as far as strategic weapons were concerned (see pp. 135–8). Washington had come out of the Cuban crisis strengthened. That made it relatively easy for Kennedy to advocate a re-evaluation of relations with the Soviet Union, as he did in his speech at American University on 10 June 1963. With the ambitions Kennedy and not least Lyndon B. Johnson had on the domestic scene, freeing funds from the defense budget was desirable. Now poverty was to be eradicated by means of sweeping social policy measures. After the former increase, the defense budget was actually reduced in the mid-1960s (until the war in Vietnam reversed this trend).

The fact that the Soviet Union gradually became the equal of the United States in the military sphere could cause problems for Washington, but it had its advantages as well. Equality helped establish favorable conditions for arms limitations, especially the SALT I treaty. The Soviet Union was not willing to make agreements on any other basis than equality. The development of technologically highly sophisticated satellites made it possible to use them for the verification the United States so firmly insisted on. Thus the Soviet resistance against the demand for inspection on Soviet soil could be circumvented.

The United States knew that the pace of Soviet strategic armament was greater than its own, which meant that it could be useful to set a ceiling on Moscow's build-up. There was even a certain feeling in Washington that the US was in relative decline compared to the Soviet Union and Western Europe. The policy of détente was also an expression of this sentiment and an attempt to limit the rise of others.

The Vietnam War would gradually influence the US attitude towards détente. Some Americans became more hostile towards the Soviet Union because of the country's support of North Vietnam. On the other hand, the growing opposition to the war meant that in many ways increased détente was to be desired. This could weaken the opposition against the Vietnam War and increase the possibilities that Moscow would help Washington achieve a favorable agreement with Hanoi in order to end the war. Finally, the protest movement contributed to the growth of new attitudes towards the Soviet Union and towards the defense budget. If the United States was 'guilty' in the Vietnam War, perhaps the United States would also have to bear a large share of the responsibility for the Cold War and the global arms race.

The policy of détente also represented economic advantages for the United States, although the Americans were more reserved than the Western Europeans about exploiting the opportunities that presented themselves. Congress was rather lukewarm about terminating the many trade restrictions that had been built up during the 1940s and 1950s. The American trade union movement, with its strong anti-communist streak, was opposed to almost any increase in contact with the Soviet Union and Eastern Europe.

Even so, there was little point in the United States being so reserved while the Western European countries and Japan traded with the Soviet Union and Eastern Europe, as these restrictions punished the United States itself more than anyone else. In addition, the United States had a deficit balance of payments and from 1971 a deficit on the trade balance as well. From 1970–71, trade with the Eastern countries began to take on a certain significance for the United States. Big business entered into the contracts it had long been interested in, the farmers increased their grain deliveries substantially, and credits were given further to stimulate trade. Before 1971, US exports to the Soviet Union had seldom exceeded 100 million dollars a year. In 1976 they had reached 2.5 billion dollars. Most of this increase was due to the grain trade. Apart from in agriculture, West Germany, France, and Japan had a higher level of exports to the Soviet Union than the United States had. The United States imported much less from the Soviet Union than it exported.

Western Europe's political contacts with the Soviet Union and Eastern Europe stimu- lated political changes on the part of the United States as well. De Gaulle's overtures to the East in 1963–64 had little influence, because France was relatively isolated. Things were different when West Germany began to pursue an active policy towards the East. Brandt stressed that *Ostpolitik* was a central aspect of his foreign policy. The United States had to march somewhat in step with its Western European allies. However, the degree of conflict can easily be exaggerated, for to a great extent US and European attitudes coincided. Even during the Johnson administration the United States had been more eager for overtures to the East than West Germany was, and the desire for détente increased further in the 1970s on the part of the United States as well, although the changes here were far less dramatic than in West Germany.

Towards the close of the 1960s, Moscow's policy was more accommodating towards Western Europe in general and France in particular than towards the United States. Western Europe's increasing independence probably led the Kremlin to hope that it could drive a wedge between the Europeans and the Americans. On the part of the Soviet Union, détente was to serve such a purpose as well. However, the United States could not be excluded from the process. The resolution of central problems such as the Berlin question required US participation. The Europeans refused to take part in a European security conference without US participation. Besides, the United States held the key to agreements on arms limitation and recognized superpower status for the Soviet Union.

It was no coincidence that Richard Nixon was the US president who carried détente the furthest. As has been said, he was the first American president who didn't have to worry about Richard Nixon. During the 1940s and 1950s, Nixon had established himself as one of the toughest anti-communists among leading US politicians. Against that background, it was difficult for the conservatives to accuse the President of being 'soft' on communism when he changed the course of US policy. Nor could those who were on the left of the political spectrum easily accuse Nixon of going too far in cooperating with Moscow.

The anti-communist tradition had shown itself most clearly in the US relationship to China. Relations with 'Red China' were taboo in Washington. The meetings that took place between the two countries' ambassadors in Warsaw from 1955 were the only con- tact of any significance that existed between them. Nixon had been among those who were most critical of China. During the election campaign of 1960, he had declared that the Chinese Communists 'don't just want Quemoy and Matsu. They don't just want Formosa. They want the world.'

The growing conflict between the Soviet Union and China only gradually altered the picture. When Washington began to realize towards the end of the Kennedy administra- tion how deep the breach between China and the Soviet Union actually was, China was considered an even greater danger than the Soviet Union. The war in Vietnam became a war against the Chinese pattern for liberation of the Third World. Neither the Kennedy nor the Johnson administration had anything but a bare minimum of contact with China.

It is possible that at first the breach between the two communist countries slowed down rather than hastened the process of détente. In the ideological competition with Peking, the Soviet leaders could easily become vulnerable if they showed too great an interest in cooperation with the capitalist superpower. This cooperation could also take place at China's expense. Seen from a Chinese perspective, the test ban was thus a subtle attempt to prevent China from getting its own nuclear weapons. The Chinese reaction resembled the French reaction in the West. China's ideological criticism of the Soviet Union made it even more difficult for the Chinese than for the Soviets to make overtures towards the United States.

As the conflict between the two communist giants became more intense, the perspective changed. The breach between the Soviet Union and China became one of the most important factors behind the policy of détente. The Cultural Revolution and the border skirmishes made it clear that these two countries had a greater clash of interests between them than each one had with the United States on its own (see pp. 219–21). The fear of a confrontation with China and the United States at the same time was bound to make Moscow interested in improving relations with Washington. The Soviet Union even had feelers out to inquire as to how the Nixon administration would respond to a first strike against the Chinese nuclear arsenal before it had become too large and could represent a threat to the Soviet Union. These feelers were rejected by the administration. (In 1964 the Johnson administration had concluded against a pre-emptive nuclear strike by the United States against China.)

In 1969, when the Cultural Revolution had climaxed, the Chinese leaders made their first overtures towards improving relations with the United States. Nixon and Kissinger were prepared to respond. The time was ripe for a total restructuring of US policy towards China. The breakthrough came with Kissinger's secret visit to China in 1971 and Nixon's grander tour the following year. The change in course was effected without noticeable domestic political dispute. Nixon was the right man once more to unite the country behind a new policy. It is possible that the changes caused greater problems on the Chinese side. At least Mao told Nixon in 1972 that Vice-Chairman Lin Piao's attempt to seize power in 1969 had been a reaction against the overtures towards the capitalist superpower.

Washington did not play the so-called 'China card' very directly. That might have contributed to bringing the two communist countries closer together again, or it could have intensified the breach to a dangerous level. But as Kissinger expressed it, 'we could not "exploit" that rivalry; it exploited itself.'

Both Moscow and Peking had to see to it that the other party did not achieve excessive gains in Washington. The Soviet desire for détente with the United States must have been stimulated by that fact. In many ways the years from 1970 to 1972 represented a climax for détente. It was certainly no coincidence that relations between the United States and the Soviet Union were at their best precisely during the years when rapprochement between the United States and China was in its most dramatic stage.

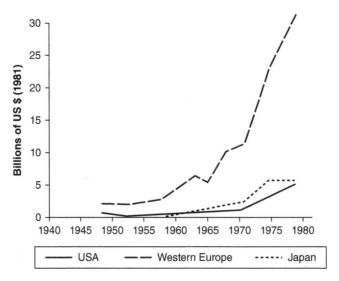

Figure 4.1 Total Soviet Foreign Trade

DÉTENTE AND GEOGRAPHIC EXPANSION OF THE EAST-WEST CONFLICT

Geographically, the policy of détente meant détente first and foremost in Europe. There were also unmistakable signs that the two superpowers had acquired a greater interest in respecting each other's influence in other regions. However, détente did not mean the end of further geographic expansion of the Cold War by any means. Rivalry in the Middle East increased, and the Vietnam War culminated just as détente reached its climax. This war was the most expensive, in both human and material terms, of any conflict in the postwar period. Only the Korean War could to some extent be compared to Vietnam.

Respect for Each Other's Vital Regions

The most evident signs of restraint were to be found in the respective vital regions, Latin America for the United States and Eastern Europe for the Soviet Union. As far as Latin America was concerned, the Cuban crisis had strongly emphasized both US strength and the superpower's willingness to use force to protect its interests. Nor can the huge Soviet subsidies of the Cuban economy have been alluring for the Kremlin. In many ways, one Cuba in the Western hemisphere was enough.

Castro was eager to spread the Cuban revolution to other countries in Latin America. He supported various guerilla movements and criticized even the Soviet Union and the local Communist parties for passivity in the struggle against reactionary regimes. In 1968, however, Cuba's policy showed a change of course. The guerilla strategy seemed to have proven bankrupt, and the island's economic dependence on the Soviet Union had become so great that the country began to pursue a course that was openly pro-Soviet.

Moscow had little sympathy for the guerilla strategy and placed priority on ordinary diplomatic relations with the countries in the region. However, economic assistance to Latin America was very limited, except for Cuba and to a much lesser degree Chile and Argentina. The only country except Cuba that received Soviet military assistance was the relatively radical government of Peru in the early 1970s.

In 1965, the United States intervened in the Dominican Republic with 20,000 men in order to prevent the radical Juan Bosch from assuming power. Bosch was said to be supported by Communists and could allegedly represent the danger of a new Cuba. The Soviet reaction was not much stronger than that of many of the United States' allies. Moscow raised the issue in the UN Security Council and denounced the US intervention, but even the language used was moderate.

In many ways, policy towards Allende's popular front government in Chile (1970–73) also demonstrated Soviet restraint in the United States' vital region. Allende did not request military assistance, so Moscow did not have to take a stand on that issue. Economic support was given, but its extent was far from overwhelming. In June 1972 Santiago was granted trade credits for a possible total value of 260 million dollars. The Soviet Union also expressed its willingness to import copper from Chile when other importers withdrew because of the dispute concerning compensation for the national-ized American copper mines. It appears that Allende hoped for an additional 500 million dollars at the end of the year. He received only 30 to 50 million. The fall of Allende in 1973 was due mainly to local conditions, but also the US policy of destabiliza-tion. His fall caused a limited reaction in the Soviet Union. Declarations of sympathy were moderate in tone, but the Kremlin broke off diplomatic and trade relations with the new military regime.

In Western Europe, Soviet policy towards Portugal after the revolution in 1974 was somewhat more obscure. Moscow gave economic support to the pro-Soviet Communist party and obviously hoped that radicalization of the country would strengthen the position of both the party and the Soviet Union. But it was probably a question of exploiting the local situation rather than challenging the Western position, unless the Western powers more or less voluntarily let themselves be outmaneuvered. After the pendulum had swung quite a way to the left for a while, it swung back towards the political center. Local forces determined the course of development in Portugal as in most other places.

If Soviet policy was relatively restrained, especially in Latin America, the same can be said about US policy towards the vital region of the Soviet Union, Eastern Europe. Washington tried to strengthen relations with the more independent countries, espe-cially Romania and to a certain extent Poland, but US moderation was clearly illustrated in Czechoslovakia. In the first place, the Western powers were on the whole cautious about giving support to the liberalization policies of the Dubcek government (see pp. 198–9), because this could only increase Moscow's skepticism about develop-ments in the country. In the second place, the Soviet invasion in August 1968 produced fairly limited reactions. President Johnson reluctantly cancelled a planned summit meeting, and negotiations on the SALT treaty were thus drawn out. The United States and the other Western powers, with the partial exception of Britain, were still intent on continuing the policy of détente after a reasonable interval to underscore their disapproval of the invasion. Johnson revived his proposal for a summit as early as

November, but by then it was already clear that Nixon would be the new president. The summit meeting had to wait.

There was a growing sentiment in the United States that the country had assumed excessive commitments and that a reduction was necessary. The United States could not bear the primary responsibility for any regime that was threatened by some type of aggression. This attitude represented first and foremost the fear of a new Vietnam and was in no way intended to increase Soviet influence. Nevertheless, it limited Washington's possibilities of assuming large-scale involvement. This attitude was most clearly presented in the so-called Nixon Doctrine of November 1969. In his speech on Guam, Nixon maintained that the United States would stand by its treaties and protect vital regions against aggression by major powers.

> In cases involving other types of aggression we shall furnish military and economic assistance when requested in accordance with our treaty commitments. But we shall look to the nation directly threatened to assume the primary responsibility of providing the manpower for its defense.

US forces on the Asian mainland were reduced considerably, not only in Vietnam, but in most countries where US troops were stationed.

The Grey Zones between East and West

The two superpowers were prepared to exercise moderation, particularly in each others' vital regions. The existence of a number of 'grey zones' where the superpowers and others competed to gain influence represented a problem. Almost all of them were in the Third World, where many countries were characterized by little domestic stability, and there was always a danger of the superpowers being drawn into local disputes. Circumstances beyond the control of Washington and Moscow might cause a clash between them. In addition, there were numerous instances in which the two were actively engaged in trying to strengthen their influence.

A local conflict that had a degree of influence on superpower relations was the conflict between India and Pakistan. The antagonism went back to the period before independence in 1947 and flared up from time to time, in part because of the situation in Kashmir. (Most of Kashmir belonged to India, although a majority of the population was Muslim.) Even though the United States and the Soviet Union would have liked to have good relations with both India and Pakistan, the United States was linked to Pakistan through SEATO and CENTO, while the Soviet Union tried to establish close relations with India in particular. However, Prime Minister Kosygin acted as a mediator after two brief rounds of Indo–Pakistan war over Kashmir in 1965. Although the conflict was not resolved, a cease-fire was effected.

In the early 1970s the Soviet Union oriented itself more and more towards India, because of Pakistan's good relations with China and the danger of a civil war in which India would support the independence of East Pakistan. The 1971 cooperation and friendship agreement between the Soviet Union and India gave New Delhi the backing against China that was needed for the Indians to intervene on the side of East Pakistan.

The subsequent war ended with victory for India and the establishment of the new country of Bangladesh. The Nixon administration sent a fleet to the region, primarily to prevent the spread of the war to West Pakistan. If any such danger existed, it was averted. All in all, the policy of détente did not suffer much damage from this conflict.

The Middle East, 1967–1975

The threat to détente was greater in the Middle East. Soviet influence was on the increase, in part as a result of US ties with Israel. The Soviet Union gave substantial military and economic assistance to countries such as Egypt, Syria, and Iraq. The Soviets had also built up a fleet in the Mediterranean that could underscore Soviet diplomacy.

There is little reason to believe that the Soviet Union wanted war in the Middle East in 1967. On the other hand, Moscow did not want to weaken its relations with the radical Arab countries. The escalation began when the Soviet Union – probably to help the Syrian government – spread rumors that Israel was preparing an attack on Syria. In order to prevent such an attack, Egypt mobilized forces in Sinai. Nasser demanded that the UN forces there be withdrawn. Events began to acquire a momentum of their own that probably exceeded both what Moscow desired and what Nasser originally seems to have planned. Egypt blockaded the Strait of Tiran, which gave Israel access to the Red Sea and the Indian Ocean. Verbal hostility escalated dramatically; troops were concentrated along the Israeli borders. Israel chose to strike first. In the course of six days Egypt, Jordan, and Syria were defeated.

In the short term, the war represented a defeat for the Soviet Union. Moscow did not send military supplies of any magnitude to help the Arabs. Nor was the Soviet fleet in the Mediterranean engaged in the action. The Soviet Union had to accept a cease-fire without Israeli withdrawal to the prewar boundaries. Moreover, Moscow accepted UN Resolution 242, which entailed recognition of Israel in return for Israeli withdrawal from 'territories occupied in the recent conflict.'

However, shifts in relations between the Soviets and the Egyptians could be abrupt. In 1971, the Soviet Union and Egypt signed a friendship and cooperation agreement. Twenty thousand Soviet soldiers were stationed in Egypt, and Soviet bases were established. In the following year the soldiers were sent home and the Soviet Union suffered one of its worst setbacks. One of the reasons for the reversal was that Sadat, who had taken over after the death of Nasser in 1970, was not promised the necessary support in the event of a new war with Israel. When Sadat did not receive the welcome he had hoped for in the West, he turned to the Soviet Union once more. Moscow now wanted to recover what it had lost and sent large supplies of weapons.

Soviet policy was more active in 1973 than in 1967. The Soviet Union probably still did not want war but did nothing to prevent it. Information as to Arab intentions was not given to the United States, although many leaders in Washington claimed that this was required by the 1972 agreement on 'The basic principles of mutual relations between the Soviet Union and the United States.' After war had broken out, the Soviet Union advocated an immediate cease-fire. That would have benefited the attacking Arabs considerably. When the fortunes of war were reversed, the Soviet Union gave substantial military assistance. The Arab countries which were not involved in the conflict were

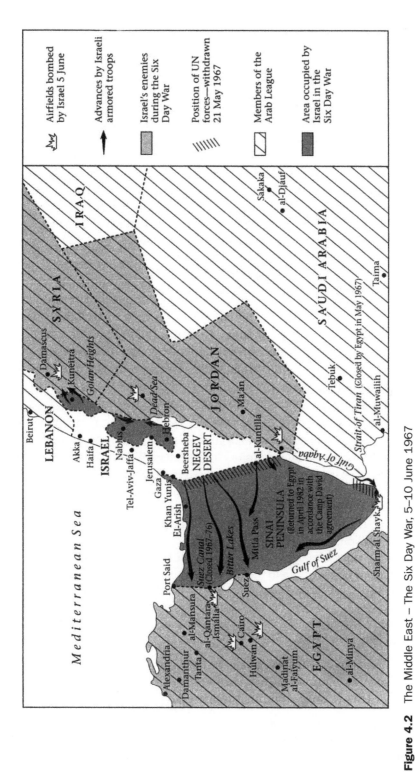

Figure 4.2 The Middle East – The Six Day War, 5–10 June 1967

encouraged to assist their brethren. When Israel did not respect the cease-fire agreement that the United States and the Soviet Union brought about, the Soviet Union threatened to intervene directly on the side of the Arabs. It is not known how genuine this threat was, but Soviet troops were placed on alert. The United States, which had increased its assistance to Israel, also placed troops on alert. The danger of a conflict between the United States and the Soviet Union in the Middle East increased, but passed when the Israelis halted their advance before the Egyptians were defeated entirely.

The Middle East conflict of 1973 was a strain on the policy of détente. The Soviet Union was opposed to the area being considered a Western sphere of influence. Moscow had just as much right to influence there as Washington had. The Western powers reacted against the increasing Soviet involvement. Many policy-makers asked whether no price was too high for the Kremlin to increase its influence in the Middle East.

Even so, many Arabs were disappointed with the insufficient Soviet support. After the 1973 war, Egypt returned to a pro-Western course. The war had given Sadat the backing that was needed to promote a diplomatic solution. The key to such a solution was in Washington, as only the United States could pressure Israel to make concessions. In 1976 Sadat terminated the cooperation agreement of 1971. The last Soviet base rights vanished. The Soviet military presence, which had been so great, was reduced to nothing.

The Vietnam War

According to most criteria, the Vietnam War was the most comprehensive conflict after the Second World War. It was certainly the most lasting. After France's defeat in 1954, the United States took over as North Vietnam's chief enemy. This new war lasted for about 20 years. It exceeded all other wars in use of fire power. By 1970, with much of the bombing yet to come, more bombs had been dropped in Vietnam than the sum total of all other targets in human history. The Vietnam War was also the most expensive economically. US expenses alone have been estimated at 150 billion dollars. There are no reliable estimates as to how much it cost the communist side. The number of American casualties was about 58,000 (as compared to approximately 33,500 during the Korean War). However, the total number of civilian and military deaths did not exceed the 3.5 to 4 million killed during the Korean War.

US involvement was escalated gradually. From 1954 to 1961, military, political, and economic assistance was given to the Diem regime in South Vietnam but the extent was fairly moderate. In November 1961 there were still 'only' 948 military advisers in the country. The years from 1962 to 1965 were an interim period in which the US role was expanded considerably, but it was still subject to clear limitations. The number of military personnel rose to 12,000 by the end of 1962 and to 75,000 in the middle of 1965. Their functions were increased, although they still primarily lent support to South Vietnamese combat troops.

From 1965 to 1968, most of the restrictions on the US warfare disappeared. In March 1965 the first combat troops were landed. The first bombing raids over North Vietnam had taken place as early as in 1964. From February 1965 they became a regular element of the war, although all in all more bombs were dropped in the south than in the north. At the end of 1968 the number of US soldiers had reached 540,000.

There were many reasons for US policy. Vietnam was only one of many places where Washington tried to contain 'communist aggression' during the postwar period. The policy of containment was generally accepted in the United States, and at least until 1965 there was little reaction against the way the war was carried out. To the extent the official stance was criticized, most of the criticism came from the right, in the form of demands for more intensive warfare.

Behind the policy of containment was the belief that a communist victory in one area would result in further expansion. This was the domino theory. Once again this was a belief that was widely held. This is how President Johnson's leading advisers summed up their view in 1965:

> Thailand could not be held if South Vietnam were taken over, and ... the effects on Japan and India could be most serious ... the effect in Europe might also be most serious, and ... de Gaulle would find many takers for his argument that the U.S. could not be counted on to defend Europe ... South Vietnam was *a crucial test* of the ability of the free world and the U.S. to counter the Communist tactic of 'wars of national liberation' and ... a U.S. defeat would necessarily lead to worldwide questioning whether U.S. commitments could be relied on.

These general explanations of the US involvement can be subdivided. During the first years after the Second World War, the primary objective was to strengthen France in Western Europe (see pp. 17–18). Then defense against 'world communism' became the primary motivation. When the breach between the Soviet Union and China was perceived in earnest by Washington in 1962–63, the war was justified as a defense against the 'Chinese' pattern for wars of national liberation. A defeat for the United States would mean new guerilla thrusts in other parts of the world, whereas a victory would frighten other movements from taking such a course of action. From the mid-1960s, the fact that the United States had already invested so much prestige became a primary element preventing a re-evaluation of US policy.

While the Cold War context was undoubtedly important for the US intervention, some historians have emphasized the more personal role of leading American politicians. There has been some speculation about what Kennedy would have done, if alive – an impossible question to answer. Many have focused on Lyndon Johnson and underlined his personal responsibility for the dramatic escalation of the war in his presidential years. He may have harbored his private doubts about the war, but in all discussions, both public and private, he held to a firm line, strongly discouraging discussion about alternatives. Nixon, while reducing the number of US troops in Vietnam, was prepared to use intensive bombing to strengthen the US negotiating position.

US economic interests in Indochina were small. In the abundance of sources available, there are few indications that they had much significance for the judgments of the leading politicians. Most of the references to the significance of the natural resources in the area are to be found in the Eisenhower period. On the other hand, the domino theory virtually abolished the distinction between strategic, political, and economic considerations. For any of these dimensions, a defeat for the United States would have highly negative consequences.

There were instances in which the United States had not been particularly active in trying to prevent communist expansion, such as in China in 1945–49. This example could not have encouraged moderation in American warfare. The fall of China had resulted in bitter strife within the United States and had undoubtedly been an important factor behind McCarthyism in the 1950s. The Democrats had struggled with the problem ever since. They were not about to be blamed for the fall of Indochina as well.

The differences between China in the 1940s and Vietnam in the 1960s were interesting. The material resources of the United States had increased tremendously. The Americans' belief in themselves as the world's leading nation had increased at an even faster pace. The situation in Europe had stabilized, so that efforts could be concentrated on the new type of conflicts arising in Asia and Africa. Vietnam appeared to be a problem that would be much easier to handle than China had been. There was no reason not to believe that Washington could take on Hanoi. The danger of Peking or Moscow intervening was considered minimal as long as the United States did not invade North Vietnam and observed certain self-imposed limitations with regard to bombing it.

However, the relative position of the United States was weakened in many ways, and time would show that the American capacity to exert influence in Vietnam was much less than nearly everyone had assumed.

Until 1964–65, Soviet involvement in Vietnam was very limited. In 1957 the Soviet Union had advocated that both North and South Vietnam become members of the UN. Economic and military assistance to North Vietnam was moderate and was actually reduced in 1964. This was possibly a reflection of increasing Chinese influence in Hanoi. The Cuban crisis and the conflict between China and India probably also curbed Soviet interest in major new commitments.

But as the war in Vietnam increased in intensity, the Soviet Union became more active. The Kremlin could not entrust Peking, which dispatched large forces to North Vietnam as Hanoi sent its troops south, with the defense against 'capitalist aggression.' The conflict in Indochina also tied up substantial US resources. That was advantageous for the Soviet Union in many different ways, ranging from the reaction against the war in US and European public opinion, to reduced appropriations to the sections of US defense that were not involved in Vietnam. Soviet economic and military assistance increased rapidly. In 1964 it had probably amounted to about 40 million dollars. In the years from 1967 to 1972 it was about one billion dollars annually. Soviet support clearly came to exceed Chinese assistance, although Hanoi was fairly successful at playing these two countries off against each other in order to achieve maximum gains. However, relations between Peking and Hanoi deteriorated rapidly after North Vietnam began to negotiate with the United States, and the Chinese troops were withdrawn. North Vietnam's eminent leader, Ho Chi Minh, died in 1969.

In June 1962, Secretary of Defense Robert McNamara declared that: 'Every quantitative measurement we have shows we're winning this war.' However, there was a lot that was not quantifiable. Morale was much higher on the side of North Vietnam and the Viet Cong than on the side of the United States and the South Vietnamese government. To a certain extent it appeared that US involvement was counter-productive. The more the Americans fought, the less motivated the South Vietnamese were to bear their part of the burden. To an ever-increasing extent, the South Vietnamese governments were considered US-dominated and thus forced upon the country by foreigners. Moreover, governments came and went every few months after the fall of President Diem in 1963, until the generals, first Ky and then Thieu, managed to achieve a degree of stability after 1965.

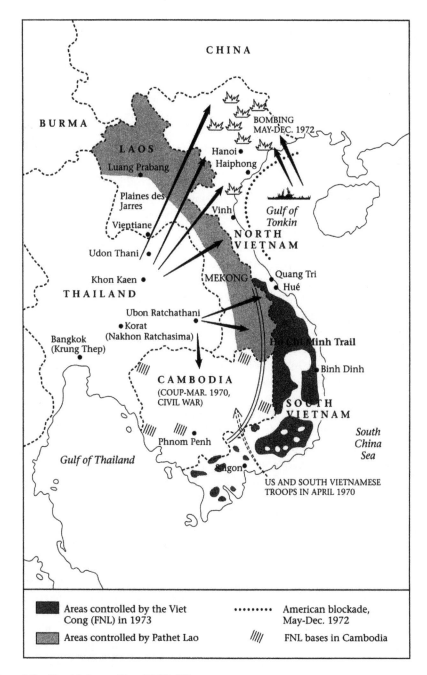

Figure 4.3 The Vietnam War, 1969–73

The extensive US bombing probably contributed to the relative stability in the south after 1965, but it could not prevent an escalation of the war on the part of North Vietnam. Official US estimates showed that the influx of troops from the north increased from 35,000 in 1965 to 90,000 in 1967. The bombing seems to have had little negative effect on Hanoi's willingness to carry on the war, and probably contributed first and foremost to drawing the North Vietnamese more closely together.

The US warfare in general, and the bombing in particular, led to widespread reactions in many countries, including among Americans themselves. The protests spread from the universities to large segments of US society. US objectives in Indochina seemed unclear for increasing numbers of people. The means were all the clearer and were portrayed in detail daily in the first televised war. The fact that the massive effort did not result in any visible success further strengthened the opposition to the war, especially after the Tet offensive of North Vietnam and the Viet Cong in 1968.

Johnson decided not to run for re-election. Nixon had no alternative when he assumed the office of president: the ground forces had to be reduced in number. By the turn of the year 1970–71 they had been reduced to 280,000. In other ways the war was intensified. The air force and the navy were used even more actively than formerly, and the South Vietnamese government received even more support. Geographically, the war was extended in 1970 by the US–Vietnamese invasion of Cambodia, in the following year by the invasion of Laos. The bombing of North Vietnam was at its most intense in 1972.

In January 1973 a cease-fire was established. The US troops were to be withdrawn, while the North Vietnamese were allowed to remain in South Vietnam. Hanoi did have to agree to let Thieu remain in power in Saigon for the time being, but negotiations were to be initiated concerning the establishment of a government comprised of the two competing local factions as well as the political forces that represented views between these two factions. In the polarization of the war there were not many who still took a middle stance. Nor could water and fire be unified. Nothing ever came of a political solution for South Vietnam.

The cease-fire collapsed. The US forces had not been able to win militarily, but had prevented a North Vietnamese victory. Public opinion and attitudes in Congress now made it impossible for the Ford administration to continue the bombing raids. A well-equipped South Vietnamese force consisting of one million men proved insufficient to resist the North Vietnamese offensive which came in 1974–75. The Viet Cong had suffered great losses, particularly during the Tet offensive, and the North Vietnamese played an ever-increasing role in the south. The Thieu regime collapsed in the course of a few months. The military dispositions of the regime were unwise, the political support slight, economic chaos reigned, and the Americans could no longer do much to influence the result. On 30 April 1975 the Communist forces conquered Saigon, or Ho Chi Minh City as it was now called. The Khmer Rouge had then already been victorious in Cambodia. Just after the fall of Saigon the Communists gained complete control in Laos. The Vietnam War was over.

However, even the war in Vietnam had limited influence on relations between the United States and the Soviet Union – how limited was most clearly illustrated by Nixon's visit to Moscow in May 1972. Just two weeks prior to his visit, the United States mined seven North Vietnamese ports and escalated the bombing. The White House expected these dramatic measures to result in a postponement of the summit with Brezhnev. This did not happen. Moscow was prepared to carry out the scheduled talks, which would actually represent one of the zeniths of the policy of détente. No one can say with any certainty whether this policy could have been carried even further if it had not been for Vietnam, but at least Vietnam did not prevent détente in any way.

The Vietnam War also illustrated how limited the influence of the superpowers could be. Even a total expenditure of 150 billion dollars and the employment of more than 500,000 US soldiers could not prevent the events in Vietnam from resulting in victory for North Vietnam and the Viet Cong, a victory that could not be explained by foreign support. Soviet assistance did not amount to more than approximately one-thirtieth of the American assistance. Once more, local conditions proved to be decisive.

DÉTENTE BETWEEN EAST AND WEST, 1962-1975: THE LITERATURE

Two key works on Soviet policy during this period are still Michel Tatu, *Power in the Kremlin: From Khrushchev to Kosygin* (New York, 1972) and Robin Edmonds, *Soviet Foreign Policy: The Brezhnev Years* (Oxford, 1983).

For US policy, Henry Kissinger's monumental *White House Years* (Boston, 1979), *Years of Upheaval* (Boston, 1982) and *Years of Renewal* (New York, 1999) are indispensable. They may well be supplemented by Jussi Hanhimäki, *The Flawed Architect: Henry Kissinger and American Foreign Policy* (Oxford, 2004) and even Seymour M. Hersh, *The Price of Power: Kissinger in the Nixon White House* (New York, 1983). A useful book on the Nixon–Kissinger years is also William Bundy, *A Tangled Web: The Making of Foreign Policy in the Nixon Presidency* (New York, 1998). A still fascinating analysis of the relationship between foreign and domestic policy in the United States, based on the Jackson–Vanik amendment, can be found in Paula Stern, *Water's Edge: Domestic Politics and the Making of American Foreign Policy* (Westport, CT, 1979). An ambitious, if not entirely successful attempt to explain détente in terms of domestic politics is found in Jeremi Suri, *Power and Protest. Global Revolution and the Rise of Détente* (Cambridge, MA, 2003).

On the Helsinki process, Daniel C. Thomas, *The Helsinki Effect: International Norms, Human Rights, and the Demise of Communism* (Princeton, NJ, 2001) is most useful. See also Oliver Bange and Gottfried Niedhart, *Helsinki 1975 and the Transformation of Europe* (New York, 2008). On Ostpolitik see also Carole Fink and Bernd Schaefer (eds), *Ostpolitik, 1969-1974. European and Global Responses* (Cambridge, 2009). The most satisfactory contemporary presentation of the SALT I talks is John Newhouse, *Cold Dawn: The Story of SALT* (New York, 1973). With regard to the Middle East, William B. Quandt, *Peace Process: American Diplomacy and the Arab–Israeli Conflict Since 1967* (Washington, DC, 2005) is excellent. Ritchie Ovendale, *The Origins of the Arab–Israeli Wars* (London, 1984 and subsequent editions) and Nadav Safran, *Israel: The Embattled Ally* (Cambridge, 1982) can also be recommended, although the former is relatively brief and the latter, as the title indicates, places greatest emphasis on the role of Israel.

As far as Vietnam is concerned, too much of the literature is focused on the United States. Most useful among these books are still George C. Herring, Jr.,

(Continued)

(Continued)

America's Longest War: The United States and Vietnam, 1950–1975 (New York, 1979 and subsequent editions), Leslie H. Gelb and Richard K. Betts, *The Irony of Vietnam: The System Worked* (Washington, DC, 1979), Robert Schulzinger, *A Time for War: The United States and Vietnam, 1941–1975* (New York, 1997) and Fredrik Logevall, *Choosing War: The Lost Chance for Peace and the Escalation of War in Vietnam* (Berkeley, CA, 1999). For the international dimensions of the Vietnam War, see Peter Lowe (ed.), *The Vietnam War* (Houndmills, 1998). See also Logevall's *Embers of War: The Fall of an Empire and the Making of America's Vietnam* (New York, 2012).

RENEWED TENSION BETWEEN EAST AND WEST, 1975-1984

The policy of détente had primarily meant détente in Europe. Here the status quo was acceptable to both power blocs. Détente also contributed to regulating the arms race through certain limitation agreements.

After 1975 this policy lost its momentum. Relations between East and West, particularly between the United States and the Soviet Union, soon became so poor that many people felt the Cold War had returned, or not only that: more and more people claimed that it had never actually ceased.

Few new agreements on arms limitations were reached. SALT II was signed but not ratified by the United States. The intensity of the arms race increased (see pp. 142–5).

It became evident that the point of departure for détente had differed in the two blocs. The Soviet Union combined cooperation in certain areas with conflict in others. Moscow was prepared to accept the status quo in Europe, but normalization there went hand in hand with more active policies in other regions of the world: in southern Africa, the Horn of Africa, Indochina, and Afghanistan. The United States had had higher expectations for détente; there, disappointment over new conflicts gave added fuel to those who opposed cooperation with the Soviet Union – a sentiment that had always existed in parts of the population. Vietnam faded somewhat into the background. The United States' need for self-assertion increased, and this need was further stimulated by various setbacks around the world.

In a sense, détente in Europe had overshadowed conflicts in other regions. Now détente was almost taken for granted in that part of the world, while the many conflicts outside Europe assumed greater significance than previously. The United States and the Soviet Union were determined to pursue more active policies, even in the adversary's backyard. Washington considered the end of liberalization in Poland a greater setback than the Soviet invasion of Czechoslovakia. Cuba, with the assistance of the Soviet Union, began once more to support revolutionary movements in several Central American countries. In the many conflicts outside of Europe the two superpowers, important as they were, had to face many diferent regional and local factors, which were often beyond their control.

THE SOVIET UNION: A NEW GLOBALISM

It is important to point out what détente was not. Moscow stressed that while the policy of détente was necessary, not least to avoid another major war, the ideological differences between communism and capitalism would still remain. Both at home and abroad, the Kremlin emphasized that there could be no question of ideological coexistence. The struggle between ideologies would continue until communism had won its final victory throughout the entire world. Anything else was inconceivable from a communist ideological point of departure.

Even when détente was at its peak, *Pravda* wrote:

> Only those politically naive can argue that what we are witnessing is some understanding between capitalism and socialism, its costs to be borne by the Third World. The Soviet Union will continue to rebuff any aggressive attempts by the forces of imperialism and render extensive help to the patriots of Angola ... Mozambique, Zimbabwe, South Africa ...

And at the Twenty-fifth Party Congress in 1976 Brezhnev claimed that

> detente does not in the slightest way abolish, and cannot abolish or change the laws of the class struggle. We do not conceal the fact that we see detente as a way to create more favorable conditions for peaceful socialist and communist construction.

According to the Soviets, the policy of détente meant that the Soviet Union would be recognized as a superpower on a level with the United States. No major international question was to be resolved without Soviet participation. Moscow's train of thought showed clear tendencies towards superpower hegemony. The United States had long had both the will and the capacity to use military force almost anywhere in the world. After 1945 the United States had intervened a total of more than 200 times to promote its policies. Such intervention took place close to home, such as in Guatemala, Cuba, and the Dominican Republic, as well as in more distant parts, such as Berlin, the Middle East, Vietnam, and Quemoy-Matsu. Not all US interventions had been equally successful, but the Soviet Union too had experienced defeat when it occasionally ventured far from its borders.

During the 1960s and 1970s, Moscow strengthened its capacity to pursue a more global policy. This was not a sudden change, but a gradual increase throughout the two decades. In the strategic sphere, the Soviet Union achieved approximate parity with the United States around 1970. The overall level of defense was increased. An important aspect of this increase was the improved facility for so-called power projection. The air force gained the capacity to undertake large transfers over long distances, and the navy was strengthened extensively. After Khrushchev had first reduced the conventional surface fleet, it was expanded once more. By the mid-1960s the Soviet navy had established a fairly permanent presence in the Mediterranean, a few years later in the Indian Ocean and the Caribbean Sea. At the end of the decade there were several instances in which it was employed to support foreign policy objectives (Yemen, 1967 and Ghana, 1969).

The Soviet Union obtained bunkering rights in Africa, in the Middle East, and on Cuba, a fact that further increased the possibilities of pursuing this type of policy.

The Soviet Union also became more active in the export of armaments. Traditionally, US weapon exports had been much greater than those of the Soviet Union. This trend changed from the mid-1970s, and in the early 1980s the Soviet Union was responsible for slightly more than 30 per cent of the world's weapon exports, whereas the US share was slightly less than 30 per cent. The major recipients of Soviet equipment were Syria, Libya, Iraq, India, and Vietnam. On the whole, Moscow placed greater emphasis on military assistance than on economic assistance. For the years 1976–80, military transfers to the Third World were four times as great as economic transfers. On the part of the United States, the economic share remained somewhat greater than the military share.

The Soviet military build-up reflected first and foremost the fact that Moscow placed high priority on defense, more so than the United States did during this period (see pp. 138–41). This took place without any corresponding shift in the relative economic strengths of the two superpowers, although the rate of growth in the Soviet Union seems to have been higher than in the United States even in the late 1960s. According to rough Western estimates, the Soviet gross national product equalled approximately 40 per cent of the US GNP in 1960. In 1970 this figure had risen to 49 per cent, and to 50 per cent in 1980. (Russian calculations from the 1990s indicate that these Western estimates may have been considerably too high, but at least they represent perceptions at the time.)

All in all, the Soviet Union was still clearly inferior to the United States in terms of its capacity for power projection in the Third World. What was new was that the Soviet Union had at least achieved the capacity to pursue a more ambitious course of policy than previously. In step with its increasing capacity, its will had also grown stronger, although Soviet expansion seems to have been more a response to opportunities that were created locally in various parts of the world than the expression of a 'grand design' behind Moscow's policy.

After the fall of Ben Bella in Algeria, Nkrumah in Ghana, and Keita in Mali in the years 1965–68, Soviet presence in Africa was minimal for a long time. On the whole, Brezhnev's first years were somewhat characterized by a reaction against the policies Khrushchev had pursued. Now the limited resources were to be concentrated on key countries, such as Algeria and Morocco, or on the few more progressive regimes that existed, such as in Guinea and Congo-Brazzaville. Africa's share of Moscow's economic assistance to the Third World sank from 47 per cent of the total amount during the decade 1954–64 to only 13 per cent in the years 1965–74. For North Africa, this figure declined from 34 to 9 per cent and for Africa south of the Sahara from 13 to 4 per cent. Most of the Soviet advisers were sent home from Sudan in 1971 and in the following year from Egypt.

However, new opportunities for Soviet policy in Africa presented themselves in the mid-1970s. In 1974 the Salazar–Caetano regime in Portugal collapsed. Thus the Portuguese colonial empire moved quickly towards its end. In Guinea-Bissau and in Mozambique, unified independence movements had achieved substantial results even before the revolution in Portugal and were ready to assume power.

In Angola, however, there were several rival liberation movements, and they had only liberated small parts of the country. The three combatants, the MPLA, the FNLA, and UNITA, had all received assistance from abroad for many years. The Soviet Union supported the MPLA, the United States and China the FNLA. Supplies from abroad continued after an agreement was reached in January 1975 for a coalition government. The first Cuban advisers arrived to support the MPLA, while Zaire and South Africa supported the FNLA. The antagonism between the three groups – particularly between the MPLA, on the one hand, and FNLA–UNITA, on the other – was great, and the attempt at cooperation soon disintegrated. Warfare escalated, and the assistance from abroad increased. Portugal would withdraw altogether in November 1975, and what mattered for each faction was to achieve the best possible point of departure for seizing power then.

There is little doubt that Soviet support to its faction was more comprehensive than US support to its faction. In December 1975 the Senate stopped the assistance the United States had given to FNLA–UNITA. Nor was the US fleet sent to the region to neutralize any Soviet presence. Cuban intervention began somewhat earlier and became considerably more extensive on the whole than that of South Africa. Cuba would send a total of about 20,000 men to Angola. Even so, the South African intervention proved to be most significant for the attitude of black Africa, in disfavor of FNLA–UNITA. Even though the MPLA was victorious for the most part, warfare continued in parts of Angola.

Cuba had long had advisers in various African countries. It had proved difficult to spread the revolution to Latin America, so Castro concentrated all the more on Africa. However, before Angola, Cuba's contribution had been limited to a relatively moderate number of advisers. There were clear differences between Soviet and Cuban policies in Africa, even though the two countries had mutual interests for the most part. Both financially and in terms of transport, the Cubans were dependent on Soviet assistance for their presence in Angola and several other places in Africa. Obvious reasons of language, race, and great power politics made Cuban troops highly preferable to Soviet troops.

On the Horn of Africa, the Soviet Union had signed a friendship and cooperation agreement with Somalia in 1974, and acquired an important naval base in Berbera. After Emperor Haile Selassie's fall in 1974, and particularly after Haile Mengistu had taken over the leadership of the revolutionary council in 1977, Ethiopia changed to a more pro-Soviet course of policy. The Kremlin wanted to have its cake and eat it too, but as Somalia and Ethiopia were at war over the Ogaden province, it was difficult to support both sides at the same time. The Soviet plans for a socialist federation of Ethiopia, Somalia, Eritrea, and Djibouti were rejected.

Somalia terminated its agreement with the Soviet Union. The Soviet Union then concentrated its efforts on Ethiopia, the larger and more influential of the two countries. Once more, Cuba and the Soviet Union intervened, now with about 17,000 men. In November 1978 the Soviet Union and Ethiopia signed a friendship and cooperation agreement. Soviet weapon assistance has been estimated at about one billion dollars in a single year.

Again the US reaction was modest, in part because of its Vietnam complex, in part because Somalia's claim on Ogaden was not recognized by the other African countries. However, the United States gradually drifted towards Somalia. When the fortunes of war turned in favor of Ethiopia, the United States supported Somalia directly, and Ethiopia and the Soviet Union were warned not to invade Somalia. They did not do so.

In South Yemen, too, the Soviet Union had gained a foothold after the British withdrew in 1967. In February 1979, North Yemen was invaded by troops from South Yemen. The Soviet Union had given substantial military assistance to the South, but tried to maintain good relations with the North as well. Now Washington was prepared to send supplies and advisers. The United States cooperated with Saudi Arabia. Even radical Arab countries spoke out against the invasion. A cease-fire was declared and the troops from South Yemen withdrawn, although guerilla combat continued until 1982.

In Indochina, the Soviet Union cooperated with Vietnam. After their victory over the US-backed Thieu government in 1975, the Vietnamese became increasingly dependent on Moscow. To a great extent this was because Hanoi's relations with Peking became very strained owing to border disputes and differing policies in relation to Cambodia. When the Vietnamese invaded Cambodia in December 1978 and deposed the Pol Pot regime, they could count on Soviet support. Thus the most brutal regime the world had experienced after 1945 had fallen. From 1975 to 1979 the Khmer Rouge killed between 1 and 2 million people, out of a total population of 7–8 million.

However, the invasion was such a clear example of encroachment on another country that the new government won only modest international support. Once more there were many in the West who spoke of Soviet-backed expansion. After Deng Xiaoping had first proclaimed his intentions in Washington, China responded in February 1979 by sending troops into Vietnam. The Soviet Union sent warnings to China, although a direct invasion does not seem to have been planned. The war went badly for the Chinese, and they withdrew from Vietnam after a brief campaign.

The clearest example of Moscow's expansive role was the invasion of Afghanistan in 1979. The Soviet Union had traditionally had close relations with the changing Afghan governments. Relations with Afghanistan and Finland were considered exemplary for relations with non-communist countries. In April 1978, a pro-Communist government assumed power in Afghanistan. The coup seems to have taken Moscow by surprise. The Afghan Communist party was divided into rival factions. Many of the reforms that were instituted were moderate in a Western context: land reforms, general access to education, a reduction in marriage taxes. In Afghanistan, however, they were radical.

The combination of a rapidly growing Soviet influence, political repression and opposition to the reforms mentioned led to a large-scale Muslim guerilla war against the Marxist government. There was a very real danger of its collapse despite the 10,000 Soviet advisers/troops that were already in the country. Moscow also feared that the unstable communist ruler, Amin, could turn to the United States. In December 1979 Moscow intervened. The total number of troops rose to 90,000 men. Amin was killed and the Soviet-friendly Babrak Karmal installed as the new leader. With the possible exception of the events in Eastern Europe in the wake of the Second World War, this was the most direct Soviet intervention anywhere. The reaction was sharp, not only in the United States and many other Western countries, but also in nonaligned countries, particularly the Islamic ones.

Soviet policy in Latin America had also become more active. In 1983 Moscow had diplomatic relations with 19 countries, as compared to only four 25 years earlier. Trade with this part of the world had increased considerably, although it was still relatively limited, with the partial exception of Argentina. The increased Soviet presence was due not only to an altered Soviet stance, but also to a widespread desire in Latin America itself for improved contacts to the East.

In addition to Cuba, the Soviet Union had particularly close relations with Nicaragua after the Sandinista government assumed power in 1979, and with Grenada, from 1979 as well. They were both referred to in Moscow as 'people's democracies' and received military and economic assistance from Cuba and the Soviet Union. Even so, the Kremlin seemed determined to avoid more comprehensive commitments towards governments that were under such strong pressure from the United States.

The Soviet Union wanted both continued détente with the United States and increased influence around the world. The Soviet leaders had not concealed their intentions, even their duty, to support 'wars of national liberation.' Why should such assistance endanger détente? After all, the Soviet Union had been willing to continue détente even when the Vietnam War was at its most intense.

However, it is likely that the leaders in the Kremlin gradually began to feel that they had less to gain by the policy of détente than they had hoped. SALT II was in difficulties. In December 1979 NATO decided to deploy US intermediate-range missiles in Western Europe in response to the Soviet SS–20 missiles if a solution was not reached through negotiations (see pp. 144–5).

The Soviet Union received less economic and technological help from the United States than they had expected. On the other hand, Washington showed an ever-increasing willingness to grant China advantages in the economic and even in the semi-military sphere (see pp. 219–21). In 1971–72 the US opening to China had contributed to accelerating détente. Now the consequences seemed to be the opposite. This difference

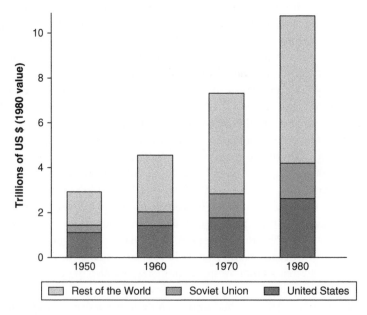

Figure 5.1 The United States, the Soviet Union, and the World's Total GNP

Source: Block, 1981, *The Planetary Product in 1980: A Creative Pause*

could possibly be explained by two considerations. In the first place, Moscow's fears as to how far US rapprochement would go were greatest at the time of the sensational events of 1971–72. In the second place, the overtures towards China at that time were accompanied by a strong desire in Washington for détente with the Soviet Union. This was much less the case at the turn of the decade from the 1970s to the 1980s.

If the advantages of détente were smaller, it is possible that the gains from a more aggressive policy in Africa and Asia were greater than the leaders in the Kremlin may have expected. In Africa in particular the Soviet Union had attained a position at the beginning of the 1980s that few would have considered possible ten years earlier.

THE UNITED STATES: REACTION TO DÉTENTE

On the part of the United States, the policy of détente was viewed with high expectations. US–Soviet relations had moved from confrontation to negotiation. The rhetorical descriptions of the new relations could reach great heights. At the signing of SALT I in 1972, President Nixon declared: 'The historians of some future age will write of year 1972 … that this was the year when America helped to lead the world out of the lowlands of constant war to the high plateau of peace.' Even when Nixon wanted to caution against excessive expectations in relation to détente, his choice of words could indicate the opposite. In his speech to Congress after returning from the SALT conference, he said that 'we did not bring back from Moscow the promise of instant peace, but we do bring back the beginning of a process that can lead to lasting peace.' This type of statement was partly a result of genuine optimism and partly an attempt to upstage the skeptics, not least in Congress, who would oppose some of the many agreements that had been signed by the United States and the Soviet Union.

Some segments of public opinion swung from one extreme to the other. Whereas the Soviet Union had previously been considered practically the embodiment of evil, the policy of détente was now to usher in peace and cooperation. Gallup polls showed that confidence in the Soviet Union was greater in 1973 than at any time after the outbreak of the Cold War. Forty-five per cent of the respondents had a positive perception of Soviet intentions, whereas the corresponding figure as late as in 1967 had been 19 per cent and in the 1950s as low as 3 per cent.

Much of the public had difficulty in accepting the fact that relations with the Soviet Union were to consist of cooperation in some areas and conflict in others. It had to be one or the other. In the short term, this meant that the possibilities for agreement were exaggerated. In a somewhat longer perspective, this type of attitude paved the way for a strong reaction when the disappointments set in.

Despite the optimism that existed during the period of détente, even in 1972–73 a greater share of the population had little or no confidence in the Soviet Union than those who had a more positive perception. The trade union movement was basically on the skeptical side. Senator Henry Jackson was the chief spokesman for the skeptics in Congress. He got Congress to pass an amendment to SALT I establishing that in future agreements there would have to be equality between the United States and the Soviet Union with respect to the number of weapon launchers (despite the lead the United States had in terms of multiple warheads).

However, Jackson enjoyed limited support for his skepticism of arms control. On the other hand, he gained more widespread support when he tried to bring about freer emigration from the Soviet Union. In October 1972 he presented a proposal that the 'most favored nation clause' for liberalizing trade between the United States and the Soviet Union, as agreed on by Nixon and Brezhnev, should only be ratified by Congress if Moscow allowed free emigration. It was particularly Jews who wanted to leave the Soviet Union. Jackson's proposal soon acquired a majority, as both conservatives and liberals could support it. The Nixon administration was skeptical about interfering directly in the Soviet Union's domestic affairs. However, there were few who were in favor of the most favored nation clause. Parts of big business and the farmers were those who showed the greatest interest. Moreover, the administration's authority in relation to Congress was weakened considerably by the Vietnam War and the Watergate scandal.

The Soviet Union was willing to make certain concessions in relation to Jewish emigration, but Kissinger's negotiations to reach a compromise between Jackson and Moscow failed. Not only did nothing come of the most favored nation clause, but Congress voted that the Soviet Union should not be able to borrow more than 300 million dollars during the course of the three-year period the trade agreement lasted.

Trade between the United States and the Soviet Union increased nevertheless, but most of the increase was due to Soviet imports of large quantities of grain. Here, many Americans felt that they as capitalists had been outsmarted at their own game by the fantastic bargain the Soviet Union had made in 1972, the so-called 'great grain robbery.' Moreover, the emigration of Jews began to decline. Fluctuations in Jewish emigration often reflected the extent of Moscow's interest in improving relations with the United States.

The Nixon administration's foreign policy was continued to a great extent during Ford's short presidency (August 1974–January 1977). Kissinger represented the continuity, although an increasing opposition to the policy of détente was noticeable. The reaction came from at least two different quarters. On the part of the conservatives, it found expression in Ronald Reagan's campaign to become the Republican presidential candidate in 1976. Reagan felt that détente had benefited the Soviet Union alone. Even though Reagan lost to Ford, he received widespread support, and it was illustrative that the word détente now dropped out of the Republican vocabulary.

The other reaction was among liberals. Most of the people who were left of center claimed that the policy of détente was beneficial. However, as practised by the Republicans it had its drawbacks. Too little emphasis was placed on relations with Japan and the allies in Western Europe, as these countries themselves claimed. Moreover, Nixon and Kissinger's policies were not sufficiently in accordance with American ideals, in the sense that their policies ostensibly lacked a moral dimension. Where, for instance, were human rights in all these pragmatic policies towards the Soviet Union? The need for a moral awakening was strengthened by the crises the United States had experienced during the Vietnam War and Watergate. After all, the latter had forced Nixon to resign from the presidency.

The United States would try both methods of approach. In 1976 the relatively liberal Jimmy Carter won the presidential election. Carter wanted to retain much of Nixon and Kissinger's foreign policy, more than he admitted publicly, but new elements were also to be introduced. However, there was less agreement within the Carter administration than in any other administration after the Second World War. One small circle was associated with UN Ambassador Andrew Young, emphasizing human rights, cooperation with the Third World, and less emphasis on East–West issues. Two other circles were stronger. One of them was linked to national security adviser Zbigniew Brzezinski, representing in part a continuation of Kissinger's policies, but with a sharper tone towards the Soviet Union, even more cooperation with China and emphasis on US self-assertion. The other one was associated with Secretary of State Cyrus Vance, representing a pragmatic course. Each issue should be considered in isolation, caution was to be exercised in any change of course, and moralism and grand design could both easily lead the United States astray.

Each of these factions represented elements in Carter's own thinking. The new president lacked foreign policy experience and a dominant overall perspective. It was equally significant that these factions represented various attitudes in the United States as a whole. They had been there during the entire postwar period, but the conflict between them had never been as great as it was now. The United States was in a period of transition. Realism existed side by side with idealism, anti-communism with the desire for détente, great power politics with an aversion against such politics.

The Soviet reaction to Carter was reserved at first but gradually became openly more skeptical. The administration exhibited a willingness to follow up the SALT negotiations, but confused the Soviets by proposing much greater reductions in the weapons arsenals than had been the premise at Vladivostok in 1974. When a new SALT agreement was finally signed in 1979, it was doubtful whether the Senate would ratify it with the necessary two-thirds majority.

Carter placed greater emphasis on the issue of human rights than previous presidents had, but here, too, there was considerable wavering. Washington stressed that it was not only concerned about such conditions in communist countries, and a harder line was undoubtedly pursued towards rightist dictatorships, for instance in Latin America. But the administration's attitude towards countries such as Iran and South Korea showed that this dimension had to be balanced against other considerations. Moscow considered support to champions of human rights to be interference in domestic affairs, and disagreement on this account contributed to poorer relations, although the Carter administration gradually pursued a more cautious policy towards the Soviet Union in terms of human rights.

In the Middle East, the United States first based its efforts for achieving a comprehensive peace treaty on cooperation with the Soviet Union. However, as soon as the United States and the Soviet Union had reached agreement on a joint outline in October 1977, the Carter administration – under pressure from the Congress, from Israel, and more indirectly from President Sadat in Egypt as well – dropped the entire scheme and staked everything on following up Sadat's dramatic journey to Jerusalem in November 1977. In September 1978, Egypt and Israel signed the Camp David accords, which were drawn up with Carter's personal participation. Israel withdrew from the Sinai Peninsula, and Egypt recognized the state of Israel. It was unclear what would happen to the rights of the Palestinians. In March 1979, Egypt and Israel reached a peace agreement. The Soviet Union became even more determined to win influence in the radical Arab countries and to cooperate with the Palestine Liberation Organization, the PLO.

The United States brought up Soviet–Cuban policies in Africa in several talks with Soviet leaders, but its relatively mild criticism could hardly have a deterrent effect on

Moscow. This was the case in regard to both Angola and Ethiopia–Somalia. In North Yemen and to some extent in the question of Shaba in 1977–78, where the United States assisted France, Belgium, and Morocco in repelling an Angola-backed invasion of the Katanga province in Zaire, Washington intervened more actively and was successful.

Considering the general attitude of the United States after the Second World War, it was surprising how little the country did to limit the increasing Soviet influence, particularly in Africa. Kissinger argued that Soviet intervention in Angola was

> the first time since the aftermath of World War II that the Soviets have moved militarily at long distances to impose a regime of their choice. It is the first time that the U.S. has failed to respond to Soviet military moves outside their immediate orbit.

The limited US reaction was first and foremost an aftermath of the Vietnam conflict. But it was also partly a way of expressing the conviction that the East–West dimension was subordinate to local conditions in the countries in question. Moscow's gains did not need to be particularly long-lived. The close partners of the Soviet Union one year – such as Egypt, Sudan, and Somalia – could become the most bitter enemies of the Soviet Union the next year.

The coup in Afghanistan in April 1978 gave rise to few reactions. The US response to the Soviet invasion in December 1979 would be all the stronger. SALT II was put on ice. Carter proposed major increases in the defense budget, the grain trade was limited, exports of high technology were halted, and the Olympic games in Moscow were boycotted. It was not possible to trust the Soviets. The level of distrust in public opinion rose to old heights once more. Only 13 per cent now had a positive opinion of the Soviet Union. Although reactions in Western Europe were far more cautious, particularly in France and West Germany, the events in Afghanistan sharpened attitudes towards the Soviet Union there as well.

The invasion in Afghanistan came on top of other humiliations the United States had experienced. The allies in Western Europe wanted to preserve the results of détente and proved less willing than before to follow US leadership. The United States' economic dependence on the outside world increased, with increased oil imports and higher oil prices as the most obvious manifestation of this fact. Of utmost importance, however, were the events in Iran. The rule of the Shah had disintegrated at the turn of the year 1978–79; in November 1979 US embassy personnel were taken hostage by Iranian students and held in confinement for more than a year. A feeling spread that it was time the United States again let its voice be heard, whether in the face of communists, ayatollahs, or lukewarm allies.

The experiences of Vietnam faded somewhat into the background. The United States was prepared to assume new commitments in vital threatened areas. The clearest manifestation of this attitude was the so-called Carter Doctrine of January 1980. The President stressed that:

> any attempt by any outside force to gain control of the Persian Gulf region will be regarded as an assault on the vital interests of the United States. It will be repelled by the use of any means necessary, including military force.

The combination of an anti-Soviet and a nationalistic wave would contribute to Ronald Reagan's victory over Jimmy Carter in the presidential election of 1980, although domestic affairs were more important than foreign policy for most voters. Moscow had come to despair of Carter's vacillation and his gradually more antagonistic attitude to such an extent that even the leaders in the Kremlin apparently preferred Reagan to Carter. Reagan's harsh criticism of the Soviet Union was attributed to the election campaign. Perhaps he could even become a new Nixon with Kissinger at his side, a president who cooperated with the Soviet Union, but who had such an anti-communist point of departure that opposition to this policy would be moderated.

If that was the analysis of the Kremlin, it was long wrong. Reagan's anti-communism seemed firmly established, whereas Nixon's had been more dependent on the situation at hand. Reagan had always opposed détente. In his opinion, it was based on the dangerous illusion that the United States and the Soviet Union had significant mutual interests. Attitudes in the United States were different than they had been during and after the Vietnam War eight to ten years earlier. Skepticism of the Soviet Union was growing in all segments of the population; the need for an increase in the defense budget was generally accepted. The United States had to act as the leader of the 'free world' once more and dispel the doubt as to its own role that the Vietnam War had caused. Finally, the international situation was rather different in 1980 from what it had been at the outset of the 1970s.

Even in Reagan's policies there were certain changes which showed that as president he would not be quite the same as in a position of opposition. US relations with Taiwan were not strengthened to the degree he had advocated (see p. 220). SALT II was respected, even though it had been denounced during the election campaign as 'totally flawed.' Negotiations with Moscow on arms limitations – START, as the further SALT process was now called, and the INF negotiations on intermediate-range weapons in Europe – were begun before the United States had acquired the desired position of strength.

Even so, it was surprising how small the changes were. To a great extent Reagan pursued the policies that he had said he would promote and that he had represented throughout the 1970s. The defense budget would be increased dramatically (see pp. 143–4). The verbal attacks on the Soviet Union were many and harsh. No US president after the Second World War had publicly so strongly cast doubt on the legitimacy of the Soviet system. Reagan claimed that:

> The march of freedom and democracy will leave Marxism-Leninism on the ash heap of history as it has left other tyrannies which stifle the freedom and muzzle the self-expression of the people.

The Reagan administration steadily found new evidence that its analysis of Soviet intentions was correct. The war in Afghanistan continued. There were no signs that the Soviet Union intended to withdraw. In December 1981, a state of emergency was declared in Poland. Even though the Soviet Union did not intervene directly, most leaders in Washington felt that Moscow was behind the tough policies in Poland (see pp. 199–201). In September 1983, a South Korean passenger plane was shot down over Soviet territory, and all 269 on board perished. This was considered new evidence of the true nature of the Soviet regime. Confidence in the Soviet Union was weakened further. Only 9 per cent of the US population had a somewhat positive perception of the Soviet Union.

In Reagan's opinion, the United States had ceased to lead the free world. This would now be changed. However, it became evident that the United States and Western Europe had different perceptions of what results had been achieved by the policy of détente. The Europeans felt that it had had many positive effects and that it ought to continue, though perhaps in a modified form. The United States felt that détente had failed and ought to be abandoned. The Europeans insisted that they should have a say in the formulation of Western policies to an entirely different degree than previously. The United States could no longer decide more or less on its own, whether in terms of nuclear strategy, negotiations on arms limitation, or limitations on Western trade with the Soviet Union (see pp. 171–2).

The European perspective was greatly affected by the fact that the policy of détente had produced more beneficial results in Europe than in the rest of the world. But even in Europe this policy had lost its momentum, and tension increased once more. This was in part a result of the events in Poland, but even more so of the developments with regard to intermediate-range weapons and the generally deteriorating relations between East and West.

Even so, the greatest conflicts were linked to areas outside of Europe. Reagan was convinced that most of the unrest in the world could be attributed to the Soviet Union. Communist expansion was to be opposed, in Central America, in the Middle East, and everywhere else, whether the Soviet Union was directly behind it or tried to use others as its instrument. For Reagan, a defensive stance was not enough. The United States would also support the 'freedom fighters' who were prepared to take up the struggle against Soviet-Communist regimes. This offensive stance became known as the Reagan Doctrine. In some ways the Reagan Doctrine resembled the Eisenhower administration's emphasis on 'liberation,' but there were distinct differences. Eisenhower's policy applied mostly to Eastern Europe and was mainly rhetorical. The Reagan Doctrine was primarily directed at the Third World, and support was both military and economic.

In Central America, the large landowners, the army, and the Church had tradition-ally been dominant. In the course of the 1970s this alliance began to crack. The Church became more liberal, and new ideas also penetrated parts of the officer corps. In Nicaragua, the Somoza family's power base had become so narrow that the regime collapsed in 1979. The new Sandinista government was at first a broad coalition, but then it too began to lose some of its popular support.

The Carter administration swung from half-hearted support of the Sandinistas to a more skeptical attitude. Under Reagan the objective was openly to undermine and preferably overthrow the government as an element in 'the defense of the Western hemisphere against Soviet–Cuban expansion.' In El Salvador the United States defended the existing government, whereas in Nicaragua it now supported the politi-cal and military opposition. US aid increased steadily, with only limited success. The fear of a new Vietnam placed clear limitations on the willingness of Congress and public opinion to send military personnel to the region, although the United States built up bases in the neighboring country of Honduras. The US invasion of Grenada in the autumn of 1983 was also defended as necessary to halt Soviet–Cuban expansion.

The Marxist government on the island was deposed and the Cuban advisers sent home, but the invasion was denounced even by most of the United States' allies.

The Middle East was the other area that became a focal point of attention. In 1975 civil war had broken out in Lebanon, and the Syrian troops that advanced across the border the following year had remained. Israel intervened in Lebanon twice, first in 1978 and again in 1982. After the second invasion US troops were employed as part of an international peace-keeping force that was to oversee conditions in the chaotic city of Beirut. Gradually the troops were drawn in on the side of the Christian-Falangist government in the ongoing civil war. Thus they became an instrument directed against the Syrian influence. Washington saw Moscow behind Syria, as there were 7,000 Soviet advisers in Syria.

But in Lebanon the domestic situation was so chaotic, the objective of the US presence so unclear, the losses so great – 241 US soldiers were killed in a terrorist attack in Beirut – and the opposition to the United States so strong that Reagan was forced to withdraw the troops early in 1984. This action showed that the president could act pragmatically despite his harsh, uncompromising verbal stance.

The Reagan administration expected the Soviet Union to yield if only the United States conducted itself firmly enough. For instance, when it became evident that Washington would deploy new intermediate-range missiles in Western Europe, Moscow would make the concessions that were necessary to attain a negotiated solution.

The Kremlin was willing to make some concessions, but not as many as the White House wanted. Instead, verbal attacks on the Reagan administration were increased. Yuri Andropov, who had assumed leadership after the death of Brezhnev in November 1982, said in September 1983 that 'if anyone had any illusions about a possible evolution for the better in the policy of the present American Administration, such illusions have been completely dispelled by the latest developments.' In December 1983, deployment of intermediate-range missiles was begun in the West. This resulted in Moscow breaking off the arms limitation negotiations between East and West (see p. 145). In February 1984 Andropov died and Konstantin Chernenko replaced him. This change meant little for the climate between the two power blocs. Relations between the United States and the Soviet Union were worse than at any time since the Cuban crisis in 1962.

RENEWED TENSION BETWEEN EAST AND WEST, 1975-1984: THE LITERATURE

The most exhaustive treatment of détente and what went wrong is to be found in Raymond L. Garthoff, *Detente and Confrontation: American–Soviet Relations from Nixon to Reagan* (Washington, DC, 1985, revised edition 1994). Garthoff's sequel to that book is *The Great Transition: American–Soviet Relations and the End of the Cold War* (Washington, DC, 1994). Adam Ulam has written the sequel to *Expansion and Coexistence* in *Dangerous Relations: The Soviet Union in World Politics, 1970–1982* (Oxford, 1983). Mike Bower and Phil Williams present a brief, engaging discussion in *Superpower Detente: A Reappraisal* (London, 1988). Anatoly Dobrynin's *In Confidence: Moscow's Ambassador to America's Six Cold*

(Continued)

(Continued)

War Presidents (New York, 1995) is fascinating reading. For some good essays and many interesting sources on the demise of détente, see Odd Arne Westad (ed.), *The Fall of Détente: Soviet–American Relations during the Carter Years* (Oslo, 1997). Westad's *The Global Cold War: Third World Interventions and the Making of Our Times* (Cambridge, 2005) is indispensable.

Among the many memoirs from the Carter period, Zbigniew Brzezinski, *Power and Principle: Memoirs of the National Security Adviser 1977–1981* (New York, 1983) is the most candid. Most useful from the Reagan era is George P. Shultz, *Turmoil and Triumph: My Years as Secretary of State* (New York, 1993). An early collection of articles on the Reagan administration's foreign policy is to be found in David E. Kyvig (ed.), *Reagan and the World* (New York, 1990).

For a description of conflicts throughout the world, see Patrick Brogan, *World Conflicts* (London, 1998). Strobe Talbott, *Endgame: The Inside Story of SALT II* (New York, 1979) is the best work in its field.

THE END OF THE COLD WAR, 1984-1990

DIFFERENT THEORIES ABOUT THE END OF THE COLD WAR

With the dissolution first of Soviet rule in Eastern Europe and then of the Soviet Union itself, the Cold War was over. The West, primarily the United States, appeared to be the winner of a contest that had lasted more than 40 years.

This outcome created a strong temptation to analyze the end of the Cold War in terms of a Western triumph. And 'triumphalism' is indeed one school of thought in analyzing the end of the Cold War. Triumphalism comes in two main versions. One version stresses the particular contributions of the Reagan administration (Peter Schweizer and some of the many members of the Reagan administration who have written about these events). These writers see Ronald Reagan as different from his predecessors in that he gave up the containment policy based on the status quo and instead tried to bring about the 'victory' of the West and the collapse of the 'evil empire.' Schweizer highlights a number of measures – military, economic, political, and psychological – which helped bring about the desired outcome. This interpretation has received support from Russians who regret the collapse of the Soviet Union and see this outcome as the result of Western machinations.

The more moderate version of triumphalism sees the end of the Cold War as reflecting not primarily the policies of the Reagan administration, but rather the general containment policy pursued by all American presidents from Truman to Reagan. Thus, Robert Gates writes that 'Two generations of us accepted George Kennan's 1947 analysis that if Soviet expansionism could be contained, eventually the fundamental contradictions in the Soviet system would bring it down.' In this version, this was what happened, although the process went rather more quickly than virtually any observer expected, especially in the late 1970s.

A moderate group sees the end of the Cold War as a result both of Western, primarily American, policies and the fundamental changes brought about in the Soviet Union by Mikhail Gorbachev. Don Oberdorfer is in this group. Prominent members of the Reagan administration, such as Secretary of State George Shultz and Ambassador to the Soviet Union Jack Matlock, see Ronald Reagan as adopting the right blend of policies even before Gorbachev came to power, although they clearly think that these policies would never have had the effect they had without Gorbachev abandoning the old Marxist–Leninist ideology. In these accounts Reagan and Gorbachev both emerge as great heroes. John Gaddis basically supports this group. Gorbachev was important, but he allowed 'circumstances – and often the firmer views of more far-sighted contemporaries – to determine his own priorities.' The most far-sighted of them all was presumably Ronald Reagan, ably assisted by George Shultz.

Others insist on the primary role of Gorbachev while also giving Reagan his due. This attitude is reflected in the recent studies by Melvyn Leffler, Vladislav Zubok, and Andrei Grachev. All three give considerable credit to Reagan, particularly for his willingness to negotiate with Soviet leaders, especially Gorbachev. Yet, they clearly give most of the credit to Gorbachev. So does even James Mann in his very sympathetic study of Reagan. No one did more to bring the Cold War to an end than did Gorbachev.

Others again take a more critical view of Reagan's contributions. Thus, Raymond Garthoff explicitly argues that

> The West did not, as is widely believed, win the Cold War through geopolitical containment and military deterrence. Still less was the Cold War won by the Reagan build-up and the Reagan Doctrine, as some have suggested. Instead 'victory' came when a new generation of Soviet leaders realized how badly their system at home and their policies abroad had failed.

Still, Garthoff sees some importance in Western policies, and then primarily in the form of containment, which precluded any temptation Moscow may have had to advance its cause through military means.

Then, there are those (Archie Brown, Jacques Lévesque, some Russian supporters of Gorbachev) who give virtually all the credit for the end of the Cold War to Gorbachev and who see at least certain aspects of Reagan's hard-line anti-communism as probably having slowed down the cessation of the Cold War. The decisive factor was Gorbachev's 'idealistic view of the world, based on universal reconciliation.' If Gorbachev had not come to power, the Cold War would presumably still be continuing.

Little attention has been paid to the policies of George H. W. Bush. Many of the crucial developments actually took place during his administration, from the collapse of the Communist regimes in Central and Eastern Europe and in the Soviet Union itself to the unification of Germany. Yet, Bush was relatively slow in recognizing the revolutionary nature of the changes in the Soviet Union.

Finally, many Western European but also some other scholars emphasize different European contributions to the end of the Cold War, whether in the form of France's policies from de Gaulle to Mitterrand (Bozo), German *Ostpolitik* (Niedhart, Bange, Haftendorn, Soutou, Loth) or the unintended effects of CSCE (Daniel Thomas).

It is too early to develop a truly historical perspective on the end of the Cold War. As we see, much of the literature is still being written by the participants themselves. The present account is definitely critical of triumphalism. Yet, while strongly emphasizing the role of Gorbachev in ending the Cold War, it also gives some importance to the policies of the West in general, and the United States in particular.

There would, however, seem to be an obvious need for the literature to move beyond the endless fascination with individuals and try to relate the end of the Cold War to much deeper national and international structures, as has been done in the analysis of previous conflicts.

WHAT HAPPENED - AND WHY?

In the autumn of 1984 there were signs that the icy climate between East and West, and particularly between the Soviet Union and the United States, was beginning to thaw. For the first time, Reagan met with a representative of the top-level Soviet leadership, Foreign Minister Gromyko. The rhetoric used about the other side was moderated both in Washington and in Moscow. This was important in itself, especially in the light of the harsh invectives that had dominated previously. Both sides again showed greater interest in talks and other forms of contact. Reagan's attitude towards the Soviet Union was clearly more conciliatory than during his first years as president.

Chernenko died in March 1985, and Mikhail Gorbachev assumed the leadership of the party. Gorbachev had been born in 1931. Thus he was far younger than his predecessors; he had different attitudes and he was much more dynamic. It quickly became evident that he intended to implement sweeping changes in Soviet foreign policy. In December 1984 Margaret Thatcher had met Gorbachev and concluded that 'I like Gorbachev. We can do business together.' In November 1985 he and Reagan met for the first time. This meeting, in Geneva, was the first summit since Brezhnev and Carter had met in Vienna in 1979. The talks did not lead to any concrete results, but they showed that the two leaders were interested in developing a dialogue between East and West. In October 1986 Reagan and Gorbachev met again, this time in Reykjavik. Their talks on arms control and disarmament were the most dramatic ever held between leaders of the two superpowers, even though no agreements were reached (see p. 145).

Reagan and Gorbachev met three more times. In Washington in December 1987 they signed an agreement on land-based intermediate-range missiles (the INF treaty). This agreement represented something completly new, for the superpowers now agreed to eliminate an entire class of weapons, rather than merely setting limitations on further growth as they had done previously. When Reagan went to Moscow in June 1988, all mention of 'the evil empire' had ceased, and instead the two leaders could be seen hand in hand in Red Square. 'Gorbiemania' swept across the United States. Gorbachev's book *Perestroika* was advertised as 'the book of the year by the statesman of the year.' Gorbachev's popularity did not match Reagan's within the United States, but in many Western European countries the leader of the Soviet Communist party was more popular than the US president. This was definitely something new in the history of the Cold War. When Reagan and Gorbachev met for the last time, in New York in December 1988, it actually appeared as though the two leaders parted with considerable poignancy.

The new Bush administration did not merely continue the policy of détente that Reagan had begun to pursue. Several of Bush's advisers had been in the Ford administration when the previous period of détente began to give way to renewed tension.

They felt that it was best to be prepared for new setbacks. At least it was prudent to reconsider before proceeding.

Nevertheless, this pause for reflection was brief. At the summit meeting in Malta in December 1989, Bush showed that he was prepared to continue where Reagan had left off. Plans were laid for the two sides to conclude a START treaty, an agreement on chemical weapons and one on conventional disarmament, all this during the course of 1990 (see pp. 145–6). On several occasions Bush made it clear that he was eager for Gorbachev to succeed with his reform policies. For that reason the administration was willing to make substantial concessions with regard to lifting restrictions on trade and credit. Numerous articles were written on the theme 'From Yalta to Malta.' The Cold War, which was supposed to have begun in Yalta in February 1945, was now declared over.

Part of the Cold War had been waged on the ideological level. Major ideological changes now took place on both sides, especially in Moscow. The concept of peaceful coexistence between capitalistic and socialistic nations went back to Lenin, but both during Lenin's regime and later under Khrushchev and Brezhnev, peaceful coexistence was envisioned as a temporary condition. As we have seen, Brezhnev made it clear on several occasions that détente did not annul the laws of class struggle. The two blocs had to cooperate in order to prevent a conflict between the major powers, but Moscow still had an obligation to help 'wars of national liberation.' The fundamental ideological conflict would inevitably end in the victory of socialism and communism.

Gorbachev separated peaceful coexistence from the class struggle, conceiving of cooperation as a more permanent condition. This cooperation was also to encompass a much wider range of activities than previously. Avoiding a conflict between the major powers was not enough. In his book *Perestroika*, Gorbachev wrote:

> On the whole, we have long lived in peace. But the current international situation can't be described as satisfactory. The arms race, especially the nuclear arms race, goes on. Regional conflicts are raging. The war danger grows. To make international relations more humane is the only way out – and that is a difficult thing to do. This is how we pose the question: it is essential to rise above ideological differences. Let everyone make his own choice, and let us all respect that choice.

There would still be competition between the social systems, and of course Gorbachev hoped that socialism would eventually triumph throughout the world, but this competition would be peaceful and subordinate to the many shared challenges facing mankind. Gorbachev repeatedly likened the nations of today's world to a group of mountain climbers who were tied together with a climbing rope: 'They can either climb on together to the mountain peak or fall together into an abyss.'

This ideological shift made it substantially easier to reach agreements on arms control and disarmament. The Soviet stance on regional conflicts also changed dramatically. The many Soviet ventures, particularly during the 1970s, had not proved at all as successful as the Kremlin had hoped. In Afghanistan the Red Army met fierce opposition and had great difficulty establishing control outside the major urban areas. Local wars also continued in Angola, Ethiopia, and Cambodia. In Nicaragua the Sandinista government consolidated its position, but Moscow's involvement here was a source of particular irritation to Washington.

The regional conflicts were now to be resolved, but not necessarily won. The Soviet attitude towards the United Nations changed. Moscow paid its debt to the UN and supported peacekeeping operations. In the war between Iran and Iraq, the cease-fire that was reached in July 1988 was due in part to the concerted efforts of the superpowers, as well as the participants' re-evaluation of the situation in the wake of massive losses and small gains.

Coalition governments or elections were the preferred solutions for turbulent countries. The withdrawal of Soviet troops from Afghanistan in February 1989 was the most prominent manifestation of the transformation of Soviet policy. A change in Soviet outlook was also essential for the Namibia–Angola agreement of December 1988, an agreement negotiated by US Assistant Secretary of State for African Affairs Chester Crocker between Angola, Cuba, and South Africa. Of course the local participants also had good reason for ending a prolonged conflict that none of them seemed capable of winning. Free elections were to be held in Namibia, and the country was to attain formal independence. As expected, the elections in November 1989 were won by the South-West African People's Organization (SWAPO). The Cuban troops were gradually to be withdrawn from Angola in an operation scheduled to be completed by July 1991.

In Indochina, Hanoi declared in the spring of 1988 that all Vietnamese troops would be out of Cambodia by 1990, a deadline that was later moved up by several months. Again Moscow's stance was assumed to have contributed to a change of course by a local government, in this case Vietnam. When the United States invaded Panama in December 1989 and arrested the country's leader, Manuel Noriega, Moscow scarcely reacted. Soviet influence in Nicaragua was limited, and the willingness of the Sandinistas to hold free elections in February 1990 arose primarily from regional and local considerations, the country's strained economic situation and the United States' hard line. Soviet policy was oriented towards compromise once more. After the opposition candidate Violeta Chamorro had defeated the Sandinista leader Daniel Ortega in the election, Moscow actually continued its assistance to Nicaragua under the new regime. In Ethiopia it became increasingly evident that Moscow would reduce its comprehensive support to the Mengistu regime in its struggle against various resistance groups.

The new Soviet policy in Eastern Europe and Germany was an extremely important condition for the change in climate between East and West. Gorbachev not only removed the established system of sanctions represented by the Brezhnev Doctrine and the Red Army; he also encouraged the Eastern European regimes to implement extensive political changes in order to accommodate the growing opposition. In the space of six months in 1989, from free elections in Poland in June to the fall of Ceauşescu in Romania in December, the established order fell apart at the seams (see pp. 203–4).

Soviet restraint was also demonstrated in East Germany, a country of great strategic significance. It quickly became evident that the East German population was in favor of rapid unification with West Germany. West German Chancellor Helmut Kohl for his part made German unification a leading issue, but events occurred at a much more rapid pace than even Kohl could have foreseen. The demolition of the Berlin Wall took place in November 1989; in July 1990 the two nations were merged in an economic and social union, and in October political unification was accomplished. Although Moscow was skeptical about this process at first, the Kremlin ultimately accepted German unification (see pp. 173–5).

It is easier to describe the dramatic changes in the climate between East and West than to explain them. On the part of the United States, Reagan had been surprised to learn that Soviet leaders actually thought that the United States might attack the Soviet Union. He also wanted to show the electorate before the 1984 election that he not only represented firmness, but that he was also capable of establishing good relations with the Soviet Union. Public opinion in the United States wanted both strength in relation to the Soviet Union and 'peace' with arms reductions. The Democratic majority in Congress shared this aspiration. Moreover, a change in US policy would improve relations with Western Europe. Détente was never criticized as strongly in Western Europe as in the United States. Détente afforded substantial advantages in political, economic, and human terms, precisely in Europe, and Soviet expansion outside Europe made less of an impression in Europe than in the US. Politically and ideologically Reagan could claim that it was not the United States but the Soviet Union that had changed its course. And this change of course was seen as a result of the firm policy that had been pursued during the first years of his presidency. Critical voices included even Nixon and Kissinger who soon thought Reagan went too far, particularly in arms control; however, in the end the critics were few, and they enjoyed limited support both among the general public and in Congress. Reagan carried much of the US right wing with him in his new outlook on the USSR. The deals made between Reagan and Gorbachev were also quite simply very favorable to the United States.

Attitudes in the West were doubtless a factor that contributed to the changes in Soviet foreign policy. The West served as a model in the sense that Western society ran smoothly in the sectors where the USSR had the greatest problems. France under de Gaulle made strong efforts to break down the East–West division in Europe, but the effect was clearly smaller than Paris had hoped for. While Moscow and the Eastern European capitals appreciated France's break with NATO, with the exception of Bucharest they did not see this as having much relevance for their own policies. They would stay closely together in the Warsaw Pact. *Ostpolitik* was more important in that it took away the old image of revanchist Germany which had meant much for the cohesion of the East. West Germany quickly established close economic and political relations with many of these Central and Eastern European countries (see pp. 69–70). Despite the initially rather limited expectations on this point, the Helsinki process greatly encouraged human rights activists in Eastern Europe and the Soviet Union. Rights were now formally adopted that an increasing number of activists were determined to follow up on, although their governments were not. There is a direct line from certain sections of the Helsinki Act of 1975 to the collapse of the regimes in Central and Eastern Europe in 1989.

In addition the United States, through its firm stance, had made it clear that the cost to Moscow of maintaining the 'old' policies would merely increase. A number of more specific factors also played a role, e.g. the failure of Soviet policy in Afghanistan and the ambiguity of 'triumphs' in the Third World (the new partners were rarely as loyal as Moscow hoped for, but they were all expensive).

The change in attitude was undoubtedly greater in the Soviet Union than in the United States. Gorbachev did more than anyone else to bring the Cold War to an end. He was convinced that domestic and foreign reform had to go hand in hand. And, unlike former Russian reformers such as Alexander II and Khrushchev, Gorbachev did not resort to force when the reforms did not yield the desired changes, but instead went much further than originally intended.

Moscow's new course was closely linked to the enormous economic, political, and social problems the nation was facing. The cost to the USSR of the arms race and an expansive foreign policy was immense, representing at least 20 per cent of the gross national product, or probably much more – a national product with a growth rate that was declining in relation to that of the United States. The rate of economic growth had been decreasing throughout the 1970s and came almost to a halt at the end of the decade. That meant that even reduced growth in the defense budget, from 4 to 2 per cent annually, took an increasing share of the national product. The fact that oil prices were quite low in the mid-1980s also contributed to the difficult economic situation in the Soviet Union. Reform seemed the only way out.

In political terms Gorbachev was convinced that the Soviet Union had to pursue a policy of *glasnost*, or greater openness, if for no other reason than because in the Soviet Union an economic *perestroika* appeared impossible without *glasnost*. Once the Soviet Union had started down the road of *glasnost*, it was difficult to reverse the process without undermining the credibility of Gorbachev. Such a reversal would also greatly harm relations with the West at a time when Gorbachev wanted to transform the entire East–West relationship. The efforts to play down the effects of the explosion in the nuclear power plant at Chernobyl had also backfired badly.

On the foreign policy side, *glasnost* enhanced confidence in the Soviet Union abroad, but at the same time greater openness made it more difficult for Moscow to control events in Eastern Europe. Even when the Soviet state itself began to be threatened, the willingness to make concessions to the West continued to increase (see pp. 206–8). Thus Foreign Minister Shevardnadze could claim that *perestroika* had been successful precisely because it had advanced the most important aim of Soviet foreign policy, which was 'to create the conditions that can make the greatest contribution to the domestic transformation of the country.' Domestic policy controlled foreign policy.

Yet, towards the end of his rule it was becoming evident to Gorbachev and others that his economic policies were not succeeding. The economic reforms helped undermine the old system, but a true market economy was not established. The problems seemed to be growing rather than abating. Not until the autumn of 1990 was the decision made to convert to a market economy. And it was still a long way from resolution to reality, not to mention economic results. In fact, the setbacks in growth and production were much larger under Gorbachev than before he took over. Once this began to dawn on the leadership, the temptation increased to seek glory and success abroad rather than at home. Gorbachev was celebrated more and more abroad and less and less at home, suspended as he was between those who thought reform went too far and the increasing number who thought it did not go far enough.

THE END OF THE COLD WAR, 1984-1990: THE LITERATURE

In addition to the books by Garthoff and Shultz already mentioned in the bibliography to Chapter 5, the following authors are mentioned in the text: Peter Schweizer, *Victory: The Reagan Administration's Secret Strategy that Hastened the Collapse of the Soviet Union* (New York, 1994); Robert M. Gates, *From the Shadows: The Ultimate Insider's Story of Five Presidents and How They Won the Cold War* (New York, 1996); Don Oberdorfer, *From the Cold War to a New Era: The United States and the Soviet Union, 1983–1991* (Baltimore, MD, 1998); Jack Matlock, *Autopsy of an Empire: An American Ambassador's Account of the Collapse of the Soviet Union* (New York, 1995); Melvyn P. Leffler, *For the Soul of Mankind: The United States, the Soviet Union, and the Cold War* (New York, 2007); Vladislav M. Zubok, A *Failed Empire. The Soviet Union in the Cold War from Stalin to Gorbachev* (Chapel Hill, NC, 2007); Andrei Grachev, *Gorbachev's Gamble: Soviet Foreign Policy and the End of the Cold War* (Cambridge, 2008); James Mann, *The Rebellion of Ronald Reagan. A History of the End of the Cold War* (New York, 2009); Archie Brown, *The Gorbachev Factor* (Oxford, 1996); Jacques Lévesque, *The Enigma of 1989: The USSR and the Liberation of Eastern Europe* (Berkeley, CA, 1997). See also Olav Njølstad (ed.), *The Last Decade of the Cold War: From Conflict Escalation to Conflict Transformation* (London, 2004). Unfortunately Vladimir Pechatnov's main work is only available in Russian. John Gaddis's important interpretations of the Cold War are found in *We Now Know. Rethinking Cold War History* (Oxford, 1997) and *The Cold War* (New York, 2006).

Frédéric Bozo, *Mitterrand, the End of the Cold War and German Unification* (New York, 2009); Oliver Bange and Gottfried Niedhart (eds), *Helsinki 1975 and the Transformation of Europe* (New York, 2008). Helga Haftendorn, *Coming of Age: German Foreign Policy since 1945* (Lanham, MD, 2006); Georges-Henri Soutou and Winifried Loth (eds), *The Making of Détente: Eastern Europe and Western Europe in the Cold War, 1965–75* (London, 2008); Daniel Thomas, *The Helsinki Effect: Internation Norms, Human Rights, and the Demise of Communism* (Princeton, NJ, 2001).

Gorbachev's own stories are told in *Perestroika: New Thinking for Our Country and the World* (New York, 1987) and *Memoirs* (London, 1996).

MAJOR POWERS AND LOCAL CONFLICTS AFTER THE COLD WAR, 1990-2016

THE MAJOR POWERS IN THE NEW WORLD

The Cold War had been characterized by antagonism between East and West. When the Soviet Union had finally attained military parity with the United States in most areas, with a considerable capacity for power projection in remote regions, the entire country disintegrated. The Soviet Union could not continue to hold its own as an equal of the US when its economic, cultural, and ideological power base was in no way as strong as that of the United States.

The demise of the Soviet empire in Eastern Europe was more painless than anyone could have imagined. Apart from the unification of Germany, the division of Czechoslovakia in 1993 into the Czech Republic and Slovakia was the only territorial change that took place, and this partition was effected peacefully. Nearly all the former Soviet partners in Eastern Europe attempted to establish as close ties to NATO and the European Union as possible, but attaining membership in these organizations would take time.

For Russia the 1990s was a highly turbulent decade both in foreign and domestic policy (see pp. 208–11). As the clear leader of the 15 nations into which the USSR was divided, Russia assumed the role of the Soviet Union in many arenas, such as in the UN Security Council. The association formed by 10–12 of these nations, the Commonwealth of Independent States, had little practical significance, although the Muslim-dominated countries in particular maintained considerable contact with Moscow. The old economic ties could not be severed entirely, and Russia used its military strength to create close ties with some of the new states.

On the other hand, the Baltic countries in particular were determined to pursue an independent line, cooperating as closely as possible with the Western powers. Relations between Russia and Ukraine, the two principal nations, were strained regarding the division of the inheritance after the Soviet Union, particularly the status of the Crimea, the Black Sea fleet, and the price of energy deliveries. There was strife between Armenia and Azerbaijan owing to the conflict about Nagorno-Karabakh as an Armenian-dominated enclave in the middle of Azerbaijan. Armenia maintained close security ties with Russia. Georgia pursued an increasingly nationalist course, in part in response to Moscow's interest in enclaves on its territory (South Ossetia, Abkhazia).

Within Russia, Chechnya declared its independence as a separate nation in October 1991. A Russian invasion in December brought the situation under only partial control, as seen from Moscow. In May 1997 a peace treaty was finally concluded. Although the status of Chechnya remained formally unresolved, Moscow gave up the effort to control Chechen territory. Other provinces developed considerable autonomy, but within Russia. Toward the end of 1999, Russian forces entered Chechnya once more. Heavy fighting ensued. Brutal means were used by both sides, including large-scale Chechen terrorist actions. Moscow and its local supporters were now clearly on the offensive, although opposition still lingered.

The position of the United States within the Western world proved to be far stronger than that of the Soviet Union within the Eastern bloc. The US military dominance was further emphasized by the collapse of the Soviet Union, and in political and ideological terms the end of the Cold War could be seen as a victory for democracy and market economics, both vital pillars of US politics.

Many saw the new world as unipolar, as entirely dominated by the United States. Even so, the position of the United States was weaker than the unique dominance it had attained during the first decades after 1945. Of course the US economy was vastly larger in 1990 than in 1945. In fixed prices the gross national product had almost tripled. However, the growth rate had been even greater in other key countries. In 1945 the United States had produced nearly half of the world's goods. This was due in part to the destruction caused by the war in other countries. By 1960 the US share of world production had sunk to approximately 30 per cent. From the mid-1970s it has remained around 25 per cent.

In the 1980s and 1990s economic growth in the United States was so strong that the country's share of world GNP actually increased slightly, at least temporarily. However, in a number of significant areas there were unfavorable developments also in the 1980s. The United States experienced large deficits in its federal budget and in its balance of payments. In the course of a few years during the Reagan administration the country went from a position as the world's leading creditor nation to the largest debtor. During the 1950s the United States had produced up to half of the world's oil, importing only modest amounts. In the 1970s almost half of the oil used in the US was imported, and following a reduction in the early 1980s the import share rose again, this time to more than 50 per cent. These economic realities limited the United States in its foreign policy options.

Important changes also took place in the foreign policy attitudes of the American public. After the Cold War was over, the question was raised as to the need for a comprehensive foreign policy involvement, particularly in the military sphere. The exception was in the event of an obvious, striking threat, such as Saddam Hussein's invasion of Kuwait in August 1990.

Bill Clinton, elected president in 1992, showed little interest in foreign policy especially during his first two years in office. Attention was turned inwards, and the greatest foreign policy involvement was now linked to promoting US economic interests. There was a strong aversion to risking American lives in conflicts anywhere in the world. In 1998 Washington became increasingly preoccupied with the Lewinsky scandal, the result of President Clinton's sexual relations with a young White House intern. The Republican majority in Congress pressed for the impeachment of the President, but he was eventually found not guilty by the Senate.

Nevertheless, even under Clinton the United States intervened militarily, although quite reluctantly, in several countries (Bosnia and Kosovo in Europe, Somalia in Africa, and Haiti in Latin America). The United States was the only country that could undertake a major military intervention anywhere in the world. The remarkable growth in the US economy during the Clinton years strengthened the country's position abroad; domestically this growth created a surplus in the 1998–99 federal budget.

Yet the relative decline in the economic position of the United States was most clearly evident in comparison with the two adversaries from the Second World War, Germany and Japan. During the 1980s German exports came to equal those of the US, although only for a short time. Japan produced just as many cars as the United States did and surpassed the US lead within household electronics and in the production of semiconductors.

However, neither Japan nor a united Germany had in any sense the same breadth as the United States in terms of the criteria for superpower status in the military, political, economic, and ideological spheres. Moreover, in 1992 Japan entered into its most serious economic and political crisis since the early 1950s. Germany was now potentially the leading power within the EU, particularly in the economic sphere, but the German GNP was considerably smaller than that of Japan, and the countries of the EU had great problems reaching agreement on the central foreign policy issues of the 1990s. Even a united Germany was not inclined to take a key military or diplomatic role internationally. In these areas the United Kingdom and France remained the leading Western European powers.

During the 1990s China, with its rapid economic growth and modernization of its military forces, acquired a key role in international politics in earnest. Yet, in the 1990s China's power was still more potential than real. More dramatic changes would occur in the next decade.

HOPES FOR PEACE - AND THE REALITY OF LOCAL CONFLICTS

The end of the Cold War created high hopes of a more peaceful world. And the key source of tension in international politics, the antagonism between East and West, disappeared. The fear of total annihilation through nuclear war was also reduced substantially. However, the world did not immediately become more peaceful after the Cold War. The Cold War had been characterized by a high level of tension, but also by stability and predictability, particularly in Europe. After the Cold War the level of tension was reduced in many ways, but stability decreased as well.

Thus, the end of the Cold War sparked a number of conflicts, many involving the former territories of the Soviet Union and Yugoslavia. National disputes that had earlier been suppressed by authoritarian regimes did now break out in the open. Conflicts were also raging in the Middle East and in various parts of Africa. After a high in the early 1990s, the number of conflicts around the world actually seemed to diminish. There are several possible explanations for this: colonial and post-colonial conflicts had become fewer; Cold War 'proxy wars' more or less ended; international activism increased, focusing on various forms of preventive diplomacy, peacemaking missions, and peacekeeping operations, often performed by the UN and the African Union. In the long run, the growing strength of democracy probably also helped promote peace, although the wave of democracy from the 1990s died down. Still, due to the optimism connected with the end of the Cold War, as with the end of earlier Great Power conflicts, many were disappointed by the continued bloodshed in several different parts of the world, particularly in Africa and in the Middle East and Western Asia. And, in 2014, there was again a significant increase in the number of conflicts in the world, although the number remained lower than in the early 1990s.

The hopes for a peaceful Europe were dashed in earnest by developments in Yugoslavia. To some extent Yugoslavia had been held together by the threat of Soviet interference, but the country's dissolution in 1991 was due primarily to internal circumstances. Yugoslavia was a country with two alphabets, three religions, four or five different languages, and at least 20 different ethnic groups. Moreover, there was a wide economic gap between the more prosperous north and the much poorer south. The tensions between ethnic groups had also manifested themselves earlier, particularly during the Second World War, but in the postwar period there had been considerable contact. This could be seen in the increase in mixed marriages between ethnic groups. Tito's authoritarian style of governing had put a lid on the ethnic tensions, but when he died in 1980 they emerged more openly. Nationalism became a means for politicians to gain support, and particularly the Serbian leader Slobodan Milosevic, who came to power in 1987, played this card for all it was worth.

In June 1991 Slovenia and Croatia declared their independence. The Serb-dominated Yugoslavian army was put into action against the ethnically relatively homogeneous Slovenia, but after a short time it had to concentrate on Croatia where the Serbs constituted a substantial minority. However, a cease-fire was achieved after six months of fighting. In February 1992 Bosnia-Herzegovina declared its independence, with three large ethnic groups – Muslims, Serbs, and Croatians – competing for control. The war in Bosnia was lasting and bloody, with many instances of 'ethnic cleansing,' particularly by the Serbs. The three wars of 1991–95 cost perhaps 150,000 lives and left over 2 million refugees.

Various initiatives by the United Nations and the European Union to achieve a cease-fire and a political solution failed. However, by autumn of 1995 Milosevic was more amenable to peace. The economic and political pressure on Serbia from abroad was strong, and the Serbs had difficulties holding the territory they had captured. Croatia had built up its military forces substantially and drove the Serbs out of most of Croatia. The United States and NATO decided to use tougher means after the Bosnian Serbs had captured and ethnically cleansed some of the 'safe areas' the UN troops were supposed to protect, including Srebrenica where thousands of Muslims were killed. Comprehensive bombing raids were launched against Serbian positions. All of these factors changed the balance of power considerably in disfavor of the Serbs.

Following an active negotiating round in Dayton, Ohio, the Americans pushed through a political agreement for Bosnia in November–December 1995. Bosnia would be one country formally, but the two parts – a Muslim–Croatian segment comprising 51 per cent of the territory and a Serbian segment comprising the remaining 49 per cent – would enjoy a substantial degree of self-government. A large-scale NATO presence secured the peace, but there was little reconciliation among the warring parties.

In 1998 the fighting spread to the province of Kosovo. Here Serbian rule was fiercely opposed by the vast Albanian majority. Now the Serbs used massive force to suppress the growing Albanian demand for independence. The conflict in Kosovo threatened peace in the whole Balkan area, since it could easily spill over into not only Albania, but also Macedonia, which has a substantial Albanian minority. In 1999, after eleven weeks of bombing, the US and NATO forced the Serbs to retreat. In 2008 a largely independent Kosovo was established.

In the Middle East, superpower rivalry had represented only one dimension of the conflicts, which had deep local roots. Relations between Israelis and Palestinians grew increasingly troubled during the course of the 1980s. In December 1987 demonstrations against the Israeli government broke out on the West Bank and in Gaza. This *intifada* proved to be considerably more lasting than previous uprisings had been. The tough Israeli policies served to isolate Israel politically and reinforced conflicts within Israel, but the governing party, Likud, maintained that at most the Palestinians could achieve a severely limited regional self-government. An independent nation was entirely out of the question.

In August 1990 Iraq invaded Kuwait, annexing this neighboring country. The military operation was uncomplicated, but the invasion was condemned by nearly the entire world community. The United States and a number of Western European, Arab, and other countries sent troops to the Persian Gulf region. Once again the United States held the key military role, but its new position was demonstrated by the considerable military and not least economic support the US received from a number of other countries.

The United States could cooperate with the Soviet Union, formerly an ally of Iraq, to a considerable extent, dramatically illustrating the transformed international climate. This meant that the United Nations could play an important role. The UN Security Council insisted that Iraq withdraw from Kuwait. Iraq refused to give in. On 17 January 1991 the United States and its allies launched a major bombing offensive against key military targets in Iraq. When the US and its allies launched their ground offensive on 24 February, the Iraqi troops were defeated in the course of four days.

In addition to withdrawing from Kuwait, Iraq had to accept limits to its sovereignty in the northern and southern parts of the country in order to protect the groups – particularly the Kurds in the north – who had fought against Saddam Hussein. Iraq also had to agree to dismantle installations that could be used to produce nuclear, chemical, or biological weapons. The United States and its allies in turn tolerated the fact that Saddam Hussein put down the rebellions against him in the south and remained in power. They feared that his fall could result in a division of Iraq which would have unfortunate consequences for the balance of power in the Middle East. When Iraq later violated the conditions of the cease-fire, the United States, often with the support of the British, carried out bombing raids without achieving any political results.

The end of the Cold War and of the Gulf War would each, in different ways, contribute to better relations between Israel and the PLO. The collapse of the Soviet Union meant that the PLO lost an important source of support. The Gulf War, during which the PLO supported Iraq, strengthened the moderate Arab countries, made the PLO lose most of its economic support from these countries and emphasized the key role of the United States in the Middle East. The emergence of extremist fundamentalist groups among the Palestinians also threatened to outmaneuver Yasir Arafat's PLO.

In Israel the Labour party victory over Likud in the 1992 election was most significant. For several years the PLO had been interested in contact with Israel. Now the organization found a negotiating partner. The Labour party had a much more open view of ceding Israeli-occupied territories. Moreover, it was important for Israel to curb the more fundamentalist groups among the Palestinians.

With the help of Norway, Israel and the PLO negotiated the Oslo agreement which was formally signed in Washington on 13 September 1993. This agreement granted the Palestinians limited self-government in Israeli-occupied territories. Starting with Gaza and the city of Jericho on the West Bank, this self-rule was to be extended to the entire West Bank. The Jewish settlements were to remain under Israeli control. The status of Jerusalem was to be determined in the final peace agreement, to be completed by September 1998.

The Oslo agreement not only resulted in mutual recognition between the PLO and Israel; to a considerable degree it also normalized relations between Israel and moderate Arab countries, particularly Jordan. However, the agreement was met with fierce opposition from, on the one hand, fundamentalist Islamic groups, supported by Iran and Syria, and, on the other hand, by Likud and Jewish fundamentalist circles. A number of terrorist attacks threatened to derail the peace process, but at first it continued, even though the negotiators did not manage to meet the deadlines outlined in the original plan.

With the election of Benyamin Netanyahu as prime minister and a Likud-led government in May 1996, the peace process soon came to a halt. Even the active efforts of the Clinton administration to revive it appeared to make little difference, until in October 1998 the administration finally managed to persuade Netanyahu to cede an additional 13 per cent of West Bank territory to the PLO for a total of 40 per cent and Arafat to clamp down further on security threats to Israel. In the end, Netanyahu did not implement this agreement after all.

Following Israeli elections in May 1999, the Labour party candidate Ehud Barak became prime minister. The peace process with the Palestinians was resumed. Not only did relations with the Palestinians improve, but also the same was true to a certain extent of relations with Syria and Lebanon.

At the very end of his term of office, Clinton combined forces with Israel and the PLO itself in a dramatic attempt to reach a peace agreement between the Israelis and the Palestinians. Particularly in Taba, Egypt in January 2001 the parties seemed near an agreement that would have granted the Palestinians control over more than 90 per cent of the West Bank. However, vital questions remained as to the status of Jerusalem, the Israeli settlements on the West Bank and the Palestinians' right to repatriation. Moreover, time was running out. Barak was succeeded by Ariel Sharon as prime minister of Israel, and Clinton was succeeded by George W. Bush. A new *intifada* had erupted in September 2000, making the climate between the parties increasingly bitter once more. After negotiations broke down, acts of terror escalated further.

The end of the Cold War made it possible for the United Nations to take a much more active role than previously. The UN helped end conflicts in Namibia, Mozambique, and El Salvador, and the organization tried to moderate conflicts in Angola and in Cambodia, although the latter two were far from resolved. All the new operations clearly overburdened the UN. In many countries the situation was so deadlocked that there was little the United Nations could do. In former Yugoslavia the UN made a significant contribution in humanitarian aid, but political negotiations showed little progress until the United States became involved in earnest. In Somalia, which was stricken by famine and where various clans waged fierce struggles against each other, the United States withdrew its troops from the UN mission in 1994 after 19 US soldiers had been killed. Years of chaos followed. Somalia no longer had an effective government.

In Rwanda the deep and lasting conflict between Hutus and Tutsis resulted in the slaughter of about 800,000 Tutsis and moderate Hutus in 1994 without the world community doing much about it. The UN in fact reduced its presence in the country; the US was traumatized by the loss of the soldiers in Somalia; the French vacillated, but finally sent a relief force which saved some lives. The situation in Rwanda had serious consequences in Burundi where more than 100,000, mostly Hutus, were killed. The influx of refugees from Rwanda also helped further undermine the Mobutu 'kleptocracy' in Zaire. In May 1997 Tutsi-aided rebel forces finally overthrew the regime. The country was renamed Congo, but few other changes were made. As a result, rebels aided by Rwanda, Burundi, and Uganda soon tried to overthrow the new Kabila government which in turn was saved by the intervention of Zimbabwe, Angola, Namibia, and even Chad and Sudan.

In Liberia and in Sierra Leone bloody civil wars raged, to some extent also after Nigerian forces intervened in early 1997. In Sudan several rounds of civil wars had taken place starting in 1963 between the Muslim north and the Christian south. By the late 1990s more than one million people had been killed, in part because of the wars themselves, in part because of the resulting starvation. In Algeria a virtual civil war was raging between the ruling army and Islamic terrorists, after the army had cancelled elections in January 1992 as a result of the large Islamic party having won the first round in December 1991. In this, as in so many other conflicts, it was obvious that the end of the Cold War meant little or nothing.

Even so, the international picture was far from entirely dismal. In South Africa, where many people had believed that apartheid could only be abolished through civil war, the Nationalists under F.W. de Klerk and the dominant black party the African National Congress (ANC) under Nelson Mandela managed to establish a broad coalition government in 1993–94 with Mandela as president and ANC as the dominant party. In Northern Ireland, where there had been more or less open strife between extremist Catholic and Protestant groups since 1968–69, the British and the Irish governments in April 1998 secured a multi-party peace agreement. A vast majority of the Catholics supported the agreement while the Protestants were more divided.

Thus old and new situations coexisted around the world. The Cold War was over, but that did not mean that even all areas of conflict between Russia and the West ceased to exist. Russia was eager to secure its international position, despite its grave domestic problems. The most difficult controversy was linked to the desire of the Eastern European countries to join NATO, which Russia came to oppose. It was particularly opposed to NATO membership first for the Baltic states, then potentially for Ukraine and Georgia. Russia also pursued its own separate aims vis-à-vis Yugoslavia, Iraq, and Iran.

There were a number of bloody conflicts throughout the globe. In Africa they were usually called clan or tribal conflicts, in other parts of the world ethnic or national conflicts. Developments in former Yugoslavia and in the Caucasus showed

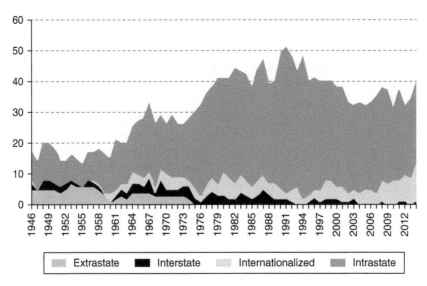

Figure 7.1 Number of armed conflicts by type, 1946–2011

Source: Journal of Peace Research, 2015, 52: 4, 539

that these conflicts were also to be found in Europe. The difference from previously was that the one remaining superpower, the United States, and the other major powers, for better or for worse, were now much less inclined to intervene in most of these local conflicts.

11 SEPTEMBER 2001, AFGHANISTAN AND IRAQ

After the end of the Cold War, no unifying dominant theme for international politics had emerged. In Washington the Clinton administration had claimed that consolidating an international democratic market economy was one such unifying theme, but it was evident that this was only adequate for describing developments in certain leading parts of the world. Others claimed that globalization in a broader sense was the key theme. There was no doubt that the rate of globalization accelerated in the 1990s, but in principle the process had begun long before. In the economic sphere, it had taken several decades after 1945 until the world became more integrated than it had been in the years prior to the First World War. In terms of immigration, even the market-oriented part of the world is not as integrated now as it was then.

The dramatic attacks by radical Islamists on the World Trade Center in New York and the Pentagon in Washington, DC on 11 September 2001 moved a new concern to center stage: the war on international terrorism. Terrorism as such was not a new phenomenon in international affairs (cf. Russian and Irish terrorism in the 1800s and early 1900s). What was new was the increasing tendency to target not only key figures of authority, but the population at large.

Islamic terrorism had emerged in the 1960s and 1970s, but for an extended period it was limited to certain Muslim countries and Israel. Politics in most Muslim countries was still dominated by secular leaders and movements. The revolution in Iran in 1979 changed this picture. So many different alternatives had failed in the Muslim world. Now increasing numbers felt it was time to return to the deepest religious roots. The developments in Iran encouraged radical and violent movements. Some of them, such as Hizbollah in Lebanon and even Hamas in the Palestinian territories, were directly supported by Iran. Al Qaeda, which was behind the terrorist attacks on 11 September (9/11) was not aided by Iran, since the two had quite divergent religious interpretations. After 11 September 2001 the focus of US and, to some extent, of international politics was radically altered. Suicide attacks proliferated and took place in many different countries. Most countries supported the United States in its war on terrorism, although circles in various countries, particularly in the Muslim part of the world, encouraged the terrorists in varying degrees. Some analysts claimed that this was a conflict between civilizations, but even though the leading terror groups were mostly Muslim, they were also to be found within other religions; most Islamic countries denounced international terrorism. Most of the victims were also Muslim.

When George W. Bush was elected president in November 2000 with the smallest possible margin, he made it clear that the United States would pursue a more nation-ally oriented foreign policy. His emphasis on the national orientation was meant as a criticism of Clinton, who ostensibly sacrificed vital US interests on the altar of multi-lateralism. The armed forces were to be built up considerably and a national missile defense was to be established (p. 147). The United States rejected a number of inter-national agreements, from various measures to limit US weapons of mass destruction to an international criminal court and a protocol on climate change; all of these were denounced much more strongly than under Clinton because they would limit US lati-tude of action. On the other hand, Washington would avoid the types of involvement in Middle Eastern diplomacy and conflicts in the Balkan region that Clinton had engaged in. However, like Clinton, Bush would soon discover that even the world's only superpower was also at the mercy of others. Even a relatively small group such as al Qaeda proved how vulnerable the United States could be. This was a new, important aspect of globalization.

The United States enjoyed broad international support for the use of a wide-ranging arsenal of measures in the war on terrorism. The greatest changes were naturally within the United States. The fact that the US mainland had been attacked for the first time since 1814 led to a dramatic re-evaluation of US security policy. (The attack on Pearl Harbor in December 1941 had been in Hawaii, although that led to even greater changes than those brought about by the events of 11 September.) Now the American giant had been awakened in earnest. The fear of military losses, which had been latent ever since Vietnam, was considerably diminished. An already growing defense budget enjoyed further dramatic budget hikes; the defense of the US itself was completely reorganized; the United States made it clear that a condition for cooperation with other countries was their stance in the war on international terror; the security needs of the US were decisive and nothing could induce Washington to compromise in safeguarding these needs. The objective was quite simply to eradicate international terrorism and those who supported such terrorism anywhere in the world.

Attention was focused on Afghanistan, where Osama bin Laden, the head of the al Qaeda network, was hiding and where the local Taliban regime had championed an extreme form of Islamic fundamentalism. A great many governments were willing to provide support for the United States in its war against the Taliban, but the Bush administration chose not to involve NATO so as to have complete control over the warfare. As was said in Washington, 'the mission should determine the coalition; the coalition should not determine the mission.' Apart from Britain, and Australia to some extent, the most important allies for the United States were the many local partners in the region: from the Northern Alliance in Afghanistan itself, which already enjoyed the support of Russia, India, and Iran, to countries such as Pakistan and Uzbekistan. The role of the United States in the former Soviet republics of central Asia was dramatically changed. Vladimir Putin's Russia reluctantly accepted this fact, perceiving the war on terrorism as an opportunity for improving relations with the United States and for mustering support in its own war against the Chechens. Even China considered the war on terrorism a factor that could improve the climate vis-à-vis the United States, as well as provide a chance to reap sympathy for its efforts to quash separatism at home, particularly in Xinjiang. Countries such as Pakistan and Saudi Arabia tried to clamp down on terrorism, not always with success, particularly in the case of Pakistan.

In the course of a few weeks, the United States and its allies managed to defeat the Taliban regime and assume control in Afghanistan. Now forces from other countries, particularly from NATO allies, were allowed to join in the more limited peacekeeping tasks. Washington also needed help in economic reconstruction. It was one thing to install a friendly regime under the leadership of Hamid Karzai, but an entirely different thing to unify a country with powerful regional warlords and then bring about economic development.

In his January 2002 State of the Union address, President Bush designated Iraq, Iran, and North Korea as the 'axis of evil.' After achieving a military victory in Afghanistan, the United States soon turned its focus to Iraq. For the most conservative members of the Bush administration, Saddam Hussein had been a thorn in the flesh ever since the end of the 1991 Gulf War. Saddam's attempt to assassinate George Bush Sr. during a visit to Kuwait had made the climate even worse. George W. Bush and his administration were eager to find a link between Saddam and al Qaeda. It also assumed that Iraq had resumed its program to develop weapons of mass destruction after the Gulf War and after the UN weapons inspectors were expelled in 1998. Iraq's vast oil resources played a part, as did relations with Israel and not least the example the United States believed it could set in the region as a whole following a successful war against Saddam. The United States could develop a democratic, capitalistic form of government in Iraq that would influence developments throughout the Middle East.

The Bush administration would have liked to oust Saddam with the support of the UN, but was willing to do it alone if necessary. Many of Washington's political judgments proved wrong in the prelude to the war against Saddam. The United States received strong support from Blair's Britain, whereas Chirac's France made it clear that it would not support the use of force through the UN until the weapons inspectors had been granted sufficient time to investigate whether Iraq actually had weapons of mass destruction. When France signaled its opposition to a hasty war against Iraq, Putin's Russia and China could also express criticism of US policy. They feared the consequences if the United States alone could depose governments it did not like. Washington had also counted on Turkish consent for the establishment of a northern front into Iraq. However, the Muslim-oriented government in Ankara refused to acquiesce.

Nevertheless, the military campaign by the United States and Britain in Iraq in March–April 2003 was a resounding success. Coordination between the various branches of the military was dramatically improved compared to previous wars; precision-guided weapons played a new and key role. And when they suffered setbacks, the Iraqi troops surrounding Baghdad soon capitulated. The greatest disappointment for the Americans was the fact that Saddam himself escaped, just as Osama bin Laden had evaded them following the war in Afghanistan.

However, the war proved not as decisive politically as the Americans had hoped. Most Iraqis were probably glad to be rid of the despot Saddam, but they were suspicious about the role the Americans were to play. Washington had instigated the harsh sanctions in the 1990s that had caused great suffering in Iraq; the Americans were unprepared for the vast problems they were facing as they set out to govern Iraq more or less on their own during an interim period. The Iraqi army was disbanded and ruling Baathists purged. This stimulated the growing chaos. Widespread looting broke out and the infrastructure of the country collapsed. Many US soldiers were killed by Iraqis who were still fighting against the United States. All of these problems made the Bush administration more interested in involving the UN and NATO, and the Iraqis themselves, in the governing of Iraq, but that did not mean that Washington wanted to relinquish the overall control. Resentment from the diplomatic skirmishes in the UN before the war broke out remained, and US policy in Iraq was slow in gathering support internationally. The fact that no weapons of mass destruction were found undermined support for the war. The arrest and execution of Saddam alleviated the situation very little. There was growing strife, particularly in the Sunni-dominated regions around Baghdad, soon even in Shia areas.

The massive focus on Iraq pushed other conflicts into the background. Washington had made it clear that it would not accept the development of nuclear weapons by Iran or North Korea, but it now intended to use primarily political and economic means to attain this ambitious objective. Thus the United States could gather relatively broad international support for its efforts here. It was difficult to envision the United States attacking North Korea, since the latter could so easily respond with a military assault on Seoul. And all the problems in Iraq meant that the regime in Teheran was less vulnerable than it would otherwise have been.

Just as had been the case with the Gulf War of 1991, the war in Iraq in 2003 gave rise to a US diplomatic offensive to solve the conflict between Israelis and Palestinians. In collaboration with the UN, the EU, and Russia, the Bush administration drew up a road map in three stages that was to result in peace and the recognition of a Palestinian state. The United States marginalized Yasir Arafat because he would not denounce those among the Palestinians who used terror. Support for Prime Minister Ariel Sharon's tough stance in Israel was stronger, although it was unclear how far he would go to obtain an agreement with the Palestinians.

Conflicts that had existed for years were now assessed according to how they related to international terrorism. For the United States, as mentioned, this affected its relationship to Arafat. There had been renewed skirmishes in Kashmir in 1999. After 11 September 2001, Pakistan's policies were partially perceived as support for terrorist movements. Thus Pakistan was a close ally of the United States in Afghanistan, but at the same time it was criticized for its policies in relation to Kashmir. Following various episodes both in New Delhi and in Kashmir, tensions mounted rapidly between India and Pakistan. These two nuclear powers both embarked on comprehensive mobilization before the crisis was again defused, in part with the aid of the United States. However, there was little sign of a solution to the Kashmir problem. The United States now had greater sympathy for India than it had had during the Cold War. After the demise of the Soviet Union and the Cold War, these two countries grew considerably closer.

The tragic developments in a number of African countries faded completely into the background in the focus of international politics. Hundreds of thousands have lost their lives in the war in Congo since 1998. Although foreign troops were gradually withdrawn for the most part, except for many from neighboring Rwanda, fighting between various Congolese groups persisted. Intervention by the UN and the EU, under French military command, did attain only a limited degree of success. The devastating civil war in Liberia raged on until a Nigerian-led force was brought in, while French intervention in the Ivory Coast and British intervention in Sierra Leone stabilized the situation in these two countries. The protracted civil war in Angola was brought to a swift close in 2002 after the rebel leader Jonas Savimbi had been killed.

Few dramatic changes were to take place during George W. Bush's second term. Considerable work was done to improve the various crisis situations that had arisen in his first four years. The American response in Afghanistan was widened to include NATO allies and even other partners, but despite a strong international mandate and a popularly elected president, Hamid Karzai, attacks from the Taliban and al Qaeda only increased. Karzai's writ did not run much beyond the capital. The situation in Iraq got somewhat better, due to increased cooperation between Shia and Sunni elements, local opposition to the terrorism of al Qaeda, a somewhat improved economy and an increase in the American troop presence. In Iran the government continued to refuse extensive international inspection of its nuclear program. International sanctions were introduced, but they had limited effect. North Korea continued its on-and-off diplomacy. An agreement to dismantle its nuclear program was signed but soon partly abandoned, or so it seemed, in the rather impenetrable politics of North Korea. In the Middle East Bush committed the United States to a two-state solution, but the administration in fact continued to give strong support to Israel. With the Palestinians even more badly divided after Arafat's death in November 2004 between the PLO – now led by Mahmoud Abbas – and Hamas, the situation only got worse. In December 2008 Israel invaded Hamas-led Gaza, which it had left in 2005. In August 2008 war broke out between Russia and Georgia (see p. 210).

Less related to the role of the United States, the tense situation in Kashmir and new Islamic terrorist activities in India, widely seen as supported by Pakistani elements, led to new crises in relations between India and Pakistan – both states being armed with nuclear weapons. In Sudan, particularly in Darfur, thousands and thousands were killed, despite a significant presence from the African Union. In July 2011 South Sudan became independent under challenging circumstances. In Congo the even bloodier war continued only somewhat abated by an international presence, at least until 2008–09 when there were signs that the worst might be over.

BARACK OBAMA AND THE GREATER MIDDLE EAST

In November 2008 Barack Obama was elected the first black president in US history. Expectations were extremely high almost all over the world. There was little reason to believe that he could live up to these expectations. The United States was clearly still the leading power in the world, but it had many problems of its own to cope with, including the most severe economic crisis since the Great Depression of the 1930s. Obama brought a new rhetoric and a new style to the White House. The need for international cooperation and negotiation was emphasized, often in the most inspiring of terms. The war on terror was downplayed. A new environmental policy was introduced; Guantanamo was to be closed; torture was to end. America's prestige rose again virtually all over the world, but particularly in Western Europe.

The more concrete issues remained, however. The situation in Iraq had improved somewhat, but it was still difficult. In 2011 most US troops pulled out due to a lack of agreement with the Iraqi authorities. In Afghanistan the United States, despite large-scale withdrawals, was forced to maintain a significant number of troops due to Taliban bombings and attacks. The Europeans, however, only reinforced their troop contributions marginally. In Iran and North Korea no solutions were found, despite Washington's renewed interest in dialogue (see p. 180). Most ominously, Pakistan was coming under increasing pressure from the Taliban and other radical Islamists. Free elections had been held in Pakistan in February 2008, but there had been a drastic increase in political violence. In the provinces nearest to Afghanistan the government had only very limited control. Pashtuns lived on both sides of the border, along with warlords, drug barons, arms dealers, and Taliban fighters. The use of drones increased dramatically under Obama.

In 2012–13 the United States and its allies started to pull out of Afghanistan. The massive foreign intervention had resulted in improvements in education and in health. In May 2011 Osama bin Laden had been captured and killed in Pakistan. Yet, the Taliban had gradually become stronger in part as a response to the foreign intervention. No one could be certain what would be the political future of Afghanistan. In the circumstances, it was decided that US troops would have to remain in the country even after Obama had left office.

The most spectacular changes were taking place in the Arab world. The countries in the region faced many problems. The regimes were virtually all more or less authoritarian; economic growth was slow, even some of the oil states were facing financial challenges; education, certainly including universities, was inferior; cultural impulses from the outside world were weak; conspiracy theories proliferated; demographic pressure was severe, with a big youth bulge; corruption endemic. The most noticeable change was the increased popularity of the social media, to some extent undermining state monopolies on information.

Yet, the changes in 2010–11 came as a surprise. In December 2010 street vendor Mohamed Bouazizi set fire to himself in Tunis. This was the spark that led to the Arab spring. In the course of a year the governments in Tunisia, Egypt, and Yemen all collapsed after widespread demonstrations. The new regimes that emerged were dominated mostly by Muslim parties and movements. Instability seemed likely. In Libya the Gaddafi regime fought back, but the demonstrators were supported by the UN

Security Council, and by NATO with France and Britain in the lead, although it soon became clear that the military campaign was increasingly dependent on US military resources. Gaddafi was captured and killed in October 2011. In Syria the situation developed into a civil war, but here the Western intervention was limited, in part due to the opposition of Russia and China to forcing the Assad government out. In 2013 French troops intervened in Mali to drive Islamic extremists out of the country. While the Obama administration had gradually come to favor change in the region, Washington still had close ties with the regimes in strategic Bahrain and oil-rich Saudi Arabia. Israel remained the closest ally of the US in the Middle East. Little progress was made in the peace negotiations with the Palestinians. The expansion of Israeli settlements on the West Bank continued at a brisk pace, making the two-state policy less and less realistic. Local circumstances and US policies thus varied considerably from country to country.

In Egypt the military returned to power after a year of controversial rule by the Muslim Brotherhood. In Yemen the old regime was overthrown, but a complex civil war resulted with the Shia and Sunni parties being supported respectively by Iran and Saudi Arabia. The most ominous situation emerged in Syria. Contrary to Western expectations, the Assad regime remained in power. The opposition was badly divided among numerous forces. The search for Western-oriented democratic groups was largely futile. Instead the Islamic State (of Iraq and the Levant, IS), a Sunni jihadist extreme militant group, took control of large parts of Syria and Iraq. Its success was explained in part by the collapse first of Iraq and then of Syria. IS proclaimed a caliphate with claims on the loyalty of all Muslims and the leader allegedly being a successor to the prophet Muhammad. IS combined very traditional religious views with advanced use of social media. It received some, but limited support from Sunnis in Syria and Iraqi, but also attracted jihadist followers from many different countries. In late 2015, with the United States backing the opposition to Assad and Russia now strongly supporting the regime, a delicate situation arose with the potential for further renewed tension between Washington and Moscow. More than 400,000 people were killed in the Syrian civil war. Millions fled Syria for the neighboring countries and for Europe.

In November 2015 IS was behind horrendous terrorist acts in Paris that killed around 130 people. It also became clear that IS was responsible for the blowing up of a Russian plane over Egypt in October that resulted in many deaths. This meant that the United States, France, and Russia now all shared a strong hostility to IS, but that hostility was not yet strong enough to paper over the differences with regard to Assad's future role.

While the number of Great Power armed conflicts had become very few indeed and the number of wars between states had also almost disappeared, around 2015 the number of intrastate conflicts, civil wars, that had been going down since the early 1990s again increased. Most of these wars were related to IS, with wars going on in Iraq, Syria, and Lebanon and also in Afghanistan, Libya, Russia, Yemen, Nigeria, and even Egypt (Sinai). In addition there were the civil war in South Sudan and the conflict in Eastern Ukraine.

In November 2012 Barack Obama had been re-elected to a second term as President of the United States, despite the lingering effects of the economic recession and a certain disillusionment after the high hopes of 2008. The Obama administration seemed determined not to intervene in force again in the countries of the Greater Middle East, with the partial exception of Afghanistan and Iraq and the extensive use of drones.

In July 2015 the United States, in cooperation with Russia and leading Western powers, was finally able to get that long-sought agreement with Iran that the country would refrain from developing nuclear weapons, at least for a 15-year period. In return, the sanctions against Iran would be lifted. In the fall of 2016 Iraqi forces, supported by the Kurds in Northern Iraq, and with the assistance of the United States and even other international elements, started an offensive against IS. The offensive made only slow progress.

American–Russian relations deteriorated sharply in the last years of the Obama administration. Putin came to dislike the strong Western role in some of the former Soviet allies. The West responded negatively to the events in Ukraine. Popular uprisings forced President Yanukovich, elected in 2010, out of power in February 2014 due to his pro-Russian policies at the expense of the EU. Russia responded by taking control of the Crimea, incorporating it into Russia. Russia also increased its support to separatists in the Donbass area of Ukraine. This in turn led to Western sanctions against Russia. In addition there were the events in Syria.

In the presidential election in November 2016 Donald Trump surprisingly defeated Hillary Clinton. In the campaign Trump presented a foreign policy dramatically different from that of his predecessors: an end to free trade agreements and to the work against global warming; building a wall against Mexico and expelling illegal immigrants; a lower foreign policy profile in general with increased contributions from America's European and Asian allies and improved relations with Russia. It remained to be seen how this approach would be followed up in practice when Trump took office in January 2017. The early signals were quite mixed.

In some cases it was clearly beyond the powers even of the United States to determine whether there should be war or peace, cooperation or conflict. Many disputes had their own local causes, not always easily influenced by outsiders.

MAJOR POWERS AND LOCAL CONFLICTS
AFTER THE COLD WAR, 1990-2016: THE LITERATURE

On the presidency of George H. W. Bush, George Bush and Brent Scowcroft, *A World Transformed: The Collapse of the Soviet Empire* (New York, 1998) is useful. Philip Zelikow and Condoleezza Rice, *Germany Unified and Europe Transformed: A Study in Statecraft* (Cambridge, 1995) is fascinating about Germany's unification. The best book on the United States in the 1990s is Derek Chollet and James Goldgeier, *America Between the Wars: From 11/9 to 9/11. The Misunderstood Years Between the Fall of the Berlin Wall and the Start of the War on Terror* (New York, 2008). David Halberstam, *War in Time of Peace: Bush, Clinton, and the Generals* (New York, 2002) is enjoyable. On Clinton's Russia policy Strobe Talbot, *The Russia Hand: A Memoir of Presidential Diplomacy* (New York, 2002) is enlightening.

Among the many books on the years of George W. Bush, James Mann, *Rise of the Vulcans: the History of Bush's War Cabinet* (New York, 2004) is both enlightening and entertaining. Derek Chollet, *The Long Game. How Obama Defied Washington and Redefined America's Role in the World* (New York: Public Affairs, 2016) is the first cut from an administration insider. George W. Bush's own story is told in

(Continued)

(Continued)

his *Decision Points* (New York, 2010). Zbigniew Brzezinski, *Second Chance: Three Presidents and the Crisis of American Superpower* (Cambridge, MA, 2007) is useful and relatively open-minded. An excellent study is Robert S. Litwak, *Regime Change: U.S. Strategy through the Prism of 9/11* (Washington, DC, 2007). Ahmed Rashid, *Descent into Chaos: The World's Most Unstable Region and the Threat to Global Security* (Penguin, 2008) is a fine journalistic account of developments in an increasingly important area. Gilles Kepel, *The War for Muslim Minds: Islam and the West* (Cambridge, MA, 2004) is stimulating. Adeed Dawisha, *Iraq: A Political History from Independence to Occupation* (Princeton, NJ, 2009) is useful. John Mueller's work is fascinating with many original observations. One good example is his *The Remnants of War* (Ithaca, NY, 2004). On the Obama administration, James Mann's *The Obamians: The Struggle Inside the White House to Redefine American Power* (New York, 2012) provides a lively first account. On the new issues after the Cold War, see my edited volume *International Relations Since the End of the Cold War: New and Old Dimensions* (Oxford, 2013).

THE ARMS RACE, 1945-2016

PERSPECTIVE AND MOTIVATING FORCES

The development of destructive weapons has been a part of life since time immemorial. But the arms race after 1945 was still unique in many ways.

One of the greatest changes of the postwar period was to be found in the level of military expenditure. The absolute and probably even the relative figures had never been higher in peacetime. During the Second World War, the Soviet Union and Britain used at the most about 60 per cent of their national products and the United States between 30 and 40 per cent of its national product for arms production and warfare. After 1945, this figure never exceeded 14 per cent on the part of the United States. Not even in the Soviet Union, where these expenses surely accounted for at least 20 per cent of GNP, could expenditure after the war compare with that during the war. However, compared with other peacetime periods the costs were great. Arms expenditure represented approximately 6–8 per cent of the world's total production. In the years preceding the First World War and during the interwar years, the corresponding figure had been about 3–3.5 per cent. In the 1980s, total world military expenditure equalled the income of the poorer half of the world's population. The two superpowers spent roughly half of that total.

In addition, an entirely new range of weapons was developed: the nuclear weapons. These weapons had a destructive capability that was unique. Humanity might face its own demise if a new major war broke out. Nuclear weapons and the new launchers, long-range bombers, and missiles united the world. A future war could affect everyone – military or civilian, belligerent or neutral.

Moreover, the pace of new invention was faster than it had ever been. The question of armaments still had a quantitative dimension, but the qualitative aspect played an increasingly greater role. More and more new weapons systems were developed. Those involved were constantly preparing for the worst possible scenario that could materialize, not only tomorrow, but 10, 15, or 20 years into the future.

To simplify, it can be said that there are two main interpretations of the motivating forces behind the arms race. The first one places greatest emphasis on the foreign policy environment. The arms race between East and West, like previous arms races, arose from international anarchy (anarchy in the sense that there is no supranational body that can effectively regulate relations between nations). Distrust and fear cause nations to try to protect themselves by amassing armaments. The competing sides then impel each other on through a pattern of action and reaction. Initiatives by one side result in counter-measures on the other side, which again lead to new measures, and so on. Thus the arms spiral continues.

The other interpretation places greatest emphasis on internal causes. Armament is pursued to satisfy various pressure groups. The military establishment seldom or never gets enough weapons. The weapons industry endeavors to earn profits and secure employment. These groups in turn receive support from politicians. According to this theory, there were actually two parallel arms races, one in the West and one in the East.

There are also combinations of these two main views. They provide the basis for the present discussion. Primary emphasis will be placed on the foreign policy environment and the pattern of action and reaction. However, a number of other factors also contributed to the arms race. Economic trends, prevailing economic theories, and the priority given to defense within the total national economy were significant. The same was true of technological developments and the influence of scientists, the military, and the weapons industry. The relative importance of the various factors could vary considerably from case to case. It also makes a difference whether the focus is on total arms expenditure or the development of specific weapons projects. Internal factors probably played a greater role for specific weapons projects than for aggregate defense expenditure, which is the primary focus of this presentation.

The end of the Cold War would dramatically influence developments in some areas. As should be expected from the action–reaction theory, the collapse of the Soviet Union led to extensive disarmament in Russia, as well as to important new agreements on disarmament between Russia and the United States. Defense budgets shrank substantially in almost all the European countries. In the United States, however, these changes were considerably smaller in scale. Following some years of cuts, the defense budget grew quickly once more. There were obviously strong forces within the country that had a vested interest in a large defense budget and the development of ever new weapons systems.

The events of 11 September 2001 accelerated this process. When attacks of this nature could occur, the United States needed to be prepared to face practically any conceivable type of threat. In various other parts of the world, regional arms races persisted.

HIROSHIMA, ATOMIC WEAPONS, AND CONVENTIONAL FORCES, 1945-1949

When Franklin Roosevelt decided in the autumn of 1941 that the United States should substantially increase its level of research on nuclear weapons, two considerations seem to have been crucial. The first one was the international situation, or more specifically the fear that Germany would be the first country to acquire such weapons. The decision was made before the United States had entered the war. The second consideration was technological; the probability that an atomic bomb could be produced. In the summer of 1941, the British had reached the conclusion that not only could such weapons be constructed, but that they could be developed within a two-year period.

As would frequently prove to be the case, the possibility of developing a weapon very often meant that the decision to develop it would be made.

Research concerning the US motive for dropping atomic bombs over Hiroshima and Nagasaki in August 1945 has been intense. Today there is a high degree of consensus that the primary motive was to defeat Japan as quickly as possible. In order to achieve this objective, the weapons that were available were employed. In this sense it was not a major decision for Truman and his advisers to determine that the bomb should be used. They almost took it for granted. The more quickly the war was brought to an end, the fewer lives would be lost, particularly on the US side.

An important decision seldom has a single motive, nor was that the case in this instance. A number of leading politicians, including President Truman, Secretary of State Byrnes, and Secretary of War Stimson, all felt that demonstrating the bomb in the war would prove clearly advantageous in relation to the Soviet Union as well. Perhaps a rapid end to the war could reduce the role the Soviet Union would play in Asia, although it was difficult to renege on the concessions that had been made to Stalin at Yalta, concessions that were particularly unfavorable for China. Even more important was the consideration that the bomb would underscore the power of the United States and thus, presumably, get the Soviet leaders to show greater consideration for US interests in international politics.

Domestic policy considerations also favored the use of the bomb. Many policy-makers feared that the administration would suffer a political defeat when it one day became known that millions of dollars had been spent developing a weapon that then was not used to hasten Japan's capitulation. Finally, some people, particularly a number of the scientists who were engaged in the Manhattan Project, as the bomb project was called, felt that only a realistic use of the new weapon could force the revolution in attitudes that was needed to avoid a new major war in the future.

After the war, a few initiatives were taken in an attempt to ensure that the new source of energy came under the control of the UN and that it was exploited for peaceful purposes. The Baruch plan was the most important initiative on the part of the United States. According to this plan, an international authority was to control all aspects of development, from mining to the finished weapon. The United States declared that it was willing in principle to relinquish its atomic weapons.

This plan was not acceptable to the Soviet Union. The United States was to relinquish its atomic weapons only as the final step in a number of measures. The Americans would still retain their monopoly on the know-how of atomic bomb production. Finally, a comprehensive international control system would violate the Soviet policy of seclusion from the rest of the world.

It was equally obvious that the United States could not accept the Soviet plan. It quite simply prohibited the use of atomic weapons under any circumstances and called for the destruction of all such weapons within three months. No international system of control was to be established. Each country was to promise to adopt stiff punishments for any breach of agreement within its own boundaries.

The role of the atomic bomb in US strategy during the first years after the Second World War can easily be exaggerated. Everyone was aware that it was a weapon of entirely new dimensions. Even so, military planning did not presume that the bomb would immediately revolutionize warfare.

In the first place, US war plans until 1948–49 were based on the assumption that a war with the Soviet Union could extend over a long period of time. Because of its conventional superiority the Red Army would probably conquer most of the European continent. The atomic bomb would be a part of the US general mobilization strategy. Only after a considerable build-up in a number of areas could the United States expect to repulse a Soviet offensive. In principle, atomic bombs would function as conventional bombs, but with a much greater explosive force.

In the second place, the United States only had a few atomic weapons, and those they had were unwieldy. After Nagasaki, Washington seems to have had only one for a time. By the end of 1948 the country still had only 50, and none of them was ready for immediate use. Moreover, the navy and the army were reluctant to place primary emphasis on a weapon that would be under the control of the air force.

Gradually, however, politicians began to do just that. A primary reason was that atomic weapons were so cheap compared to conventional forces.

The greatest military significance of the atomic bomb probably lay in its deterrent effect. Washington and most of the capitals of Western Europe considered the chances of a Soviet attack small, in part precisely because of the US atomic monopoly. When the NATO treaty was signed, the implicit atomic guarantee, combined with the US troops in Europe as a sort of trigger mechanism, was the very foundation of the US contribution, at least in the short term.

The political advantages of the new weapon soon proved to be much smaller than the leaders in Washington had hoped. Threatening the Soviet Union directly with the atomic bomb was politically impossible, so what was needed was that the Soviet Union itself should feel the need to take into consideration the reality the bomb represented in terms of power politics. However, the Truman administration soon concluded that it was difficult to perceive any such moderation.

Outwardly the Kremlin played down the significance of atomic weapons. Stalin ostensibly placed little emphasis on the information he received when Truman, in general terms and very briefly, told him about the bomb at the Potsdam conference in July 1945. Molotov practically laughed it off at the meetings of foreign ministers in London and Moscow later in 1945. Soviet military journals did not have a single article on the new weapon until 1953.

Stalin's military conservatism was one reason for this attitude. However, of more significance was the fact that the Soviet leaders must have felt almost obliged to dismiss the significance of a weapon held only by the adversary and not by themselves. Admitting the revolutionary effect of this weapon would be admitting Soviet inferiority at the same time.

Under the official surface, however, the Soviets worked energetically on developing their own atomic weapons. These efforts had begun in earnest in 1942. The Soviet Union, like the United States, wanted to develop the weapons it was possible to develop. It merely appeared that Stalin made light of the information Truman gave him in Potsdam. In reality, this information, combined with what Moscow knew through Soviet espionage and finally from the bombs over Hiroshima and Nagasaki, led to a strong escalation of Soviet research. Developments in one country influenced others. The Soviet Union also stepped up its efforts in missile research, a field on which it concentrated more than the United States did.

In most areas the Americans had the lead over the Soviets. Only in terms of conventional forces could the Soviet Union be said to be stronger than the United States. The Soviet Union was widely assumed to have had four to five million men under arms when demobilization after the Second World War was completed. These figures were too high. Khrushchev later claimed that 2.8 million was the correct figure, but even this was considerably higher than the corresponding figure for the US side. US forces totaled approximately 1.4 million from 1947 to 1950. The leaders in Washington complained about the rapid demobilization, but it was considered political suicide for the Truman administration to try to slow the process.

THE US TURNABOUT, 1949-1953

In August 1949 the US atomic monopoly came to an end. The Soviet Union detonated its first atomic bomb, earlier than most experts had expected. At first, Truman actually doubted whether it could be true that the Soviet Union had carried out such a test. When it became evident that this was the case, the mood reversed. After having underestimated Soviet nuclear potential, Washington now overestimated it.

The United States decided to increase its production of atomic weapons, a decision that was not particularly controversial. On the other hand, there was considerable discussion about the step that was taken in January 1950: production of an even more powerful weapon, the hydrogen bomb. Whereas several of his advisers were in doubt or opposed to the new weapon, at least at that time, Truman felt that the decision was relatively easy. The United States had to keep ahead of the Soviet Union at all times in the nuclear field.

Uncertainty spread in Washington. The Soviet Union had been underestimated militarily. Politically, Mao's victory in China represented a major defeat for the United States. In January 1950, Klaus Fuchs, a British scientist who had cooperated with the Americans in atomic matters, was arrested for espionage. In February, Senator Joseph McCarthy made his first vigorous attacks on ostensible communist sympathizers in the State Department.

In this atmosphere, the State Department and the Department of Defense carried out one of the formative studies for US foreign policy after the Second World War, *NSC 68*, which was completed on 7 April 1950. Its main author was Paul Nitze. What was new was not the fact that the US leaders were skeptical as to Soviet political intentions, but that Soviet military strength was evaluated as much greater than previously. The threat from Moscow was considered much more direct now. The United States was still superior to the Soviet Union in nuclear terms, but *NSC 68* assumed that with a rapid build-up the Soviet Union would have 200 long-range atomic charges in 1954. Then even continued US superiority would be much less reassuring.

The solution was to be found in large-scale rearmament on the part of the United States, in both conventional and nuclear terms. The nuclear part of the program was already being implemented. The men behind *NSC 68* had not suggested specific sums for the implementation of their proposals, but a defense budget of about 40 billion dollars seemed realistic. This was far too high for Truman; after all, it meant nearly trebling what he had previously considered a maximum figure.

The outbreak of the Korean War was highly significant for further developments. On 30 September, Truman approved *NSC 68*. In the course of two or three years the defense budget was increased to more than 50 billion dollars. Little was now to be heard about the United States 'bleeding to death' if more than 15 billion dollars was used for defense, as had earlier been claimed. Rearmament was effected so rapidly that the four branches of the military could not possibly use all the appropriations. Even so, they would not agree to a reduction.

The United States sent four new divisions to Western Europe, to the great embitterment of the right wing of the Republican party. Although Western Europe received substantial support for its military rearmament, the Europeans, too, would have to increase their defense budgets dramatically. The most ambitious conventional plans were drawn up at NATO's Lisbon conference in February 1952, where the alliance committed itself to having 50 divisions in 1952, 75 in 1953, and 96 in 1954.

West Germany was included in the defense of Europe. This was decided in principle as early as September 1950. The reluctance most of the Western European governments felt about German rearmament faded alongside the increased threat from the Soviet Union. Only with a German contribution was it possible to plan a forward defense along the East–West border, and not, as previously, a defense strategy based on the loss of the area east of the Rhine.

In order to safeguard against a new German national army and to increase the efficiency of the individual countries' defense build-up, the Western powers aimed at a high degree of military cooperation. NATO evolved from a treaty into an organization. The alliance acquired a joint staff that was to make preparations for complete integration in the event of war. General Dwight D. Eisenhower was the first Supreme Commander. He would be succeeded by a series of other US generals. The Europeans in particular considered it advantageous to have a US Supreme Commander. That would tie the United States more closely to Western Europe.

A number of important changes took place outside Europe as well (see pp. 49–54). All in all, John Lewis Gaddis thus seems to be right when he claims that at least in the military field, the greatest change in US postwar policy came with *NSC 68* and the outbreak of the Korean War. In order to explain this shift, it is reasonable to point out the primacy of foreign policy. The strained international situation before, and especially after, the outbreak of the Korean War was the most important single factor. However, other considerations also had an effect. The mentality of budget policy was in the process of changing. Within the Truman administration, Keynesian expansionism gained a foothold in earnest. A higher level of government activity was to result in increased production without necessarily entailing higher inflation.

The military services had long pressed for increased defense expenditures, surprisingly without the support of Secretary of Defense Louis Johnson in the years 1949–50. A number of scientists spoke out in favor of the development of new weapons, although many were opposed to the hydrogen bomb. This bureaucratic pressure had some effect. But only when the President and the leading decision-makers changed their views – and this in turn to a great extent was a reflection of the Korean War and the international situation – did this pressure achieve decisive influence in Washington.

NEW DIRECTIONS IN US AND SOVIET DEFENSE POLICIES

The 'New Look'

When Eisenhower assumed office in January 1953, major changes in US defense policy ensued. Nuclear weapons acquired an even more central position, while conventional forces were given lower priority. The new president felt that the build-up under Truman had been far too expensive. Not until 1958 did Eisenhower's defense budget reach the same level as Truman's last defense budget in 1953. The share of the gross national product that went to defense declined from 13.8 per cent in 1953 to 9.1 in 1960.

The central premise of the 'New Look,' as the new strategy was called, was that the Soviet Union was never to rest assured that nuclear weapons would not be employed. Eisenhower and Secretary of State Dulles did not state explicitly when they would be employed, but the option was to remain open to respond to even a minor conventional attack with nuclear weapons. Whereas Truman's policy of containment had had as its point of departure the premise that Soviet aggression should be answered in the region where the attack had taken place, the 'New Look' meant that a US response could possibly come in an entirely different area and with completely different means.

What was it that made a former army general promote a strategy which in many ways meant that his own branch of the service was given lowest priority? For the air force was again the focal point. The air force's share of total defense expenditure rose from 26 per cent in 1950 to 47 per cent in 1957. The navy's share remained relatively constant, while army appropriations declined in step with the air force increase. By 1957 the army's share had dropped to 22 per cent.

The 'New Look' was in part a reaction to the Korean War. The United States had been drawn into a lengthy conventional war that had ended as a draw. The threat of massive retaliation was to compel the Soviet Union to refrain from similar aggression. If a war broke out nonetheless, it was to be decided swiftly in favor of the United States.

Strong economic considerations spoke in favor of the 'New Look.' Eisenhower and the Republicans had a different view of the federal government's responsibilities from the one that had developed particularly towards the end of the Truman administration. Washington was to limit its expenditures, including defense expenditure. Eisenhower was firmly convinced that large expenditures, with the taxes they entailed, could destroy the capitalist system. Moreover, his administration based itself on the assumption that the threat the Soviet Union represented was lasting, without any specific critical point, whereas *NSC 68* had singled out 1954 as a particularly dangerous year. As a former general and army commander, Eisenhower knew better than most people where cuts could be made in the defense budget, and he could do it without anyone daring to accuse him of making the United States vulnerable in relation to the Soviet Union.

Technological developments were also significant for the 'New Look.' Deployment of so-called tactical nuclear weapons started in 1953. These new, smaller weapons would be more versatile and thus ostensibly more credible than strategic weapons, in that they could more easily be employed in the event of a Soviet attack. Eisenhower himself expressed it as follows: 'Where these things [tactical nuclear weapons] are used strictly on military targets and for strictly military purposes, I see no reason why they shouldn't be used just exactly as you would use a bullet or anything else.'

In practice, the British had chosen a similar strategy. The Conservatives had assumed power in 1951, and their strategic thinking was similar to that of the Republicans on the other side of the Atlantic in many ways. However, the British Labour party, like the Democrats in the United States, placed somewhat greater emphasis on conventional forces.

Even so, the most important factor for the introduction of the 'New Look' was the simple fact that the concentration on conventional weapons that had been so clearly stated previously – most recently at NATO's Lisbon meeting in 1952 – had proved unrealistic. Truman's last defense budget pointed towards many of the same conclusions that Eisenhower reached, placing greater emphasis on nuclear weapons and the air force. Instead of 96 divisions, NATO had 25 in 1954, with an additional 25 in reserve. Finally, the international climate had become somewhat less strained from 1953 onwards. That made it easier to be in favor of reductions in the defense budget.

As long as the United States was clearly superior, there seemed to be little reason to doubt the country's willingness to use nuclear weapons in the event of a Soviet attack. But as the Soviet Union developed atomic and hydrogen weapons with suitable means of delivery, many people began to question the credibility of US nuclear policy. This doubt came from some so-called strategic thinkers in the West, thinkers who partly reflected developments in weapons technology but who also influenced them in turn. Their views were supported by those for whom such criticism was politically or militarily advantageous. In US politics that meant the Democrats, and, within the military establishment, primarily circles within the army and to some extent the navy.

The attitude of the Eisenhower administration changed somewhat in the course of the 1950s. Tactical nuclear weapons played an ever-increasing role, although calculations showed that even they would cause destruction to such a degree that the discussion of credibility soon expanded to include them as well.

Even so, US nuclear superiority was so great in the 1950s that the 'New Look' could be sustained. A certain degree of unpredictability was a deliberate aspect of this strategy. This uncertainty could be exploited politically by Washington more or less directly threatening to go to war to attain specific objectives. This was what Dulles liked to call 'brinkmanship.' He emphasized his conviction that 'the ability to go to the verge without getting into the war is the necessary art.'

On at least three or four occasions the Eisenhower administration threatened to employ nuclear weapons. In April 1953, Dulles warned Peking through diplomatic channels that such weapons could be employed if a peaceful solution was not reached in Korea. This threat probably contributed to the difficult question of repatriation of prisoners of war being brought closer to a solution 11 days later.

In 1954, Washington threatened to use nuclear weapons in Vietnam to prevent Chinese intervention. It is unlikely that the Chinese had any plans of intervening at all. In the following year, the use of atomic weapons on the Chinese mainland to prevent a Chinese landing on Quemoy and Matsu was discussed fairly openly. When the Chinese pressure decreased, these plans were put aside. It is difficult to make any conclusive judgment concerning the question of Chinese motivation in this case. In 1958 the Chinese began to shell the islands once more, without achieving much.

Even with Eisenhower's reduced defense budget, close ties existed between the various branches of the military, leading politicians, and large companies linked to the arms industry. On several occasions, most emphatically in his farewell address, the President himself gave a warning about the strength of the combination formed by this military–industrial complex.

There was undoubtedly strong pressure to put into production the many new weapons the researchers first developed, the companies then wanted to manufacture, and the military so strongly wanted to acquire. Those who had a vested interest in a new weapons system had a natural tendency to depict the situation in black and white. If 'their' system was not developed, the adversary could gain a lead that at worst would result in defeat in the event of war. One service was unwilling to see its weapons in relation to those a different service had. Rival groups were to be found even within a single service. With regard to strategic weapons, some members of the air force campaigned for bombers, others for missiles. The fact that the navy got its first submarine with long-range missiles in 1960 did not result in a reduced need for planes and missiles within the air force. The exact opposite tended to be the result.

However, the extent of technological-military pressure can be exaggerated, for there were counter-forces at work. Overall economic goals could, as in the Eisenhower years, reduce the appropriations that were made available to the military. Many officers were technologically conservative, precisely owing to bureaucratic considerations. Thus leading circles in the air force were actually quite skeptical about intercontinental ballistic missiles (ICBMs) for a long time. The air force had always been based on manned planes and ought to be so in the future as well. In 1955, the civilian leadership, with the support of a minority within the air force, more or less had to compel the air force to give top priority to the development of ICBMs. But then of course the air force was to have both planes and missiles. In the navy, too, certain vested interests showed reluctance to accept the development of the new Polaris submarines. However, the opposition within the navy towards Polaris was less than the air force's towards ICBMs, not least because the missile era had already begun to establish itself.

The 'New Look' in the Soviet Union

Developments in the Soviet Union were also determined both by the international situation, including US military dispositions, and by domestic factors within the Soviet Union. The possibility of carrying out detailed analyses is limited by the lack of information about the various weapons systems and even about such things as the actual size of the defense budget. Roughly, however, developments on the Soviet side followed those in the United States. The early 1950s were characterized by rearmament, emphasizing both nuclear weapons and conventional forces. From the middle of the decade the conventional forces were reduced substantially and nuclear weapons granted priority.

Outwardly, Stalin continued to claim until his death that the areas in which the Soviet Union was strong were the only ones that meant anything. Still, he pressed for the development of atomic and hydrogen weapons with the accompanying means of delivery. In August 1953 the Soviet Union detonated its first hydrogen bomb, less than a year after the United States. Whereas the Soviet atomic bomb had been based to a substantial degree on espionage, the hydrogen bomb was designed independently. It appears that mass production of Soviet intermediate-range missiles began in 1955. The Soviet Union could also compete with the United States in terms of intermediate-range bombers. This was all the result of decisions that must have been taken during the Stalin period.

Despite this build-up, developments were much less dramatic than assumed in *NSC 68*. This was particularly true in the strategic field. The estimates that the Soviet Union would have 200 long-range atomic charges in 1954 proved to be considerably exaggerated. Not until the mid-1950s did the Soviet Union develop a bomber that could reach the United States and return. After this plane had taken part in the May Day parade in Moscow in 1955, rumors sprang up concerning a bomber gap in the Soviet favor. They proved to be wrong. The Soviet Union concentrated on the production of intermediate-range planes aimed at Europe rather than on long-range planes intended for use against the United States. The technology was less complicated and the costs were smaller.

The United States remained far ahead of the Soviet Union in the strategic field. In 1956, the Strategic Air Command (SAC) had at least 540 planes with an intercontinental range. As late as 1960 the Soviet Union probably had only 135 such planes, while US intelligence sources had considered it likely that they had three times that number. In addition, the US planes were considerably more advanced technologically than the Soviet planes.

Soviet conventional forces grew from approximately 2.8 million men in 1948 to approximately 5.7 million in 1955. The United States had 2.9 million men under arms in 1955. Although the Red Army had not reached the number of divisions Western intelligence attributed to it, the Soviet Union and the Eastern European countries remained superior to NATO in conventional terms.

In 1955 West Germany joined NATO. That increased Western conventional strength rather dramatically. The fear of a strong Germany once more was genuine in the Soviet Union and a not unexpected result of the fact that the country had suffered tremendous losses during the Second World War. The creation of the Warsaw Pact was partially a response to this fact, although to a great extent the Pact represented a formalization of relations that already existed in Eastern Europe.

In August 1957 the Soviet Union carried out its first test of an intercontinental missile. Then in October the Soviets launched Sputnik I, the first satellite. Sputnik in particular came as a shock to the United States. This shock was even greater than when the Soviet Union developed its first atomic bomb in 1949. Its launch struck at the belief in US technological superiority.

Khrushchev now adopted a public strategy that was the opposite of the one Stalin had pursued. Nuclear weapons were given primary importance. Khrushchev loudly proclaimed Soviet superiority in the intercontinental sphere. That obviously did not reduce the level of concern in the United States. Many Washington policy-makers chose to take the Soviet leader literally when he stated for instance that the Soviet Union had enough nuclear weapons to wipe any aggressor off the face of the earth.

Like Eisenhower, Khrushchev placed great emphasis on expanding the sectors of the air force that were based on nuclear weapons. Missiles were given higher priority than planes, although in this matter he met resistance from much of the air force, as was the case in the United States as well. In 1959 the strategic missile forces were established as a separate military service. The Soviet Union was far behind the United States in the development of nuclear submarines.

In the light of the new weapons, an economic change of priorities within the Soviet Union and the incipient détente in the mid-1950s, Khrushchev began to reduce the level of conventional defense. Defense expenditures sank towards the end of the 1950s. The conventional navy was reduced substantially, especially the surface fleet. The armed forces were reduced. Cutbacks were effected in three stages. From 1955 to 1957 the armed forces were reduced from 5.7 to 3.9 million men. In 1958–59 the number was reduced by another 300,000. In January 1960 Khrushchev announced a new cutback, to 2.4 million. It was only halfway achieved by the time of the Berlin crisis in 1961, and it is unclear how much ever came of the second half of this reduction. By way of comparison, US forces under the 'New Look' were reduced from 3.5 million men in 1953 to 2.4 million in 1960.

KENNEDY, MCNAMARA, AND FLEXIBLE RESPONSE

The Eisenhower administration stuck to a relatively low defense budget until the very last. The necessary condition for achieving this was an emphasis on strategic deterrence entailing a willingness to employ nuclear weapons, especially tactical ones. Soviet development of intercontinental missiles further accelerated this concentration on nuclear weapons. As the Pentagon had to contribute more in the nuclear sphere, this took place at the expense of the conventional forces once more.

When John F. Kennedy assumed the presidency in 1961, he planned to make major changes in US defense policy. The defense budget would have to be increased substantially, and, as under *NSC 68*, emphasis was to be placed on both strategic armament and conventional forces. In the former field especially a dramatic effort was needed. In the light of the launching of Sputnik and Khrushchev's declarations of Soviet superiority, the belief had spread that there was a missile gap in favor of the Soviets. Kennedy made much of this in his election campaign, promising to overtake the Soviet lead.

Eisenhower had not credited the alleged missile gap. In part, he wanted to shelter the administration from accusations of negligence. In part, he relied on intelligence reports showing that the Soviet Union deployed far fewer missiles than Moscow's own statements would indicate. Information from the U-2 spy plane was important in this context. The Kremlin chose to develop a new and better missile rather than rely on the first, relatively primitive ICBMs.

Kennedy and Robert McNamara, his dynamic Secretary of Defense, increased the pace of production of ICBMs, based on the promises Kennedy had made during his election campaign. However, quite early in 1961 it became evident that the talk of a Soviet lead had been misleading, as pictures from new satellites showed. The decision to increase production had already been made. The Kennedy administration felt that it could not reverse its decision without seriously undermining public confidence. The result was that at the end of 1963 the Soviet Union still had less than 100 ICBMs. The United States had by then acquired at least 550.

This was probably an important reason for the Soviet attempt to deploy intermediate-range missiles on Cuba in 1962. Khrushchev's bluff had been called. The Soviet Union had never had the strength he had tried to give the impression of. Instead the United

States now had a great, rapidly growing lead. The cheapest and fastest way for Moscow to counterbalance this lead was to install shorter-range missiles on Cuba. Deployment would not give the Soviet Union any superiority at first, but of course the number of missiles could later be increased (see pp. 60–1).

The foundation for subsequent US strategy was laid under McNamara. Quantitative growth was comprehensive and continued even after Kennedy's death in 1963. McNamara set the ceilings on US strategic weapons that applied for decades: 1,056 ICBMs and 656 submarine-launched ballistic missiles (SLBMs). These levels were reached in 1967.

It was more a question of expanding existing weapon systems than of developing new ones. McNamara stopped the plans for a new bomber, the B-70. He considered planes the least important part of the US triad of strategic weapons. As far as missiles were concerned, Minuteman II and III were developed, but they were not dramatically innovative. Skybolt was stopped. The greatest change occurred in terms of submarines, with the major emphasis that was now placed on Polaris and later on Poseidon. With their survival capacity in the event of war, submarines were McNamara's favorites. The most important entirely new program was multiple independently targetable re-entry vehicles (MIRVs). McNamara was skeptical of anti-ballistic missiles. He felt that offensive weapons would be superior to defensive weapons. However, political and military pressure got him to support a limited program of development and deployment. With regard to the strategic doctrine, key concepts such as mutual assured destruction (MAD), damage limitation, counterforce-countercity, and flexible response were all developed in the early 1960s.

However, conflicting interests created problems for McNamara, as they had done for most of the preceding Secretaries of Defense. Tension developed, for instance, between the strategies of complete avoidance of war, which was a primary objective of MAD, and of limiting a war to military targets if it should occur. Moscow denounced the belief in a limited nuclear war. Western Europeans feared that deterrence would be reduced if the United States was no longer willing to meet Soviet aggression with an unlimited response. Other critics expressed their fear that a strategy based on striking military targets would result in a race to strike first.

The result, at least verbally, was to push the strategy of damage limitation into the background and again stress that a nuclear war could not be limited. Thus there was little purpose in distinguishing between military and civilian targets. However, the concrete US war plans appear to have followed the verbal fluctuations only to a slight degree. Both civilian and military targets were considered, in a number of different possible combinations, under both Eisenhower and Kennedy.

Eisenhower's policy of massive retaliation had built on the principle that local aggression could be met with a nuclear response. But the Vietnam War showed even in the 1950s that it was easier said than done to use or even threaten to use nuclear weapons in limited conflicts. There was no getting past the fact that even tactical nuclear weapons would mean a dramatic escalation. Nuclear weapons could have a deterrent effect with regard to large-scale aggression, but in limited local conflicts they almost seemed irrelevant.

Kennedy's flexible response meant that, if possible, the enemy should be met with the same means he himself had employed. The United States had to improve its ability to fight wars without resorting to nuclear weapons. Thus the conventional forces had to be built up. If the Soviet Union, contrary to all expectations, instigated a comprehensive attack, and the West was in the process of being defeated, the premise was now as previously that NATO would be the first to use nuclear weapons. But if that occurred it would be at a later time than under Eisenhower's insufficient conventional readiness.

In 1967, flexible response was adopted as NATO strategy. De Gaulle had opposed this approach, and the new strategy could only be adopted by NATO when France had withdrawn from NATO's military command. This decision resulted in a certain, though fairly limited, degree of reinforcement of conventional defense. Western Europe was not willing to make much of an effort in this field (see p. 164). The United States built up its forces in the course of the 1960s, from 2.4 million men in 1960 to 3.4 million in 1969, but the Vietnam War made the practical consequences small in Western Europe. On the other hand, the Kennedy administration would implement a dramatic increase in the number of tactical nuclear weapons in Europe, paradoxically enough. This was due partly to the fact that changes were not made in plans that were already being realized, and partly to the fact that the conventional build-up was smaller than had been planned at first.

As far as the size of the US defense budget was concerned, substantial growth took place in nominal figures, from 45.9 billion dollars in 1960 to 81.2 billion in 1969. However, the share of the gross national product that went to defense declined, mostly because the 1960s were a period of flourishing growth in the US economy.

Whereas it can roughly be said that Eisenhower had taken as his point of departure the amount he felt was available for defense on an economic and political basis, after which he worked out a doctrine that fitted this amount and let the services decide rather freely within this framework, McNamara worked in the opposite direction. He began with a doctrine, found out how much it would require in weapons and appropriations, and then tried to ensure that the individual services followed up through coordination rather than each of them planning their own war against the Soviet Union. McNamara's strategy was apparently logical and coherent, but it was also considerably more expensive than Eisenhower's, without anyone being able to claim that the latter had endangered the security of the United States.

The most concrete inheritance from McNamara was the quantitative growth, partly in the defense budget as a whole, but most particularly in the number of ICBMs and SLBMs. What was the cause of this growth? As we have seen, to a great extent it was determined by foreign policy interpretations – or rather misinterpretations – of Soviet strength at the time Kennedy assumed office. The program that was initiated on an erroneous basis was continued, even after the true strength of the Soviet Union had been disclosed.

This quantitative growth was also strongly related to new attitudes in domestic policy, particularly the attitude towards government activity. Kennedy and Johnson promoted a far higher level of activity than Eisenhower had done. They were willing to use larger amounts of tax money in many areas, including defense. It was paradoxical that although the Republicans in general were even more skeptical of the Soviet Union than the Democrats, the latter were willing to spend more on defense because of their attitude towards the role of the government in economic policy.

THE SOVIET BUILD-UP

Developments in the strategic sphere brought the Soviet Union on a level with, and in certain areas even beyond, the United States during the course of the 1960s and 1970s.

In the Soviet Union, as in the United States, least emphasis was placed on bombers. 'Backfire,' in the 1970s, was the first new type of plane with possible intercontinental range. There was actually a slight decrease in the total number of planes. Thus the Soviet Union continued to lag behind the United States in this regard. In 1985, the United States had 2,520 airborne nuclear warheads, as compared to the Soviet Union's 680.

The changes were greater with regard to strategic submarines. In this field, too, the Soviet Union continued to lag behind the United States, but they applied considerable efforts to reducing this gap. In 1967–68, the Soviet Union developed a submarine that could compare with the US Polaris to some extent. In 1973–74 they developed an even newer model. Although the Soviets now began to retire their old submarines so that the total number no longer increased, the Soviet Union soon had more strategic submarines than the United States. However, the United States' new Poseidon and Trident were technologically superior to the Soviet submarines, and because the United States had much more advanced MIRV technology, especially at sea, it kept its lead in terms of the number of nuclear warheads. In 1985, the United States had 5,536 nuclear warheads as compared to the Soviet Union's 3,123.

Whereas the Americans had a reasonable balance among the elements of the so-called triad, especially between the navy's submarine-based missiles and the air force's land-based missiles, the Soviets concentrated primarily on land-based missiles. This difference can be explained to a great extent by tradition and geographic conditions. The Soviet concentration was both quantitative and qualitative. The Soviet Union's arsenal increased from approximately 100 ICBMs in 1963 to approximately 1,400 in 1970, outstripping the United States in numbers.

On the whole the Soviet missiles were larger than the US missiles. This compensated for the greater accuracy of the US weapons. But the Soviets gradually approached the US level of accuracy. The lead the United States had long enjoyed in terms of MIRV technology was also diminishing, particularly as far as land-based missiles were concerned. In 1985 the Soviet Union had 1,398 land-based missiles with 6,420 warheads. The corresponding figures for the United States were 1,018 and 2,118.

From the time the United States had withdrawn its intermediate-range missiles from Western Europe in the early 1960s, the Soviet Union had enjoyed a clear lead in terms of such weapons. At the end of the 1970s, Moscow deployed modern SS-20 missiles, partially to replace the old SS-4 and SS-5. This emphasized a new Soviet superiority in relation to NATO. Roughly one-third of the rapidly increasing number of SS-20s were aimed primarily at China and other targets in Asia.

In a number of other areas as well a considerable build-up took place. The Soviet navy expanded rapidly during the 1960s and 1970s. Whereas Khrushchev had made drastic cutbacks in the number of conventional surface vessels, this policy was reversed from the mid-1960s. Now the Soviet Union was not only to have a modern submarine fleet – for that had been the assumption all along – but a modern surface fleet as well. The Soviet navy gradually appeared on all the oceans of the world (see pp. 88–9). The merchant fleet was doubled from 1964 to 1969.

In the mid-1960s the Soviet Union began to build up its conventional forces again in earnest. This could partly be seen as a reflection of the US strategy of flexible response. In part it must be linked to the tense situation along the Chinese border. The build-up was concentrated in that region. The number of Soviet troops in Eastern Europe remained constant at approximately 500,000.

It is difficult to state conclusively when the Soviet build-up began and even more difficult to analyze Soviet motives. Political scientist David Holloway claims that it probably started as early as in 1959–60. In any case, most of the new projects must have been initiated under Khrushchev. For a long time, he had hoped to balance the nuclear build-up with reductions in the conventional forces. That proved not possible in the 1960s. The pace was probably stepped up even further under Brezhnev, when greater emphasis was again placed on conventional forces.

If the build-up was begun in 1959–60, it was stimulated by developments in US policy under McNamara and by the defeat on Cuba. The Soviet Union considered itself one of the two superpowers and wanted the rest of the world to share that view. Superpower status had to be secured primarily on a military basis for want of other alternatives. Khrushchev attempted to build up the needed strength in the cheapest possible way. The very cheapest way was by exaggerating Soviet military strength. After this had been exposed as a bluff and had only strengthened the US military lead, he had attempted to deploy intermediate-range missiles on Cuba. When that, too, failed, there was only one option left: to build up the necessary strength, especially in the form of intercontinental missiles.

In the short term, at least, the Soviet objective must have been to attain military equality with the United States. In the early 1960s such a goal was still a long way off. To aim for superiority must have seemed rather illusory. The costs would be enormous. Equality would give the Soviet Union greater freedom of action without threatening international stability. In the course of the 1970s the SALT negotiations probably reinforced this course of policy. By approving the SALT agreements, the Soviet Union imposed limitations on itself that were more in line with a policy of equality than of superiority. (Agreements on arms limitations are discussed on pp. 68–9.)

In the early 1970s, the increase in the number of intercontinental missiles leveled off. It was true that old missiles were replaced with new ones, and the Soviet Union gradually mastered MIRV technology, but even this did not introduce any dramatic new elements into the situation. The Americans had a tendency to place primary emphasis on land-based missiles in comparing their strength with that of the Soviet Union, veiling the fact that for the United States this component of the triad was less important than for the Soviet Union.

During the 1960s and the first half of the 1970s, the annual growth of the Soviet defense budget was 4 or 5 per cent. In itself this growth was not extraordinarily high. What was more important was that it was sustained over such a long period. It probably declined towards the end of the 1970s. At least the CIA estimated that the annual growth after 1976 was about 2 per cent.

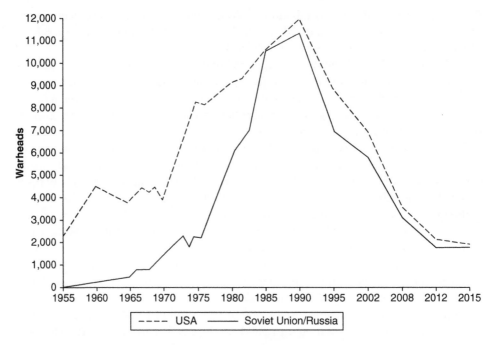

Figure 8.1A Nuclear warheads on strategic nuclear delivery vehicles

Sources: The Harvard Nuclear Study Group, *Living with Nuclear Weapons* (Toronto 1983), 74. *Economist*, 11 Oct. 1985, 50 and *Economist*, 9 June, 1990, 50. *Arms Control Today*, Nov. 1995, 30. *SIPRI Yearbook 2008* (Oxford, 2008), 366–81. *SIPRI Yearbook 2012* (Oxford, 2012), 308. *SIPRI Yearbook 2016* (Oxford: Oxford University Press, 2016), 610.

Figure 8.1B Strategic nuclear delivery vehicles

Sources: The Harvard Nuclear Study Group, *Living with Nuclear Weapons* (Toronto 1983), 74. *Economist*, 11 Oct. 1985, 50 and *Economist*, 9 June, 1990, 50. *Arms Control Today*, Nov. 1995, 30. *SIPRI Yearbook 2008* (Oxford, 2008), 366–81. *SIPRI Yearbook 2012* (Oxford, 2012), 316. *SIPRI Yearbook 2016* (Oxford: Oxford University Press, 2016), 610.

THE US REACTION

The First Phase: Prior to 1973–1974

For a long time, the US reaction to the Soviet build-up was limited. Early in the 1960s the United States had substantially increased its lead in the strategic sphere. Washington's first appraisal was that the Soviet Union would develop only the minimum force needed to deter the United States and to maintain its superpower status. When Secretary of Defense McNamara felt that the Soviet Union had reached that level in the mid-1960s, he began to claim that there was no sign that the Soviet Union aimed at developing a force equal to that of the United States.

The Soviet build-up was also underestimated, at least during the 1960s, by the US intelligence agencies that were responsible for predicting these developments. This underestimation may be largely considered an overreaction to the many erroneous statements from the late 1950s concerning the missile gap that it was later known had never existed.

Moreover, part of the reason the number of Soviet missiles increased so rapidly was that Moscow did not retire old missiles to the same extent Washington did. The fact that the Soviet Union developed missiles that were considerably heavier than the US missiles was mainly interpreted as evidence that the Soviet Union had to make up for their lacking accuracy with more blast effect. All in all, McNamara saw little reason to react as long as the United States was certain the country could survive a Soviet first strike and still have the capacity for adequate retaliation. This capacity in itself would deter the Soviet Union from considering such a first strike.

In many ways, Nixon and Kissinger had the same reaction to the Soviet build-up as McNamara had shown. The United States continued to retire old ICBMs and bombers. A total of approximately 1,000 ICBMs and 300 B-52 bombers were withdrawn during the period from the early 1960s until the mid-1970s. The relative strengths would have been quite different if these had been retained. The share of the defense budget that was used for strategic weapons continued to decline. Many people had the feeling that the stockpiles of nuclear weapons were now so large that further increases would have little significance. As Kissinger exclaimed, in what has become an almost classic quote, in response to opposition to the SALT I agreement in Washington:

> And one of the questions which we have to ask ourselves as a country is what in the name of God is strategic superiority? What is the significance of it, politically, militarily, operationally, at these levels of numbers? What do you do with it?

The Nixon administration shifted from talking of the need for US superiority to the use of expressions such as 'parity' and 'sufficiency.' Why have more weapons than necessary? It was easy to air such thoughts when the United States was still believed to have a slight lead in the strategic race. When the United States also had a more than sufficient defense capacity and when Soviet intentions were judged more optimistically than at any previous time during the Cold War, there was little reason to react to the Soviet build-up. After all, the policy of détente reached its peak in the early 1970s.

The new arms limitation measures made it less necessary and politically more difficult to initiate a new round of rearmament in the United States. The Vietnam War heightened criticism of the defense budget in public opinion. Beginning in the late 1960s and continuing until the mid-1970s, a clear majority felt that the defense budget was too large. This influenced not only members of Congress, but also the Johnson and Nixon administrations.

Even so, weapons development continued in the United States. During the SALT I negotiations the US military establishment insisted that MIRV technology was not to be included, and their wishes were observed. Thus, even though the SALT agreement limited the number of missiles on each side, it could not prevent a huge increase in the number of warheads on those same missiles. Later in the 1970s the United States insisted on keeping the MX missile out of a new agreement. The same was true of most aspects of the new cruise missile technology.

The Second Phase: The Years up to 1984

The United States allowed the Soviet Union to reach its level in the strategic sphere and even to surpass it in certain limited areas. However, the Soviet build-up gradually led to major changes in US policy. First the existing strategic doctrine was altered, then the defense budget was increased substantially.

A new strategy was introduced as early as in 1973–74 and was associated with the name of Secretary of Defense James Schlesinger. Schlesinger's point of departure was that it was no longer credible that the United States would start a full-scale nuclear war to defend anything other than extremely vital interests. In his opinion, MAD had been based on a US superiority that no longer existed. The country needed a strategy for the flexible use of nuclear weapons, in part to limit the destruction in the event of war. Military targets were assigned top priority, and strikes against large cities and other civilian targets were ranked correspondingly lower.

This was a return to thoughts McNamara had presented in his early phase as Secretary of Defense. He had later abandoned them, but his retreat was more evident on the verbal level than in relation to the targets US strategic weapons were actually aimed at. Schlesinger did away with this contradiction. Moreover, military technology had become more advanced. The accuracy of the weapons increased the possibilities for a selective choice of targets.

However, the problems of this strategy were the same ones McNamara had encountered. Many people felt that preventing war now came second to being able to fight a limited war. The Soviet Union still did not express any conviction that such limitations were possible. The Western Europeans remained skeptical, if not to the same degree as previously.

For a long time Carter and Secretary of Defense Harold Brown were hesitant about various aspects of Schlesinger's strategy, but in practice they accepted the major components of his scheme. Schlesinger had concentrated primarily on military targets. Brown would include economic and political targets to a greater extent. The Carter administration's view was established in Presidential Directive 59 in 1980.

The idea of a flexible use of nuclear weapons gained further momentum under Reagan and Weinberger. The result was that the US and Soviet doctrines converged. The United States, which had placed strong emphasis on deterrence, placed greater priority on analyses of how a nuclear war should be conducted and possibly even won. Soviet military leaders had long placed relatively little emphasis on deterrence, as interpreted in the West, and stressed that the Soviet Union would be capable of winning even a nuclear war. However, a number of statements by top politicians now concluded that in a nuclear war there would be no victor.

In nominal figures, the US defense budget increased throughout most of the 1960s and the 1970s. This was a reflection of the Vietnam War and rising inflation, for apart from expenditure on the war in Vietnam there was no real growth. The share of the federal budget that was used for defense was halved in the course of these two decades. This was first and foremost a result of major increases within health and social services, education, etc. Defense expenditure as a percentage of the gross national product decreased as well. In 1960 this percentage had been 9.1. In 1978 it reached its lowest level since 1950, 5.0 per cent, or several times smaller than the corresponding Soviet figure. On the other hand, the US national product was at least twice the size of the Soviet GNP.

From 1975–76, the policy of détente was subject to strong pressure (see Chapter 5). Even so, it took time before the political reversal resulted in significant increases in arms expenditure. When Carter was elected president in 1976, he promised to cut back the defense budget. Nothing came of this. The budget increased, and towards the end of his four-year term there were substantial increases. Public opinion was now in favor of the United States again building up a stronger defense.

The high growth rate in the defense budget at the end of Carter's term was accelerated further under Reagan. He proposed 14 per cent real growth for 1982, and subsequently 7 per cent annually, as compared to the 5 per cent Carter had recommended for 1982–86. Even though Congress reduced this increase somewhat, most of it remained.

In his second term, however, Reagan was able to get only very small increases from Congress, since public support for dramatic defense outlays quickly dwindled after the rapid growth during the first Reagan years.

In the perspective of party politics, Reagan's defense policy was an innovation. Republicans had traditionally placed priority on keeping down expenditures, including defense expenditure. Only in that way could government activity be reduced, allowing for tax cuts. Reagan was highly in favor of reducing government activity, but made one major exception for defense. Contrary to the pattern from earlier in the postwar period, it was now a Republican president who went furthest not only in general anti-communism, but also in armament to strengthen the United States in the contest against the Soviet Union.

New weapon systems were to be developed, while production of those Carter had already approved was to be escalated. In terms of aircraft, the decision to cancel the B-1 was reversed, at the same time that the new Stealth plane was also to be built. In terms of missiles, the MX was retained, although the Reagan administration had great problems deciding how it should be deployed. In addition, the Midgetman, a new single warhead missile, was to be developed. In terms of submarines, the pace of production of the new Trident was stepped up. Carter's decision not to assemble the neutron bomb was reversed, although it proved impossible to deploy the new weapon in Western Europe because of the opposition there. The build-up was almost as pronounced in conventional terms. The navy and the air force in particular were strengthened.

The foundation was laid for a new round in the arms race. Cruise missiles became continuously more advanced. They were so small and easy to hide that they could undermine the possibilities of further arms limitation. The first anti-satellite weapons were produced, first in the Soviet Union, then in the United States. Most important were the attempts to develop a defense against the opponent's missiles, based partly on laser and particle beam weapons. The Soviet Union was also doing research in this field, but Reagan's speech to the nation on 23 March 1983 signaled a dramatic acceleration of the US effort to develop 'a program to counter the awesome Soviet missile threat with measures that are defensive … I am directing a comprehensive and intensive effort to define a long-term research and development program to begin to achieve our ultimate goal of eliminating the threat posed by strategic nuclear missiles.' It was far from clear how effective such a defense system could be, but in any case these were qualitatively new questions. This development represented a clear threat to the most important arms limitation measure, the ABM treaty of 1972.

The Reagan administration justified the large increases in the defense budget by stating that they were necessary in order to eliminate the lead the Soviet Union had supposedly taken. Accordingly, Washington's primary objective in future negotiations on arms control would be to achieve substantial reductions in the areas where Soviet strength was the greatest. Western reductions were to be much smaller than Soviet reductions. Several statements by the administration could be interpreted to mean that equality should preferably be combined with an 'extra margin for safety.' The need felt by many policy-makers in Washington to carry out negotiations from a position of strength could also suggest that the objective was more than mere equality with the Soviet Union. Reagan's view of relations between East and West (see pp. 97–9) opened the way for development of virtually all the new weapons technology was capable of producing.

US armament frightened not only the adversary, but also allied countries and US citizens, a paradox that had appeared on several occasions during the postwar period. The reactions in the early 1980s were stronger than at any previous time. The protests appeared first and most strongly in many Western European countries, then in the United States itself. They were directed against many different aspects of the military build-up: armaments in general; the new strategic doctrines with less emphasis on deterrence and more emphasis on how nuclear weapons could be used in a war; and the proliferation of new weapons.

However, the most important single factor in Western Europe was Carter's and NATO's decision in December 1979 to deploy 572 cruise and Pershing II missiles in Western Europe. They were to be a response to the Soviet SS-20 build-up. The German chancellor, Helmut Schmidt, had been among the first to warn against this build-up, although he preferred that the SS-20s were negotiated away rather than met with new US weapons. Moscow on its part claimed that the SS-20 merely compensated for British and French nuclear weapons as well as US bombers in Europe. However, there was little doubt that the Soviet Union had a growing lead in terms of intermediate-range weapons in Europe.

The NATO decision was also intended to link the United States more closely to Western Europe. The theory was that the United States would have to build up an escalation ladder. A step was needed between the tactical and strategic nuclear weapons. Such an intermediate weapon could make the defense of Europe more credible than the other weapons alone could do. However, in large segments of public opinion the deployment decision was interpreted as a sign that the United States was preparing to fight a limited nuclear war, but not on American soil. This fear was reinforced by confusing statements, not least by President Reagan himself, on how nuclear weapons could possibly be employed in a war.

During the 1970s, the importance of Western Europe within NATO had grown (see pp. 182–3). This fact, combined with the intensity of the points of view that surfaced in most of the European NATO countries and the opposition even within the United States, forced the Reagan administration to place greater emphasis on arms control than could have been expected given Reagan's ideology and former statements. After a time, negotiations were entered into with the Soviet Union regarding limitations on both strategic weapons and the intermediate-range missiles that had caused such uneasiness in Western Europe.

There was little progress to be seen. In December 1983, deployment of the cruise and Pershing II missiles began. Negotiations broke down altogether (see p. 99).

COOPERATION, DISARMAMENT, AND REARMAMENT ONCE MORE

In late 1984 it became evident that both the United States and the Soviet Union were again interested in an improved climate (see p. 103). Moscow abandoned its demand that the US intermediate-range missiles had to be withdrawn from Western Europe before arms control negotiations could be reopened. Negotiations were resumed in March 1985.

Little progress was made at the first summit meeting, in Geneva. The next one, in Reykjavik, was highly dramatic although no accord was reached on this occasion either. Reagan and Gorbachev were apparently close to agreeing on considerable reductions in the number of strategic weapons. Even the possibility of doing away with this class of weapons altogether was discussed. The meeting broke down over disagreement about the Strategic Defense Initiative (SDI), Reagan's scheme for a defense shield against Soviet missiles. Gorbachev insisted on limitations to SDI research that Reagan could not accept.

The political climate improved rapidly. Gorbachev's rise to power in the Soviet Union resulted in major changes in the Soviet stance. In the field of arms control there was little doubt that substantial concessions were now being made by the USSR. First Gorbachev agreed to abandon the demand that a treaty on intermediate-range weapons would have to apply to the British and French as well as the US nuclear forces. Then he relinquished the link to SDI. Of equal importance was Moscow's complete turnabout on the issue of verification. The differences of opinion here had obstructed agreement on treaties in several areas. Now the Soviets were prepared to open up their society in a manner that had previously been unknown. They agreed to a comprehensive system of 'on site' inspections, first in relation to the 1986 Stockholm treaty on confidence-building measures at the Conference on Security and Cooperation in Europe (CSCE) and later in relation to intermediate-range missiles. In December 1987, agreement was reached on an INF agreement which would do away with all US and Soviet land-based intermediate-range missiles. This was the first time the two sides actually agreed to do away with an entire class of weapons.

Whereas it had proved difficult to reach agreements on arms control when the political climate was not conducive to this, the situation changed during the rapid relaxation of tension at the transition from the 1980s to the 1990s. It became difficult for the negotiators to keep pace with the actual reductions that the two sides were implementing more or less on their own. This process was undoubtedly influenced by developments in Eastern Europe and by the existence of economic problems, particularly within the Soviet Union but in the United States as well.

Negotiations on reductions in conventional forces in Europe at the Conference on Security and Cooperation in Europe provided the best illustration of the new climate. At a grand ceremony in Paris in November 1990, leaders of the 34 countries of the conference signed an agreement after less than two years of negotiations. By way of comparison, the negotiations on mutual and balanced force reductions (MBFR) had lasted from 1973 to 1988 without achieving significant results. Once again it was the USSR that made the greatest concessions. The overriding principle was that the two blocs should be equal. In this context that meant reductions of up to 50 per cent on the part of the Eastern bloc, as compared to only around 10 per cent for the Western bloc. The Soviet Union relinquished its superiority in terms of tanks and heavy artillery. Although the USSR remained the greatest single power in Europe in military terms, the Warsaw Pact had disintegrated. Even though the number of troops was not directly affected by the agreement, Moscow first implemented substantial unilateral reductions, and then the Kremlin was prepared to concede the United States the right to equal numbers. Each of the two superpowers would be entitled to have 195,000 men stationed in Central Europe. Then developments in Germany and Eastern Europe made it illusory for Moscow to have even 195,000 men in the region in question. The Russian soldiers in East Germany were to be withdrawn by the end of 1994, and it was unlikely that other countries in Eastern Europe any longer desired Russian military presence.

The end of the Cold War laid the basis for an entirely new pace of disarmament, illustrating the great significance of the foreign policy climate for the superpowers' weapons arsenals. After nine years of negotiations the United States and the Soviet Union signed the START I agreement in July 1991. During the course of a seven-year period the two superpowers were to implement a reduction from a level of 11,000 or 12,000 nuclear warheads on their strategic arms carriers to 6,000 warheads on a maximum of 1,600 strategic arms carriers.

The dissolution of the Soviet Union in December 1991 meant that Belarus, Ukraine, and Kazakhstan also became nuclear powers because nearly one-third of the Soviet arsenals were located within the borders of these three republics. Through the Lisbon agreement of March 1992, these three states agreed to eliminate all nuclear weapons on their soil. In practice some of them were to be destroyed, others transferred to Russia. After some delay this agreement was in fact implemented despite the political problems between Russia and Ukraine.

Already in June 1992 George Bush and Boris Yeltsin reached agreement on substantial new reductions, an agreement that was formalized in the START II treaty of 3 January 1993. During the course of a maximum of 10 years the United States and Russia would reduce the number of nuclear weapons to between 3,000 and 3,500 each. (Each country could decide how many they wanted to have within these limits.) The treaty prohibited MIRVs on land-based missiles. This meant that the threat from Russian land-based missiles that the Americans had been so concerned about was greatly reduced. The focus of the nuclear arsenals had now in earnest shifted to submarine-based weapons.

Even though the two powers still had more than enough nuclear weapons to destroy each other several times, the START II reductions appeared dramatic and made a significant contribution to reducing the level of fear of nuclear weapons. Substantial reductions in the numbers of tactical nuclear weapons reinforced this change of climate. Through unilateral but parallel commitments the United States and Russia decided that they would implement comprehensive reductions in the numbers of such weapons as well. Certain types of tactical weapons were eliminated entirely, and both the United States and Russia stopped carrying tactical nuclear weapons on naval vessels. However, tactical nuclear weapons still had a place in their arsenals. The United States retained the option to launch such weapons from airplanes in Europe. Destroying such a large number of weapons as the United States and Russia now set about to do was an expensive and technically complicated proposition. For that reason the United States agreed to give Russia various forms of support to facilitate this process.

After the end of the Cold War, defense budgets were reduced in most countries, particularly within NATO and what had been the Warsaw Pact. The US defense budget decreased from approximately 300 billion dollars in 1990 to approximately 260 billion in 1995. The United States did, however, remain by far the biggest spender on arms. The development of new weapons projects continued almost unabated, despite the demise of the Cold War. Russia intended to remain a military superpower, but the difficult economic situation brought about both a sharp decrease in defense spending and a sudden drop in the production of new weapons systems.

In December 1997 a global convention to ban landmines was signed by more than 120 countries, but not by several major powers – the United States, Russia, and China. Landmines are a major humanitarian problem in many conflict areas, particularly in the Third World. While there was a general reduction in global spending on arms, in certain regions the build-up continued. This was especially the case in the Balkans, the Middle East, and in East Asia.

The Clinton administration increased the defense budget substantially during the last years of his presidency. Even so, the Republicans criticized these hikes as being far from enough. Thus when George W. Bush took office in 2001, significant changes were made in US defense policy. The budget grew rapidly, particularly in the wake of the terrorist attacks on 11 September 2001. The United States now spent almost as much on defense as the rest of the world together. The increase from one year to the next could be as large as the entire defense budget in Britain. The ability to intervene quickly in any part of the world was the fundamental objective. If necessary, the United States should be able to stage an offensive against other countries and against terrorist groups before being attacked itself. This new doctrine of pre-emptive strike was met with massive criticism internationally. Precision-guided weapons were developed that placed the United States in a class by itself militarily. The administration was also determined to develop a national missile defense, a modified version of

Reagan's SDI, even though it was uncertain how effective such a defense system could be. For this reason the ABM agreement with Russia was revoked.

The end of the Cold War and the nature of qualitative developments made quantitative measures in certain areas even less meaningful than before. In May 2002 Bush and Putin signed a brief but dramatic agreement, SORT (Strategic Offensive Reductions Treaty), as SALT and START were now called. Thus START II would in practice not enter into force. The new treaty, SORT, stipulated that the number of operative strategic warheads was to be reduced to between 1,700 and 2,200 for each side by 31 December 2012. New president Barack Obama in fact expressed support for a world without nuclear weapons, although he added that he did not expect to see this goal realized in his own lifetime. In April 2010 the United States and Russia signed the New START agreement, which was a follow-up to START I and replaced the recently signed SORT agreement. Under the terms of the treaty, the number of strategic nuclear missile launchers will be reduced by half. The number of deployed strategic nuclear warheads will be cut to 1,550, which is down two-thirds from the original START treaty. Reductions were actually then made in the number of both warheads and the means of delivery (see Figure 8.1 on p. 140). Britain and France also reduced their strategic arsenals somewhat. Still, Washington and NATO's plans for a European missile defense, while scaled down under Obama, nevertheless continued to disturb relations with Moscow, particularly the plans that affected NATO's new and Moscow's old allies in Eastern and Central Europe. The general climate between Russia and the West was also deteriorating in 2012–13 with differences over the Western intervention in Libya, the Russian veto against an intervention in Syria, and the weakening of democracy in Russia (see p. 210).

In 1995 an agreement was reached to make the non-proliferation treaty of 1968 permanent. This was an important step in efforts to prevent an increase in the number of nuclear powers. In return, many of the countries that did not possess such weapons demanded that the nuclear powers not only continue to reduce their arsenals, but that they should also impose a complete ban on all testing of such weapons. The United States, Russia, and the United Kingdom had practiced a moratorium on testing since 1992. China and France continued their test programs, but the strong international reactions to the French underground nuclear tests in the Pacific in the autumn of 1995 helped influence the French government's decision to cease such testing from 1996. China has also observed a self-imposed testing moratorium since 1996. In 1998, however, India and Pakistan both staged nuclear weapons tests. A Pakistani network helped spread nuclear technology to Libya (the nuclear program was still abandoned in 2003), Iran, and North Korea.

Further proliferation of nuclear weapons cannot be ruled out. Iraq promised to halt its existing program after the Gulf War; the United States assumed that Saddam Hussein had failed to do so, but the war in Iraq in 2003 revealed that Iraq had in fact more or less closed down its earlier nuclear program. Iran has an ambitious nuclear program, and its refusal to consent to effective international inspections might indicate that the program has a military objective. In 2015 this program was put on hold. North Korea promised to discontinue its nuclear program in agreements with the United States in 1994–95 and again in 2007, but it soon became evident that the program had not been closed down; North Korea in fact developed a nuclear weapon. Some delivery vehicles were already in place. The confusing developments in North Korea could have a significant ripple effect throughout the region. A North Korean nuclear bomb could put pressure on South Korea to follow suit. In addition, there is always the possibility that Japan will reconsider its negative attitude toward nuclear weapons. The Bush administration was committed to halting the development of nuclear weapons in both Iran and North Korea, but after the Iraq war had few instruments to implement its policy. Israel was also strongly against an Iranian nuclear bomb. The Obama administration would not accept such an outcome either. The 2015 agreement appeared to solve the problem with Iran at least temporarily. The dispute with North Korea remained unsolved, with the temperature in the region going up significantly.

Although the Cold War was over and key arms limitation treaties had been signed, the development of new weapons and the spread of existing ones continued. In certain regions, such as the Middle East, Southern Asia, and North-Eastern Asia, tensions ran high. Both Washington and Moscow had a definite interest in reducing the number of strategic weapons further and in maintaining a system of effective verification, but their modernization programs continued with considerable force after the deterioration in relations after the events in Ukraine in 2014. Many challenges thus remained.

THE SMALLER NUCLEAR STATES

Nuclear developments illustrated the prominent leadership of the two superpowers. Here, even more than in most other fields, the United States and the Soviet Union were the primary actors. In 1986 these two countries had 96 per cent of the world's nuclear weapons. Even so, they did not have an absolute monopoly.

The United States and Britain had cooperated closely in developing the atomic bomb during the Second World War. During the initial stages in particular the British contribution had been highly significant. But the agreements made in 1943 and 1944 by Roosevelt and Churchill concerning continued cooperation after the war were soon set aside when the war was over. This was due partly to the fact that the agreements were not known outside a very narrow circle, and partly to the fact that the politicians in Washington, and especially in the Senate, were firmly determined to safeguard the US monopoly, even in relation to Britain. The US Atomic Energy Act of 1946 was an expression of this view.

In January 1947 the British government decided to develop atomic weapons on its own. This decision seems to have been based on three considerations. In the first place, atomic weapons could come to play an important strategic role. They represented a qualitative new step in weapons development and it was essential that Britain take part. In the second place, there was the question of Britain's political role. Even though it would inevitably be diminished compared to the period between the wars, atomic weapons would strengthen the position of the United Kingdom in relation to both the Soviet Union and the United States. Finally, London hoped that having its own nuclear force would open the way to cooperation with Washington at a later date. This could be significant not only in the nuclear sphere, important as that was, but also far beyond that.

The first British detonation took place in October 1952. It contributed to moderating the US attitude to some extent, but it was the test of a hydrogen bomb in May 1957 that truly liberalized Washington's policy.

With regard to delivery systems, London became entirely dependent on US assistance from the late 1950s. When the Americans stopped development of the planned Skybolt missile in 1962, and Britain was thus left without the launcher the country had based itself on, Kennedy promised Prime Minister Harold Macmillan in December 1962 that Britain would get the new Polaris missile instead. The British nuclear submarines were to be placed under NATO joint command, but could be withdrawn if the British felt that their 'supreme national interests' were at stake. France would receive a similar offer.

France had enjoyed a relatively strong position in the field of nuclear physics during the period between the wars. However, the country's position in international politics was even more weakened than that of Britain after the Second World War. It is difficult to single out any specific time when the decision was made to develop a separate French atomic force. Technology, economics, and politics were closely intertwined.

To a great extent the French process had the same basis as the British. Strategic considerations were significant, as were political considerations. The Suez incident in 1956 was important because it convinced French decision-makers that something had to be done to strengthen France's position. Relations with Germany and Britain were also of significance. France wanted to counterbalance the Germans' rapidly growing role in the military field. If London was capable of producing nuclear weapons, Paris ought to be so as well.

De Gaulle first increased the pace of development of the French atomic force and then made it far more independent of NATO than previous French governments had intended. He was also much more concerned about a problem that would gradually interest increasing numbers of people: Could one truly trust the United States to use nuclear weapons to defend Western Europe when the Soviet Union had achieved the possibility of striking the United States directly?

The first French test detonation took place in 1960. The French president, de Gaulle, was not interested in the US Polaris offer. He preferred to continue work on a separate French nuclear force. Moreover, the agreement between Kennedy and Macmillan probably contributed to de Gaulle's rejection of British membership of the EEC of 1963. In de Gaulle's eyes, the British had once more demonstrated their dependence on the United States.

The number of nuclear powers has grown more slowly than most observers expected around 1960. In 1957 the Soviet Union promised to help China develop nuclear weapons. However, two years later Moscow backed out of this agreement, a fact that contributed strongly to the growing antagonism between the two communist countries (see p. 191). It is not clear how much help the Chinese actually received from the Soviet Union during the two years this cooperation lasted. In 1964, the first Chinese nuclear test detonation took place. China was clearly far behind Britain and France in terms of both nuclear technology and delivery systems. A decade passed before the nuclear club gained a new member. In 1974, India carried out what the government called a 'peaceful nuclear explosion.' New Delhi was thus capable of producing nuclear bombs for military use. In 1998 India and then Pakistan carried out a series of nuclear tests. Over several decades Israel had also developed a substantial nuclear capacity. In 2006 North Korea conducted a nuclear test. It did so again, with more success, in May 2009 and again in 2013 and 2015. It also carried out numerous missile tests. The new states developed their weapons for the same basic reasons as did the older ones: security needs and status considerations, often stimulated by various domestic considerations, including popular support, sometimes even enthusiasm.

Some states did, however, abandon their nuclear projects. South Africa actually developed a bomb, in part probably in cooperation with Israel, but discontinued its further nuclear efforts even before the fall of the apartheid regime, although that change was probably anticipated when it ended its project. Ukraine, Belarus, and Kazakhstan similarly ended their projects after the dissolution of the Soviet Union, although it has to be added that the weapons in question were still under Russian control and not under that of the three new countries. In 2003 Libya abandoned its program; it simply cost too much diplomatically, politically, and economically. Libya also had problems with the basic science involved. Many other countries, from Argentina and Brazil to Sweden and Yugoslavia, had also considered the nuclear option before they gave it up. Thus, developments did not go all in one direction. Some countries did give up their nuclear projects.

In the 1980s there was a growing fear that chemical weapons could become the 'nuclear weapon' of the poor nations. After gas had been employed during the First World War, the Geneva Convention of 1925 prohibited the use, but not the production and stockpiling of such weapons. Some 20 nations are believed to have chemical weapons. The technology required is relatively simple, and it is not easily distinguished from civilian chemical technology. During the 1980s Iraq demonstrated that such weapons could be used, both against Iran and against its own Kurdish population. Iraq even had a program to develop biological weapons. In 1990 the United States and the Soviet Union reached an agreement to reduce their chemical weapons stockpiles by 80 per cent. In 1993 an international convention was signed which prohibited the production and stockpiling of chemical weapons. It came into force in 1997, but several countries were widely perceived as still having such weapons.

THE ARMS RACE, 1945-2016: THE LITERATURE

Four key discussions of the arms race are Lawrence Freedman, *The Evolution of Nuclear Strategy* (New York, 1981, revised edition 2003); Michael Mandelbaum, *The Nuclear Question: The United States and Nuclear Weapons, 1945–1976* (Cambridge, 1979); David Holloway, *The Soviet Union and the Arms Race* (New Haven, CT, 1983); and McGeorge Bundy, *Danger and Survival: Choices about the Bomb in the First Fifty Years* (New York, 1988). Thomas Wolfe, *Soviet Power and Europe, 1945–1970* (Baltimore, MD, 1970) and the Harvard Nuclear Study Group, *Living with Nuclear Weapons* (Toronto, 1983) are also useful. Michael Quinlan, *Thinking about Nuclear Weapons. Principles, Problems, Prospects* (Oxford, 2009) is more philosophical than historical in approach, but still quite helpful.

In the abundant literature on why the atom bomb was dropped on Hiroshima and Nagasaki and the role of the new weapon in US strategy, two books stand out from the rest. They are Martin J. Sherwin, *A World Destroyed: The Atomic Bomb and the Grand Alliance* (New York, 1973) and Gregg Herken, *The Winning Weapon:*

(Continued)

(Continued)

The Atomic Bomb in the Cold War, 1945–1950 (New York, 1980). Campbell Craig and Sergey Radchenko, *The Atomic Bomb and the Origins of the Cold War* (New Haven, CT, 2008) is a recent interesting interpretation. David Holloway's *Stalin and the Bomb: The Soviet Union and Atomic Energy* (New Haven, CT, 1994) is excellent on the development of the atomic bomb by the Soviets.

A superb general presentation of overall US security policy is John Lewis Gaddis, *Strategies of Containment: A Critical Appraisal of Postwar American National Security Policy* (Oxford, 1982). Jozef Goldblat, *Arms Control: A Guide to Negotiations and Agreements* (Oslo, 1994) is a most useful guide to the various arms control agreements. The annual yearbooks from the Stockholm International Peace Research Institute (SIPRI), published by Oxford University Press, are particularly valuable for statistics on armaments.

In June 2009 the Norwegian Nobel Institute held a useful symposium entitled 'Peace, security and nuclear order.' The book from the symposium is Olav Njølstad (ed.), *Nuclear Proliferation and International Order: Challenges to the Non-Proliferation Treaty* (London, 2011).

THE UNITED STATES AND WESTERN EUROPE, 1945-2016

After the Second World War the United States acquired a dominant position in world politics. The greatest difference in relation to the period between the wars was the new role the country would play in Western Europe and Japan. (Japan is dealt with in Chapter 11.) The US influence was based on many different elements: US participation in the occupation of vital countries such as West Germany, Japan, and Italy; the United States' economic strength at a time when economic needs were acute; the country's military strength, combined with a growing interest – especially in Western Europe – in military guarantees in relation to the Soviet Union; and the pervasive cultural and political influence of the United States.

Relations between the United States, Western Europe, and Japan gradually changed in character. US economic assistance ceased, the extent of US economic superiority declined, and relations were characterized by a mixture of cooperation and competition. Occupation came to an end, and West Germany and Japan in particular became central actors in international politics. Japan would become the stronger of the two economically, but West Germany played a more active role politically and militarily nonetheless. In France, de Gaulle designed an alternative to the prevailing US-dominated politics. Economic and political integration in Western Europe strengthened Europe in relation to the United States. The end of the Cold War, the unification of Germany, and the deepening of content and geographic expansion of the European Union (EU) further fueled this process. The basis of cooperation within the Western bloc would have to be redefined, but it would prove difficult to find a replacement for US hegemony.

EXPANSION BY INVITATION, 1945-1950

The main features of relations between the United States and Western Europe were established in the years before 1950. The United States had great power and strong interests in many different parts of the world. It was only natural that Washington wanted to promote these interests. But the situation in Western Europe in particular could be described as expansion by invitation.

There was a widespread fear in Western Europe that the United States would revert to the policy of the period between the wars. The politicians of the day knew little of what the future would bring. However, they well remembered how the United States had retreated into 'splendid isolation' after the First World War. Most Europeans wanted to prevent history from repeating itself.

The British government was the most prominent example of this. Although London overestimated the position of the United Kingdom, both Churchill's coalition government during the war and Attlee's Labour party government after the war were actively engaged in linking the United States more closely to Western Europe. They favored obtaining both economic and military support from the United States, for that was the only possible source of substantial assistance. Britain no longer had the resources to play such a central role as formerly, neither in the world economy nor in the global or even European balance of power. Good relations with the United States could compensate to some extent for this decline.

The British were thus highly disappointed at the US reductions in Lend-Lease assistance in May and September of 1945. The Attlee government had hoped for an even larger and even cheaper loan than the 3.75 billion dollars on fairly favorable terms the two countries agreed on in December 1945. When the US and British zones in Germany were unified in 1946–47, the British were strongly in favor of the Americans paying a larger share of the joint expenses. Both the Churchill and the Attlee governments wanted to maintain the Anglo-American combined boards that had been established during the war, the most important of which was the Combined Chiefs of Staff. The British also wanted to continue cooperation on nuclear weapons. For London, a final objective was to bind the US occupation forces to Western Europe for as long as possible.

In 1946, Congress put a halt to the scheme Churchill and Roosevelt had agreed on with regard to nuclear weapons. The Combined Chiefs of Staff committee was dissolved. In a number of other areas, however, cooperation between the United States and Britain continued after the war. The British wanted this to take place relatively openly, but because of political misgivings in Washington most of it was kept secret.

In January–February 1947, the British, led by Foreign Secretary Bevin, were actively engaged in efforts to get the United States to assume the role Britain had traditionally played in containing Soviet-Russian influence in South-Eastern Europe. The dramatic way in which the British announced their withdrawal from Greece contributed to the willingness with which the United States, through the Truman Doctrine, assumed this responsibility. Bevin also played a significant role in shaping Marshall's speech of 5 June 1947 into what would become the Marshall Plan. Finally, London's role was important for the changes in March–April 1948 that transformed Washington's role from that of an encouraging adviser to a full partner in Atlantic military cooperation (see p. 19).

Although relations between the United States and Britain were unique, attitudes similar to those in Britain were to be found in a number of countries. In the economic sphere there was a nearly unanimous desire for help. The countries of Western Europe requested far more than the 7.4 billion dollars they received from the end of the war until July 1947. Under the Marshall Plan the Europeans originally requested 28 billion dollars from the United States. The Truman administration reduced the amount to 17 billion, and Congress finally granted 14 billion. Only Moscow's opposition prevented Finland, Czechoslovakia, and Poland from participating. Spain wanted to be included as well, but Truman was opposed to Franco's participation.

The pattern was largely the same when it came to US military ties to Western Europe. Although there were distinct differences among the various countries' views, France, Belgium, the Netherlands, and Luxembourg all joined the efforts in 1948 to persuade the United States to increase its commitments. In the short term they wanted to receive as much weapon assistance as possible; in a somewhat longer perspective the objective was some sort of treaty system. Just as there were many countries that wanted to take part in the Marshall Plan, there were also many that wanted to participate in NATO. In addition to the countries mentioned, Italy, Portugal, Iceland, Norway, and Denmark joined, although the last two or three would probably have preferred somewhat looser ties to the alliance than they acquired. Once more there were countries that were not allowed to join. Spain was still barred from membership. Nor did Washington want to include Greece, Turkey, and Iran. The Western European NATO countries were all eager to make the US guarantees in the event of a Soviet attack as automatic as possible, whereas the Truman administration, not least in consideration of Congress, was concerned about incorporating a certain degree of flexibility.

The interest in binding the United States to Western Europe continued after the establishment of NATO. Most countries favored involving the United States directly in the various regional planning groups that were to be established within NATO. After the outbreak of the Korean War the European pressure to increase Washington's involvement was further intensified. Four new divisions were sent to Europe. US military assistance was stepped up substantially. Most importantly, a joint command structure was developed (see pp. 129–131).

All in all, the countries of Western Europe actively applied pressure to get the United States to play a greater role in European affairs. This was not only the policy of the governments. To the extent that satisfactory material on public opinion exists, the public mostly rallied round this policy. But of course there were differences among the countries, and in occupied or more or less authoritarian countries it was hardly meaningful to speak of any public opinion.

The Europeans could not force the Americans to do anything against their own will. US policy was primarily determined by Americans themselves, but influential circles in the United States supported the policy most of the Western European governments pursued. Even so, the attitudes of the Western Europeans must be said to have contributed to strengthening US involvement and to hastening a clarification of US relations with Europe.

With increased involvement came increased influence; economic assistance was not given without return favors. Under the Marshall Plan, trade within Western Europe had to be liberalized, contact with Eastern Europe limited, and the United States given a certain degree of influence in the formulation of the individual countries' economic policies. Politically, the US influence spanned from opposition to socialization in the Bi-zone in Germany to interference in the Italian elections in 1948. Within NATO, the formulation of the organization's strategy became mainly a US concern. Washington also brought about the rearmament of West Germany after the outbreak of the Korean War.

As soon as US assistance was secured, European criticism of certain aspects of US policy increased. The support was too limited, the return favors too many, US policy too variable, the Americans too moralistic, and so on.

However, the level of both US assistance and US influence can be exaggerated. Marshall funds did not account for more than 10 to 20 per cent of the various European countries' capital formation in the years 1948–49 and less than 10 per cent in 1950–51. Washington's direct intervention in domestic political affairs was also modest, apart from in the occupied countries and in countries such as Greece and Turkey, where the domestic conditions were rather special.

The main point in the first years after the Second World War was that the United States and Western Europe to a great extent had corresponding interests. Western Europe faced enormous tasks of reconstruction and needed assistance from abroad. Only the United States could offer assistance of any magnitude. This assistance would be advantageous for the Americans themselves as it would generate large-scale purchasing from the United States. The Truman administration and most of the European governments also had mutual interests in preventing increased Soviet influence in Western Europe. Only the United States could represent a political and military counterweight to the Red Army.

EUROPEAN INTEGRATION, 1945-1973

The United States wanted to weave the Western European countries into a comprehensive international network. Economically, what was needed in 1945–46 was to attain their support for the World Bank and the International Monetary Fund. In 1947–48, the Marshall Plan was based on close cooperation across the Atlantic, although the United States did not join the organization that administered the assistance, the Organization for European Economic Cooperation (OEEC). The European economies were also to be made more open through the establishment of the International Trade Organization, which never materialized, and through the General Agreement on Tariffs and Trade (GATT). NATO brought the United States and Western Europe closer together militarily and politically.

At the same time, the Americans encouraged much closer cooperation among the countries of Western Europe. Truman, and to an even greater extent the Eisenhower administration, actively supported the Western European efforts at integration. This was evident on a number of occasions. Washington would have preferred the OEEC to become as binding as possible in the form of a permanent customs union, but the OEEC did not go that far. The Americans showed all the more support for the continental countries when they joined together in supranational organizations.

It can roughly be said that there were two main attitudes towards integration in Western Europe during the postwar period, later often called the federalist and confederalist views. The former dominated on the continent and aimed at supranational cooperation within certain sectors, or preferably in general. The latter accepted a certain degree of coordination of policies in the various countries, but without them relinquishing any of their independence and without any sweeping institutionalization. This view dominated in Britain, in the Scandinavian countries, and in Switzerland and Austria.

The federalist way of thinking was behind the Coal and Steel Community (1950), the proposal for a European army (1950–54), Euratom (1958), and the European Economic

Community (1958). The confederalist philosophy formed the basis for the OEEC (1948), the European Council (1949), and the European Free Trade Association (EFTA) (1960). Despite these divergent attitudes, historically the extent of cooperation and integration in Western Europe was an important new phenomenon. Several factors must be included to explain this development in the 1940s and 1950s.

On the international level, the influence of the United States and the Soviet Union was important, although in different ways. As mentioned, the United States encouraged the Western Europeans to cooperate, clearly preferring what is here called a federalist approach to a confederalist one. The Soviet contribution was based on the fact that European integration was also a means of containing Soviet and communist influence.

The international standing of the United States and the Soviet Union showed that the traditional European powers had become second- and third-ranking nations. The French and British colonial empires began to disintegrate. Only through European cooperation could Western Europe make its voice heard once more. Later, experiences such as the Suez conflict (see pp. 56–7) would explicitly confirm how reduced the role of Britain and France had become, and especially that of France.

A number of political conditions can explain why the continent was dominated by the federalist philosophy, while confederalism was strongest in Northern Europe. In the first place, the experiences of the Second World War had influenced the various countries in different ways. In countries such as Germany and Italy nationalism was discredited for obvious reasons. In France, nationalism was waning, at least in some segments of the population, although de Gaulle did his best to restore the country's self-respect. It was no coincidence that the idea of integration was strong within much of the European resistance movement. Peace was to be secured through an integrated Europe. Small countries such as Belgium, the Netherlands, and Luxembourg were naturally in favor of plans that could put an end to the destructive German–French conflicts.

In Northern Europe, on the other hand, the Second World War had contributed to strengthening nationalism in many ways rather than weakening it. The British were extremely proud of their performance during the war. Many people, both within Britain and outside the country, felt that they had fought the most glorious struggle of all the allied nations. In Norway, too, self-esteem flourished in the wake of the resistance against the Germans and the local Nazis. Sweden and Switzerland had managed to preserve their neutrality once more.

In the second place, the continental countries were strongly under the influence of the Christian Democratic parties, which to a great extent had a shared political and religious perspective that made it easier for them to cooperate. Cooperation was further stimulated by the fact that several of their leading representatives came from border districts that had suffered greatly from the European conflicts: Robert Schuman in France, Konrad Adenauer in West Germany, and Alcide de Gasperi in Italy. The continental Socialists were more divided, although the majority of them also supported the integration efforts. The best-known spokesmen for this group were Paul-Henri Spaak in Belgium and Guy Mollet in France.

The fact that the Christian Democrats, most of them Catholics, enjoyed such a strong position on the continent, was bound to increase the opposition between these countries and the Northern European countries. In Britain and Scandinavia Socialism and

Protestantism held a strong position, without providing a sufficient basis for such close cooperation between them as had been established on the continent.

In the third place, Britain in particular still had comprehensive political and economic commitments outside Europe that made it difficult to establish exclusive links to the rest of Western Europe. As the British government made clear in its response to the plans for a Coal and Steel Community in 1950: 'A political federation, limited to Western Europe, is not compatible either with our Commonwealth ties, our obligations as a member of the wider Atlantic community, or as a world power.' This type of consideration was decisive for the changing British governments during the course of the 1950s. Norway and Denmark were in turn linked to Britain economically, politically, and militarily. It was nearly inconceivable that they should join European organizations to which Britain did not belong. The same was true of Sweden.

Considerations of economy and communications were also significant for integration in general and for developments on the continent in particular. The countries in the geographic center of Europe cooperated, while what may roughly be called the northern and southern periphery did not take part. Improved communications had made distances shorter. Trade increased and tourism flourished.

There were clear economies of scale linked to a European market. For many people, the United States was the pattern to be emulated. In the continental countries, leading financial circles were enthusiastic spokesmen for European integration, with the partial exception of France. French industry was relatively protectionistic and afraid of competition, especially from Germany. On the other hand, the French farmers could attain significant advantages. In Britain and Scandinavia this was not the case, in part because the trade patterns were different. Contact with the continent was more limited, whereas there was more trade with other regions.

Finally, there were a number of 'local' conditions on the continent that stimulated the idea of integration. Germany could only achieve sovereignty through integration. No one dared give the Germans an entirely free rein. Italy was seeking both political protection against an internal communist threat and economic progress through European cooperation. France could only become a major power again as the spokesman for a fairly unified Western Europe.

France played a central role in the political decision-making process on the continent. Here were both the strongest and most influential adherents of integration (Monnet, Schuman, etc.) and the strongest opponents. The large Communist party received support from de Gaulle's nationalists in their opposition to supranational Western European cooperation. It was these two groups, with scattered support from others, that toppled the plans for a European army in 1954.

After de Gaulle assumed power in 1958, he reconciled himself with French membership in the European Economic Community (EEC). He even became interested in using the organization to achieve coordination of the member countries' foreign policies. But foreign policy cooperation, like cooperation in other areas, was to take place between independent countries and not be based on supranational bodies. The so-called Luxembourg compromise of January 1966 was in reality a victory for de Gaulle's view in this matter.

However, at this time nothing much came of the foreign policy cooperation the French president advocated. The main reason was the differing attitudes among the

EEC countries towards Britain and the United States. Washington worked actively to do away with the breach between the EEC and EFTA, on the terms of the EEC. Five of the six EEC member countries supported British membership. However, de Gaulle thwarted the British application both in 1963 and in 1967. In his opinion the 'Anglo-Saxon' countries would attain too much influence, at the expense of France in particular.

De Gaulle's successor, Georges Pompidou, admitted the United Kingdom in 1972. Britain was followed by Denmark and Ireland. Following a referendum, Norway chose to remain outside the EEC, or the European Community (EC) as the organization was called from 1967. Pompidou was generally somewhat less nationalistic than de Gaulle. The growing political independence West Germany exhibited, combined with the country's economic strength, increased France's need to be able to counterbalance the German influence within the EC. Moreover, the then British government under Edward Heath was the most pro-European government Britain had had.

There were several reasons why the British had re-evaluated their stance, from choosing to remain outside the EEC at first, to then applying for membership and finally to working more actively to become a member of the EC. In the long run Britain did not manage to sustain what the British loved to call their 'special relationship' with the United States. Washington did not consider it either desirable or necessary to have a mediator in its contacts with continental Europe, especially not when British influence was dwindling, while French and German influence was growing. London's long-standing relations with the British Commonwealth became less significant as well. Trade with continental Europe was growing much more rapidly than with the Commonwealth. The new countries of Africa and Asia were only mildly interested in following Britain's lead in political and economic matters. The Commonwealth became an increasingly loosely knit organization.

Nor could building up EFTA as a counterweight to the EC succeed. EFTA was too randomly composed. The political and economic center of Europe was located on the continent. If Britain was to play a role in world politics once more, and, not least, attain economic growth on a level with the other countries of Europe, membership of the EC seemed to be their only option.

In the final analysis, Britain's membership in the EC reflected the country's declining position not only politically, but economically as well. As late as 1950 the British economy was still the third largest in the world. During the course of the 1950s it was surpassed first by West Germany, then by Japan and France. This relative decline in fact persisted after Britain joined the EC. By the end of the 1980s the Italian economy had also outstripped the British.

Explanations for the US Stance

It can be argued that in terms of power politics it would have been much better for the United States to establish ties with the European countries individually rather than through European unity. How then can the strong US emphasis on European integration be explained?

In the 1940s and 1950s, it was largely assumed in Washington, as in most of the European capitals, that the United States and Western Europe would have similar, if not identical, interests in most matters of any significance. Of greatest importance in this context was their shared attitude towards the Soviet Union and communism. Cooperation in Europe would strengthen the entire 'free world.'

The problem of Germany greatly influenced the US stance. It was important that Germany be drawn into international politics, both in the joint front against the Soviet Union and in the reconstruction of and further growth in Western Europe. West Germany would have to become independent but not be granted complete freedom. Integration was to grant Germany equal status with other countries and take into consideration Europe's need for German resources, while minimizing the danger of German nationalism.

The Americans also considered themselves and their own course of development a natural model for others. In the United States, the growth of a large market had resulted in the highest standard of living in the world. The Europeans would have to be willing to tear down trade barriers if they wanted rapid economic growth. Many Americans even drew a parallel with the United States of some 200 years ago. As originally separate states had grown together into the United States, the same process should take place in Europe.

The traditional American isolationism had died. However, there were still remnants of isolationist tendencies, especially within the right wing of the Republican party. For instance, former President Herbert Hoover and Senator Robert Taft wanted to reduce the US role in Europe economically and militarily. This could more easily be accomplished if the Europeans cooperated to assume the responsibilities the Americans now had to fulfill against the wishes of the right wing. Although Eisenhower's foreign policy was far from that of Hoover and Taft, he shared their overall view of the need to exercise restraint in the use of US resources.

The general assessment of the Truman and Eisenhower administrations was that supporting European integration was desirable despite the disadvantages this might entail for US trade. It was expected that the combination of common external tariff barriers and the abolition of internal trade restrictions would result in increased inter-European trade, at the partial expense of trade with countries from outside the region. To a great extent, this proved to be the case. From 1958 to 1967, trade among the EEC countries was doubled, measured as a percentage of their total trade.

However, even this type of shift could have positive side effects seen from a US perspective. The alternative could well have been that the United States would have had to continue to subsidize Western Europe by paying these countries' dollar deficits. Washington made it plain as early as 1947–48 that there was no chance of such a subsidy after the four-year period of the Marshall Plan ended.

Nor did initial US willingness to bear the anticipated economic consequences prevent the Americans from attempting to secure certain economic benefits. European cooperation was first and foremost to be adapted to a wider international – particularly Atlantic – framework. But in addition there were a number of conditions, especially in the Marshall Plan, that directly promoted US interests, for instance within agriculture and shipping. Moreover, as time passed it became evident that with the rapid economic growth in Europe, US–European trade increased as well, although this increase was much smaller than for trade within Europe.

Friction gradually developed in relations between the United States and several of the Western European countries. This friction in turn contributed to the United States becoming ever more concerned that cooperation in Europe should not weaken the position of NATO. Nor should it discriminate against US trade interests. The United States was no longer as willing to assume an economic burden in order to promote over-riding political objectives. Finally, Europe's economic situation was entirely different from what it had been during the reconstruction years just after the Second World War. The breakthrough for a new US policy came in 1971 (see pp. 166–8).

US-EUROPEAN RELATIONS, 1950-1973

Cooperation Prior to 1962

Through its support for European integration, the United States to some extent encouraged arrangements that could limit US influence in Western Europe. The Western Europeans, on the other hand, were still interested in increasing the US pres-ence in many fields, although the main pattern was established by around 1950. This showed that the 1950s were characterized by good relations between these two parts of the world.

For the most part, the United States and Western Europe had a shared assessment of the threat the Soviet Union represented. The Americans needed the Europeans, and the Western Europeans needed the Americans just as much. The US nuclear guarantee and US troops in West Germany were the central elements in NATO's policy of deterrence. US military assistance to Europe was substantial. From 1950 to 1959 it amounted to 13.7 billion dollars.

Western Europe was not only dependent on military support from the United States. Economic assistance was still significant, although it was in the process of being reduced. Washington had insisted at first that Europe should stand on its own feet when the Marshall Plan ended in 1951–52. But assistance was given to some countries even after that, to a total value of approximately three billion dollars from the time the plan ceased until 1960. In addition, most of the Western European countries made active efforts to attract US investment.

In 1961, the OEEC, originally established to administer the Marshall Plan, was restructured as the Organization for Economic Cooperation and Development (OECD). The United States and Canada became full members, and the objective was to link the two sides of the Atlantic more closely together. They were also to cooperate on matters outside the Atlantic region, such as aid to developing countries.

Throughout the postwar period, the Americans had been concerned with reducing trade restrictions in general, especially across the Atlantic. In that way, the disadvantages of remaining outside a common European market could be reduced. Through five rounds of negotiations within GATT, the barriers were reduced. Throughout this pro-cess, the initiative was taken by the United States, which made major concessions in order to attain a successful result.

For a long time, US and European politics were dominated by leaders who were marked by the fellowship that was created during the Second World War and through the establishment of the Marshall Plan and NATO. Close friendships devel-oped between Acheson and Bevin, Eisenhower and Churchill, Dulles and Adenauer.

The relationship between the considerably younger Kennedy and Macmillan was also warm, although time would show that to a great extent the close personal ties were linked to one particular generation.

Relations across the Atlantic were probably strengthened by the conservatism that was the strongest political movement in the 1950s, both in the United States and in Western Europe. The elections in Italy in 1948, in Britain in 1950–51, in France in 1951, in the United States in 1952, and in West Germany in 1953 all signaled a period of conservative dominance and a decline for the more radical parties. Even so, in many ways the popularity of the United States in Western Europe reached its peak during Kennedy's brief presidency and then subsequently declined.

Even during this period, there were shades of difference in US and Western European attitudes towards the Soviet Union. Thus in 1953 Churchill was more eager than Eisenhower to exploit the possibilities for détente that might present themselves after Stalin's death. Likewise, later in the 1950s the British governments of Anthony Eden and Harold Macmillan tried to ease the strained relations between East and West. From the end of the 1950s and the early 1960s, the Europeans would generally be more interested than the Americans in increasing trade with the Soviet Union and Eastern Europe. West Germany was no exception in this respect.

However, there was no doubt that US relations with the Soviet Union were also strengthened in the course of the 1950s. Perhaps most importantly, attitudes varied considerably both among and within the various countries of Western Europe, so that on many occasions Washington was more willing to negotiate than several of the European capitals were.

The Germans consistently pressed for German unification as the first item on any East–West agenda. Towards the end of the Eisenhower administration and particularly under Kennedy, the Americans considered the German stance both unrealistic and negative. The fact that the US position was often in the middle, in addition to US military and economic superiority, strengthened the leadership of the country within the Western world.

There were only slight differences between the United States and the European countries with regard to their attitudes towards the Soviet Union. Other issues would cause greater tension across the Atlantic during the 1950s, although there were seldom dramatic differences nor a truly unified European perspective.

The most important controversy in Europe was German rearmament. From September 1950 onwards, the United States insisted that West Germany had to find its place within the Western military cooperation. France was naturally highly skeptical, whereas the other NATO countries, more or less reluctantly, were prepared to follow the United States in this matter. When the French government under Prime Minister René Pleven proposed in October 1950 that rearmament should take place within the framework of an integrated European army, the Americans supported this plan. But when France hesitated to ratify the treaty for a European army, Paris was subject to strong pressure from Washington, without that preventing the national assembly from rejecting the proposal in 1954. In 1955, West Germany was granted direct membership in NATO instead.

Differences of opinion between the United States and Western Europe were more numerous with regard to issues outside Europe, but even here most of the differences were limited in scope. Britain, followed by certain other Western European countries, recognized communist China. The United States did not. The Europeans supported the basic outlines of US policy during the Korean War, but the nuances that existed indicated that many Europeans were more cautious: they dissociated themselves from even threats of the use of nuclear weapons and evidenced greater understanding for Chinese wishes. Many European governments were skeptical of the growing US support to Chiang Kai-shek on Taiwan in the course of the 1950s.

During the Indochina crisis of 1954 as well, most Europeans were more hesitant than the Eisenhower administration, with the partial exception of the French, who wavered between the desire for a military victory, on the one hand, and the need for a complete withdrawal, on the other hand (see pp. 50–1). Under Eisenhower and Dulles, the Americans could be sharper in their denunciation of neutral governments, such as that of India, than most Europeans were.

Even so, there were clear instances in which the United States evidenced a more moderate stance towards radical regimes in the Third World than Western Europe did. Most striking was the Suez conflict in 1956, perhaps the most important controversy between Washington, on the one hand, and Paris and London, on the other, during the 1950s. Before the Israeli–British–French invasion of Egypt, the policy of the Americans was rather unclear: after the invasion, Eisenhower applied political and economic pressure to bring it to a halt as quickly as possible. The humiliating British–French retreat undoubtedly contributed to the rise of anti-American sentiments in certain segments of the population, especially in France. (For US–European differences on colonial issues, see also pp. 229–30.)

Political and Military Controversy, 1962–1973

In the 1960s it became increasingly evident that the premise that in many ways had been the foundation for US policy towards Europe – the assumption that the United States and Western Europe had coinciding interests on most of the important issues – could no longer be taken for granted.

Several attempts were made to absorb and adjust to the great changes that had taken place between and within the two regions. Europe would have to attain greater influence, and the growing European cooperation would have to be more firmly incorporated in the Atlantic framework. However, these attempts could not prevent the transatlantic cooperation from beginning to crack.

The first major reform proposal was Kennedy's program for 'Atlantic interdependence,' which he proclaimed in a speech on US Independence Day, 4 July 1962:

> I will say here and now, on this Day of Independence, that the United States will be ready for a declaration of interdependence, that we will be prepared to discuss with a United Europe the ways and means of forming a concrete Atlantic partnership, a mutually beneficial partnership between the new union now emerging in Europe and the old Union founded here 173 years ago.

Militarily and politically, little came of Kennedy's Atlantic partnership. There was no unified Europe for the United States to cooperate with. Britain did not join the EEC, an important condition for Kennedy's plan. De Gaulle was preoccupied with limiting French policy towards the United States.

In fact, there were strong elements of French independence even before de Gaulle. During the first postwar years, France had pursued a separate policy on the German question, in which Paris advocated a weakest possible Germany (see p. 26). However, the rapidly increasing tension in the Cold War and US–British concessions with regard to the Saar region contributed to drawing France into the Western cooperation. As early as 1948–49, the French government first aired the idea that the Western military alliance should be led by a triumvirate consisting of the United States, Britain, and France. Preparations for an independent French nuclear force were proceeding before de Gaulle assumed power in 1958.

Only gradually did de Gaulle's policies become more independent of US policies. For a long time the French president was at least as harsh in his anti-communism as Washington was. He advocated firm policies both in Berlin and during the Cuban crisis in 1962 and was concerned about combating Soviet influence in Africa, especially in Algeria.

Until de Gaulle's veto of British membership in the EEC in 1963, the French showed their independence primarily by emphasizing anew the old triumvirate plans and by withdrawing the French Mediterranean fleet from NATO control. In 1963, the Atlantic fleet was withdrawn from NATO control as well, and in 1966 France withdrew entirely from NATO's military program, although the country remained a member of NATO and kept its troops in West Germany. Criticism of the United States increased sharply, and Britain continued to be kept out of the EEC in part to limit Anglo-American influence in Western Europe. Relations with the Soviet Union and the Eastern European countries were expanded, and France soon became the Western country with the best political contacts with the East.

For a long time de Gaulle was isolated in Western Europe in his attitude towards the East–West conflict and the two superpowers. Towards the close of the 1960s, however, the attitudes of the European countries began to change, and the desire for détente with the Soviet Union was more clearly formulated throughout most of Western Europe.

This increased Western European independence can primarily be linked to two circumstances: the Vietnam War and the new German policy towards the Eastern bloc. Criticism of US warfare in Vietnam was harshest in France and in some of the smaller European countries. But even in Britain and West Germany such criticism was growing under the official surface of agreement with Washington.

In 1963, after de Gaulle had vetoed British membership in the EEC and de Gaulle and Adenauer had followed this up by signing a treaty promoting Franco-German cooperation, President Kennedy forced the Germans to dilute the treaty by affirming the primacy of NATO. Moreover, West Germany had to cancel its plans to contribute to an oil pipeline from the Soviet Union.

Even more importantly, West Germany abandoned its tough stance vis-à-vis the Soviet Union and Eastern Europe. The first signs of a more flexible eastern policy had been apparent before Adenauer's term expired in 1963, but at that time there was much talk of reluctantly adjusting to new signals from Washington. The breakthrough came in two stages, first under Kiesinger and Brandt's coalition government (1966–69) and then in earnest under Brandt and Scheel in the years following 1969. The German *Ostpolitik* paralleled the general movement towards détente, but Nixon and Kissinger were still uneasy about the independence of the initiative, the pace and the way in which *Ostpolitik* was practiced (see pp. 69–70). In the military sphere, more and more of the burden of conventional defense was borne by West Germany, with the political consequences this entailed. An imbalance could easily arise between West Germany's military and economic strength, on the one hand, and on the other hand, the fact that the country – in contrast to Britain and France – did not have nuclear weapons.

This was part of the background for plans for a multilateral nuclear force (MLF) within NATO. The initiative originally came from experts on Europe in the US State Department as early as during the Eisenhower administration. The plans were then developed further in a number of variations under Kennedy, and now the West Germans became more and more interested. Even though the United States was still to have control over the nuclear weapons, at least the guidelines for their use were to be drawn up by the member countries, and manning and financing the vessels the force was to consist of was to be multilateral. West Germany was to acquire a say in NATO's nuclear policy, without the country actually having a finger on the button, at least not in the foreseeable future.

However, from the turn of the year 1964–65 the plans for a multilateral nuclear force faded into the background. Secretary of Defense Robert McNamara showed little interest in the idea. Congress grew ever more skeptical. Many policy-makers both in the United States and in Western Europe felt that the entire scheme was too complicated. Britain and France feared that a joint force would entail pressure on their own more independent nuclear forces. The Soviet Union was opposed to anything that could give West Germany a say in nuclear policy.

Instead of MLF, a nuclear planning group was established within NATO that was to give the Western Europeans greater insight into and perhaps a greater influence on US nuclear planning. It did reestablish a calmer atmosphere concerning the role of nuclear weapons, but the entire process had probably worsened rather than improved the Atlantic climate. Even so, the main differences of opinion regarding MLF were among the European countries, not between the United States, on the one hand, and Western Europe, on the other.

However, when it came to changing NATO's strategy from massive retaliation to flexible response (see pp. 136–7), the differences were greatest between the two sides of the Atlantic. The Western Europeans were basically satisfied with the strategy of massive retaliation. This strategy linked the United States firmly to the countries of Western Europe while demanding little of them. In 1967, flexible response was formally accepted by NATO nonetheless, without any major changes on the part of the Europeans. This was similar to what had happened after the Lisbon meeting in 1952: ambitious plans for contributions to conventional defense, but few concrete results.

Washington applied pressure to get the Europeans to assume a larger share of NATO's defense expenses. In 1960, the United States bore 74 per cent of the alliance's total expenditure. Here, too, the Americans accomplished little during the 1960s. The US share was just as high in 1970 as it had been ten years earlier (expenditure in Vietnam not excluded). On several occasions, however, West Germany increased the compensation paid for the US troops stationed there. Partly to limit US criticism, the European members of NATO (with the exception of France, Iceland, and Portugal) established a EURO-group within the alliance in 1968 for the purpose of strengthening and coordinating the European contribution.

There were strong US reactions against Europe's insufficient willingness to contribute more to its own defense, especially in the Congress. Western Europe had the economic strength to do far more than previously. A large number of US forces were tied up in Vietnam. In 1968, most of a US division was withdrawn from Europe.

The pressure for Western Europe to pay more for NATO defense increased in 1970–71 and culminated in 1973. The Nixon administration found itself in a difficult position between Congress and Western Europe. On this issue, however, the difficulties were solved surprisingly easily, at least for the moment. In part, the Western Europeans assumed more of the cost, so that the US share had declined to 60 per cent by 1975. (This decline was also due to the phase-out of the Vietnam War and a new exchange rate on the dollar.) In part, the West Germans again increased their compensation for the US forces stationed in the country. Finally, Brezhnev helped the situation by agreeing to start negotiations on mutual force reductions in Europe.

While the United States had initially been skeptical of many European colonial engagements, in the light of decolonization, Vietnam, and the overall burden-sharing of expenses in containing communism, Washington came to support the British presence in Asia. So, when in 1967 the Labour government under Harold Wilson decided to withdraw all British forces east of Suez, with the exception of those in Hong Kong, this was disliked in the American capital. Still the policy was confirmed by Edward Heath when the Conservatives came to power in 1970.

Economic Relations, 1962–1973

The controversies between the United States and Europe were due in large part to the changes that had taken place in the relative economic strengths of the two parts of the alliance. Just after the Second World War, the United States alone was responsible for almost half of the world's production. This share was bound to sink as the razed countries were rebuilt after the war. However, the decline continued even after reconstruction. In 1960 the US share had sunk to about 30 per cent. From the moment Britain joined the EC, the total GNP of the EC was just as great as that of the United States, at least if measured in market prices.

One of the results of these economic realities was that US assistance to Western Europe gradually ceased. The economic assistance had been discontinued at the end of the 1950s. In the course of the 1960s, the program of military assistance was also phased out. The purely economic advantages that Western Europe enjoyed through cooperation with the United States were reduced.

Kennedy's plans for 'two pillar' cooperation between the United States and Western Europe failed in the political and military spheres. However, better results were achieved in the economic sphere. The Kennedy Round, the sixth in the series of tariff negotiations within GATT, was the most important event. The participating countries together represented 75 per cent of total world trade. In 1967, these negotiations resulted in major reductions in tariff rates. Two-thirds of the reductions on tariffs for industrial goods were of the order of 50 per cent or more. Tariff duties on such products in the United States, Western Europe, and Japan were now approximately 10 per cent. However, little was accomplished with regard to agricultural trade.

The EEC had negotiated as a single entity during the Kennedy Round. This was a victory for European integration. The liberalization that resulted from the negotiations could be said to be a victory for the philosophy of Atlantic cooperation, although GATT comprised many more countries than the United States and the Western European nations.

The dollar was the most important international currency. It was for Western economic cooperation what nuclear weapons were for military cooperation. More than three-fourths of the trade among non-communist countries and of the central banks' reserves was in dollars. In the course of 1967–68, however, the most important currencies – the dollar, the pound, the franc, and the mark – all experienced crises, demonstrating that the foreign exchange market was not effectively under control.

In 1969, a system of special drawing rights (SDR) was established to try to stabilize the market. In a longer perspective, SDR could possibly replace the dollar as the most important currency unit. The new value of currencies was not to be controlled by the United States alone, but by a group consisting of the ten most important industrialized countries within the International Monetary Fund.

In many ways the negotiations during the Kennedy Round and the agreement on SDR represented a climax of the postwar period in terms of Western cooperation on trade and currency. US imports from what later became the nine EC countries rose sharply during the 1960s, in both absolute and relative figures. US exports to the same countries also increased. Both imports and exports represented about 25 per cent of the total US figures in 1968. Most dramatic were the changes with regard to US investments in Western Europe. Their value rose from approximately 4 billion dollars in 1957 to approximately 24 billion in 1970, or from 15 to 30 per cent of total US foreign investments. All in all, the United States became more dependent on the outside world economically than it had been previously, although foreign trade was still less significant for the United States than for nearly all the other industrialized countries.

Even so, the signals of a new and more difficult era were strong even at this stage. After 1968 the volume of US imports from Western Europe initially declined, while exports to Western Europe were better sustained. Western Europe's trade with the rest of the world, and not least the EC countries' trade with each other, increased much more rapidly than trade with the United States. On the part of the United States, the Pacific region became increasingly interesting during the course of the 1970s.

In 1962–66, the EEC had reached agreement on an agricultural policy that was clearly protectionist, particularly in relation to the United States. US exports of the goods the Europeans protected fell dramatically. The EEC's various preference agreements with countries outside Europe created new problems. An enlargement of the EEC would have political advantages, but economically the discrimination against the United States would be extended further. In Asia, Japan's flourishing economy and new status as an economic superpower caused major adjustment problems for the international trade system.

The United States had long struggled with a deficit balance of payments, largely as a result of the military and economic commitments Washington had assumed. In 1971, the country experienced a trade deficit as well for the first time since 1883.

This was mainly due to the large deficit in trade with Japan, but in the following year even the United States' traditional trade surplus in relation to Western Europe was changed to a deficit.

The complicated SDR system proved not to be a success. The foreign exchange market was still not under effective control. The dollar remained the currency all the others were measured against, and the Europeans became increasingly irritated at being tied to a currency they did not have the slightest control over.

The many and complicated economic problems of the United States diminished Washington's willingness to sustain its internationally oriented economic policy. The measures of the Nixon administration in August 1971 represented a breakthrough in that respect. The convertibility of the dollar vis-à-vis gold was abolished, and a 10 per cent import duty was levied on all dutiable goods. When this duty was removed shortly thereafter, the United States devalued the dollar. International exchange rates were allowed to float. Washington also demanded changes in the EC's agricultural policies and in the organization's general preference system. Here, however, little was achieved. All in all, the new policy could be said to signal the collapse of parts of the Bretton Woods system as it had been established in 1945.

THE UNITED STATES AND WESTERN EUROPE AFTER 1973: NEW TENSIONS

Expansion and Integration of the EC/EU

The most significant expansion of the EC took place in 1973, when the United Kingdom, Denmark, and Ireland all joined. In the UK and Denmark there were substantial groups which continued to oppose membership. When Labour came to power in Britain in 1974, the Wilson government renegotiated the conditions. After the EC had accepted minor changes, the party leadership sanctioned membership, which was then approved in a referendum. Britain's unrelenting struggle against the financing arrangements, which resulted in a number of crises, was not resolved until 1984. Following a new referendum in Denmark in 1986, sentiments calmed down somewhat there as well. In reality, once a country had joined the EC, membership entailed economic ties that made it virtually impossible to withdraw again.

As a result of the 1973 expansion, even more countries wanted to join the EC. Following many years of negotiations, Greece became the tenth member in 1981, and in 1986 Spain and Portugal were admitted as the eleventh and twelfth member states.

It would be reasonable to expect that the geographic expansion of the EC would obstruct efforts to increase the degree of integration. Britain and Denmark in particular were skeptical of political supranationality and all the new members tended to be interested first and foremost in the economic advantages of membership. This view was expressed clearly in the UK during Margaret Thatcher's many years as prime minister, from 1979 to 1990, although she too was prepared to make greater concessions in practical politics than her rhetoric might have seemed to indicate.

In fact, EC cooperation was extended significantly. Ever since the German–French treaty of 1963, the initiative in the EC had been located largely along the Paris–Bonn axis. In many ways France and Germany were the driving forces behind European cooperation. This was particularly the case under Valéry Giscard d'Estaing and Helmut Schmidt from 1974 to 1981, but the German–French cooperation continued in the 1980s under François Mitterrand and Helmut Kohl. The Benelux countries and Italy also subscribed to the view that expanding the EC should not entail the end of efforts to enhance the substance of European cooperation.

At the meeting in The Hague in December 1969, the EC countries laid the foundation for an expansion of the EC. At the same time they tried to pave the way for increased economic and political cooperation. Monetary cooperation had long been an objective of the EC, but an attempt in 1972 to design a joint fluctuation margin within the new international floating currency system did not succeed. However, in 1978 Schmidt and d'Estaing agreed on the framework for a European Monetary System (EMS). Although the UK was only loosely linked to this system until 1990, it represented a crucial step nevertheless along the path to monetary cooperation.

The European political cooperation which was established in 1970 also arose from a French–German joint initiative. This was an attempt to coordinate the foreign policy stances of the EC member countries. Such coordination was to be achieved primarily through regular meetings of the foreign ministers. In 1974 this cooperation was elevated to a higher level by the establishment of the European Council, which consists of the heads of state of the member countries and the president of the European Commission.

In many ways, 1975 was a year of breakthrough for European political cooperation. At the Conference on Security and Cooperation in Europe in Helsinki, the EC position was presented by a joint spokesman. At the vast international conference in Paris on economic cooperation between North and South (CIEC), the EC had joint representation for the first time. The Lomé agreement between the EC and 46 developing countries was also signed in 1975. In 1979 it was renewed and extended, this time with 58 developing countries.

In a number of areas the EC countries proved capable of promoting views that were, if not jointly held, at least coordinated. This was particularly true in relation to the Middle East. There was an increasing degree of coordination among EC countries at the UN. It was substantially more difficult to attain such coordination vis-à-vis NATO, particularly because France did not participate in the military aspect of the alliance and Ireland was not a member of NATO.

In December 1985, the Single European Act was launched. Its objective was to achieve greater integration within the EC in three ways. In the first place, an internal market was to be realized by the end of 1992. This internal market would be an area without boundaries, within which the free movement of goods, persons, services, and capital would be ensured. In the second place, the Single European Act was a treaty formalizing European political cooperation and establishing new areas of cooperation such as environmental protection, research and development, and social reforms. Finally, the Single European Act opened up increased use of majority decisions to ensure the implementation of the internal market, modifying the veto right of the member countries. All in all, the Single European Act was the most significant formal agreement to be concluded within the EC since the founding Treaty of Rome in 1957.

On the institutional level, the European Commission played a prominent role, but the most important decisions were still made at the ministerial meetings. In 1979 the first direct elections for the European Parliament were held, but the position of the

Parliament within the EC system was still fairly weak. Outside the EC several attempts were made, particularly by the French, to strengthen the Western European Union as a body for cooperation in the sphere of foreign policy and security policy, without attaining any concrete results.

In December 1990 the EC embarked upon its most extensive revision since its establishment in 1957. At a meeting in Maastricht, the Netherlands, in December 1991 the EC decided to institute the European Union (EU). The EU was to be based on three pillars, the most important of which was still the traditional economic cooperation. The aim was to implement an Economic and Monetary Union (EMU) by 1999 with a common currency and a joint central bank for all the member countries. The other two pillars were foreign and security policy and legal cooperation. The Maastricht treaty even proclaimed the establishment of a joint foreign and security policy. The member countries intended to coordinate their foreign policies to the greatest possible extent. With free movement of goods and services, capital and labor across national boundaries a need arose for joint control of criminals, terrorists, narcotics, etc. This was the background for cooperation within the legal pillar. A joint police force (Europol) was established, and through the Schengen treaty most of the members of the EU agreed to do away with border controls between member nations.

Economic cooperation was to be governed by the traditional EU bodies, but with a further reduction in the member countries' veto rights. Within the other two pillars the Council of Ministers remained the key body, and this entity was based on independent nations with little or no supranationality. The foreign policy dimension largely represented an intensification of the previous cooperation.

The traditional cooperation within the EU had gradually won widespread support in the member countries. However, the Maastricht treaty was controversial in many countries. A referendum in France resulted in a slim majority in favor of Maastricht, and in Denmark two referendums had to be held even though Denmark, like the UK, had exemptions in relation to certain aspects of the treaty.

The end of the Cold War made it easier for neutral countries to approach the EC/EU. The integration of the EU made it more difficult to remain outside economically, although the establishment of the 'European Economic Area' (EEA) in 1992 increased integration between the EC and EFTA considerably. As a result, Austria, Sweden, and Finland joined the EU from 1995, while Switzerland and Norway decided to reject membership following referendums. Thus the EU still managed to combine policy deepening with geographic widening.

The success in combining deepening and widening seemed to continue in the late 1990s. On the widening side, virtually all the countries of what had been Eastern Europe wanted to join the EU as well as NATO. So did Mediterranean countries such as Cyprus and Turkey. Turkey faced special problems because of its human rights record and the 1974 occupation of northern Cyprus.

On the deepening side, at first the efforts to establish the Economic and Monetary Union seemed to face almost insuperable hurdles. In 1992, in fact, the UK and Italy found it necessary to withdraw even from the European Monetary System, and Spain devalued its currency. France postponed its participation in the Schengen cooperation. Yet, a few years later most of the EU countries initiated relatively drastic policies with the aim of meeting the rather ambitious economic criteria laid down in Maastricht for the establishment of EMU. To the surprise of many observers, virtually all of them made such progress that 11 of the 15 member countries joined EMU when it was formally established on 1 January 1999. Greece did not initially meet the criteria and Britain, Sweden, and Denmark, which met the criteria, did not want to join for political-economic reasons.

In the economic sphere the EU had proved to be a considerable success. Politically, however, cooperation was still based largely on the individual nation state. The Economic and Monetary Union applied substantial pressure to the nation state, but a European identity had not developed in the member countries. It remained to be seen how the EU would resolve these tensions.

From the Year of Europe to German Reunification

There had almost continually been some forms of disagreement within the Atlantic cooperation, but the differences had often been between the United States and perhaps only one of the European countries, especially France, or they had been linked to specific problems, such as the Suez crisis or the Vietnam War. At the close of the 1960s, differences of opinion began to appear between the United States, on the one hand, and most of the countries of Western Europe, on the other. This tendency would be somewhat reinforced during the 1970s and 1980s, although the Europeans continued to have problems in reaching joint positions.

Every president since Kennedy had accused his predecessor of having let relations with Western Europe decay. Kennedy's own plan for 'Atlantic interdependence' had been a success in one area at best: the economic sphere. Nixon and Kissinger's Year of Europe in 1973 was the next major initiative on the part of the Americans. The Year of Europe was an attempt to give allied cooperation primary importance after US diplomacy had long been concentrated on the Soviet Union, China, and Vietnam. As under Kennedy, these efforts were supposed to lead to a statement that would partly outline the foundation for the existing cooperation and partly bring new life to it.

The Year of Europe was not a success. The Nixon administration was so weakened by Vietnam and Watergate that its negotiating strength was minimal. 1973 was dominated by conflict in the Middle East and the subsequent oil crisis, resulting in new tensions across the Atlantic. Europe expressed a clearly more pro-Arab attitude than the United States did. Moreover, the French stood by their resolve and were still not interested in laying a new foundation for Atlantic cooperation.

The coordination of foreign policy within Western Europe did not contribute to reducing tension across the Atlantic. However, Carter felt that a change of president would improve relations. Now the US allies would finally receive at least as much attention as the country's adversaries. Consultations were to replace dramatic initiatives in US policy.

The Carter administration could not prevent new difficulties from developing in US–European relations. The most important concrete controversy concerned the deployment of neutron weapons in Western Europe. Carter did not want to effect deployment unless the European countries in question, Germany in particular, expressed a desire for the new weapon. The Western Europeans would have preferred the United States to assume the responsibility for such a controversial decision.

The entire matter was postponed and died out. Neither the decision itself nor even less the process leading up to it strengthened Atlantic unity.

The economic problems between the United States and Western Europe merely continued to grow. The international recession in the 1970s reinforced the difficulties, as protectionism and the subsidizing of industries in difficulties, such as the steel industry, showed. In 1979, the so-called Tokyo Round within GATT was completed after more than six years of negotiations. A certain degree of further liberalization was achieved for trade in industrial products, but despite the lofty phrases in other areas the actual results were small. The discussion between the United States and Western Europe concerning the agricultural policies of the EC became ever sharper, especially as both sides tried to solve their surplus problems through exports.

The rate of economic growth in Western Europe was now lower than in the United States. In contrast, the Asian countries in the Pacific region still enjoyed substantial growth. US trade with these countries increased rapidly, in 1978 for the first time becoming greater than trade across the Atlantic. Economic interdependence between the Western countries became stronger, but international control had diminished. No single organization could assume the leadership role the United States had previously exercised.

After Carter's vacillation, Reagan wanted to re-create unity through firm leadership. 'The free world' was to be unified under American leadership against the communist threat. Defense was to be strengthened substantially and contacts with the Soviet Union reduced (see pp. 97–9). However, the traditional system based on US leadership could not be re-established. The Reagan administration lacked the necessary insight. Even more important was the fact that the United States no longer held the same leading position and, partly for that reason, was not willing to make the generous contributions that had helped sustain the previous order.

When the United States at the end of the Carter administration and particularly under Reagan shifted to a harsher policy towards the Soviet Union, it was only partially followed by Western Europe. Even the conservative governments in Britain and West Germany favored maintaining a greater degree of contact with the Soviet Union and also placed greater emphasis on negotiations for arms control than the United States did. An example of the altered relations was the fact that whereas Washington had managed to persuade Bonn to halt the gas pipeline deal with Moscow in 1963, not only Bonn, but London and Paris as well refused to give in to similar requests in 1982–83. Most of the Western European governments were also skeptical about the Reagan administration's aggressive policy towards the Third World as expressed in the Reagan Doctrine.

When the Reagan administration assumed a course of greater cooperation with the Soviet Union in 1984–85, US policy and Western European policy were more in line once again. On the whole, relations between the United States and Western Europe were quite good during the second Reagan administration. However, Reagan's new policy could also pose problems. This was most clearly illustrated at the summit in Reykjavik (see p. 103). The more conservative wing in Europe was appalled that Reagan was apparently prepared to take dramatic strides in doing away with nuclear weapons. The left was disappointed that he remained steadfast on the issue of the Strategic Defense Initiative. And most of the European leaders were shocked that such major changes in US nuclear policy could be discussed with Moscow without their being consulted in advance.

In the economic sphere, the Single European Act of 1985 brought new life to the EC. In the course of a short period of time, references to 'Eurosclerosis' – the concept that economic growth was in the process of being strangled by various institutional problems – were replaced by a new optimism. The United States had traditionally supported European integration and continued to do so on one level, but the country had substantial economic interests to maintain in relation to a more unified and dynamic Western Europe. Agricultural policy had long been a difficult area between the US and Western Europe, but Washington now pointed out in more general terms that 'the establishment of a common market that reserves Europe for the Europeans would be detrimental for Europe, the United States and the multilateral economic system.'

The climate of cooperation between the United States and Western Europe improved under the first Bush administration. In the political sphere, Washington and most of the European capitals had fairly similar views on developments in the Soviet Union, although the Bush administration was relatively reserved for some time with regard to economic assistance. Margaret Thatcher gave great priority to close relations with the US, though not with quite the same success under the Bush administration as under Reagan. George Bush expressed strong support for Helmut Kohl's policy of German unification, a fact which strengthened relations between the US and Germany. Nearly all of the Western European countries supported the US stance on the conflict between Iraq and Kuwait, although Washington wanted even stronger support in both economic and military terms as well as politically. In terms of the economic situation, the US stance on the internal market became more relaxed as signals were given that this market would pursue a relatively open policy in relation to the outside world.

During the period from 1870 to 1945, the German question had been one of the most central issues, or for many even the most central issue, of international politics. Both world wars were fought to keep Germany from dominating the European continent. This problem was solved in 1945–49 by the division of Germany. 'The German problem' in the postwar era arose from this division of Germany, but the division was primarily a problem for the Germans themselves. For the major powers and for Germany's neighbors it was largely considered an advantage. The Berlin Wall in 1961, Brandt's *Ostpolitik*, and the Helsinki Declaration of 1975 represented the de facto, if not the formal, recognition of the existence of two German states.

In 1989–90, in the course of less than a year, this situation was changed entirely. The liberalization of Poland and Hungary during the summer and autumn of 1989 placed pressure on the East German authorities (see pp. 202–5). Its most concrete manifestation was when Hungary began to allow East Germans passage to West Germany. It became clear that Gorbachev would not intervene with military force in East Germany either. On the contrary, he encouraged Honecker and his successor Krenz to implement reforms when it became evident that the old regime was doomed.

On 9 November 1989 the Berlin Wall was opened, allowing for massive emigration from East Germany. On 28 November Kohl presented his ten-point plan for German unification. The aim was a German confederation, a loose union of East and West Germany to be developed over a number of years. The plan was considered dramatic, both in Germany and internationally, and it was presented without any prior discussion with the three Western powers. However, it was soon superseded by the actual events. By October 1990, unification was formally accomplished. 3 October became the new national holiday instead of 17 June, which had been the national holiday in West Germany (in memory of the revolt in East Germany in 1953). East Germany ceased to exist and was fully absorbed by West Germany. The five East German *Länder* were now on equal terms with the 11 *Länder* of West Germany.

The pace of developments was primarily determined by those who had been the weakest part throughout the entire postwar era: the people of East Germany. Once they were given the opportunity to decide, it became evident that they had few ties to the East German government in its various manifestations. Many East Germans moved to West Germany, and most of those who remained were in favor of swift and complete unification. At the elections in March 1990, the Christian Democrats, who were the strongest proponents of this course, received 48 per cent of the votes, emerging as the largest party. The pace of unification was further increased by the collapse of the East German economy. The old system disintegrated, in part because decisions were postponed pending unification. This, too, accelerated the process of unification beyond all expectation.

The United States strongly supported Kohl's strategy for unification. The UK and France had no choice but to follow the stream of events, although Thatcher in London and in part even Mitterrand in Paris disliked at least the tremendous pace of the process. The Soviet Union was definitely the most skeptical about unification, but the Soviets no longer had the will to stop the process. Moscow tried to ensure that a unified Germany would be neutral, but had to relinquish that objective as well. The new Germany became a member of NATO, but in the eastern part only limited German forces were to be stationed. The Soviet troops were to be withdrawn completely in the course of 1994. The weak negotiating position of the USSR meant that the most important result for Moscow after having dismantled 'the East German workers' and farmers' state' was substantial West German economic support. In addition, the Germans agreed to make major reductions in their armed forces.

West Germany was already the strongest power in Western Europe in economic terms. East Germany's production was equivalent to about 15 per cent of that of West Germany. Thus, a unified Germany was the indisputable economic leader of Europe. Politically, Germany had finally achieved formal independence, freed from the last restrictions from 1945. Germany's geographical location in the heart of Europe gave it a considerable advantage in political and strategic terms.

Even so, there was little reason to believe that a unified Germany would represent a power threat in the sense that Germany had in 1870–1945. In the first place, the country's relative position was still much weaker now than then, in terms of both territory and population. The Soviet Union/Russia and the United States in particular were both active in international politics in an entirely different way than during the previous period. In the second place, the new Germany would be integrated in the EC and NATO. Within the EC, the joint German economy was smaller than the sum of the British and the French economies. In the third place, the political attitudes in Germany were far more democratic now than they had been during the previous period. The unification of Germany in 1989–90 took place through 'words and money,' not 'blood and iron' as under Bismarck's rule. In terms of foreign policy, the newly united Germany was skeptical about taking on military commitments outside of NATO.

Politically it was surprisingly easy to incorporate Eastern Germany into Western Germany. Economically and not least psychologically, particularly for the citizens of East Germany, the rapprochement between the two segments was much slower. Even with the attention unification required on the domestic front, a unified Germany rapidly proved to be the key driving force within European integration. In fact, Kohl clearly thought that German unification made it essential for Germany to pursue further integration. In France, President François Mitterrand also concluded that unification necessitated new efforts at integration. Thus the reunification of East and West Germany became an important driving force behind the Maastricht treaty.

The US and the EU from Clinton to Donald Trump

When Bill Clinton assumed the office of president in 1993, he showed little interest in Europe initially. Europe was ostensibly to be given less priority in US foreign policy. However, the Clinton administration soon took an active interest in the new European 'architecture.' Clinton supported the policy integration that Maastricht and the EU represented. He also endorsed the geographic expansion of the EU from 12 to 15 member countries. When the United States was to reduce its foreign policy activity, it was considered advantageous that other friendly nations would play a correspondingly larger role.

However, the Clinton administration, too, was eager to fit European integration into a security policy and economic framework that ensured US interests. In the field of security policy nothing should be done that would weaken the overall significance of NATO. With Germany's support, the United States controlled the process of NATO enlargement. In economic terms, the effect of the EU was to be reduced through a continued liberalization of world trade. Thus, it was important that the 117 countries in GATT, led by the United States, the EU, and Japan, completed the Uruguay Round in December 1993. This meant a further reduction in tariff rates on industrial goods, and several service sectors and parts of agriculture were included in the liberalization process. GATT was replaced by a new and stronger organization, the World Trade Organization (WTO). However, once the WTO had been established, disagreement arose between the United States and the EU on how and to what extent the liberalization process should proceed.

The US contribution in the conflict in Bosnia during the autumn of 1995, and in Kosovo in 1998–99, showed that the United States, after some hesitancy, was now a key player even in the Balkans (see pp. 112–13). Thus the Clinton administration took on a much more active role in Europe than it had planned at the outset.

At the turn of the millennium, relations between Europe and the United States appeared to be better than they had been in several decades. There were several reasons for this rather surprising development. First, the end of the Cold War had initially created a great deal of uncertainty about this relationship. The Americans reduced the number of their troops in Europe to 100,000 and then even further, and the Europeans emphasized their greater independence. Soon, however, the unification of Germany, the unpredictable state of affairs in Russia, and, more than anything, the conflicts in the former Yugoslavia underlined Europe's continued dependence on the US. So, in a way, the European invitations to the Americans to stay in Europe had to be reissued, although in a distinctly modified form. The United States, for its part, realized how much its global position depended on close relations with Europe. Despite the many problems in relations between the US and Europe, Washington's closest and most reliable allies were to be found in Europe.

Second, as long as the supremacy of NATO was recognized, the Clinton administration was prepared to let the Europeans go quite far in setting up their own institutions. Even a common military policy within the EU could be accepted provided that the links to NATO were sufficiently strong. On their part, most European countries also had their special reasons for cooperating closely with the United States. Kohl's Germany was grateful for the strong American support for unification; Britain under John Major from 1990 and, even more, Tony Blair's leadership from 1997, again tried to strengthen its position through its 'special relationship' with the US; a more pragmatic France re-evaluated its position towards the United States and NATO in the wake of German unification, the Gulf war, and the war in Bosnia. Although France did not join NATO's integrated military structure as Jacques Chirac, president from 1995, had signaled it would at one stage, it did make a partial move in that direction, and the countries of Central Europe strongly wanted American military guarantees through NATO.

Among the major European powers, the greatest changes took place in Germany. There was an emerging normalization of foreign policy in the sense that Germany gradually shed some of its self-imposed restrictions. It began to participate in military operations outside NATO territory. Berlin sent peacekeeping forces to take part in monitoring of the peace treaty in Bosnia, and in the Kosovo conflict German military units were involved in direct combat for the first time. Helmut Kohl had become increasingly recognized as the leading European statesman, but in 1998 his 16 years as chancellor came to an end. After the elections the German Social Democrats formed the government with the support of the Greens, and with Gerhard Schroeder as the new chancellor. Serious allegations of corruption were raised against Kohl, if not personally, at least on behalf of his party, the Christian Democratic Union.

Third, despite the rapid growth in trade across the Pacific, trade across the Atlantic also increased. US investments were much larger in Europe than in Asia. Most Americans were still of European ancestry and felt closer to Europe than to most other parts of the world. American culture was still dominant in Europe.

However, there were distinct differences between the United States and the European countries. Clinton had originally intended to pursue a relatively multilateral foreign policy, based on cooperation with the UN, other international organizations, and US allies. For a country as large and self-assured as the United States, such a policy could easily become more explicit in rhetoric than in reality. The United States expected to be the leader of the world in any case, but the Republican dominance in the Congress after the 1994 elections helped place even greater emphasis on national interests. The United States refused to sign the convention to ban landmines; the Kyoto protocol to reduce the greenhouse effect was not saleable in US politics; the agreement to create an International Criminal Court (the ICC) was even less acceptable for many Americans; and a permanent agreement to ban all nuclear testing was rejected by the Congress.

Clinton was a master at convincing the European allies that he was indeed on their side, but that domestic policy considerations made it impossible to follow this up at all times. This would change dramatically when George W. Bush took office as president in January 2001. He made a point of emphasizing that US national interests would be paramount. The defense budget would be increased dramatically; a national missile defense system was assigned top priority; the United States appropriated the right to use preventive strikes against nations or groups perceived as a threat; the agreements rejected by Clinton were rejected by Bush as well, along with other measures that limited US freedom of action, and the rejection of the Kyoto protocol and the ICC was reiterated on stronger grounds of principle. If organizations such as the UN and even NATO did not follow US leadership, they would lose further sympathy and relevance. Now 'the mission should determine the coalition; the coalition should not determine the mission' (see pp. 117–18). There was to be an end to warfare by committee, as had ostensibly been the case during the war in Kosovo. Influential circles wanted to withdraw the US forces from the Balkans, but this was prevented by the more moderate members of the administration under the leadership of Secretary of State Colin Powell. The list of economic disputes between the United States and the EU, which had already become extensive during the Clinton years, became even lengthier under Bush. Various aspects of EU agricultural policy and US subsidies of domestic steel production were among the most critical conflicts.

Washington placed great emphasis on membership by the countries of Central and Eastern Europe in NATO. With their strong desire for US security guarantees, they could become close allies. In addition to Poland, Hungary, and the Czech Republic, which had joined NATO in 1999, the three Baltic countries plus Slovenia, Slovakia, Bulgaria, and Romania would become members in 2004. NATO would assume a more global role. EU security and defense policy would have to be adapted to NATO policies. Any mention of the EU as a counterbalance to US influence was rejected as hostile.

The EU in turn had achieved successes that increased its self-confidence considerably. The European economic and monetary union was complete from January 2002 when the new single currency, the euro, was put into circulation in 12 of the member states. (Greece had also qualified the previous year.) Objectives for joint military forces had been defined. In the course of 60 days, the EU would be able to deploy a force of 60,000 troops that could be operative for a year in an international conflict.

The terrorist attacks on New York and Washington on 11 September 2001 resulted in concerted support for the United States. For the first time, NATO invoked Article 5 of the NATO treaty. Even *Le Monde* declared that 'we are all Americans now.' Germany expressed a strong desire to take part in the war against Afghanistan. However, with a partial exception for the UK, the Bush administration made it clear that it did not see any need for the comprehensive military assistance offered by its European allies. Sympathy for the US cause helped ease the European disappointment arising from this decision.

After Afghanistan, the US focus was turned to Iraq. Influential circles in the Bush administration had long wanted to settle accounts with Saddam Hussein (pp. 118–19). The United Kingdom again expressed its support for US policy, not necessarily because the two countries agreed in all respects, but because Tony Blair himself was keenly involved in the war on terrorism and against weapons of mass destruction, and because

London believed it could best influence Washington through close cooperation. Ever since the adverse experience of the Suez crisis in 1956, the British had rejected any attempt to unify Europe against the United States. The relatively rapid economic growth in the UK during the past decade had boosted British self-confidence. Britain's GNP had now surpassed that of both France and Italy.

The British stance enjoyed considerable support among the governments of Italy, Spain and the smaller Atlantic-oriented allies, although none of them had plans for taking part in a war with more than largely symbolic forces. These countries also objected strongly to what France and Germany saw as their more or less obvious right to define what should be EU foreign policy. Under the leadership of Poland, most of the governments among the new and potential NATO allies in Eastern Europe also supported this view.

It was a major disappointment for the Bush administration that Turkey, which had strong military and economic ties with the US, ultimately decided not to let the United States attack Iraq from Turkey. It would simply be too dramatic for the Turkish government, which was dominated by committed Muslims, as well as for public opinion, which was highly critical of the United States. The disappointment in Washington was particularly profound because US involvement had been great in getting a NATO guarantee of support for Turkey in the event of an Iraqi attack, which had given rise to a serious crisis within NATO until a solution had been found that was accepted by France and Germany.

It gradually became evident that France would use its seat on the UN Security Council to veto a war led by the United States against Iraq unless the UN weapons inspectors had been given sufficient time to complete their work first. Germany assumed an even more uncompromising stance. Schroeder made it clear that Germany would not provide any direct support, whether military or economic, for a US war on Iraq. This was surprising in the light of the ostensible normalization that had been evidenced in German foreign policy in relation to Bosnia, Kosovo, and Afghanistan. This resolute stance appears to have helped Schroeder stay in power in Germany after the elections in September 2002. For the first time, a German election had been won based on opposition to the United States. The election results did not primarily reflect anti-American sentiments; they probably arose more from an anti-militarism that was more deeply rooted in the German population than many were aware of. However, this did not prevent Germany from soon having 10,000 troops stationed abroad, particularly in Afghanistan, on various peace-keeping missions. The Franco-German policy enjoyed the support of the governments of Belgium, Luxembourg, Greece, and most of the formerly neutral EU countries. Thus the EU was split right down the middle. Strikingly enough, public opinion in almost all the European countries was in support of the Franco-German policy. With a partial exception for the Vietnam War, such a massive difference of public opinion between the two sides of the Atlantic had never existed in the years after the Second World War.

This deep rift, and the combination of a highly successful American–British war against Saddam Hussein, and subsequent significant political and economic problems within Iraq, made both sides in the bitter transatlantic dispute interested in improving the climate of relations. The United States wanted to maintain its control over developments in Iraq, but it now called for both military contributions and economic help from its European allies. France and Germany in turn wanted to improve relations with the

Bush administration without making any concessions that their previous policy had been wrong. Thus they increased their participation in Afghanistan rather than in Iraq. Major differences therefore remained.

In the course of a few brief years, the two sides of the Atlantic had drifted apart substantially. The differences between Americans and Europeans had grown, even though they were toned down by support for the United States among several European governments. They were also tempered by the fact that Europe was still dependent on the US militarily. The attempts to establish a stronger defense among the countries of the EU had made significant progress on paper; the concrete increases in military capacity had been considerably smaller.

An underlying set of more long-range factors could help explain the dramatic strains on relations between the United States and Europe. The Cold War was over, and the new terror threat was not a similarly cohesive factor. Dominant forces on the two sides of the Atlantic had divergent views on how acute the threat was and how it should be countered. The United States had become more unilateralist, while the EU had become ever more determined to define its own identity – for many also vis-à-vis the United States. Work on a constitution for the EU progressed smoothly for a time, but in May–June 2005 the French and Dutch voters turned it down. Ten new member states would join the EU in 2004: Poland, Hungary, Slovenia, the Czech Republic, the Baltic countries of Estonia, Latvia and Lithuania, Slovakia, Cyprus (the Greek-Cypriotic part of the island), and Malta.

What had been known as the golden days of NATO had largely been based on cooperation primarily in Europe; outside Europe conflicts had often been more prominent than cooperation. Now Europe was stabilized, and practically all the serious international conflicts took place outside Europe. The economic disputes had gradually multiplied. Moreover, despite many attempts no new foundation for NATO cooperation – in line with the substantial changes that had taken place in the US and in Europe, and in relations between them – had been defined. Almost more clearly than ever before, the United States wanted to be recognized as the leader; at the same time the EU wanted greater influence more than ever.

After the Iraq war, at first the transatlantic rift seemed to widen further. Elections in Spain in April 2004 and in Italy in April 2006 brought left-of-center governments to power. The two countries then shifted from the pro-US to the pro-France and Germany camp. More important, however, elections in Germany and in France themselves led to victories for more pro-US parties. In the German elections in September 2005 Angela Merkel and the CDU won at the expense of Gerhard Schroeder and the SPD, although a coalition was formed between the two parties. The victory was narrow, but Merkel was determined to build bridges not only inside Germany, but also inside the EU and certainly also vis-à-vis the United States. Even more dramatic was Nicolas Sarkozy's victory in the presidential elections in France in May 2007 and then in the national assembly elections. Sarkozy was a conservative, but still a rebel who thought France was in great need of reform. He liked the United States, was pro-Israel and very skeptical of Iran. He wanted to improve relations with Washington a great deal and even promised to reintegrate France into NATO militarily, which he then proceeded to do in April 2009. In return he expected greater American sympathy for a stronger EU, and also in the security area. The EU could only become more united if it ended its many fights over relations with the United States.

These changes in Europe balanced the changes in the United States. George W. Bush was forced to conclude that his intervention in Iraq had met with great problems. The United States could not act more or less on its own. It needed allies. Its best allies were still found in Europe. Bush therefore spent much of his second term trying to repair the damage that had occurred during his first. In 2006 the Democrats won the Congressional election. That strengthened the need for change further.

Atlantic relations did not improve so much over Iraq. There the parties had made their positions just too explicit. The change was seen in Afghanistan, Iran, and North Korea. In Afghanistan, Washington wanted the NATO allies to increase their role. Most of them did, temporarily. On Iran the Bush administration left the initiative to the EU in trying to produce a diplomatic solution to the problem of that country's nuclear program. The military option was no longer so attractive. In North Korea the United States worked with China, Russia, Japan, and South Korea to end its nuclear program. Regime change was out; cooperation with allies was in.

The election of Barack Obama in November 2008 was greeted with loud applause all over Europe. The United States, which had been perceived as an increasingly conservative country, had elected a black president. The negative image of the US that had developed in most of Europe was transformed almost overnight. Theories about transatlantic rift were largely abandoned. The emphasis was now on cooperation. Yet, most of the difficult issues remained: Iraq, Afghanistan, North Korea, Pakistan, the Middle East. They were not easily solved, not even by the new miracle man in the White House. The United States was back in the driver's seat, although the Europeans expected to be widely consulted. And the roots of the conflicts were almost always local; the problems, therefore, were not easily resolved by outsiders, not even by Obama's United States.

The financial crisis after 2007–08 presented the EU with huge problems. Greece in particular, but also Spain, Italy, Portugal, and Ireland were close to collapsing under the debts of governments, banks, and individuals. In 2012–13 the crisis finally appeared to be under better control, although most of the EU countries, now including even Germany, experienced little or no growth. The economic crisis led to further integration in the EU. The banks had to be placed under tighter control, and even governments now had to clear their budgets with Brussels. Germany under Merkel was clearly in the lead, although cooperation with France, after May 2012 under Socialist president François Hollande who had defeated Sarkozy, remained desirable. The European Central Bank also played an increasingly important role.

The continued integration collided with a revival of skepticism of the EU in Britain. The Conservative party appreciated the single market, but disliked many other features of the EU. Not only was London opposed to further integration, but it also wanted to transfer certain powers back to the British government. Immigration from Eastern Europe became a more and more contentious issue. After the Conservative election victory in Britain in May 2015, Prime Minister Cameron had promised a referendum on EU membership in an effort to end the quarreling among Conservatives on this point. The referendum was held in June 2016 and to the surprise of most observers it ended in favor of British withdrawal from the EU: Brexit. As a result Cameron stepped down and Theresa May became the new Prime Minister. After more than 40 years as a member of the EU, Britain had decided to withdraw. Integration was no longer a one-directional issue. It would take years to sort out what the new relationship between Britain and the EU would be. To complicate matters further, Scotland and Northern Ireland wanted to maintain the existing close ties with the EU.

The United States and Europe continued to be important economic partners both on the trade and, particularly, on the investment side. The recession after 2008 re-emphasized the interdependence of the two continents. The recession had started in the United States, but quickly spread to Europe. The European problems were in turn holding back the US recovery. In 2013 the two sides started negotiations on a transatlantic trade and investment partnership. In 2016 it became clear, however, that the negotiations were going nowhere. Opposition in the United States, in France and elsewhere was too strong.

On wider security matters the two sides of the Atlantic were less dependent on each other than they had been during the Cold War. America's emphasis was now on the Greater Middle East and, more and more, on the rise of China and the situation in East Asia. The European Union had to focus on its internal matters in facing the economic crisis in Greece, Spain, Italy, Ireland and even other countries. How much were the relatively well-functioning member states of the North, with Germany in the lead, to aid the crisis countries in the South, with Greece as the most critical country?

In the war against Gaddafi's Libya (see pp. 121–2) the United States left the early initiative with France and Britain. Washington was to 'lead from behind,' although it quickly became evident that, while accepting NATO's continued existence, the Europeans really could not conduct a military campaign without many different US resources from intelligence information to precision-guided weapons. Europe was also divided in that Germany and several other countries refused to take part in the Libya operation at all.

In Syria neither Washington nor the European capitals had any solution to the prolonged civil war in the country. The refugee crisis in Syria (p. 122) and other countries in the region also forced the EU to take on added powers. It was clearly impossible for Greece and Italy alone to accept the many refugees who entered these two countries. Germany and Sweden were willing to admit tens of thousands, even hundreds of thousands, but many felt the burden should be shared in a more equitable way. Under German leadership plans for a more joint EU approach were worked out, with limited success, however. The downside was that popular opposition to admitting so many refugees was quickly increasing. This also made the EU as such much more controversial in many of the member countries.

Thus, on the whole American–European relations continued to be close. At the same time, however, the two continents simply meant less to each other than they had done some decades earlier. The Cold War had been based on the centrality of Europe. Europe had been the scene of the major conflict and here the United States had its most important allies. The European allies were still significant, although less so than before. The conflicts had moved elsewhere. The election of Donald Trump as US president in 2016 came as a great surprise also to Europeans who had great difficulties in taking him seriously as a presidential candidate. The new president, however, made it perfectly clear that the Europeans would have to do more on their own and expect reduced contributions from the United States. It remained to be seen what the new relationship would be.

THE UNITED STATES AND WESTERN EUROPE, 1945-2016: THE LITERATURE

For the American–British relationship in long-term perspective, see Kathleen Burk, *Old World, New World: The Story of Britain and America* (New York, 2007). Robert Hathaway, *Ambiguous Partnership: Britain and America, 1944–1947* (New York, 1981) is an excellent book on relations between Britain and the United States early in the postwar period. Robert Osgood, *NATO: The Entangling Alliance* (Chicago, 1962) is still an important work. Alfred Grosser, *The Western Alliance: European–American Relations Since 1945* (London, 1980) contains a wealth of useful information, but is quite poorly organized. For the American–European relationship, see also my own books *'Empire' by Integration: The United States and European Integration, 1945–1997* (Oxford, 1998) and, edited by me, *No End to Alliance. The United States and Western Europe: Past, Present, and Future* (London, 1998). My newest efforts are *The United States and Western Europe Since 1945* (Oxford, 2003) and, again edited by me, *Just Another Major Crisis? The United States and Europe Since 2000* (Oxford, 2008). David W. Ellwood, *The Shock of America. Europe and the Challenge of the Century* (Oxford, 2012) is very useful.

A general survey of developments in Western Europe can be found in D. W. Urwin, *Western Europe Since 1945: A Short Political History* (London, 1981 and subsequent editions) and in William I. Hitchcock, *The Struggle for Europe: The History of the Continent Since 1945* (New York, 2003). Tony Judt, *Postwar: A History of Europe Since 1945* (New York, 2005) is masterly. Herbert Tint, *French Foreign Policy Since the Second World War* (London, 1972) provides a useful survey of French foreign policy in the early Cold War decades. A similar survey for the United Kingdom is presented in Joseph Frankel, *British Foreign Policy 1945–1973* (London, 1975).

More updated presentations of the respective themes are to be found in Derek W. Urwin, *The Community of Europe: A History of European Integration Since 1945* (London, 1991); John W. Young, *Britain and European Unity 1945–1992* (London, 1993); Philip H. Gordon, *France, Germany, and the Western Alliance* (Boulder, CO, 1995); Frédéric Bozo, *Two Strategies for Europe: De Gaulle, the United States and the Atlantic Alliance* (Lanham, MD, 2001) and his *History of the Iraq Crisis* (New York, 2016); Helga Haftendorn, *Coming of Age: German Foreign Policy Since 1945* (Oxford, 2006). Philip Zelikow and Condoleezza Rice, *Germany Unified and Europe Transformed: A Study in Statecraft* (Cambridge, 1995) is excellent on Germany. Alan S. Milward has done indispensable work on European reconstruction and integration. See particularly his *The Reconstruction of Western Europe, 1945–51* (Berkeley, CA, 1984). Charles S. Maier sums up his work also on postwar American–European relations in *Among Empires: American Ascendancy and its Predecessors* (Cambridge, MA, 2006). The most recent works on their respective topics are David W. Ellwood, *The Shock of America. Europe and the Challenge of the Century* (Oxford: Oxford University Press, 2012), Frederic Bozo, *French Foreign Policy since 1945* (New York: Berghahn, 2016) and David Sanders and David Patrick Houghton, *Losing an Empire, Finding a Role* (London: Palgrave, 2017).

THE SOVIET UNION/RUSSIA AND THE (FORMERLY) COMMUNIST COUNTRIES, 1945-2016

During the first years after the Second World War, Communists gained control in vast new areas: Eastern Europe, North Korea, China, and North Vietnam. Later, new Moscow-oriented regimes emerged – on Cuba, in Indochina, and in Afghanistan. The Soviet Union obtained a footing in African countries such as Angola and Ethiopia.

Even so, in some ways the position of the Soviet Union became weaker as the postwar era progressed. There was no longer a unified communist movement with the Soviet Union as its indisputable leader. As early as 1948, Tito's Yugoslavia had shown that a victory for communism was not necessarily a victory for the Soviet Union. In time, there would be more instances illustrating this fact, despite Soviet interventions in Hungary and Czechoslovakia.

Most important of all was the conflict with China, which in the late 1960s and during the 1970s surpassed the Cold War with the United States in intensity. In Eastern Europe, the 'satellite states' would choose different courses: a few relatively independent of the Soviet Union, most of them still more traditional. What was significant was that the national Communist parties, within certain limits, could decide for themselves exactly how closely they wanted to follow Moscow. This was true to an even greater extent outside Eastern Europe, in countries such as North Vietnam and Cuba and in the Communist parties of Western Europe.

During the course of half a year in 1989 an incredible development took place: the communist system in Eastern Europe was dismantled. Moscow decided not to intervene to sustain the sitting governments. Thus their days were numbered. The Kremlin had more than enough to do keeping up with developments within the Soviet Union. In 1991 the Soviet Union itself was divided into Russia and 14 other republics, with only a loose cooperation between some of these new countries.

In Eastern Europe, democracy and market economics soon prevailed, with certain local adaptations. Virtually all the countries in the region soon became eager to join the West in the form of NATO and the EU. In Russia and several of the new countries on what was formerly Soviet territory, more or less democratic regimes governed with varying degrees of openness for free market economics. Other formerly Soviet republics, particularly Muslim ones, tried to limit change as best they could. In China a strong degree of market economics was combined with the existing nationalist–communist political system. Vietnam followed the Chinese model to a certain extent, while Cuba had its own rather conservative model and North Korea tried to avoid change almost entirely. Thus, by 2016 there was little left of the communist world as it had emerged during the first years after 1945.

EXPANSION AND CONFORMISM, 1945-1953

Whereas to a great extent the United States was invited to play an active role in Western Europe in the years immediately following the Second World War, this was seldom the case for the Soviet Union in Eastern Europe. The United States had a considerably wider range of instruments to choose among in implementing its foreign policy than the Soviet Union had. The capitalist superpower could offer economic assistance and military guarantees. The Soviet Union had little to contribute economically. With the partial exception of West Germany, in cooperation with the United States, the Western powers were never considered the threat – at least not at the popular level – in Eastern Europe that the Soviet Union came to represent in Western Europe, which meant that the question of military guarantees was seen in a different light in Eastern Europe.

The level of support for the Soviet Union and the Communist party varied in Eastern Europe. It was undoubtedly highest in Bulgaria and Czechoslovakia, lowest in Hungary, Poland, and Romania. Bulgaria had cooperated with the USSR/Russia on many occasions. Moreover, Bulgaria and Czechoslovakia had a past history that was characterized by skepticism of the Western powers. In Bulgaria, this went back to the 1870s, in Czechoslovakia to the Munich settlement of 1938.

In Poland, Hungary, and Romania, hostility towards the Soviet Union had deep roots. Although the fear of a new strong Germany could increase understanding for the Soviet Union, especially in Poland, and although more or less opportunistic reasons dictated support for the governing party, there was a weak local basis for the dominant position the Soviet Union assumed.

Soviet expansion in Eastern Europe was primarily based on the Red Army (see pp. 21–6). Hungary, Bulgaria, and Romania had fought on the side of the Axis powers. That made Soviet control especially extensive here in the first years after the war. Washington and London granted Moscow the key role in the occupation of these countries. The Red Army also assumed a central role in developments in Poland, as it soon became evident that the Lublin group of pro-Soviet Poles enjoyed limited local support. Czechoslovakia was the only country from which the Soviets withdrew – which they did in December 1945 – but where Moscow and the strong local Communists obtained full control nonetheless. (With regard to the situation in East Germany, see pp. 26–30.)

Politically, the countries in the region were governed at first by coalition governments under varying degrees of Communist/Soviet influence. In 1947–48, these coalitions were dissolved. The non-Communist parties disappeared as independent entities. They were soon followed by the Communist leaders who could be suspected of wanting national independence. In Hungary, Rajk had to pay with his life, as did Kostov in Bulgaria; in Romania, Patrascanu was purged, as was Gomulka in Poland. Even Communists with strong loyalties to Moscow disappeared from power. In 1951–52 Slansky in Czechoslovakia and Pauker in Romania, both known for their subservience to Moscow and both of them Jews, were purged. Slansky, general secretary of the Communist party, was even executed.

The Eastern European economies were subjugated to the Soviet economy. Not only was trade skewed to the East, but the conditions of trade were to the advantage of the Soviet Union to an extreme degree. The joint Soviet–Eastern European companies were often a mere cover for Soviet exploitation. By demanding war reparations and by confiscating German-controlled property, Moscow could further consolidate its position. All in all, the Soviet Union's transfers from Eastern Europe probably amounted to more than the assistance the United States gave Western Europe under the Marshall Plan.

After a few years of relatively balanced reconstruction, from 1949–50 onwards Eastern Europe was built up according to the Soviet pattern, with five-year plans that clearly favored large-scale and heavy industry. In most countries the government even took over small craftsmen's firms. Much of agriculture was collectivized, although the pace varied somewhat from one country to another. An organization for economic cooperation, COMECON, was established in 1949, but acquired little significance at this time. As the various Eastern European countries placed priority on many of the same areas, there was little need for trade and cooperation. Moreover, the boundaries between countries were under close surveillance.

This enforced conformity can be explained on the basis of several considerations. The Soviet Union, like other powers in similar situations, transferred its own system of government to the countries it controlled. As the United States exported Western capitalism with considerable strains of pluralism, the Soviet Union exported communism, a communism in which divergence from prevailing norms was not allowed, especially during the Stalin era. Eastern Europe held a central position in ensuring Soviet security, and that strengthened Moscow's demands on the regimes that were established.

The demands for loyalty gradually increased. This was partly a result of the fact that Moscow got more time to shape the region in its own image and partly a reflection of international and local factors. The increasingly chilly temperature of the Cold War meant that fewer and fewer deviations were tolerated. The lines between East and West were to be drawn even more sharply than previously. Several of the Eastern European countries, most particularly Czechoslovakia, were interested in participating in the Marshall Plan. The Kremlin's dissatisfaction on this account was part of the background for the Communist coup in Czechoslovakia in February 1948, a coup that quickly brought the country in line with the rest of Eastern Europe. Locally, the first important act of the Communist Information Bureau (COMINFORM), established in October 1947, was to expel Yugoslavia. The split between Stalin and Tito in June 1948 meant the initiation of a witch hunt for any elements that could be said to represent the slightest degree of independence in relation to Moscow.

The Yugoslavs were accused of having embraced ideological deviation. The fact that they had gone far in encouraging revolution in Western Europe was seen as 'leftist deviation.' Tito had pursued a harsh course in relation to the United States and Britain, particularly in Trieste and by supporting the insurrection in Greece. Nationalization of industry and collectivization of agriculture had also begun earlier and progressed further than otherwise in Eastern Europe. Tito's 'national' deviations were examples of 'rightist deviation,' such as his opposition to joint companies and Soviet exploitation, control, and surveillance. Tito was now compared to Trotsky; it was not possible to sink much lower.

The most important basis for the split was the fact that Tito and the Yugoslavian Communists had risen to power on their own, with little help from the Red Army. This was also the primary reason why Yugoslavia survived the total isolation the country was subjected to from the other Communist countries and parties. Tito had built up an army, a party, and an administration that for the most part remained loyal to him.

In only one other Eastern European country was the situation similar to that of Yugoslavia, and that was in Albania under Enver Hoxha. But here the bitter conflict between Yugoslavia and Albania contributed to Hoxha seeking close cooperation with the Soviet Union to prevent the country from being absorbed as a province of Yugoslavia. Thus the independent power base of the regime could, for the time being, be combined with a pro-Moscow policy.

The Chinese Communists had at least an equally independent power base, but even they naturally looked to Moscow as the world's Communist capital. The cooperation agreement of 1950 linked the two countries to each other. For the Chinese, the leadership of Stalin and the Soviet Union was a matter of course. When Stalin died on 5 March 1953, Mao Tse-tung spoke of his 'sublime wisdom' and 'burning love' for the Chinese people. (For the stance of the Soviet Union during the Chinese Civil War, see pp. 37–40.)

THE REINS ARE LOOSENED (1953-1956) AND TIGHTENED (1956-1958)

A number of conditions diminished Soviet control over Eastern Europe and the worldwide communist movement during the course of the 1950s.

The most important single factor was Stalin's death. No one could take the place of 'the greatest genius of the present age' to use another of Mao's phrases at the time of Stalin's death. Although Khrushchev gradually emerged as the unmistakable top man, he never attained the authority Stalin had had, neither in the Soviet Union itself and in Eastern Europe, nor in the other Communist countries and parties.

The Soviet Union was still the model for the other countries, but with the thaw that was now taking place the content of this model was no longer so clear-cut. Power was shared among more persons and bodies, first in the Soviet Union and then in Eastern Europe. The role of the security police was reduced, and most of the political prisoners released. There were signs of discussion, and the various factions in the Eastern European parties could – with varying degrees of justice – invoke support from different centers of power in Moscow.

The moral and political position of the Soviet Union grew weaker. Trade agreements were revised, and the joint companies were changed in character or dismantled. Greatest were the concessions in relation to China (see pp. 190–1). These changes were partly a result of freer conditions, but it was also admitted that Stalin had made grave mistakes. Khrushchev's denunciation of the deceased leader at the Twentieth Party Congress in February 1956 tore the former deity down from his pedestal in earnest. This denunciation probably strengthened Khrushchev's position at that moment, but in a somewhat longer perspective it was bound to weaken his and the Soviet Union's possibilities of assuming the same leadership role as before. The Soviet Union had made serious mistakes in the past. That meant it could happen again.

One of Stalin's greatest mistakes, in Khrushchev's opinion, was the fact that he had thrust Tito out into the cold. The split in 1948 was considered unnecessary. Yugoslavia was again to be brought into the fold of communist countries. In 1955, Khrushchev journeyed to Belgrade for reconciliation. Tito was rehabilitated and declared a good Communist. That could gain Moscow greater influence in Yugoslavia, but in the rest of Eastern Europe the consequences were the exact opposite. If there were now different roads to communism, that had to apply not only in Yugoslavia, but in other countries as well. Reconciliation with Tito was also bound to have consequences for the many Eastern European leaders who had been accused of 'Titoism' and 'national deviation.' They had not all lost their lives. In April 1956 the COMINFORM was dissolved.

Destalinization was far from painless in the Soviet Union. Even so, the problems were small compared to those in Eastern Europe. In the Soviet Union, nationalism had been absorbed in the communist system to a great extent, in contrast to what was the case in Eastern Europe; there, nationalism was an anti-Soviet and anti-communist force in most of the countries. The domestic political situation in these countries was less stable in other ways as well. The Communists had only been in power for a few years, and the attachment to traditions other than communism was far stronger than in the Soviet Union.

The new tensions were first expressed in the June 1953 demonstrations in Czechoslovakia and East Germany. In Czechoslovakia, the authorities managed to quell the unrest in Pilsen and other cities. In East Germany, a strong desire for liberalization coincided with a power struggle in the local party – a power struggle with ramifications in various factions in Moscow – and with the continuation of harsh economic policies. Only direct intervention by the Soviet occupation troops re-established socialist law and order in East Berlin and other East German cities.

The Revolts in Poland and Hungary in 1956

Revolts erupted during the summer and autumn of 1956, first in Poland and immediately thereafter in Hungary. In many ways, it was only to be expected that the problems were greatest in these two countries.

Poland and Hungary had long historical traditions of struggling to resist foreign subjugation and sustain national independence. Moreover, the most deeply rooted anti-Russian sentiments were to be found in Hungary and especially Poland (and in Romania as well). The economic tensions were great. Whereas East Germany and Czechoslovakia were industrialized countries and Bulgaria and Romania were agricultural countries, Poland and Hungary were in an intermediate position. The rate of investment had been very high, with the sacrifices that had necessarily entailed. Even more importantly, in 1956 the party leadership was in a period of transition which stimulated expectations and uncertainty. In Poland, Bierut died after having heard Khrushchev's disclosures of Stalin's outrages. In Hungary, the hated Rakosi had to resign after having tried various strategies to survive politically.

In Poland, the workers' revolt in Poznan in June was aimed at economic conditions such as wages and prices. The authorities never managed to bring the situation fully under control. Ochab, the new party leader, could not unite the party, much less the nation. The party's leading 'revisionist,' Gomulka, had been sentenced to prison and thus escaped execution. In April he was released from prison; in October he was elected leader of the Communist party.

The Soviet leadership, which in many ways had initiated the thaw, was skeptical of Gomulka. It tried to prevent his being elected general secretary. But considering the support he enjoyed in the party, in the population, in the police force, and in much of the army, Gomulka was the only person who could unite the country. If the Soviets chose to intervene with military force, it could be that they would be met with open opposition. Gomulka had to be given a chance. Then the revolt in Hungary broke out. Moscow soon became more preoccupied with Hungary than with the situation in Poland.

Rakosi's Hungary had pursued what was perhaps the harshest policy of repression in all of Eastern Europe. In July, this dictator had been forced to resign under Soviet pressure, a situation that could partially be seen as a result of the rapprochement with Tito.

The new party leader, Gerö, was so discredited that his takeover could not have any other purpose than to discourage Rakosi's supporters. As in Poland, Hungary moved into a transitional phase in which the new leaders did not manage to get the situation under control. The events in Poland stimulated developments in Hungary.

In Poland, the party had rallied around Gomulka. In Hungary, Imre Nagy was appointed prime minister on 24 October following large-scale demonstrations in Budapest. But the party was still divided. An appeal was sent to the Soviet troops to re-establish the socialist order. Clashes ensued in several places. Janos Kadar replaced Gerö as general secretary of the party.

The Soviet troops were withdrawn from Budapest, at the same time as preparations were made to send reinforcements into Hungary. Events unfolded rapidly. Pressured by the oppositional groups that sprang up everywhere, Nagy first allowed several parties and then established a coalition government. Thereafter he announced Hungary's withdrawal from the Warsaw Pact and established the country's neutrality. On 4 November, the Red Army intervened with its full force. In the course of a few days it had taken control. Kadar became the new strong man.

After the dramatic events of October–November 1956, Moscow tightened the reins once more. Khrushchev's policy of destalinization had suffered a defeat. Although he survived the 1957 challenge from his conservative rivals in the Soviet leadership, his course had to be altered. The attitude of the Soviet Union towards Tito became more skeptical. The cultural and political thaw was replaced by a colder climate once more. Collectivization accelerated anew in the Eastern European countries. COMECON and the Warsaw Pact were to be used more actively as instruments to control developments in Eastern Europe. In December 1957, a new communist world conference was held. Soviet leadership was emphasized. Attacks on 'revisionists' were far stronger than attacks on 'dogmatists.'

Despite its tighter grip, Moscow's dominance could never again be what it had been. Instead, the split in the communist camp would soon be greater than ever before.

THE SPLIT BETWEEN THE SOVIET UNION AND CHINA

There was no doubt that friction between the Soviet and the Chinese party leaders had existed for a long time. It was natural, at least in retrospect, for the Chinese to reproach

Stalin for his cooperation with the Kuomintang which had resulted in the massacre of the Communists in 1927. The popular front policy of the mid-1930s suited the Chinese well in their struggle against Japan, whereas the 1941 Soviet non-aggression treaty with the same adversary cannot have been in the interest of the Chinese. Likewise, it is likely that Stalin's recognition of Chiang Kai-shek as China's legitimate leader in August 1945 was hardly pleasing to Mao.

As we have seen, the Soviet support to the Chinese Communists during the civil war was quite limited (see pp. 39–40). Both before and after the Communist takeover, there were unmistakable signs that Moscow would try to maintain a special position in the parts of China that bordered on the Soviet Union. It is highly likely that Mao wanted to limit Soviet influence within the Chinese Communist party. Those who were considered most pro-Soviet were isolated. Kao Kang was frozen out of the leadership, and Wang Ming does not even seem to have been granted entrance into China.

Figure 10.1   China–Soviet friendship will safeguard peace

Source: Woodcut by Li Hua, 1950

From Cooperation to Armed Struggle

Despite these occurrences and despite the harsh statements Mao himself issued after the split between the Soviet Union and China had become open and bitter, caution should be observed in describing Sino-Soviet relations as strained at too early a date. Throughout most of the 1950s, these two countries cooperated rather well.

In the first place, their systems of government were based on a shared Marxist–Leninist ideology. There were shades of difference in the two countries' interpretation and practice of this shared legacy. But there was no disagreement as to the fact that the Soviet Union was the undisputed leader within the communist movement.

For the most part Mao followed Soviet policies until 1958. Five-year plans were drawn up, the level of investment was very high, and giant projects within heavy industry were given priority over light industry and agriculture. Within agriculture, land redistribution was soon replaced by collectivization. Political fluctuations largely followed those in the Soviet Union. Mao's large-scale campaign, launched in May 1956 under the slogan 'Let a hundred flowers bloom, and a hundred schools of thought contend' could be seen as a local variant of destalinization. Both Moscow and Peking changed their policies towards the Third World. As late as at the world conference in December 1957, there were few participants who emphasized the leadership position of the Soviet Union as clearly as the Chinese, although they stressed their conviction that this leadership had to be accompanied by a special responsibility for cracking down on revisionists within the communist movement.

In the second place, the intensity of the Cold War contributed to keeping the two countries together. The Soviet Union and China had one mutual enemy, the United States. The Chinese Communists needed Soviet support during the Korean War and in their conflict with Taiwan. As far as Korea was concerned, the Chinese may well have been disappointed at the business-like conditions on which the Soviet Union granted its military assistance. The same was true of Moscow's lukewarm stance during the Quemoy–Matsu conflicts of 1954–55 and 1958 (see pp. 50, 73), but even this was probably more evident in retrospect than at the time. Although the suspicious Stalin must have feared a new Tito in Mao, there could be no doubt in the Soviet Union that the Chinese Communists' victory had strengthened the USSR in relation to its main enemy, the United States. The 30-year alliance against Japan and countries allied with Japan that was established in February 1950 was an expression of this solidarity (see p. 43).

In the third place, Soviet assistance to China was welcome. It was true that the 300 million dollars Mao was granted in 1950 after his three-month visit in Moscow was quite certainly less than he had hoped for. However, the Soviet Union was the only country the Chinese could expect to receive economic and military assistance from. After Stalin's death this assistance was stepped up. New credits were granted, and entire factories were built by Soviet technicians, often in return for deliveries from those same factories. The Soviet Union relinquished its privileges in Port Arthur, in Dairen, in Manchuria, and Sinkiang. Stalin had promised to end them in 1952, but they had been extended because of the Korean War. Many Chinese students (6,500) went to the Soviet Union to study, and, perhaps most significantly, the Soviet leaders promised in 1957 to help China develop nuclear weapons.

However, there were developments even in the 1950s that had a negative effect on Sino-Soviet unity. Khrushchev could never attain the position Stalin had enjoyed. Moreover, the Chinese were only partially in agreement with Khrushchev's criticism of his predecessor. Moscow's overtures towards Yugoslavia, emphasizing the several possible paths to communism, meant greater scope for China as well, although the Chinese would strongly distance themselves from Tito ideologically.

The events in Eastern Europe in 1956 illustrated the Chinese role in an interesting way. The Chinese defended Gomulka and the initial phase of the events in Hungary. However, when Moscow intervened it did so with Peking's support, as Nagy had abandoned fundamental communist principles. The fact that the Soviet Union wanted international approval of its intervention strengthened China's position. Finally, the incipient policy of détente with the West reduced both the willingness and the need to stand shoulder to shoulder against the United States. As we shall see, the two communist powers would also assess the advantages of détente differently.

In 1959, the Soviet Union reneged on its agreement to help China develop nuclear weapons. In the following year, economic assistance was stopped and the Soviet technicians suddenly withdrawn. The public polemics had already begun. From 1960 to 1962, these verbal attacks were indirect as the Chinese heaped abuse on the 'revisionists,' particularly the Yugoslavs, while the Soviets thundered against 'dogmatists' and Albanians. However, few people were in doubt as to the true addressees.

The first minor border skirmishes took place as early as in July 1960. In 1962–63, the polemics were replaced by open, direct accusations. From 1965 relations between the two parties were nearly severed. In the course of the 1960s, the official relations also deteriorated rapidly, although there was never a formal diplomatic break. The border clashes increased in number and intensity, climaxing in March 1969 at the Ussuri River. On one occasion the Soviet Union suffered about 60 killed and wounded, while the figure for China was probably several hundred.

In 1967 the Soviet Union had 15 divisions along the Chinese border. In 1973 this figure had risen to 45, or 25 per cent of the total Soviet forces. The Chinese had even more men on their side. Mao feared a Soviet attack and asked the Chinese people to 'store grain and dig deep tunnels' in anticipation of the war that might erupt. The situation became so strained that each of the two communist countries came to consider the United States a much lesser evil than the other side. (For the Sino–Soviet–US triangle, see pp. 219–23.)

Explanations for the Split

Many different factors must be included in order to explain the antagonism between the Soviet Union and China. They can be grouped into certain main categories. The ideological issues comprise one such group, the national issues another. The territorial disputes may be considered either a third group or an aspect of the national issues.

The ideological differences were in many ways the most conspicuous. They spanned a broad spectrum. In terms of foreign policy, Moscow emphasized its conviction that the socialist countries had now become so strong that war could be avoided and that peaceful coexistence between East and West should be possible. Peking agreed that socialism had grown stronger. It had actually become so strong that the imperialists ought to be forced to make concessions. Hand in hand with the Chinese skepticism of peaceful coexistence went an emphasis on the socialist countries' duty to support 'wars of national liberation.'

As far as relations between the socialist countries were concerned, for a long time there was concurrence regarding the Soviet leadership role. However, after the split had widened, Peking placed primary emphasis on their conviction that relations ought to be based on the principles of equality and independence.

In terms of domestic policy, the possibilities for a peaceful transition to socialism were a primary concern. At least from the time of the Twentieth Soviet Party Congress in 1956, Moscow had maintained that such a transition was possible under certain conditions. The Chinese rejected this idea and stood firm on the premise that only a revolution could lead from capitalism to socialism. The Kremlin also claimed that when the proletariat had won its struggle, such as for instance in the Soviet Union, the dictatorship of the proletariat could be modified or even come to an end. The Chinese considered this too a dangerous heresy that would merely give bourgeois elements a new chance to gain influence. They felt that this had happened in the Soviet Union.

Domestic policy differences were most prominent during Peking's most ideological periods: the Great Leap Forward (1958–61) and the Cultural Revolution (1966–76). The Great Leap Forward represented China's liberation from the Soviet model. The level of ambitions was extremely high. Instead of relying on isolated giant projects within industry, built with Soviet assistance, more emphasis was now to be placed on small- and medium-sized enterprises throughout the entire country. Agriculture was also to be incorporated in a more balanced manner than previously. Organizationally, the basic unit was to be the people's commune, which surpassed anything else within the communist world in its degree of collectivism. In many villages common eating and sleeping quarters were established.

The Great Leap Forward was far from successful, although the authorities tried at first to give the impression that it was. The results were particularly poor within agriculture. Although no one knew for certain, more than 30 million people, by one estimate more than 40 million, probably lost their lives primarily due to the chaos and production setbacks experienced in most areas. This was one of the worst famines of modern times.

The fiasco resulted in a weakening of Mao's strong position. He had to relinquish the office of president to Liu Shao-chi. However, attempts by more pro-Soviet circles, led by Defense Minister Peng Teh-huai, to exploit the situation to the advantage of rapprochement with the Soviet Union were unsuccessful. Peng was dismissed and replaced by Lin Piao.

A somewhat more moderate policy in China meant little in a larger context. The same was true of the transition from Khrushchev to Brezhnev and Kosygin. After a brief respite from the polemics following Khrushchev's demise, they were soon resumed, more bitterly than ever.

The Cultural Revolution resulted in a further escalation of the conflict. Now the enthusiasm of the masses was to save the Chinese revolution from bureaucracy and lead it on towards the highest form of communism in record-breaking time. The Soviet path was denounced in the sharpest possible terms as an attempt to reintroduce capitalism in the socialist world. At times, members of the Red Guard blockaded the Soviet embassy in Peking. Mao's standing reached new heights; he was the subject of a tremendous personality cult. He was considered the great renewer of world communism (and of the art of swimming: he ostensibly swam 15 kilometers in 65 minutes, not bad for a man of 72).

The many ideological disputes between Moscow and Peking were significant enough. But it is difficult to determine to what extent they were decisive in themselves, or whether they primarily reflected other factors that were subsequently cloaked in ideology.

On several issues, however, a substantial gap between theory and practice could be perceived. The Chinese issued exhortations on the need to combat capitalism and imperialism and proclaimed that several hundred million Chinese would survive even a nuclear war. In most practical contexts, however, they were reserved. Thus Hong Kong and Macao were allowed to continue as 'imperialist enclaves' on Chinese soil. In contrast, although the Soviet Union emphasized the possibilities of peaceful coexistence, neither in theory nor in practice did that preclude support to 'wars of national liberation' in Africa and Asia.

Moreover, there was a clear tendency for the ideological accusations to play a lesser role in the 1970s than they had done in the 1960s. Certain accusations were almost the opposite of what they had been previously. Whereas the Chinese had long accused the Soviet Union of pursuing a weak, yielding course of policy, they later claimed that the Soviets' objective was world hegemony. 'Proletarian internationalism' grew increasingly weak, while anti-Soviet sentiments grew stronger. In several countries China supported anti-communist regimes on the basis of their resistance to Soviet influence (the Shah in Iran and Pinochet in Chile).

The different ideologies were not detached from reality; they had a source. To a great extent the ideological differences mirrored differing historical developments in the two countries. For instance, it was natural that the Soviet Union emphasized the role of industrial workers as a revolutionary vanguard, whereas the Chinese placed greater emphasis on the role of the peasants. From this basic difference arose divergent assessments of the relationship between city and countryside, between heavy industry, light industry, and agriculture.

The national issues were of great significance. As in relations between the United States and Western Europe, an external threat and economic dependence could draw the two sides together. When the threat declined and dependence decreased, the antagonism became more open. This was even more evident in relations between the Soviet Union and China than between the United States and Western Europe.

Two countries seldom or never have identical interests. Two countries that were as different, as strong, and as proud as the Soviet Union and China certainly did not. The Soviet Union was a world power and was used to other communist countries submitting to Soviet leadership. Perhaps China was not a major power at the moment, but the Chinese traditionally considered themselves the center of the world and believed they had a great future.

It was as natural for the Soviet Union to want to limit the number of nuclear powers as it was for China to want to develop such weapons. After the break in Sino-Soviet nuclear cooperation in 1959, Peking was bound to perceive the signing of the test ban agreement in 1963 as one more attempt to hinder China's production of nuclear weapons. China's and the Soviet Union's respective assessments of the horrors of nuclear war were influenced by the fact that for a long time both sides took it for granted that it was the Soviets and not the Chinese who would make the decision, if any, to start such a war.

In the Quemoy–Matsu dispute, Peking's concern was the liberation of areas everyone agreed were Chinese. For the Soviets, relations with the United States were more important, a consideration which dictated the avoidance of a superpower conflict regarding these islands.

In the efforts of the Soviet leaders to improve relations with the countries of the Third World, India was of primary importance. The Chinese perspective on India was somewhat different. The boundaries were still in dispute, and this fact became more pressing after the Chinese had quelled the revolt (against China) in Tibet, and the Dalai Lama had fled to India. In 1958–59, minor skirmishes took place between India and China. In 1962, open war ensued, in which the Chinese inflicted a decisive defeat on the Indians. The Soviet Union did not commit itself to either side during the war, but carried out a planned sale of Mig fighter planes to India.

The Cuban crisis in 1962 also resulted in polemics between the two communist countries. First, Peking criticized Moscow for having evidenced unwarranted boldness by stationing intermediate-range missiles on Cuba. When the missiles were withdrawn, Chinese criticism of the Soviet Union was harsh for having given in to US pressure.

On 23 August 1968, Prime Minister Chou En-lai described the Soviet invasion of Czechoslovakia as 'the most barefaced and typical specimen of Fascist power politics played by the Soviet revisionist clique against its so-called allies.' Once again the perspectives were different. The Soviets were concerned about stopping tendencies towards dissolution within their Eastern European empire. The Chinese, who had supported the Soviet intervention in Hungary in 1956, now protested sharply. Peking was especially troubled by the so-called Brezhnev Doctrine, which assigned Moscow the role of policing developments in the other socialist countries. The Chinese leaders feared that such a doctrine could justify even an invasion of China.

The territorial disputes concerned first and foremost the boundaries between the two countries. In 1858, 1860, 1864, and 1881, China had ceded large land areas in Central Asia and along the Pacific coast, amounting to a total of 1.5 million square kilometers, to Russia. It had long been Chinese policy, supported by both Chiang Kai-shek and Mao, to consider these agreements the result of coercion and thus unjust. Lenin had shown understanding for this point of view, although Moscow never proposed concrete changes in the boundaries.

A few years after the Soviet privileges in China had been relinquished in 1954–55, the Chinese cautiously began to reopen the boundary issue. From 1963 onwards they pursued it to the full. They did not demand the return of all the territory in question. Their point of departure was that the Chinese cession was to be considered invalid in principle. Thereafter the two countries were to negotiate on boundary changes, but it remained unclear which areas China would actually claim. Until agreement was reached, Peking was prepared to accept the status quo.

The Soviet Union dismissed all changes of any significance and was only willing to negotiate on minor details. To some extent, the disputed territories were important in themselves. Moreover, concessions could establish a dangerous precedent in relation to other countries, regardless of how unjust the old Czarist agreements may have been at one time.

A number of other issues also involved the border areas. The Soviet stance on Outer Mongolia was one of them. Although China had accepted Outer Mongolia as an independent nation in 1946, it was obvious that Peking wanted to bring the country within the Chinese sphere of influence and away from its close ties with the Soviet Union.

In the 1950s, the Soviet Union first wanted to import Chinese laborers to Siberia; then it began to fear that such an import could complicate the border issue. Moscow was also interested in acquiring submarine bases and radio stations on Chinese soil. The Chinese rejected this proposal, which they considered practically an attempt to undermine China's sovereignty.

China was far too vast to be dominated by outside powers, as the Soviet Union was not the first to experience. The fact that the Communists in China had risen to power by their own efforts gave them an independence that most of the other Communists lacked. This independent power base was undoubtedly one of the most important conditions for the split between the Soviet Union and China, as it had been between the Soviet Union and Yugoslavia. Later developments between China and the Soviet Union are described on pp. 219–23.

SOVIET RELATIONS WITH EASTERN EUROPE, 1958-1985

The split between the Soviet Union and China had dramatic effects on communist unity. The fact that the world's most populous country so openly challenged Moscow had consequences in virtually all the Communist parties in the world. As long as the conflict was carried out within certain limits, Peking's criticism expanded the spectrum for what deviations in opinion the Soviet Union had to tolerate. After the breach was complete, the Kremlin's need for support in its struggle against the Chinese was exploited by the other Communist parties to their own advantage. Some of the parties even chose to follow the Chinese pattern. Moscow's authority could never be the same after the exchanges of verbal abuse between the Soviet Union and China. Finally, the strife demonstrated both that there were many paths to communism and that its victory had certainly not quashed nationalism as a driving force in relations between communist powers.

Even little Albania struck out on an independent course. The country's relations with the Soviet Union were still largely a reflection of Yugoslavia's relations with the communist superpower. After the rapprochement between Khrushchev and Tito in 1955, the Albanians distanced themselves from the Soviet Union, subsequently to enter into cooperation with China against the Yugoslavian–Soviet revisionists. When revisionism began to appear even in China at the close of the 1970s, 'Europe's lighthouse' chose to remain quite isolated ideologically.

The process towards greater scope for the various countries of Eastern Europe could not be reversed. Under a surface of loyalty to the Soviet Union and the communist system, the various governments would pursue different policies in many areas, both in domestic policy and to some extent in foreign policy as well.

The factors that had previously contributed to weakening the position of the Soviet Union continued to have an effect, including events within the Soviet Union itself. Stalin's death was the great watershed, but the fall of Khrushchev in October 1964 had a similar effect. Most of the leaders in Eastern Europe had had, or at least had developed, close relations with Khrushchev. Now the most powerful man in the Soviet Union was quite simply deposed. From the perspective of the Eastern European leaders, this could establish a dangerous precedent both in relation to their own parties and in relations with the Soviet Union. Thus they were more convinced than ever that in addition to goodwill in Moscow they needed a local power base that was preferably strong enough to make them more or less immune to shifts in the Kremlin.

Yugoslavia persisted on its independent course. After relations with the Soviet Union had been strained for a number of years because of the events in Hungary in 1956, they improved again, although they did not return to the level of 1955–early 1956. In 1964 Yugoslavia became an associate member of COMECON, but the country carried on extensive trade with the OECD and EEC countries at the same time. Yugoslavia was also one of the leading spokesmen for the nonaligned nations. This represented a substantial spectrum of contacts, which many Eastern Europeans regarded with envy.

A number of factors would further weaken the position of the Soviet Union in Eastern Europe, as in the rest of the communist world. The shared ideology deteriorated into ritual incantations, with little or no innovative thinking. In Eastern Europe, as in the Soviet Union, it became a modest superstructure over an enormous party apparatus. There was little left of the enthusiasm that had characterized at least certain parts of the population previously.

The policy of détente increased the freedom of action of Eastern Europe as well. The Kremlin established a network of contacts in the West and could not deny the Eastern Europeans the possibility of doing the same. Trade increased, as did imports of Western technology. If the Eastern Europeans were dissatisfied with the conditions Moscow had to offer, they could now turn to the West to some extent. The increased economic freedom of action was accompanied by political contacts. Both Moscow and the various capitals of Eastern Europe were, to varying degrees, interested in preventing Western ideas from creeping in with the political and economic contacts, but in several countries détente contributed to a certain degree of fragmentation of the communist power monopoly.

The policy of détente also made it difficult to use the danger from the West as an argument for solidarity within the Eastern bloc. The threat represented by 'German revanchism' had been of primary importance in this connection. Instead, for most of the Eastern European countries West Germany now became the most important trade partner and political contact in the Western world. The consequences of this new attitude would be particularly great in Poland, where anti-German feelings had been the strongest.

Eastern Europe acquired a position of increasing freedom in relation to the Soviet Union. Even so, there were clear limitations to these countries' freedom of action. The Soviet Union still had great influence, because of its geographic proximity and because of the instruments of power Moscow had at its disposal. With the exception of Yugoslavia and especially Albania, there were still close political, economic, and military ties between the Soviet Union and the countries of Eastern Europe. In addition, most of the local communist leaders had a distinct need for support from the Kremlin. Their local power bases were not so strong that they could act independently in relation to Moscow.

The countries that represented the least problem for the Soviet Union were Bulgaria and East Germany. Sofia stood by the close cooperation Bulgaria had always had with Moscow. East Germany was militarily, politically, and to some extent also economically highly dependent on the Soviet Union. Party leader Walter Ulbricht feared that the Soviet Union would enter into agreements with Bonn without his knowledge. He did not like the Soviet policy of rapprochement with West Germany, and in 1971 he was replaced by Erich Honecker.

During the 1980s, and especially in 1983–84, East Germany began to show signs of greater independence. The country appeared to have the highest standard of living in Eastern Europe. Its existence had finally been universally recognized. For both economic and political reasons, East Berlin was now more interested than Moscow in maintaining good relations with the West, particularly with West Germany. However, the Soviet Union placed clear limitations on how far Honecker could go in his efforts to sustain the policy of détente between the two German states at a time that was again characterized by frostier relations between East and West.

In the 1960s, Hungary embarked on a more liberal course of domestic policy than any other country in Eastern Europe (with the possible exception of Yugoslavia). Cultural life enjoyed greater freedom. From 1968 onwards the economy was less centrally controlled, and market forces were granted more latitude. In terms of foreign policy, Budapest pursued a course that was more loyal to Moscow. Nevertheless, Janos Kadar, the hated leader from 1956, managed to make himself relatively popular in Hungary.

The fact that there was no necessary correlation between a liberal or dogmatic domestic policy and dependence on or independence of Moscow was illustrated by developments in Albania and Hungary, and by Romania as well. Under Gheorghiu Dej, and from 1964 under Nikolae Ceauşescu, Romania pursued a dogmatic course in domestic policy. In terms of foreign policy, this country was the most independent of all the members of the Warsaw Pact.

Soviet troops were withdrawn from Romania in 1958. As soon as they were gone, new attitudes cropped up. The occasion was the Soviet attempts at division of labor and integration within COMECON. Those which were to be 'industrial countries' – the Soviet Union, East Germany, and Czechoslovakia – were far more satisfied with the plan than those which were to be responsible for agricultural production. Among the latter category, Romania, which had traditionally been skeptical of Russia, reacted the most vehemently. Instead, the country embarked on an industrial build-up based on its own resources and increased trade with the West. During the 1970s, machines and entire manufacturing plants were imported from the West.

There was no question of Romania withdrawing from the Warsaw Pact, but the country became more and more passive in this organization. The Romanian leaders even questioned the Soviet takeover of Bessarabia – northern Bukovina. In the Sino-Soviet conflict, the Romanians tried to remain as neutral as possible and were eager to act as mediators.

Relations with France were good, and Romania was often described as the France of the Eastern bloc. As the first Eastern European country after the Soviet Union, Romania recognized West Germany in 1967. During the conflict in the Middle East in that same year, Bucharest sustained its relations with Israel. The Romanians did not take part in

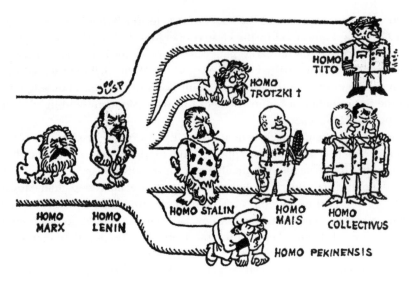

Figure 10.2 A genealogical tree

Source: Jusp in Wir Bruckenbauer, Zürich

the invasion of Czechoslovakia, and they, together with the Yugoslavs, clearly warned the Soviet Union against taking similar actions in other countries. Romania's independent foreign policy continued during the 1970s and 1980s.

Czechoslovakia – 1968

The events in Czechoslovakia in 1968 arose from internal conditions. The rate of economic growth had long been among the highest in Eastern Europe. However, it leveled off altogether in the early 1960s. In order to stimulate the economy once more, reforms were instituted. Whereas growth would stimulate cultural liberalization in Hungary, economic failure led to similar changes in Czechoslovakia.

As in Poland and Hungary in 1956, time would show that a partial dictatorship was a more difficult form of government for the authorities than a firm dictatorship. Those who favored reforms thought that the reforms fell short. The dogmatists felt they went too far and became disillusioned. In January 1968, the strong man ever since 1953, Antonin Novotny, was forced to withdraw as general secretary of the party. He was replaced by the party leader in Slovakia, Aleksander Dubček.

Dubček and his collaborators felt they had learned from the events of 1956. Liberalization had to be limited. Two limits were absolute: Czechoslovakia's participation in the Warsaw Pact could not be questioned, and a system with more than one party could not be allowed.

Even so, the course of developments soon gave rise to concern in the Soviet Union and even more so in East Germany and Poland. The repeal of press censorship meant that the authorities had sacrificed an important instrument of control. The dogmatists were pushed aside. New, independent persons took over. Parties that agreed to cooperate with the Communist party under its leadership were to be allowed. What would be next?

On 20 August, the Red Army invaded Czechoslovakia, with the support of smaller units from Poland, East Germany, Hungary, and Bulgaria. The situation in Czechoslovakia appeared to be steadily more worrying for the Kremlin. The Fourteenth Party Congress was expected to result in further replacement of elements that were loyal to the Soviet Union. Ulbricht and Gomulka applied pressure, as did the party leader in the Ukraine, Pjotr Shelest. He, too, feared that the 'Czechoslovakian disease' would spread. Domino theories were easy to resort to, in Moscow as in Washington. The risk an invasion entailed was small. The Western powers would not respond in military terms, and there were indications that even the political reaction would be limited.

The invasion was justified by the Brezhnev Doctrine. A socialist nation was duty bound to intervene in another socialist nation if the socialist form of government as such was threatened. The invasion did not meet with any military opposition, and the deaths were few. In April 1969, Dubček was replaced by Gustav Husak. Some people hoped that Husak, who himself had been imprisoned under Novotny, would become a new Kadar: a leader who would embark on a liberal course once he had got the situation under control. This would prove not to be the case. The resemblance to Gomulka was greater.

Developments in Poland

The invasion of Czechoslovakia showed that the Soviet Union had means of stopping the process of dissolution in Eastern Europe, if it went too far in the Kremlin's opinion. But such means could only be employed in extreme situations. Developments in Poland would demonstrate how difficult it had become to repeat operations such as those in East Germany in 1953, in Hungary in 1956, and in Czechoslovakia in 1968.

There had been high expectations focused on Gomulka when he assumed power in 1956. Important reforms were instituted. Collectivization of agriculture was largely done away with. The strong Catholic Church was granted a freer position than in any other Eastern European country. Soviet influence was reduced. But Gomulka was no liberal. After a short time, the grip was tightened once more. Cultural and intellectual life was closely controlled. At the end of the 1960s, the repression was the harshest since the Stalin era.

In 1970 Gomulka was aging, ailing, and exhausted. The economy was in serious difficulties. In order to increase government revenue, the prices of consumer goods were raised substantially just before Christmas. That resulted in a repetition of 1956, the only difference being even more extensive demonstrations and protests. The new man the party rallied round was Edward Gierek.

Gierek implemented large-scale imports of Western technology to increase investments and economic growth. This policy showed good results during the first years. After that the economy declined once more.

New widespread demonstrations erupted in 1976. Once again, the economic situation was the point of departure. Again the authorities had to go back on proposed price increases. The situation did not improve after 1976. The economic crisis grew steadily worse and the political base for the regime narrower. In contrast to the party's dwindling authority was the Church's ever stronger position, clearly manifested in the Polish Pope John Paul II's journey to Poland in the summer of 1979.

In August 1980, extensive strikes broke out in protest against new price increases. Effective cooperation was instituted between workers and intellectuals, who jointly demanded free trade unions.

The new trade union, Solidarity, under the leadership of Lech Walesa, soon established itself as a third center of power, alongside the party and the Church. The trade union was to pursue union concerns and keep clear of political issues that could undermine the position of the Communist party. This delimitation was bound to be unclear. Calls for the repeal of censorship, a more democratic Communist party, and finally free elections demonstrated the fact that Solidarity's demands had acquired clearly political dimensions.

The Soviet Union watched developments in Poland with the greatest unease. Through military maneuvers and other forms of pressure, the Kremlin tried to limit the party's concessions, without success. Direct intervention was hardly an alluring alternative. It could meet with considerable opposition from the Polish population in general and perhaps from parts of the army as well. The Western powers warned that a Soviet invasion would produce greater consequences than had been the case in similar situations previously. The invasion of Afghanistan had already imposed great burdens on Moscow and had soured relations with the Western powers. Further deterioration should be avoided. Poland's economic distress was considerable and its dependence on the West was great, which indicated that Moscow was bound to be interested in limiting its direct responsibility for developments in the country.

The unexpected solution was that the Polish army under General Jaruzelski took control and declared a state of emergency in December 1981. Jaruzelski had become party leader in October 1981. The Western powers, led by the United States, responded with a limited economic boycott. Although the party had practically collapsed, the new leadership managed to stabilize the situation after a fashion.

The leaders of Solidarity, headed by Lech Walesa, were forced underground, and in October 1982 the organization was formally dissolved by law. In 1983 the state of emergency was lifted, and in 1985 General Jaruzelski felt confident enough to call for 'elections.' At the Communist Party congress in June and July of 1986, the party expressed its support for Gorbachev's reform program, and the Soviet leader reciprocated by supporting Jaruzelski's government.

Moscow met the tendencies towards dissolution in Eastern Europe in the 1970s and 1980s in more or less the same fashion as previously. On the one hand, there was a willingness to emphasize the equal status of all Eastern bloc countries and parties more clearly than ever. Formally, the Soviet leaders no longer claimed their former position of leadership. On the other hand, the Kremlin tried to bolster the institutions that could reinforce cooperation between the Soviet Union and Eastern Europe. The military integration of the Warsaw Pact was to be cultivated, under Soviet leadership. COMECON was also to be expanded at a lower level in order to encourage direct cooperation between branches and firms. However, time would show that under this almost normal surface there were processes at work that would transform Eastern Europe completely.

THE SOVIET UNION AND THE COMMUNIST MOVEMENT ELSEWHERE

Certain countries outside of Eastern Europe were also highly dependent on the Soviet Union. Outer Mongolia was one such example. This country's ties to Moscow went back to the 1920s and to some extent reflected a desire for protection against China. Mongolia was admitted to COMECON in 1962, and large numbers of Soviet troops were stationed in the country. The Karmal regime in Afghanistan, which was installed in December 1979, would probably have had a short life span if it had not been for the massive Soviet military effort (see p. 91).

Cuba and North Vietnam also supported the Soviet Union. They accepted the leadership of the Soviet Union, but did so mainly for their own reasons. These regimes had not risen to power with the help of the Red Army, but on the contrary had independent power bases. It was another matter that they would gradually become more closely bound to Moscow than they may have intended at first.

After Castro's Cuba had shown clear signs of independence during the 1960s, such as in its attempts to export the Cuban revolution to other countries in Latin America, and in its attitude towards the Sino-Soviet conflict, the country gradually began to pursue a clearly pro-Moscow course. Castro approved of the invasion of Czechoslovakia, supported the Soviet Union against China, and cooperated with the Soviet Union in Africa, although partly based on motives of Cuban self-interest. In 1972 Cuba became a member of COMECON.

North Vietnam, which acquired control over South Vietnam and then in Laos in 1975, and from 1978 in Cambodia, abandoned the balancing act between Moscow and Peking that had characterized the country prior to the mid-1970s. Hanoi now supported the Soviet Union openly. In 1978 Vietnam joined COMECON and entered into a 25-year friendship and cooperation agreement with Moscow. The Soviet Union acquired base rights in Vietnam.

Cuban and Vietnamese support for the Soviet Union was to a considerable extent situational. Cuba sought protection against the United States in Moscow, and the Cuban economy had become dependent on the Soviet economy. Vietnam had also received support against the United States. After the end of the Vietnam War, Hanoi came into serious conflict with Peking over boundary issues and over developments in Cambodia. That tied Vietnam even more closely to Moscow.

The split in the communist movement expressed itself more clearly in Moscow's relations with other major Communist parties. In North Korea, the country's leader, Kim Il Sung, wanted to keep on good terms with both of its large neighbors. To a great extent he managed to secure his own and North Korea's interests during the bitter Sino-Soviet dispute.

The largest non-governing Communist parties were to be found in Indonesia and in Italy. The Indonesian party had embarked on a pro-Chinese course in the 1960s, but was completely crushed during the chaotic events of the coup and counter-coup in the autumn of 1965. The army's assumption of power ushered in a witch hunt for true and imagined Communists, and approximately 500,000 persons lost their lives.

The Italian Communist party had shown signs of independence even before the death of party leader Togliatti in 1964, but the breakthrough came with the denunciation of the Soviet invasion of Czechoslovakia. Later, the party would distance itself further from Moscow. The Italian Communist party (PCI) refused to take a stand in opposition to China and in fact accepted Italy's membership in NATO and the EC. In terms of domestic policy, the party placed emphasis on appearing both as a defender of democratic rights and as a spokesman for broad cooperation in the trade union movement and in the national assembly. Even so, the Communists were not accepted as members of the government. Nor did they effect a complete break with the Soviet Union. They still considered themselves a part of the worldwide communist movement, but with the right to determine their own policies themselves.

The Italian version of 'Euro-communism' enjoyed support to some extent in France as well. For a time the small Spanish Communist party pursued its independence even further than the Italians, whereas the French party returned to a more traditional position in 1978–79. This change of course arose primarily from domestic French considerations. Moscow no longer had the authority to dictate developments in the Western European parties.

In few places were the changes in the position of the Soviet Union greater than in Africa. Moscow could achieve success from time to time, but setbacks had a tendency to follow close on its heels. During the 1960s the Kremlin pinned its hopes on Ghana and Guinea. Ghana in particular proved a disappointment seen from a Soviet perspective. Then Egypt became the primary partner for cooperation, until the Soviets were thrown out in 1972. The same thing happened in Somalia in 1977.

The Marxist-inspired parties in Africa were quite different from ordinary Communist parties. Their ideological content could be highly syncretic. Thus Moscow wished to focus more on ideological training. At the close of the 1970s the Soviet position was the strongest in Angola and Ethiopia, and to a lesser extent in Mozambique (see pp. 89–90), Benin, and Congo-Brazzaville. The Soviet–Cuban presence was extensive in Angola and Ethiopia. Twenty-year friendship and cooperation agreements were signed with Angola in 1976, Mozambique in 1977, and Ethiopia in 1978. The Kremlin gave substantial military and economic assistance to these three countries.

However, in the 1980s Soviet influence was waning even in these countries. Mozambique signed a non-aggression treaty and Angola a cease-fire agreement with the regime in South Africa. The Africans showed an interest in reducing the Soviet–Cuban military involvement and in strengthening economic relations with the West. In December 1988 a treaty granting Namibia independence was concluded and formally ratified by the United Nations. According to the treaty, all foreign troops would be withdrawn from Angola during the course of 1991. Under Gorbachev's leadership, the Soviet Union became very eager to reduce its economic commitments abroad. In the economic sphere the communist countries were still unable to compete with the Western powers. And the focus was no longer on events in Africa, but rather on basic developments much closer to home.

THE FALL OF COMMUNISM IN EASTERN EUROPE

During the 1970s and 1980s, communism in the Eastern European countries began to assume more and more national contours, which materialized as reforms within the existing system. However, in 1989 the existing system disappeared. In the course of six months, from the relatively free elections in Poland in June until the fall of Ceauşescu in Romania in December, the entire system in Eastern Europe was dismantled. The established Communist regimes all stepped down as a result of mass demonstrations and protests. This transition was peaceful throughout Eastern Europe with the exception of Romania, where there was extensive street fighting. Events occurred at a pace no one had imagined possible. Somewhat simplified, it has been said that in Poland the process took about ten years, in Hungary ten months, in East Germany ten weeks, and in Czechoslovakia ten days.

In Poland, Solidarity had won a decisive victory in the 1989 election. This broad coalition movement won 99 of the 100 seats in the Senate as well as the vast majority of the seats it was vying for in the lower chamber. The winning parties in Hungary were the parties of the center and the right; the victory in Czechoslovakia went to Civic Forum under the leadership of Václav Havel; in East Germany the Christian Democrats, with close ties to their West German counterparts, emerged as the largest party. Bulgaria and Romania were the exceptions, where reformed Communists emerged victorious from the elections.

The fall of the old regimes can be explained in part by changes in the Soviet stance and partly by processes at work throughout Eastern Europe and within the individual countries. In retrospect we can see that it had gradually become more difficult for Moscow to intervene in the Eastern European countries. In 1956 the Red Army had singlehandedly taken action in Hungary; the 1968 intervention in Czechoslovakia was a joint operation by several of the Warsaw Pact allies; in 1980–81 in Poland the Kremlin refrained from sending in troops.

Thus there are grounds for claiming that even the old men in the Kremlin were in the process of changing their policy in relation to Eastern Europe. Mikhail Gorbachev's rise to power in 1985 did not bring about a sudden change. On the contrary, there seems to have been an evolution in Gorbachev's outlook as well. In his speech to the Polish Communist party congress in June 1986, he expressed his conviction that socialism had deep roots in Eastern Europe, and that the working people there 'could not imagine being without socialism. This means that socialistic progress is irrevocable.' And, he continued,

> threatening the socialist system, attempting to undermine it from the outside and tear a country out of the socialist fold, means violating not only the will of the people, but also the entire order since the Second World War, and in the final analysis, peace itself.

Even so, Gorbachev's politics were a decisive factor for developments in Eastern Europe. Gorbachev made it plain that there was no single communist model to follow any longer. Through his increasingly sharp criticism of the former course, he almost gave the impression that the Eastern European countries ought to avoid the Soviet path. Most important was the fact that he did not want to send the Red Army into Eastern Europe once more. Thus the Warsaw Pact's denunciation of the Brezhnev Doctrine in December 1989 represented a formal confirmation of a policy Moscow had already been pursuing for some time rather than a sign of an entirely new course.

To the extent Gorbachev had direct influence on the Eastern European regimes, it appears that he supported the pro-reform circles in both Poland and Hungary. He did not even send troops against the large-scale demonstrations in East Germany. In Czechoslovakia it appears that he wanted Milos Jakes, the relatively traditional party leader who had succeeded Husak in December 1987, to be replaced by more reform-oriented elements. However, that was not to be. The entire party was swept aside, and Havel emerged as the unifying leader.

There may have been many reasons why Gorbachev adopted a new policy in relation to Eastern Europe. He represented a policy of reform in the Soviet Union, a stance that was difficult to combine with intervention in Eastern Europe. The desire for détente with the West reinforced this new orientation. And once the system of sanctions had been removed, it was difficult to know what direction developments would take. Thus Gorbachev was taken captive by the course of events. Moreover, when the Soviet economy was seriously scrutinized, the economic costs of the Soviet role in Eastern Europe became more evident. During the first years after the Second World War the Soviet Union had extracted substantial resources from Eastern Europe. In the 1970s it began to become evident that the region was no longer profitable for the Soviets in purely economic terms. On the contrary, it represented a major expense, not only because of the military expenditure, but also through the sale of oil and gas to Eastern Europe at a low price and the purchase of Eastern European industrial products of poor quality at a high price. These increased costs revealed a pattern corresponding to that experienced by many former empires, including the British.

Developments in one country greatly influenced developments in the others. If the opposition in one country attained substantial concessions, that provided a stimulus for the opposition in the other countries. Poland led the way. The essentially free elections in Poland in June 1989 acted as a significant catalyst. A process of liberalization had been taking place in Hungary for several years, but when Hungary opened its borders in September to East Germans who wanted to emigrate to West Germany, the consequences for East Germany were great. The fall of Honecker in October and the opening of the Berlin Wall in November (see p. 105) in turn spurred on the demonstrations in Czechoslovakia, which led to the demise of Communist rule there in November–December. Jakes pointed out that 'we have completely underestimated the processes now taking place in Poland, Hungary and East Germany in particular and the influence they will have on our society.' This course of events contributed to the resignation of Zhivkov in Bulgaria and the overthrow of Ceauşescu in Romania, although the break with the past was less dramatic in these two countries than in the others. Ceauşescu's skepticism of the Soviet Union had meant that Gorbachev's example had relatively little significance in Romania, and the national base of the regime was a major reason for the bloodshed that erupted, in contrast to the other countries in the region.

Now that the Red Army was no longer a threat, the Eastern Europeans could determine their own future. Very few of the Communist governments had enjoyed mass support, but there had long been a core of supporters who were convinced that the new system represented 'light and hope.' By the late 1980s the belief in communism as the path of the future was definitely gone, and opportunism and corruption flourished in the party bureaucracies. The economic situation was bleak, and even in the countries which appeared to be best off, such as East Germany, Czechoslovakia, and Hungary, the inhabitants felt that they had been left behind, at least in comparison with their Western neighbors. Hungary had gone the farthest in implementing economic reforms, but even there they had not yielded particularly good results. Thus Karoly Grosz, who had taken over as Hungarian Communist party leader after Kadar in May 1988, said on 1 May 1989 that 'we have a huge foreign debt, an empty treasury, widespread social discontent and the population is disillusioned. We must begin afresh once more.'

Due to a number of local factors, the opposition was strongest in Poland and Hungary. Some of these factors have been mentioned in the discussion of the events of 1956 (see pp. 187–8). Poland's economic policies had proved to be particularly unsuccessful. By the end of the 1980s, the standard of living was lower than it had been ten years earlier and the inflation rate had reached three digits. Here the intellectuals, workers, and peasants had managed to cooperate closely within Solidarity under the leadership of Lech Walesa, and the opposition derived considerable strength from the influential position of the Church, a Church whose international head was now their 'own' pope. What had happened in 1956 had left deep scars in Hungary. Thus, it was a substantial victory for the Hungarian opposition in February 1989 when the events of 1956 were redefined as a 'popular revolt' rather than a 'counter-revolution,' which had been the former designation. The situation in Hungary was unique, as the Communist party there largely terminated its leading role itself.

THE FALL OF THE SOVIET UNION

The fall of communism did not stop in Eastern Europe. In 1991 three processes culminated which only a few years earlier had seemed beyond the realm of possibility: the Soviet Union collapsed, the communist dictatorship was done away with, and a sort of market economics, however precarious, was instituted. These three processes were concurrent and highly interdependent. They represented some of the most decisive changes in the history of the twentieth century.

At the end of the Brezhnev period, it was obvious that the Soviet Union was experiencing difficulties. Economic growth had been strong during the 1950s and 1960s, but in the 1970s the growth rate declined, and during the course of the 1980s it stopped altogether. The five-year plans had yielded substantial results in terms of production of iron and steel, but it was much more difficult for a centralized economy to determine developments within consumer goods and electronics. In addition, computer technology threatened to undermine the Communists' information monopoly. The most readily available raw material resources had already been exploited, and there was a shortage of labor in vital sectors. The former growth had to a great extent been based on increasing factor inputs. Now growth had to be based more on increased productivity, and that was difficult to achieve in the Soviet Union.

The foreign policy triumphs of the 1970s had concealed not only the economic, but also the moral decay. Stalin's regime had been based on terror, but idealism and belief in the future were important elements as well. Khrushchev had put an end to most of the terror, and himself expressed strong faith in the future, but there was ever greater skepticism about the party leader's constantly shifting plans to stimulate the Soviet economy. Under Brezhnev the system continued to decay. A swollen bureaucracy stifled individual initiative, and corruption blossomed. The moral decay was most clearly expressed in a sharply declining life expectancy, due to such factors as problems in the health sector, alcoholism, and work accidents.

When Mikhail Gorbachev rose to power in March 1985, he was keenly aware of the need for reforms. As he himself related in 1990: in 1984 he and another reform Communist, Eduard Shevardnadze, had strolled along the shore of the Black Sea, reaching the conclusions 'everything is rotten' and 'it is no longer possible to live like this.' Already in a speech in December 1984 Gorbachev announced that the Soviet Union was in decline and that reforms were needed to sustain the country's superpower status. The economy needed to be decentralized and price mechanisms used more freely. Workers should be allowed to participate in the formulation of their firm's policy. A moral awakening was also required.

From the very beginning Gorbachev encouraged *glasnost*, or openness about the problems of society. The concept of *perestroika*, which was introduced in the spring of 1985, was first confined to economic reform. However, it was soon given a broader meaning and applied to reform of Soviet society in general. Gorbachev envisioned that if he could only manage to sweep away the many layers of bureaucracy that separated him as the highest leader of the country from the people with their great strength, he could create a new foundation for the position of the Soviet Union.

However, Gorbachev did not have any desire to shatter the boundaries of the communist system per se. He had reached the top through the party and while in power he retained his faith in a reformed communism. He willingly turned to Lenin's new economic policies for a historic parallel to what he was attempting. Even though elements of the market were to be introduced, he was opposed to the free market as an economic governing principle, and the means of production were to remain under state ownership.

Gorbachev did not have a clear objective, and thus no clear plan for how to achieve his objectives. However, it soon became apparent to him that it was impossible to reform the communist system within the existing apparatus. Thus the dosages of *glasnost* had to be steadily increased. The most conservative leaders had to be replaced. In January 1987, Gorbachev declared that 'we need democracy as fresh air.' There were to be several candidates at elections, although the elections were still to take place within the framework of the Communist party, and there were to be clear limits to how long party leaders could remain in power, except those at the very top. Within criminal justice, elements of a state founded on legal protection began to emerge.

In June 1987 the party advocated some more profound economic reforms. Strict centralization was to be replaced by self-management of business enterprises, profits were encouraged, price policies were liberalized and credits given to new enterprises. Now the old system began to show cracks in earnest.

Politically there were splits within the party between those who wanted to proceed with reforms at an even more rapid pace and those who wanted to retain more of the status quo. Boris Yeltsin was the foremost spokesman for the reformists, while Yegor Ligachev was the leader among the more conservative circles. Gorbachev had taken the initiative for reforms, but he gradually assumed a position in the center which he deftly exploited to his own political advantage.

However, the political struggle in the Soviet Union could no longer be contained within the Communist party. Through *glasnost* it was possible not only for more independent intellectuals, but also for broader popular movements to play a part. Nationalism became the most important mobilizing force. In 1917 the Bolsheviks had represented the republics' right to self-determination, and that right had been established in the constitution. In reality the republics had lost any true self-government, apart from various cultural symbols and expressions. Gorbachev was a warm defender of the unity of the Soviet Union. In the autumn of 1986 he was asked whether he thought the ethnic differences could lead to serious conflicts. He responded that 'ethnic conflict is what worries me least in the Soviet Union.'

The first nationalist protests emerged in Kazakhstan in December 1986 when Gorbachev replaced a corrupt local first secretary with an honest but imported Russian. This resulted in revolt and a partial retreat by Moscow. The following year a dispute broke out between Armenia and Azerbaijan over Nagorno-Karabakh, an Armenian enclave in Azerbaijan. This struggle soon became violent and led to a national mobilization in both republics. Moscow was opposed to changing the existing borders, largely out of fear of the far-reaching consequences that could ensue if the existing system was tampered with. In 1989 large groups of people demonstrated for independence in Georgia. Thus three of the republics in the Caucasus had entered upon the path to independence during the course of 1988–89.

The Baltic region was the other area where demands for independence emerged early and with force. Whereas the process in the Caucasus was violent and sometimes chaotic, it was legalistic and non-violent in the Baltic countries. However, the result was the same: steadily increasing strength behind the demands for full national independence. Estonia was the first republic to declare its 'independence,' in November 1988. Demands for independence were also strong in Moldova and particularly in the western part of Ukraine. The catastrophe at the nuclear power plant in Chernobyl in 1986 spurred Ukrainian nationalism. In June 1990 Russia declared its own 'independence.'

Economically and politically Gorbachev was losing control. In the economic sphere new reform plans were continually being introduced for ever greater degrees of market economics within a basically socialist structure of ownership. One plan contradicted the next. As a result, the old system lost much of its remaining power, without anything new to replace it. Politically the situation was much the same. The old system's legitimacy was undermined without Gorbachev managing to establish a new power base. It became increasingly evident that only free elections could create new legitimacy. Gorbachev wanted elections only within the framework of the system, although this framework was broadening constantly. When Yeltsin was elected president of Russia through free elections in June 1991, he had attained a legitimacy with which Gorbachev could not compete.

As Gorbachev himself conceded in 1990: 'When we started, we did not recognize the depth of the problems we were facing.' The reform process was on the way to getting totally out of control. However, it could only be stopped by resorting to widespread use of force, which in turn would undermine Gorbachev's reform policies and be detrimental to relations with the West.

From the autumn of 1990 Gorbachev entered on a more conservative course. In October he rejected the liberal 500-day plan for economic reform. In January 1991 violence was used against nationalists in both Lithuania and Latvia. On the issue of the independence of the republics, however, Gorbachev was driven from bulwark to bulwark. In August 1991 he was forced, particularly by Yeltsin, to enter into a treaty of union which granted the republics a great degree of independence.

In an attempt to save the Soviet Union and as much of the old system as possible, a conservative group under the leadership of Vice-President Yanayev, Prime Minister Pavlov, Minister of Internal Affairs Pugo, Minister of Defense Yazov, and KGB chief Kryuchkov tried to carry out a coup in August 1991. They hoped to have Gorbachev on their side – after all, they had been appointed by Gorbachev – but when he refused to support them, the coup was directed against the Soviet president himself.

However, the coup failed because it was poorly organized, because even the military–industrial circles were split, and because Boris Yeltsin was able to mobilize a broad popular opposition, particularly in Moscow. After three days, Gorbachev could return to Moscow, but now he was in power only by the mercy of Yeltsin. The Communist party, which had dominated Soviet politics since 1917, was suspended in Russia. In December the Soviet Union was dissolved and Gorbachev was forced to resign. The Commonwealth of Independent States, which most of the new countries would belong to, would prove to play a very modest role.

DEVELOPMENTS IN RUSSIA AND EASTERN EUROPE AFTER THE FALL OF COMMUNISM

Gorbachev's policies brought down the old system. The Soviet Union collapsed, communism was discredited, and the Russian economy largely in shambles. Gorbachev had managed to bring the Cold War to an end, but the domestic problems his policies had attempted to solve had all become worse.

Under Yeltsin's leadership Russia tried to practice a form of market economics. Prices were deregulated, with a few exceptions. Foreign trade was stimulated. State-owned industry was partially privatized. However, the results were poor. The inflation rate reached 2,500 per cent in 1992 before it began to drop sharply. Privatization often meant that the local leaders who had run an enterprise for the state now ran it for themselves. Production declined dramatically. According to official statistics, the gross national product plummeted by 38 per cent from 1991 to 1994. Such a large peacetime drop in production is rare. Apart from inflation, crime seemed to be the factor most on the rise. In this area private initiatives were well organized.

Russia had no democratic tradition to speak of. The chaotic state of the economy made political stability practically impossible. The old and the new coexisted in a very uneasy mixture. As president, Yeltsin had to govern with a parliament that had been elected in 1990 and was dominated by conservatives. The constitution was from the Brezhnev period, but several hundred changes were made. The power struggle between Yeltsin and the conservatives in the Congress of People's Deputies culminated in October 1993 when Yeltsin sent in troops in a successful operation against an increasingly aggressive legislature.

The elections that were held for the reformed Russian legislature in December 1993 only partially solved Yeltsin's problem. The votes were spread among many different parties. The extreme nationalists under Zhirinovsky won the most votes. However, the new constitution gave the president such a strong position at the expense of the legislature that Yeltsin could govern more undisturbed than previously. On the other hand, his health deteriorated, and reluctantly he had to relinquish more power to Prime Minister Chernomyrdin.

The Soviet Union had been dissolved into its constituent republics. But the danger of separatism lurked within Russia as well. It was a country of 97 national or ethnic groups. All the problems in Moscow meant that in practice the regions were allowed a considerable degree of self-government. A few of them also formally demanded independence. Nationalism was strongest in Chechnya; in October 1991 it declared its status as a separate republic. Moscow waited a long time before responding, but in December 1994 the Russian Army was sent in. A bloody war ensued, weakening the forces for democracy in Russia (see p. 110).

The many great shocks the Russians had experienced bred a certain degree of yearning for the past. Inflation had impoverished pensioners and others on fixed wages. There were huge gaps between the poor and the rich. The economic reform policies were partially discredited. Wages were not paid for months at a time. Some people even began to long for the Soviet Union of the past. In many instances the economic ties between the former Soviet republics had been abruptly severed. Russia's voice in international politics could not hold a candle to that of the Soviet Union by any means.

The nationalistic-conservative currents represented a political challenge for a weakened Yeltsin. But even the Communists were affected by the new situation. The Soviet Union and communism could not be brought back. The course of the ex-Communists was therefore to try to weaken the reforms and to criticize their adverse manifestations. Following the elections to the legislature in December 1995 the communists became the strongest group, followed by the nationalists.

Despite his health problems, the state of the Russian economy, and the political challenges, Boris Yeltsin clearly remained the dominant figure in Russian politics. In June 1996 he was re-elected president. He very much hired and fired his own ministers. The national assembly repeatedly challenged the president, but in the end Yeltsin almost always won out. With the partial exception of Chechnya, Russia held together.

In August–September 1998, however, the Russian economy more or less collapsed. The short-term reasons could be found in the failure to collect taxes, the chaotic nature of the banking system, the increase in foreign debt, the decline in the price of oil and the quantity produced, and the impact of the economic crisis in East Asia. The most significant long-term reason probably had to do with the fact that Russia had no historical experience with a market system and that property rights were confused. Yeltsin was more interested in protecting his own economic and political base than in dealing with the difficult situation for the Russian economy. There was little the outside world could do. Health conditions were also rapidly deteriorating. Life expectancy among males declined to less than 60 years, a decline of almost 15 years.

On 31 December 1999, Yeltsin resigned as president and Prime Minister Vladimir Putin became acting president until he was elected to the office in March. Putin, who had begun his career in the KGB, could seem somewhat drab, particularly compared to the colorful Yeltsin. With the exception of the conflict in Chechnya, which, following the new Russian invasion in the winter of 1999–2000, temporarily deteriorated, developments now took a turn for the better in many ways. With the help of the low exchange rate following the collapse in 1998, Soviet exports experienced an upswing. High oil prices brought substantial revenues to the treasury. The newly wealthy Russians who had been sending their money abroad for a long time now started to bring it back to Russia. Putin's government was relatively competent and predictable, even though few observers were quite certain of what the president really wanted apart from political stability and economic growth. However, for weary Russians that in itself was quite a lot. Internationally, Russia still had a formidable nuclear arsenal, but statistically its gross national product was now no greater than that of the Netherlands.

Putin's and Russia's position continued to strengthen, however. Elections were held, although in many ways democratic rights were increasingly limited. Now the government won resounding victories in these elections. The chaos of the 1990s was indeed replaced by rapid economic growth and political stability. In 2008 Putin was succeeded as president by Dmitry Medvedev, but Putin continued as prime minister and the dominant leader. While in the 1990s Russia's position had been rapidly weakened in the 'near abroad' with the creation of many new states that often pursued pro-Western policies, Putin was now determined to win back some of what had been lost. The military budget increased significantly. This, again, gradually made for strained relations with most of the newly independent states as well as with the West. This was particularly the case with the United States, after some years of extensive cooperation, also with the Bush administration after 11 September. Relations with Western-oriented Ukraine and Georgia were particularly troublesome. They were both interested in NATO membership. Russia tried to exploit Ukraine's energy dependence. In August 2008 Georgia launched an attack into South Ossetia, formally part of Georgia, but under Russian control. The attack was quickly repulsed by Russian forces. South Ossetia and Abkhazia were proclaimed as independent countries. The Russia–Georgia war strengthened skepticism of Russia in the West. On the other hand, the Russian policy met with some success in countries such as Kazakhstan and some of the other Muslim republics, and even in Belarus and Armenia. With the large fall in the price of oil after 2007, Russia began to experience economic problems again. Its exports consisted almost entirely of oil and gas, some other raw materials and weapons. Its economy had not really diversified significantly.

In May 2012 Putin was elected president of Russia for a third term. His victory was overwhelming, although many questions were asked about the fairness of the election. The Russian economy had picked up again after the recession. In 2011 Russia was finally able to join the WTO, after 15 years of negotiation, although relations with the West were generally deteriorating. Putin's domestic position appeared strong, although many in the biggest cities were becoming frustrated with his increasingly authoritarian rule. In 2011–12 thousands had protested in the streets in the biggest cities against Putin's rule.

In Ukraine popularly elected president Yanukovitch was driven from office in February 2014, when he refused to sign an association agreement with the EU and instead chose to rely on Russia. Putin responded by occupying Crimea, which had been under Ukraine since 1954, and by supporting separatists in eastern Ukraine. A civil war followed in the eastern parts. Western sanctions were imposed against Russia. With the price of oil collapsing internationally and the ruble in decline the Russian economy suffered, but Putin's nationalistic message still appeared to be popular with the Russian population.

The new Eastern Europe, too, was facing problems, although not of Russia's magnitude. In the first place these countries wanted to establish democratic governments in a region where democratic traditions, except in Czechoslovakia, were weak. They were also to make the transition from a communist command system to various degrees of market economics. The ethnic–national conflicts in the region were far from resolved, although that claim had been made under the communist regimes. The number of Jews and Germans had been reduced sharply and borders had been redrawn after the Second World War, but the region was still complex.

Developments in Yugoslavia have already been described (see also pp. 112–13). In Czechoslovakia, tensions between Czechs and Slovaks were exploited by politicians in both camps, resulting in a division of the country in 1993 into the Czech Republic and Slovakia. The position of the Hungarians in Romania and in Slovakia was perhaps now the most difficult of the many minority issues in this region.

The direction in which foreign policy was developing in the Eastern and Central European countries was quite clear. Almost without exception they all wanted to become members of NATO and the EU. In that way they intended to ensure both their security, particularly vis-à-vis a potentially new, strong, Russia, and their economic development. Leading circles within both NATO and the EU were sympathetic to the idea of extending membership to include particularly the most Westernized of these countries, i.e. Poland, Hungary, and the Czech Republic. These three countries became members of NATO in 1999. In 2004 the three Baltic countries (Estonia, Latvia, and Lithuania), Slovakia, Slovenia, Bulgaria, and Romania would join NATO as well. In 2009 even Albania and Croatia followed. The Czech Republic, Poland, Hungary, the three Baltic countries, Slovakia, and Slovenia also became members of the EU in 2004, followed by Bulgaria and Romania in 2007.

Both NATO and particularly the EU required that member states should be demo-cratic and have settled any unresolved minority issues. This had great significance for developments in the region. Even so, political and economic developments varied con-siderably from country to country. Democracy and market economics were most firmly established in countries such as Slovenia, the Czech Republic, Poland, Hungary, and the Baltic countries. In countries such as Bulgaria and Romania, not to mention most of the former Soviet republics, such as Belarus and several of the Muslim states, the changes in relation to the past were much more modest. Many of the leaders in these countries had clear links back to the communist era, democracy was deficient, and the elements of market economics quite meager.

In the free elections that were held after liberation in 1989, right-wing parties enjoyed good results in most of the Eastern European countries. The transition to market eco-nomics caused many problems here, too, although they were considerably less serious than the situation in most of the former Soviet Union. Thus, in several countries there was a tendency for the reformed Communists to experience a strong come-back in the mid-1990s. In the presidential election in Poland in 1995, the incumbent, former Solidarity leader Walesa, lost to ex-communist Kwasniewski. In Hungary and Lithuania, too, the ex-communists made a good showing. But now they had virtually all become more social-democratic in their orientation. They were strongly in favor of membership in NATO and the EU, and they defended democracy and most aspects of market economics, although they turned their attention also to the economic and social problems that the transition to market economics had contributed to. Thus, even the Central European ex-communists had clearly broken with the past. Soon the variety in the make-up of the governments in Eastern Europe rivalled that in the Western half.

The Eastern Europeans wanted to become more and more like the Western Europeans. In fact, many disliked being called Eastern Europeans. They wanted to be simply Europeans, neither more nor less. Europe had made tremendous progress in integration, but major differences in living standards and cultural orientation still remained. Politically, first Hungary and then Poland took a different course, combining strong nationalism with some less democratic elements, while continuing to adhere to membership in NATO and the EU. Some Eastern European countries, with Hungary in the lead, also took an interest in developing better relations with Putin's Russia.

THE SOVIET UNION/RUSSIA AND THE (FORMERLY) COMMUNIST COUNTRIES, 1945-2016: THE LITERATURE

The key work on developments in Eastern Europe has long been François Fejtö, *A History of the People's Democracies* (Penguin Books, 1974). Zbigniew Brzezinski, *The Soviet Bloc: Unity and Conflict* (Cambridge, 1967) is also useful. Timothy Garton Ash's analyses of the events in Eastern Europe in 1989 are in a class by themselves. His articles have been compiled in *The Uses of Adversity: Essays on the Fate of Central Europe* (Cambridge, 1989) and *We the People: The Revolution of '89 Witnessed in Warsaw, Budapest, Berlin and Prague* (Cambridge, 1990). A good book on developments in Eastern Europe is Joseph Rothschild, *Return to Diversity: A Political History of East Central Europe Since World War II* (Oxford, 1993).

Two excellent surveys of the Soviet period in Russian history are Geoffrey Hosking, *A History of the Soviet Union 1917–1991* (London, 1992) and Martin Malia, *The Soviet Tragedy: A History of Socialism in Russia, 1917–1991* (New York, 1994). William Taubman's *Khrushchev – The Man and his Era* (New York, 2003) is monumental. Good presentations of recent developments in Soviet/Russian history are John Miller, *Mikhail Gorbachev and the End of Soviet Power* (New York, 1993) and Stephen White, *After Gorbachev* (Cambridge, 1993). The newest stimulating effort to explain a big topic is Archie Brown, *The Rise and Fall of Communism* (London, 2009).

An excellent source publication on relations between China and the Soviet Union is Keesing's Publications Limited, *The Sino–Soviet Dispute* (London, 1970). Also useful in their own different ways are O. Edmund Clubb, *China and Russia: The 'Great Game'* (New York, 1971), John Gittings, *The World and China, 1922–1972* (London, 1974) and Lorenz M. Lüthi, *The Sino-Soviet Split: Cold War in the Communist World* (Princeton, NJ, 2008).

Strobe Talbott (ed.), *Khrushchev Remembers: The Last Testament* (Boston, 1974) is a fascinating source from the Soviet side. This source has a sequel in *Khrushchev Remembers: The Glasnost Tapes* (Boston, MA, 1990). Chen Jian, *Mao's China and the Cold War* (Chapel Hill, NC, 2001) is a convincing presentation of Mao's foreign policy. On Mao's excesses the most dramatic accounts are found in Frank Dikötter, *Mao's Great Famine. The History of China's Most Devastating Catastrophe, 1958–62* (London, 2010) and his *The Cultural Revolution. A People's History 1962–1976* (London, 2016).

THE RISE OF EAST ASIA

While the East of the Cold War – the Soviet Union and its allies in Eastern Europe – collapsed in the years 1989–91, a different East – East Asia – was becoming increasingly important in international relations. First, the focus was on the rapidly increasing role of Japan. Then the focus shifted to China and its exceedingly fast economic growth. In 2009, Japan and China had the second and third largest economies in the world. In 2010 the order was reversed. In 2015–16, when measured in purchasing power terms, China's GDP even surpassed that of the United States. While Japan was experiencing difficulties in maintaining its growth, China had been moving ahead at a pace not seen before in economic history. It was quickly becoming more and more evident that the rise of East Asia economically was bound to have very significant long-term consequences, even politically and militarily.

In the long historical perspective, China and India had for centuries been leading countries in the world. Their productions traditionally outstripped those of Western countries. Although they were relatively advanced technologically, particularly China, the size of their economies was primarily a reflection of their great populations. In traditional economies the tendency was clear: the greater the population, the greater the economy. Only with the industrial revolutions of the West was this relationship broken. Following the Industrial Revolution, relatively small Western European nation states, particularly Britain, developed the most advanced economies. Their technological lead was also reflected in their military supremacy. Small Western armies could defeat huge non-Western ones. India came under British rule. China was too large to be controlled by a single outside power, but many Western states established their enclaves in its coastal areas. Japan largely isolated itself for more than two centuries. However, after Japan had been forcefully reopened in the 1850s, the decision was made to modernize the country as quickly as possible. This policy was so successful that in 1904–05 Japan defeated Russia in war. In the Second World War Japan tried to establish control over the Pacific and most of Asia. This effort failed.

After the Second World War a new Japan emerged. The emperor remained, but a new parliamentary democracy was introduced. The country was to be demilitarized. It was first occupied by the United States; then it pursued its foreign policy in close alliance with the US. After some years of hardship, Japan was again to become quite successful, both economically and politically. Its economy in fact became the second largest in the world, after that of the United States. In the 1990s major economic and political problems nevertheless developed.

In China the civil war ended in 1949 in victory for the Communists. In their impatience to catch up with the Great Powers of the world the Communist leaders undertook policies – the Great Leap Forward (1958–61) and the Cultural Revolution (1966–76) – which in fact led to huge setbacks. When, however, after Mao Tse-tung's death the Chinese leaders, under Deng Xiaoping, decided to pursue a pragmatic more market-oriented policy emphasizing the importance of economic growth, the results were quick in coming. China's growth was even more rapid and lasted longer than that experienced earlier by Japan, although from a much lower base.

THE UNITED STATES AND JAPAN, 1945-2016

US relations with Japan changed as much as US relations with Western Europe. During the first years after 1945, Japan was occupied by the United States, and US influence in Japan was stronger than in Europe. This continued in many areas even after the peace treaty of 1951 was signed.

From the early 1950s Japan entered an extended period of very rapid economic growth. During the 1980s the Japanese gross national product surpassed that of the Soviet Union, and Japan thus became the world's second largest economic power. Japan's economic growth contributed to a substantial degree of political stability. The Liberal-Democratic party totally dominated Japanese politics. Gradually Japan began to play a somewhat more independent role in international politics, but ties to the United States were still strong.

From the 1990s onward, the situation in Japan became more uncertain. The earlier political stability disappeared in the wake of the end of the Cold War and as a result of the decay within the Liberal-Democratic party after several decades in power. Japan also entered into a more difficult economic period of little or no economic growth. Trade and economic disputes with the United States increased in number and in strength, while Japan hesitantly struck out on a more independent course in foreign affairs. This course was, however, soon limited by the rise of China and the unpredictability of North Korea. The United States, therefore, remained Japan's protector.

1945–1960: Occupation and US Dominance

Japan was occupied by the United States alone. The role of the other allied countries here was as modest as the role of the Western powers in the former Axis states of Eastern Europe, where the Soviet Union determined the course of developments virtually alone. The Soviet Union complained about its lack of influence in Japan, as did Britain, Australia, and several other countries. Even the administration in Washington felt disregarded at times. Although Washington determined the main course of developments, the policies of the occupation authorities under General Douglas MacArthur were relatively independent.

During the US occupation, sweeping changes were instituted in Japanese society. Article 9 in the Japanese Constitution of 6 March 1946 established that Japan should not have military forces and that the country should not practice warfare. The political system came to resemble British parliamentarism on Japanese soil. The emperor was granted only a symbolic role. The national assembly, the Diet, became the seat of power, with the prime minister elected by the lower house. Women gained the right to vote, trade unions were established, comprehensive land reforms were instituted, the educational system was expanded, and decentralization encouraged.

As in Germany, the Cold War soon influenced occupation policy in Japan. The purging of nationalistic elements was limited, while the dismantling of the large companies – the *zaibatsus* – ceased, and in some cases the process was even reversed. When it became evident that Communists and left-wing socialists would have a strong position in the new trade unions, their rights were curbed.

From 1947 onwards, ever greater emphasis was placed on the reconstruction of Japan. A harsh policy of deflation was implemented in order to bring the country back on its feet. As with Germany, Japan could not be kept weak without the neighboring countries suffering serious economic consequences. But not until 1954–55 did the country again reach prewar levels by most standards.

MacArthur wanted a prompt peace treaty that could make Japan what he called a Switzerland of the East – without military forces and without US bases. This dream of his was shared by many Japanese, but in this matter Washington did not concur with the General nor, for that matter, with the Japanese. The Department of Defense in particular insisted that a peace treaty had to be accompanied by a security agreement granting the United States comprehensive base rights. After the outbreak of the Korean War and the transfer of US troops from Japan to Korea, the pressure to get Japan to build up semi-military self-defense forces increased sharply as well.

Although the peace treaty of 1951–52 formally marked Japan's reentry into the international arena, the country was still closely linked to the United States. The Soviet Union and its allies, including China, did not sign the treaty. US influence was further emphasized when the Senate, as a price for ratifying the treaty, insisted that Japan promise to recognize Taiwan. Again the Japanese had to give in, although many Japanese doubted that Japan's economy would be particularly viable without close relations with the Chinese mainland.

As early as the 1950s, however, there were signs indicating that Japan would come to play a somewhat independent role. In terms of domestic policy, a number of distinctively Japanese characteristics were preserved despite the tremendous US influence. As the decade progressed, Japan's economic growth began to accelerate in earnest. In terms of foreign policy, the Japanese criticized the US nuclear test detonations in the Pacific, re-established diplomatic relations with the Soviet Union, initiated a cautious trade with communist China, and joined the UN and international economic diplomacy through membership in the World Bank, the International Monetary Fund, and GATT. However, Japan's participation in the international economy in particular was encouraged by the United States.

1960–1990: Economic Strength and Greater Political Independence

The most obvious sign of a new climate was the rapidly growing criticism of the 1951 security agreement. The Eisenhower administration realized that comprehensive changes would have to be instituted if good relations were to be preserved and the governing

Liberal-Democratic party was to maintain its position vis-à-vis leftist groups. Thus, Washington agreed in 1960 to make the agreement valid for 10 years, with an option for renewal, instead of the apparently permanent agreement of 1951; US troops were divested of their right to interfere in domestic Japanese affairs; and changes in US policy with regard to nuclear weapons in Japan could be effected only after consultations with the Japanese government. After Eisenhower had to cancel a planned visit to Japan and Prime Minister Kishi had to resign because of all the political unrest related to the security agreement, this issue again faded into the background for a few years.

Kennedy tried to instill new life into US–Japanese relations by promising Japan, like Western Europe, 'an equal partnership' with the United States. Relations between the two countries improved in many ways, but there was no equal partnership to speak of. Militarily and politically Japan was still highly dependent on the United States.

Economically, however, Japan was in the process of becoming a major power. In the course of a seven-year period from the mid-1950s, the Japanese national product doubled, representing what was perhaps the most rapid growth any major power had experienced until then. The United States contributed to this growth by keeping the US market open for Japanese goods for the most part, while Washington accepted Japan's import restrictions on US goods – measures that to some extent went back to the occupation period. Most of the Western European countries, however, discriminated against Japanese goods even after Japan joined GATT. The primary interest of the United States in relation with Japan, as in Europe, was the establishment of an international political and economic system under US leadership. That required a willingness to pay the price certain aspects of this policy entailed.

During the course of the 1960s, new attitudes gradually began to emerge in Washington. Whereas the Americans enjoyed a large surplus in their trade with Japan until 1965, the United States then acquired a large deficit. Despite its participation in the international economic system, Japan not only had been, but in many ways still was protectionistic. Free trade had never been a dominant philosophy in Japan. The country felt vulnerable, since it had such limited natural resources. Moreover, the criticism from abroad was considered unfair, since so many countries discriminated against Japanese exports.

In 1968 Japan surpassed West Germany and became the world's third greatest power, measured in terms of gross national product. Although a liberalization of Japanese import policies did take place, Japan's exports caused problems of an increasing magnitude. From the end of the 1960s, Washington began in earnest to pursue a policy encouraging 'voluntary' Japanese limitations on exports to the United States.

The feeling that Japan did not contribute its fair share to the defense of the Western world grew as Japanese prosperity increased. It was true that the US forces in Japan were reduced to a level of about 37,000 men by 1972, and that Japan's defense appropriations were increased, but even so most Americans felt that Tokyo kept too low a profile. Defense expenditure represented less than 1 per cent of Japan's gross national product and even declined in some years. Nor did Japan offer more than superficial support to the United States in Vietnam.

Once more the security agreement with the United States became a focal point of interest. The US bases in Japan, and on Okinawa in particular, were highly significant for US warfare in Southeast Asia. Okinawa had only formally been Japanese since 1945.

For all practical purposes, the island was American. Again, Washington had to make concessions to maintain good relations with Japan. In the so-called Sato–Nixon communiqué of 1969, the United States returned Okinawa to Japan, and the bases there acquired the same status as the other bases in Japan. In return, the Japanese gave Washington reason to believe that they would play a more active role in the defense of their region, including South Korea and Taiwan.

Relations between the United States and Japan seemed to return to relative tranquility, but this was to be short-lived. In 1971 Japan suffered two blows, both inflicted by the Nixon administration. First the Americans initiated relations with China, then the United States levied a 10 per cent import duty and devalued the dollar.

Washington terminated its policy of isolating China without consulting Japan. Japan had long been interested in better relations with China but had harmonized its policies with those of the United States. Now Japan, too, recognized China. The economic measures were aimed more at Japan than at Western Europe, but again no consultations preceded Washington's actions.

The tensions between Japan and the United States induced Moscow to attempt to improve its relations with Tokyo. Political contacts were expanded, trade increased and the Kremlin showed an interest in involving Japan in major industrial projects, particularly in Siberia.

However, there were clear limitations on how good Japanese–Soviet relations could become. The crucial issue was the Soviet-controlled islands north of Japan. In 1945, Japan had had to cede the Kurile Islands, but Tokyo was not willing to relinquish its claim on the southernmost four of them. The Soviet Union, which had evidenced a certain degree of flexibility in the 1950s in particular, finally refused to honor this claim. Moreover, in the course of the 1970s the Pacific fleet became the part of the Soviet fleet that grew the most rapidly. The increased Soviet military presence near Japan could not contribute to improving mutual relations. Nor did the ambitious Japanese–Soviet industrial projects in Siberia really get off the ground.

China's entry into the international arena also caused problems. Although Japan tried to improve relations with both Communist countries at the same time, the Japanese had closer ties with China. The military and political problems were smaller, and the volume of Japanese trade with China became much greater than with the Soviet Union. Thus in 1978 Japan decided to sign a cooperation agreement with China, a decision that was not warmly received in Moscow.

During the first years following the Second World War, leading US politicians had been concerned as to whether Japan would manage to become economically self-sufficient. By the 1970s, their concerns were quite the opposite: that Japan would outstrip even the United States. By 1990 Japan's gross national product was more than half as large as the US GNP, and larger than both the Soviet economy and the unified German economy. Japan had become the world's leading creditor nation. The ten largest banks in the world were all Japanese. Japan surpassed the United States as the world's leading contributor of development assistance. Thus there was no doubt as to the country's increasingly important role in economic diplomacy.

Japan had gradually begun to play a more active role in political and military terms as well. At the May 1983 summit in Williamsburg, Virginia, the economic consultations among the leading Western industrial nations were extended to encompass military cooperation vis-à-vis the Soviet Union. Japan's defense budget increased substantially, reaching just beyond 1 per cent of GNP by the end of the 1980s, a level which had traditionally been considered the absolute maximum. Even so, the increase was considerably less than the United States desired. Slowly but surely Japan shaped its own policy in relation to China and the Soviet Union. Only half-heartedly did Tokyo take part in the sanctions against China after the Chinese authorities quelled the democracy movement in June 1989. On the other hand, Japan had a sharper profile in relation to the Soviet Union than the other Western powers had. This was evident in the question of economic support to Gorbachev's Soviet Union; here the dispute over the Soviet-controlled islands prevented a breakthrough.

1990–2016: Economic Problems and Political Uncertainty

As the 1980s gave way to the 1990s, many observers predicted that Japan would become the new superpower of the twenty-first century. Again it became evident how difficult it is to predict the future. For during the 1990s Japan entered into a difficult period, characterized by slow or non-existent economic growth, a lack of political stability, and some uncertainty as to the country's foreign policy profile.

In 1992 the Japanese economy stopped growing. The real estate and bank market had serious problems and even the large automobile manufacturers, which had become symbols of Japanese prosperity, experienced a significant drop in sales. Unemployment became a more substantial problem than official statistics showed.

The Liberal-Democratic party began to show distinct signs of wear and tear. Corruption scandals increased in number, and disagreement between various factions in the party became increasingly open. At the same time as their economic growth stopped, the Japanese were facing major problems in financing pensions for a steadily growing number of elderly while the total population was declining.

In August 1993 a broad coalition of parties came to power and the Liberal-Democratic dominance was broken. In June 1994 Japan even got a socialist prime minister, Tomoichi Murayama. This was definitely something new, even though more conservative circles still dominated in the government. In January 1996 a coalition dominated by the Liberal-Democrats returned to power under Prime Minister Ryutaro Hashimoto. By Japanese standards Hashimoto's political style appeared direct, but his economic policies only served to make the situation worse. In August 1998 he was, therefore, replaced.

The changes in foreign policy were smaller than might have been expected in the light of the economic and domestic policy shifts. Japan played an increasingly important role in international politics, but this process was very gradual. Relations with Russia remained relatively strained because of the disputed islands in the north. Relations with China were improving, but Japan's still very half-hearted acknowledgement of its actions during the Second World War placed limitations on these relations. The United States remained the key partner for Japan. However, the end of the Cold War increased the opposition to US security forces in the country, particularly on Okinawa. Nevertheless, the US–Japanese defense policy guidelines of September 1997 continued the close cooperation between these two countries, but with somewhat greater emphasis on the

Japanese contribution. Uncertainty related to developments in North Korea necessarily strengthened Japan's ties with the US. So did the rapid rise of China; Japan saw China as a rather significant potential threat.

The trade climate between the United States and Japan was at times very strained. Japan still had a substantial trade surplus in relation to the United States, and the Americans tried in ever more direct ways to get the Japanese to increase their imports from the US. Gradually, Japan's refusal to provide a major stimulus to its struggling economy caused even greater concern in the US. With the collapse of several Asian economies in the fall of 1997 (see p. 299) the situation worsened; and not only the economies of Asia, but also economies globally, were threatened. Whereas most Eastern Asian countries got back on the right track surprisingly fast, the economic difficulties in Japan persisted.

The high expectations that were held for Liberal-Democratic Junichiro Koizumi when he took over as reformist prime minister in April 2001 would not be fulfilled. The reforms were less ambitious than envisaged; economic growth was slow to really manifest itself. Only in 2003 were there signs of somewhat more robust economic growth, but no consistent pattern developed. The political problems became even worse when Koizumi left office in 2006. In 2007–09 the new economic crisis hit Japan quite badly. The Liberal-Democrats were in deep crisis. In 2009 the Democratic party took over but little happened in the way of reform. Growth was still slow. In 2011 a major earthquake and tsunami hit Japan. In December 2012 the Liberal-Democrats returned to power under Shinzo Abe who pursued a strongly expansionist economic policy in an effort finally to bring about economic growth.

No longer did anyone forecast that Japan would be the new superpower of the twenty-first century. The close cooperation between politicians, bureaucrats and businessmen that had seemed an explanation for Japan's growth for so many decades now appeared to explain the lack of growth and reform. The emphasis was now on China, not on Japan.

THE SINO-SOVIET-US TRIANGLE SINCE 1972

The story of the Chinese civil war, about developments in China after 1949 and Sino–Soviet relations until 1972 has already been told in Chapter 10. One of the chief controversies during the initial phase of the Sino–Soviet conflict had been the question of relations with the capitalist countries, especially the United States. Peking had been highly negative to Khrushchev's policy of détente. However, this condemnation could not prevent rapprochement between the United States and China in 1971–72 (see pp. 73–4).

Relations between the United States and China became steadily better throughout the 1970s, and a climax was reached in 1978–79 with full diplomatic recognition, a substantial increase in trade, and a number of cooperation agreements in various fields. Early in 1980 the United States declared its willingness to sell 'non-lethal' military equipment to China. Whereas Washington had had fairly good relations with both Moscow and Peking in the early 1970s, contact with China was much better than with the Soviet Union at the end of the decade. Both China and the West considered the Soviet Union an expansive power, in southern Africa, on the Horn of Africa, in Afghanistan, and in Indochina.

Although the border clashes between the Soviet Union and China decreased in intensity after 1969, and although attempts were made to improve relations between the two communist nations, there was no real rapprochement between Moscow and Peking during the 1970s. The climax in US–Chinese cooperation in fact coincided with a new, although temporary, deterioration in Sino–Soviet relations. In 1979 there were large-scale clashes between Vietnam and China, a situation that was mostly attributable to the Vietnamese invasion of Cambodia. Peking obviously wanted to teach Hanoi, now allied with Moscow, a lesson for having invaded a pro-Chinese country. The Soviet invasion of Afghanistan in December 1979 represented a further strain on Sino–Soviet relations.

Soon, however, cautious new signals could be perceived in Sino–Soviet relations, signals that grew stronger in the course of the 1980s. The major controversies persisted, but the polemics were toned down. Trade and other contacts increased. Meetings took place between high-ranking representatives of the two countries. Initiatives were taken to improve the situation, both in terms of border disputes and party contacts.

This new mood had several causes. Important changes occurred in China. Although the Cultural Revolution was somewhat on the wane after 1969, there were still radical elements among the party leaders. The fear of a 'Soviet-revisionist contagion' persisted. As long as Mao Tse-tung was alive, it seemed unlikely that the climate could be changed. After Mao's death in 1976 and after the moderates had consolidated their power under Deng Xiaoping's leadership in 1978–79, conditions were more favorable. The new leaders were prepared to have pragmatic relations with other countries, primarily in order to promote the large-scale modernization campaign. This dictated more tranquil relations not only with the United States, but with the Soviet Union as well.

The fear of a Soviet attack was also abating. At the close of the 1960s the atmosphere had been characterized by the Brezhnev Doctrine, extensive border clashes, and Soviet hints of the use of nuclear weapons against China. Even during the Sino–Vietnamese conflict and the Soviet invasion of Afghanistan, the tension level did not reach the heights it had manifested ten years earlier.

The two countries' relations with the United States were also significant. The situation in the 1970s had given Washington a central role. The Americans could, if they chose to, alternately favor the one or the other of the two rivals. The Soviet Union and China did not have the same maneuvering possibilities. Both Peking and Moscow must have perceived the negative consequences this situation entailed for them.

At the end of Carter's presidency, new tension arose in relations between China and the United States. The question of Taiwan was a primary reason. Both sides agreed that Taiwan was a part of China. The United States had also promised, as early as 1972, to re-evaluate its commitments to Taiwan in light of the overall situation in the region. But although US forces on the island had been reduced to 2,500 men, advanced weapons were still being sold to Taiwan.

Reagan's assumption of office resulted in increased tensions. During his election campaign he had promised to strengthen relations with Taiwan. The objective was a two-China policy. The President belonged to the Republican right wing, with its traditional partiality to Taiwan. Dissatisfaction with the new administration's stance was one factor behind China's somewhat improved relations with the Soviet Union.

Even so, Reagan did not go as far as he had first given the impression of. The need for a partner against the Soviet Union steadily increased and proved to be stronger than the conservative ties to Taiwan. The Chinese, for their part, needed US support, partly in relation to the Soviet Union, but just as much to accomplish their fourfold modernization program (industry, technology, defense, and agriculture). All in all, there were thus not such great changes in China's relations with the United States even under Reagan. In 1984–85 Reagan even approved the sale of various types of weapons to China.

Under Deng's determined leadership, the Chinese made great strides in liberalizing the economy. Government bureaucracy was reduced, private enterprise was stimulated in a number of fields, particularly within agriculture and retail trade, wages were more closely linked to work effort, and foreign investment was encouraged. China, which had chosen to use scarce resources on development assistance during the 1970s, was now the recipient of substantial foreign investment. This policy yielded good economic results, and Deng uttered the famous words: 'it doesn't matter whether the cat is black or white; as long as it catches mice, it's a good cat.'

However, this policy also entailed some problems. In the first place, it was controversial within the Communist party. In the second place, it yielded not only growth, but inflation, unemployment, and corruption as well. Third, it was difficult to combine relatively liberal economic policies with the firm control the Communist party wished to retain politically and culturally.

1989 was a crucial year in China, as it was in Eastern Europe and for East–West relations. In April and May, mass demonstrations erupted in Peking and many other cities in China. These demonstrations were dominated by students and intellectuals who were protesting against corruption and terrible conditions at the universities. They also demanded greater democracy. Soon after his rise to power Gorbachev had signaled his interest in better relations with China. In May 1989 he visited Peking, a visit which indicated improved relations. In a sense this summit represented the end of 30 years of animosity. The demonstrators were friendly towards Gorbachev as they wanted more *glasnost* in China. In comparison with Soviet policies, *perestroika* began earlier and went further in China, but, on the other hand, there was little *glasnost*. Following intense debate, on 4 June the party leadership ordered the army to take action to disperse the many demonstrators who were occupying Tiananmen Square in Peking. Hundreds were killed and thousands wounded. The movement for democracy was quashed.

The brutal methods of the authorities, captured by the cameras of the international media, led to sharp reactions throughout much of the world. Most of the Western countries responded by stopping deliveries of military equipment and suspending loans and credits. Peking made it clear that the economic reforms would continue, although in a somewhat more moderate form, but that the 'intellectual contamination' would be resisted.

However, it would not take long before relations between China and the rest of the world became more normal once again. China's rapid economic growth tempted many to engage in investment and trade. When Japan, for one, maintained normal relations to such a great extent, there was not much point in others keeping their distance. As the 1990s progressed, China finally seemed to become the enormous market many had been dreaming of for decades, if not for centuries.

Following the end of the Cold War and the collapse of the Soviet Union, relations between Russia and China changed. Russia was now a non-communist country, whereas China was determined to maintain its communist system despite the substantial strains of capitalism in its economy. Relations between these two countries became less important than previously, although both Russia and China were interested in mutually good relations, particularly in the economic sphere. Contact across the Sino–Russian border increased considerably. The two countries even proclaimed a 'strategic partnership' directed against those who would 'push the world towards a unipolar order.' Russia sold large quantities of weapons to China.

Still, China's relationship to the United States was more important than its relationship to Russia. For Sino–US relations, too, the end of the Cold War was significant. When Washington no longer needed a strong ally against the Soviet Union, the differences between the two countries again became more evident. The United States and China had different views on the two countries' roles in the world, on Taiwan, on human rights, and on Tibet. In the economic sphere, with China's rapid economic growth, there was a great increase in trade and in US investments in China. Gradually this had a positive effect on Sino–US relations. However, there were problems in incorporating China into the open international economy, with regard to such issues as membership in GATT/ WTO, exchange rates, patents, copyrights, and dumping.

While the Russians and the Americans reduced their military presence in East Asia, a partial Chinese build-up took place. A nationalistic tone could also be heard in Chinese foreign policy. As the Chinese had unresolved border disputes with nearly all their neighbors, this created uneasiness in this part of the world. Gradually, however, many of these disputes were resolved. In the United States the right wing in particular was interested in strengthening ties with Taiwan. When the President of Taiwan was allowed to visit the United States in June 1995, the climate between China and the United States became more strained. The Chinese military exercises and missile tests in connection with the first free presidential elections on Taiwan in March 1996 had an even more negative impact on relations.

After much vacillation, Bill Clinton decided to emphasize the elements of cooperation with China. Jiang Zemin, who had become the dominant leader after Deng's death in February 1997, took a distinct interest in extending the policy of economic liberalization. As the continuing rapid growth in China provided a significant inducement for strengthened relations, Jiang and Clinton met on several occasions. The handover of Hong Kong from Britain to China on 1 July 1997 also went more smoothly than many had expected. Yet at the end of the century there were still many matters of contention in relations between China and the United States. Taiwan, which increasingly asserted its independence, was the knottiest problem. The US bombing of the Chinese embassy in Belgrade during the war in Kosovo, divergent views on human rights, various trade issues, and a few spy scandals all contributed to difficult relations between the two countries.

Whereas Clinton had come to see China as a partner for 'strategic cooperation,' the new Bush administration perceived China as a 'strategic competitor' at the outset. Many right-wing Americans even considered China the greatest new threat to stability. This conclusion was strengthened when a US intelligence plane was forced to land in China in April 2001.

Soon, however, relations between Washington and Peking again improved rapidly: the events of 11 September 2001 meant that international terrorism dominated America's center stage entirely as the crucial new global threat; in the war on terror China was to a great extent an ally of the United States; US economic interests in China were still growing, and they had a considerable influence on the Republican administration. Although Russia and China had a mutual interest in reducing US dominance in the world, and trade and other relations between these two countries increased (particularly in terms of the sale of Russian weapons to China), the United States was quite simply too large and too important – also for these two countries – for there to be any comprehensive cooperation between China and Russia directed against the US. The United States meant far more to each of these two countries than did the other one. Economic growth was the primary focus in China, and in this context the United States meant a lot and Russia much less. However, the large surplus in Chinese trade with the US represented a problem to some extent.

EAST ASIA IN THE NEW WORLD SYSTEM

Great Powers have always come and gone. The Roman, Hapsburg, French and British empires had all come and gone. So, for that matter, had the Chinese, Mogul and Persian empires. In the late 1980s it had become fashionable in some circles to argue that the United States was in decline, soon to be succeeded by other powers, most likely by Japan. This did not happen, however, as the United States was rising to new heights. The Soviet Union collapsed and Japan was experiencing serious economic and political problems.

In 2008–09, however, an increasing number of observers were predicting that the new century would belong to China. China has many things going for it. As the world's most populous country, it has a huge population base, although its policy since 1979 of strict population control will probably lead to it being overtaken by India. In the 1960s Chinese women had, on average, given birth to six children each; now the number has been reduced to 1.7 children per woman. Unlike the much more diverse India, for about three thousand years China has had a common unifying culture. More than 90 per cent of the population is Han Chinese, again as opposed to the ethnic diversity of India. The Chinese are used to viewing themselves as the center of the universe and as a dominant power. Only the last two centuries represented an exception to this, although more for the outside world than for the Chinese themselves. Leadership appears firm and stable. In November 2002 Hu Jintao had taken over as party leader, a few months later also as president after Jiang Zemin. The party struggles of the past seemed to have gone. In 2012 Xi Jinping became the new leader. Even this transfer went smoothly, but the big question was still whether the economic growth would be accompanied by political reform. Xi's leadership became increasingly centralized.

India has also experienced rapid economic growth since the early 1990s. The traditional 'Hindu' rate of slow growth just barely exceeding the increase in population has been replaced by 8–10 per cent growth. This change in India certainly also contributed to the notion that a new world map is developing, with Asia again as a dominant continent. It is, however, difficult to talk about Asia as a whole. There never was a common Asian identity and virtually no common Asian institutions. The gross national product of India was also considerably smaller than that of China, only about one-third of China's. The infrastructure of India, in the form of roads, ports, education, etc., was considerably less developed than China's, as any visitor to the two countries could testify to. The growth in China was also even more rapid and has lasted much longer than in India. In 1978 China's share of world production was only 1.8 per cent; in 2007 it surpassed 6 per cent. In 2008 China's economy became the third largest in the world, behind only the United States and Japan. In 2010 China's economy surpassed even that of Japan.

Projections for the future showed that it was allegedly only a question of about ten years before the size of China's economy would surpass even that of the United States. Yet, it has to be remembered that if and when that actually happens, with a population four times that of the US, on a per capita basis China would still rank far behind the US. In fact in 2009, on an income per capita basis, China ranked only 100th among the UN members. There was also reason to be somewhat skeptical about some of the growth figures from the Chinese authorities, although there could be absolutely no doubt about the overall nature of the growth. In 2007–09 growth in China fell markedly as a result of the world economic crisis, although China was still doing much better than almost any other country in the world.

Not only China and India were rising. Growth in a whole series of East Asian countries had been very rapid indeed. Taiwan, Singapore, South Korea, even Malaysia had started their rapid growth well before China had. In a way China, after decades of failed policies, was just catching up with the living standards of neighboring areas, some of which were also dominated economically by ethnic Chinese. Soon rapid growth was also taking place in countries such as Vietnam, Thailand, and Indonesia.

The rise of China and East Asia was having dramatic consequences in the world economy and in world politics. China and India were redirecting their foreign policies with a view to securing the supplies necessary for their continued economic growth. The two countries had become largely self-sufficient in food, but were increasingly dependent on energy imports. Securing long-term energy deals became a major consideration in their foreign policy. China in particular became an important actor in ever new regions of the world. In so many of the world's hot spots China now had to be closely consulted; North Korea, Iran, Sudan, Burma, and Zimbabwe were some prominent examples.

The United States and China were also becoming increasingly interdependent. The United States had supported China's successful membership in the WTO in 2001. The open American market had been crucial for the growth of China, as it had been in Japan's case as well. In 2008 Chinese exports to the United States amounted to almost 8 per cent of China's GNP. The US was by far the world's largest importer while China rivaled Germany as the largest exporter. The huge surpluses China had in its foreign trade were then to a large extent invested in the US. China was, in fact, financing America's rapidly growing debt.

US economic policies increasingly had to be carried out with an eye on what would be the response in Beijing (Peking). China's position as the world's largest creditor had to strengthen its position tremendously. The US position as the world's largest debtor had to weaken it, although it had much smaller problems than poor countries in financing its debt. International financial structures had to be adjusted, reflecting the rise of Asia, and especially China. China was also surpassing the United States as the world's greatest polluter. There could be no effective global environmental policy unless the two countries contributed.

On her first visit to China as Secretary of State in the Obama administration Hillary Clinton stated that with reference to issues such as human rights, Tibet and Taiwan that had traditionally plagued American–Chinese relations, 'those issues can't interfere with the global economic crisis, the global climate change crisis, and the security crisis.' This clearly illustrated how China had become a crucial partner in all the most important issues of today. Traditional issues had to be downplayed. This was indeed a dramatic new situation.

In Pentagon circles and among realist political scientists, the rise of China was seen as potentially destabilizing. The rise of such new powers had, allegedly, always created conflict, even war, in the past. The rise of Britain had led to wars with Spain and with France. The rise of Germany was perceived as the underlying factor behind the First and the Second World Wars. China did strengthen its military forces substantially. It did build up its nuclear arsenal; it developed long-range missiles – so long-range in fact that it shot down a satellite in orbit. Much equipment was purchased at a low price from Russia. The Chinese navy appeared in waters where it had not been seen, at least not in centuries. China took part in UN-led operations. China was becoming an increasingly important actor in more and more regions of the world, including many parts of Africa and even Latin America. Yet, if China was still lagging behind the United States economically it was even further behind militarily.

In most of the world the rise of China was seen primarily in economic terms. It was certainly a threat to established industries in the United States and in Europe. China had long seen itself as the victim of the actions of others. Now, more and more, it emphasized the peaceful, even the inevitable nature of its rise. In 2009 some Chinese leaders openly referred to the country as a Great Power. The big difference was that while China had earlier seen itself as an outsider in opposition to the dominant powers and institutions, it was now becoming more and more of an insider trying to reform certain aspects of the system.

Many of China's territorial disputes with its neighbors, for instance with Russia, had been resolved; but others, for instance with India and concerning islands both in the South and the East China Sea remained unsolved. Tension was building over these islands. After Hong Kong and Macao had been brought into the 'homeland,' China's primary military concern still related to Taiwan's status and its potential for independence. While China held firm to the one-China policy, there was every reason to believe that Beijing understood that China's continued rapid economic growth depended on peace and stability in the region.

Yet, such a steep rise as China's had to have repercussions for existing alliances and loyalties. The fall of the Soviet Union and the rise of China were important factors behind the rapprochement that took place starting in the 1990s between the United States and India. Some of the ASEAN powers, such as Indonesia, the Philippines, and Singapore, also strengthened their ties with Washington. Allies such as Japan and to some extent South Korea moved even closer to the US, in part influenced by the situation in North Korea as well. In South Korea foreign policy conclusions were clearly influenced also by growing left–right political divisions. In diplomacy vis-à-vis North Korea, China's role was crucial. Here the US and China cooperated to some extent. Both were concerned about North Korea developing its own nuclear weapons and means of delivery. Beijing was, however, much more protective of the continued existence of the North Korean regime than was Washington. Yet, if proof were needed, North Korea's stubbornness illustrated that frequently national and local factors prevailed, even when the Great Powers cooperated.

The history of many Great Powers, most recently Japan, had shown that growth lines should not be extended indefinitely into the future. Something almost always happens that dramatically influences such lines. Naturally it was easier to maintain high growth when you were starting from a lower rather than from a higher base. The change from agriculture to industry was normally more productive than were changes within a service economy.

The rise of China had in fact been frequently predicted, but something had always happened in the past which prevented it from happening. The long-cherished American dream of the rise of a friendly China was crushed by the Communist revolution of 1949. Mao's most dramatic experiments ended in total failure. The current rise of China also faces many challenges. One is political and has to do with the political legitimacy of the regime. The Communist party remains firmly in power, but the communist ideology is largely gone. The overall priority is now to make money. The regime undoubtedly gained legitimacy through the fast growth and also the pride that most Chinese took in the country's rapidly increasing influence. Internationally China did not have the kind of universal appeal often associated with Great Powers. What was China's message to the world? In part its economic success was its message, but that went only so far.

Growth also created its own problems. The Chinese economy was still very state-dominated. All the main companies were state-owned; price controls were prevalent; competition was quite limited. Could such an economy function effectively in the long run? If it did, many Western economic textbooks would have to be rewritten. The legal system had to be strengthened if investors were to feel secure; corruption, a huge and growing problem, had to be limited. Inequalities were deep and getting deeper, with some benefitting hugely from the economic growth and others much less so, or not at all. Environmental problems were becoming increasingly serious. Pollution was high and water supplies low. The number of 'mass incidents,' as reported by the authorities, increased rapidly to more than 90,000 in 2006. Most of these protests were local and reflected accidents of several different sorts, property disputes, closed factories, increased prices, etc. It did not remain out of the question, however, that they could become more comprehensive in scope. The uprising in 1989 had comprised many different cities; it was still a festering sore. Ever new dissidents appeared on the scene. In other rapidly industrializing countries in Asia, in the long term the economic growth had strengthened political democracy. Would not this happen, even in China?

Another challenge related to the fact that although more than 90 per cent of the population is Han Chinese, 10 per cent is a vast number if the total population is more than 1,300 million. The authorities in Beijing displayed considerable uneasiness about the situation in Xinjiang and Tibet. There, ethnic-national disputes fused with an economic growth that easily disturbed native cultures, but that was also considerably slower than along the coast. In this perspective it was even possible that chaotic, but democratic India could, in some respects, be better placed to cope with certain of the long-term challenges of growth than was China. In addition, China was primarily an industrial producer; India was making progress also within the modern service economy. As a result of the one-child policy China would face serious problems with a rapidly aging population and possibly also with the so-called spoiled 'little emperors' as these young-sters were entering society with high expectations.

It had to be remembered that while trade across the Pacific had surpassed that across the Atlantic in the late 1970s and the gap had widened since, on the investment side the story was a different one. American investment in Europe and European investment in America were much larger than in China and East Asia. Americans and Europeans, despite the problems they were facing, were also ideologically and culturally much closer to each other than they were to the Japanese, not to mention the Chinese.

Thus, while there might be reason to hold off somewhat on the most optimistic pre-dictions about the future of Asia and China, there could be no doubt about their rapidly increasing importance in international relations. A new world was being created. Or, rather, elements of the old world were re-emerging.

THE RISE OF EAST ASIA: THE LITERATURE

Relations between the United States and Japan are analyzed in Edwin O. Reischauer, *The Japanese* (Cambridge, 1978); Charles E. Neu, *The Troubled Encounter: The United States and Japan* (New York, 1975); and Akira Iriye and Warren I. Cohen (eds), *The United States and Japan in the Postwar World* (Lexington, 1989). W. G. Beasley, *The Rise of Modern Japan: Political, Economic and Social Change Since 1850* (London, 1995) provides a survey of Japan's modern history.

On China's general history Jonathan D. Spence, *The Search for Modern China* (New York, 1990) is unsurpassed. On Mao's foreign policy, see Chen Jian, *Mao's China and the Cold War* (Chapel Hill, NC, 2001). For a lively account of recent devel-opments in Asia's key countries, see Bill Emmott, *Rivals: How the Power Struggle between China, India and Japan will Shape our Next Decade* (London, 2008). Odd Arne Westad's *Restless Empire: China and the World Since 1750* (London, 2012) is use-ful. For the most recent study, see David Shambaugh, *China Goes Global: The Partial Power* (Oxford: Oxford University Press, 2016).

DECOLONIZATION

When the United Nations was established in 1945, the organization had 51 member nations. By 2013, this figure had risen to 193. Most of this growth was attributable to new states in Asia and Africa. During the course of the 1940s, most of the Asian colonies became independent. In Africa there were still only four formally independent countries: Ethiopia, South Africa, Liberia, and Egypt. By 1976, when decolonization had been completed for the most part, this figure had risen to 48.

A revolution had taken place in international politics. This revolution had many different causes. Following the model developed by the historians Ronald Robinson and Wm. Roger Louis, I shall relate these causes to three levels: the international level, the national level (the colonial powers), and the local level (the colonies).

CHANGES ON THE INTERNATIONAL LEVEL

The Second World War meant a sharp reduction in the international influence of the traditional colonial powers. There was a relative shift of power away from Britain, France, and the smaller European colonial nations to the two new superpowers, the United States and the Soviet Union. They were both characterized by an anti-colonial heritage and would accelerate the process of decolonization, in their own separate ways.

The principles on which Washington's attitude was based were clear enough. The existence of colonies conflicted with the right to national self-determination. As the United States had once torn itself loose from Britain, it was inevitable that other colonies would attain their freedom. It was the Americans' duty to hasten this process.

This point of departure had not prevented the United States from acquiring colonies. The most important of them was the Philippines, which the United States took over from Spain after the Spanish–American War of 1898. The time perspective for independence could be extremely long term. Even the anti-colonialist Franklin Roosevelt was convinced during the Second World War that it could take 50 or 100 years before many of the colonies would gain their independence. After the war, opposition to colonial rule was accommodated to other objectives, such as the need to cooperate with allies and to contain communist expansion.

Even so, all these modifications could not change the fact that the United States was an important factor behind decolonization. In the first place, as early as 1935 the United States had promised the Philippines their independence. Washington actually proceeded more quickly than some of the colony's own leaders appreciated. In 1946, the Philippines became independent. Relations with the United States were still very close in both the economic and the military spheres, but even so the United States was the first country to divest itself of a non-white colony. This example was bound to have certain liberating effects.

In the second place, the US attitude helped establish a foundation for changes in the policies of the more traditional colonial powers. Especially during the Second World War, Washington encouraged the institution of reforms, and in their long-term planning the British in particular took this into consideration. When India was promised independence and the African colonies significant although far less comprehensive reforms, the US attitude was one of many factors behind these commitments. The willingness of the United States to apply direct pressure in order to influence the European colonial powers was greatest where the colonial power was weak and the liberation movement clearly anti-communist. US policy in relation to Indonesia was the best example of this fact, although Washington waited until as late as 1948–49 to take an unequivocal stand even against the Netherlands (see pp. 41–2).

In the third place, the liberation movements played on the attitude and powerful position of the United States. One of many examples of this was the fact that the Vietnamese independence declaration of 2 September 1945 followed the US declaration of independence of 1776 in several respects. This was an attempt to engage the United States on the side of the Vietnamese. But as France was an important power in European politics and the liberation movement in Vietnam was under communist leadership, US pressure here was much weaker than on the Netherlands regarding Indonesia.

The influence of the Soviet Union on the struggles for independence was also many-faceted. Moscow's policy line was clearly anti-colonial. All colonies had to be granted independence (with the exception of the areas in Asia that Russia itself had assumed control of during the 1700s and 1800s, of course). Lenin had proclaimed imperialism the highest stage of capitalism. Local Communists were often among those who were most active in the struggle for liberation. It was another matter that Moscow showed limited interest in what took place in most of Asia and Africa. Moreover, shortly after the Second World War Moscow began to consider many of the nationalist leaders 'Western lackeys.' This attitude often caused strife between Communists and others who were fighting for their country's independence.

During the postwar era, it became increasingly important for the colonial powers to institute reforms at such an early stage that the independence movements in the various areas did not become more radical and fall under communist leadership. If armed struggle ensued, the Soviet Union could supply weapons. Thus, the Soviet Union influenced the actions of the colonial powers both through its policies and by its mere existence. But once a movement had become 'communist' – and the definition of communism could vary considerably from one capital to another – the colonial powers almost always became less willing to grant independence. France's policy in Indochina was to some extent determined by such considerations.

On the international level, it was also significant that organizations were created that placed limitations on the freedom of action of the colonial powers. This had already been illustrated under the League of Nations during the period between the two world wars. The mandate system of the League hastened the process of independence. The British granted Iraq independence in 1932. In 1944–46, Syria and Lebanon, former French colonies, attained their independence, as did Jordan, a British colony. Even so, these mandates – formerly Ottoman – were considered so unique that developments there had little influence either on British and French colonial policies or on independence movements in general.

After the Second World War, the remaining mandates were placed under the UN supervision system along with the colonies Italy and Japan had to relinquish. The trusteeship system that was established tended towards reform, although it only affected a small number of areas, and although the colonial powers had a tendency to treat them in the same way as the other colonies they controlled. For instance, this was true of Britain's policies in the previously German Tanganyika, which the British took over just after the First World War. Libya, which had been Italian, represented a different course. International influence, combined with major power rivalry as to who should have control, resulted in this colony acquiring its independence as early as in 1951.

The United Nations accelerated the process of independence in other ways as well. Chapter XI of the UN Charter contained vague promises of future independence even for 'non-self-governing territories.' The new nations that gradually joined the organization were naturally preoccupied with independence for the remaining colonies. They questioned the policies of the colonial powers almost incessantly. This pressure was strongly reinforced by the support the new nations' viewpoints enjoyed around the world, primarily in the colonies, but in the Soviet Union and the United States as well – and even within the colonial powers themselves.

THE NATIONAL LEVEL: CHANGES WITHIN THE COLONIAL POWERS

After 1945, major changes took place in the colonial powers' capacity and willingness to retain their colonies. Their capacity was influenced by their weakened international position, by economic problems, and by many other considerations. These factors were important enough, although they were more relative than absolute in the sense that none of the European colonial powers actually had fewer resources than they had had in the period between the wars, at least not after the reconstruction years were over. Their will was thus at least as important as their capacity. Many politicians and segments of public opinion changed their attitudes towards colonies altogether, and even larger groups no longer wanted to use the force that was necessary to retain forms of rule that violated the ideals they acclaimed in their own countries. The significance of this factor was emphasized by the fact that the poorest and least democratic of the colonial powers, Portugal, retained its colonies for the longest time.

British Policies

The United Kingdom was the leading colonial power, both by virtue of controlling the largest areas and by setting an example, in many ways, to which the others had to accommodate themselves. The British colonial empire rested on a thin veneer of control. The British had only 4,000 bureaucrats in India in the 1930s, along with 60,000 soldiers and 90,000 civilians, mostly businessmen and ecclesiastical personnel, in a country of about 300 million inhabitants. This huge empire could only be sustained if the British enjoyed a certain amount of active or at least passive support from their Indian subjects.

For a long time the British were able to enlist such support. A combination of reforms and the use of force ensured the necessary control. Force alone was not politically acceptable in the long run. The Amritsar massacre in 1919, where British soldiers opened fire on an Indian public meeting, killing several hundred persons, had demonstrated this fact. The incident had occasioned sharp protests, not only in India, but in Britain as well. Without the use of force it was merely a question of time until the entire empire would collapse. The only difference was the somewhat unequal pace of developments in the various regions.

One theory of decolonization has been that it was more or less a logical process that would inevitably result in the dismantling of the colonial empires. This process had actually begun with the achievement of US independence from Britain in the 1770s and 1780s. The United States was followed by the white dominions of Canada, Australia, New Zealand, and South Africa. The Spanish empire collapsed as far back as after the Napoleonic wars.

India was supposedly the next rung on the ladder of history. The British gradually relinquished local control over the country. The most important stages in this process were the two Government of India Acts of 1919 and 1935. The first of these instituted an Indian Parliament with very limited power, as well as local assemblies with more extensive authority. The second Act increased the freedom of action of both the national and the local governing bodies. Independence ensued in 1947. Thus the floodgates were opened for the non-white colonies. In the wake of India followed the other British colonies in Asia, and from Asia the wave of independence swept over Africa. What Britain had begun, others had to complete: the Netherlands, France, Belgium, and finally Portugal as well.

This theory does contain elements of truth, but it is far too condensed and makes decolonization a much simpler process than it actually was. Most of the colonies were acquired after the first ones had already gained their independence. One colonial power did influence another, but there were still substantial differences among them. For a long time the purpose of the British reforms was not to prepare the colonies for future independence, but instead to lay a better foundation for retaining control more easily. Finally, it was quite clear, at least at the time, that the differences were tremendous between the policies that could be pursued in Asia and the policies that could be implemented in the far less developed Africa. For that matter, the differences were also great within Asia and Africa.

Before and during the Second World War few, if any, leading politicians foresaw the pace and extent of decolonization that would take place in Asia and particularly in Africa during the postwar era. In November 1942, Churchill stated that he had not become the King's Prime Minister in order to preside over the dissolution of the British empire. However, developments in Asia were in the process of outdistancing the British prime minister. Equally memorable, and perhaps more representative of the sentiments of the common people, was the comment of Labour's deputy leader Herbert Morrison, that independence for the African colonies would be 'like giving a child of ten a latch-key, a bank account, and a shotgun.' In France and Portugal, there was talk long after the war of an eternal union between mother country and colonies.

During the war, both the Conservatives and Labour opposed the demands of the Indian Congress Party for immediate independence. London long refused to discuss this question until the war was over, although there was little doubt that India would then have to be granted at least a high degree of self-government. The Indian 'Quit India' movement of 1942, combined with the need for support in the war against Japan and Germany, made the British prepare themselves for further concessions. It became the official policy that India would be granted full dominion status after the war, with the right even to leave the Commonwealth. Exactly how quickly this process would proceed was somewhat unclear as yet. Although Labour, assuming power in the summer of 1945, did not have a set schedule, they were more willing than the Conservatives to make concessions to the Congress Party.

In February 1947, Prime Minister Attlee declared that Britain would withdraw from India by June 1948. In reality, events would unfold even more rapidly. Because of pressure from the viceroy of India, Lord Mountbatten, from the Congress Party leaders and from Britain's strained economy, India was already declared independent in August 1947. The Attlee government also had to abandon attempts to keep India unified. Pakistan was partitioned off as a separate country. Hindus opposed Muslims, a division the British had previously tried to exploit through the tactic of 'divide and rule.' Burma and Ceylon (Sri Lanka), too, became independent in 1947–48.

Few, if any, members of the British colonial administration believed that the events in India would have much relevance for the African colonies. The Labour government envisioned a period of several decades of social and economic reforms that perhaps in the long run would lay the foundation for political independence there. In 1945 there was not yet a single party in any of the British colonies in Africa that had complete independence on its political platform.

Although they were not recognized at the time, in retrospect we can see forerunners of the events that were to ensue in the 1950s. The first of a series of sporadic Pan-African Congresses was held as early as 1900. The first elected representatives of the local legislative councils had assumed their seats at the beginning of the 1920s, and the constitutions of 1946 increased their power considerably in the Gold Coast and Nigeria. Minor reforms led to demands for more reforms, and it was not possible to halt this process without using physical force to an extent that was unacceptable.

The Sixth Pan-African Congress had been held in Manchester in October 1945. For the first time, the Africans were in a majority in relation to the American Negroes they had learned so much from. The conference approved a highly radical program: complete independence for a unified Africa based on a socialist economy. One of the participants at the conference was Kwame Nkrumah. A unified independent Africa was an unrealistic demand; the same was true of a unified West Africa. Nkrumah returned to the Gold Coast to lead the struggle for independence there.

The revolt in Accra in 1948 stimulated forces that had long undermined British control. In 1949 Nkrumah founded a new political party, the Convention People's Party, which pressed for dominion status. This party employed methods that had been developed by the nationalist leaders in India. Like them, Nkrumah landed in jail, but as had been the case for the Indian leaders, that did not diminish his popularity. In 1951 his party won an overwhelming election victory. The British had either to make concessions or resort to harsher measures. In many ways, the outcome was obvious. In 1957, the Gold Coast, under the name of Ghana, became the first of the new independent nations of West Africa. Nigeria followed suit in 1960. Major regional problems slowed the process there compared to in Ghana.

The British, and conservative circles in particular, perceived great differences between West and East Africa. In East Africa the white minority was larger and the level of cultural and economic development among the Africans not as advanced as in West Africa. In areas such as Kenya and Southern Rhodesia, the settlers had a particularly strong position, and there had been a substantial amount of immigration after 1945. Thus the white population of Kenya rose from 12,000 in 1945 to more than 50,000 ten years later. In Southern Rhodesia, the corresponding figures were 80,000 and more than 200,000. As late as in April 1959, Colonial Secretary Alan Lennox Boyd stated that he was 'unable to envisage a time when it will be possible for any British Government to surrender the ultimate responsibilities for the destinies and well-being of Kenya.'

However, the process leading to independence continued to accelerate. Sudan had acquired its independence as early as in 1956, but was considered an exception as the country had formally been governed as a British–Egyptian condominium. The concessions London had to make in West Africa could not be denied in East Africa. In Ghana, it took 32 years from the time of the election of the first members to the local assembly until the country became independent. In Tanganyika, which represented the great breakthrough in East Africa, the same course of developments took 39 months. Nigeria had nine years of local autonomy before gaining complete independence, Ghana six years, and Tanganyika 19 months. 'The wind of change has blown us away,' Prime Minister Macmillan ruefully commented in 1961.

Conservative British governments wanted to build up federations partially controlled by whites in East and Central Africa. Even so, Tanganyika's independence in 1961 was succeeded by Uganda's in 1962, and then by Kenya's in 1963. The federation that was actually established further south was short-lived. Malawi and Zambia became independent nations in 1964. Thus Southern Rhodesia was the only remaining colony. In 1965, the white minority under Ian Smith declared themselves 'independent' in an attempt to halt developments towards a majority government. Even in Southern Rhodesia, however, retaining white control proved hopeless. The major Western powers applied political and economic pressure to the country, and the nationalist movement grew steadily stronger. In 1979–80, Southern Rhodesia attained complete independence under the name Zimbabwe.

South Africa had acquired dominion status as early as 1910. Particularly after 1948, Pretoria built up a strict apartheid system between the white minority and the black majority. The country also had control over the previously German colony of Namibia. South Africa became subject to strong international condemnation and withdrew from the Commonwealth in 1961. The struggle against the racist regime increased both

Figure 12.1 Africa's liberation

within South Africa and abroad. In the autumn of 1989, F. W. de Klerk became president, and he put an end to most aspects of apartheid and initiated a dialogue with the released African National Congress (ANC) leader, Nelson Mandela. Namibia attained independence in 1990. During the course of 1993–94 the process leading to majority rule was completed, and Mandela was elected President of South Africa. Expectations for the new South Africa were extremely high. They were only partly fulfilled. South Africa became a full democracy, but dominated by one party. Economic growth was satisfactory, but poverty remained deep. South Africa did, however, go from a pariah existence to becoming Africa's leader.

French Policies

French colonial policies were quite different from those of Britain. Instead of decentralization, with local assemblies which gradually received more power, the French model was based on Paris as its center, with a strong governor general as the capital's local representative. Whereas the British policy gradually led to a considerable degree of local autonomy, finally – although somewhat reluctantly at first – to culminate in full independence, France's attitude was that the local population was gradually to be assimilated within French culture, thus in theory attaining rights as French subjects within a French union. This union was still to be controlled from Paris, but the local populations would be increasingly better represented in the national assembly there.

In the defense of French great power status, of French culture, and long-range assimilation, the French were willing to use considerably harsher means than the British were. In 1946 several thousand Vietnamese died when the French bombarded Haiphong in order to drive the Vietminh forces out of the city. In the following year more than 80,000 persons were killed on Madagascar in an attempt to quell the nationalist movement there. On the whole, Paris considered British decolonization a process that both would and should have little influence on French areas. France could sustain its rule even if the British gave up.

The French, too, realized that the Second World War was bound to produce major changes in relations between mother country and colonies. This was expressed at the Brazzaville conference of 1944, where the free French forces, together with officials in the French colonies that supported them, were represented. The educational system was to be expanded, there was to be an end to compulsory public service, and the Africans were to be granted greater electoral influence. These reforms would create a new foundation for permanent French rule, or as the Brazzaville declaration stated: 'Any idea of autonomy, any possibility of evolution outside the French bloc, as well as the eventual, even far-off, constitution of self-government in the colonies, must be set aside.'

There were differences among the attitudes of the French parties towards the colonies. However, with the exception of the Communists, particularly after they had been thrown out of the government in May 1947, these differences were small. Even many African leaders, such as Houphouet-Boigny in the Ivory Coast, long pursued a policy placing greater emphasis on having a voice in Paris than on local independence.

But French policies, too, would come up against a local reality that could not be forced into a pattern worked out in a distant capital. Indochina was France's most important colony in Asia. Here, it was more the capacity than the willingness to retain control that was lacking. In 1954, France suffered a political and military defeat, a defeat that was confirmed at the Geneva conference that same year (see pp. 50–1). Developments in Indochina merely made the French all the more determined to maintain their colonial empire in Africa.

In North Africa, British-dominated Egypt had formally gained its independence in 1922, in reality in 1952. The example of Egypt, their special status as protectorates, and a strong but moderate nationalist movement resulted in independence for Tunisia and Morocco in 1956. Although there were great differences between Africa north and south of the Sahara, this illustrated that the process of independence could not be kept out of French Africa. Concessions had to be made in Togo as well, as the country, a former German colony, was under the United Nations trusteeship system.

The reforms that were introduced through framework legislation (*loi cadre*) in 1956 still had as their objective the retention of control over the African colonies. However, the colonies were granted better representation in Paris, at the same time as local assemblies acquired significant influence for the first time. This new policy modified the course of integration that had been dominant. Assimilation was abandoned for the most part.

France's most uncompromising stand was made in relation to Algeria. This area was still considered an integrated part of France itself, and French policy had fluctuated between harsh repression of the Arab majority and attempts at assimilation. The French minority, about 10 per cent of the population, owned the best land and controlled the most important sectors of the economy. They were firmly determined to prevent any development that might reduce their dominance.

The nationalist movement, the FLN, had initiated an uprising in 1954 that quickly assumed vast dimensions. French involvement was escalated sharply in 1956 under a government led by socialist Guy Mollet. This, together with the earlier stand in Indochina, showed that the socialists, too, were part of what political scientist Tony Smith has called 'the French colonial consensus.' French participation in the Suez invasion that same year was largely dictated by the war in Algeria. Paris wanted to bring to an end the foreign support believed to sustain the FLN. The Suez expedition was a failure (see p. 56), as French policy in Algeria would also prove to be.

After de Gaulle rose to power in 1958, changes began to take place in French colonial policy in earnest. In close cooperation with Houphouet-Boigny, the government drew up the sections of the French Constitution that were to transform the French Union into the French community (*communauté*). The colonies were given the choice between independence or continued close cooperation with France, with local autonomy. With the exception of Guinea, which thus became the first independent black country in French Africa, all the colonies chose the latter alternative.

The new *communauté* was to have a joint foreign policy and a joint defense policy, as well as a common economic policy for the most part. In theory, these common policies were to be determined by an executive body consisting of the presidents from all the member states. In reality, the French viewpoint was usually decisive. On the more symbolic level, French remained the official language, the 'Marseillaise' the national anthem, and the French tricolor the common flag.

In 1960, this system was replaced by formal independence. The individual countries could now decide freely in the spheres that had previously been subject to joint policy. The ties between the French colonies and Paris long remained close, much closer than between London and the British colonies. There were many reasons for the rapid course of developments from 1958 to 1960. The example of Guinea was one reason, British decolonization another, internal rivalry among several of the colonies in French West Africa yet another.

Finally, the French war in Algeria played a part. The French colonies wanted to distance themselves further from the France that was waging a bloody war in Algeria. But the French had to yield even in Algeria – 400,000 French soldiers finally managed to bring the military situation under control, but the price proved to be extremely high. Political opposition to the war was growing, not only in Africa but in much of the rest of the world as well, and, most significantly, in France itself.

De Gaulle first tried to satisfy the interests of France, the local French population, and the FLN through a policy based on local autonomy. This course failed. The President then advocated full independence for Algeria, a course that meant a complete break with many of those who had placed their confidence in the general. In 1962, Algeria finally became independent.

Belgium and Portugal

The other colonial powers, too, had to yield, although both Belgium and Portugal long believed that they could retain their colonies despite developments elsewhere.

Belgian policy in the Congo has often been described as paternalistic. Through a general improvement in the standard of living, the Belgians expected to be able to postpone political demands, if such ever arose. They considered themselves far more conscientious than other colonialists, as in fact they were in certain ways. Great emphasis was placed on education, but only on basic education. In 1955, the Belgian authorities proclaimed with pride that 10 per cent of the population of the Congo attended school, while the corresponding figures were 7 per cent in Ghana, 6 per cent in India, and 3 per cent in French Equatorial Africa. However, there were only 16 Africans with university educations in all of the Congo in 1960.

As late as in 1958, no preparations had been made for independence. A revolt broke out in early 1959. Political factions were formed, and with them a race to declare independence as soon as possible. Belgium was not willing to use extensive force to stop this process. The objective was to retain the best possible relations with the Congo. The moderate forces had to be supported. This could be done by realizing the demands for independence. The Belgians dismantled their administration in great haste. The new state contained many tribes and languages, and the governing bodies soon collapsed. Five years of unrest ensued until the country achieved a sort of stability under the leadership of General Mobutu (see pp. 58–9).

The Portuguese were even less affected by the general decolonization than the Belgians were. Lisbon tried to pursue the French policy of assimilation even further than Paris did. The Portuguese colonies were still integrated parts of the mother country. Politically, the Africans would be allowed to participate when they had attained a specified standard of 'civilization.'

Portugal's colonial policy was closely linked to the domestic situation at home. In a dictatorship, spreading ideas of freedom and a gradual build-up of self-government were inconceivable. Decolonization could mean the collapse of the Salazar regime. But the costs of retaining control were tremendous as the independence movements grew stronger. Thus Portugal's colonial policy was much of the reason for the fall of the regime in 1974.

Even after the revolution in Lisbon, some of the new leaders spoke of decolonization taking a generation. But the radical forces in Portugal applied pressure, and the liberation movements were strengthened substantially. Guinea-Bissau became independent in 1974; Angola and Mozambique followed in 1975 (see pp. 89–90).

Why Different Attitudes?

There were many reasons for the differences in the colonial powers' attitudes. The reason that was perhaps most significant has already been mentioned: the relation between colonial policy and the dominant ideologies in the mother country.

As an extension of this factor, it was significant that Britain had a feasible pattern for its colonial policies. The white dominions had after all developed a model that could be followed when the political will to grant the colonies their independence arose.

Moreover, developments in India could create a pattern for possible events in Africa. The ultimate transfer of power was a process that was fairly undramatic for the British.

In contrast, France was caught up in a vicious circle in several areas. Partly due to its unwillingness to grant independence, Paris had to face radical liberation movements. This was most evident in Indochina and, to a lesser extent, in Algeria. Radical movements meant that France in turn became even more intransigent in its policies. Thus developments in certain colonies reinforced themselves.

The British governments were also far more viable than the French. Dismantling colonial rule required strong governments, particularly in areas where substantial interests were linked to the maintenance of the status quo, such as in Algeria and in some of the British colonies in Central and East Africa. It was easier for British governments, even Conservative ones, to resist the pressure from settlers and their supporters, than it was for the rapidly changing French governments. However, de Gaulle's rise to power paved the way for the final decisions regarding decolonization.

Considerations of prestige and great power politics were other factors influencing the attitudes of the colonial powers. Rivalry among the European powers had been a central factor in the establishment of the colonial empires. This rivalry had ceased. Both Britain and France were nations on the wane in an international perspective. The colonies were now partly seen as necessary in order to defend their roles as the third- and fourth-ranking major powers in the world.

Britain's international influence was clearly stronger than that of France. Thus it was easier for Britain to make concessions. France had a tremendous need to re-establish its prewar status to some extent. Paris was largely unwilling to make concessions to its colonies. If a war had broken out, it had to be won. Because France had lost in Indochina, it had to fight all the harder in Algeria.

The countries' relations with the United States were also significant. Washington's stance had greater impact in London than in Paris because Britain's relations with the United States were so much closer than France's. This factor was also important for the smaller colonial powers. The Netherlands, like Britain, pursued a relatively Atlantic policy. When the United States, in 1948–49, decided to support Indonesia's independence, that was bound to have great effect. Portugal dreamed of still maintaining a certain international position, and through the US need for bases on the Azores, Salazar could long secure at least neutrality from Washington.

The colonies had varying significance for the different mother countries. The British economy was only dependent on the colonies to a slight degree. In 1938, only 8.5 per cent of British imports originated in the colonies, and 12.5 per cent of their exports went to the colonies. For France, trade with the colonies accounted for almost one-third of both exports and imports. Where settlers were numerous and the economic interests especially great, such as in Southern Rhodesia for Britain and in Algeria for France, this was a factor that delayed independence. The white minority consistently opposed plans to transfer power to the local majority.

However, it gradually became clear to the colonial powers that independence did not necessarily entail such great changes in relations between mother country and colony. Economic, military, and cultural ties could still persist. The greater the chances of this happening, the easier it was to grant political independence. There could even be advantages to not having to spend large sums of money to retain administrative control.

Independence would also mean that the colonial power would be spared from having sole responsibility for local development programs.

The relation of the Philippines to the United States was a good example of this. The US bases remained, economically the country was still closely linked to the United States, and the same social groups governed in Manila now as previously. For Britain, relations with former colonies such as Canada, Australia, South Africa, and even the United States illustrated that economic relations could in fact be strengthened after the colonies had gained political independence. Even so, the British placed little emphasis on this experience during the first years after 1945. But later experience confirmed that the consequences of decolonization were often far less sweeping than they had imagined immediately after the war.

The maintenance of close ties with the mother country was also a condition for the changes that took place in French colonial policy in the years 1958–60. In Africa south of the Sahara, in Morocco and Tunisia (in contrast to in Indochina and to some extent in Algeria), the French largely succeeded in retaining the new nations' orientation towards France. The smaller colonial powers (the Netherlands, Belgium, and Portugal) had difficulties in maintaining the former ties. They were simply not strong enough, neither economically nor militarily.

THE LOCAL LEVEL: INDEPENDENCE MOVEMENTS GROW STRONGER

Independence may have been something the colonial powers granted, but it was also something the colonies seized. Although there were differences in the colonial powers' attitudes, independence was almost always something the national leaders had to struggle for, at least until developments began to unfold almost under their own momentum during the 1960s.

Local conditions in the various colonies differed tremendously. Distinctive local features were important when the individual colonies gained independence. Generalizations about the course of developments are necessarily more accurate for some colonies than for others, but certain basic features can be outlined.

The establishment and expansion of control by the colonial powers had often led to revolts, but these tended to be more or less spontaneous, without any national ideology as a unifying factor. They could be protests against taxes, against the loss of land, against enforced labor, modernization, religious repression, racial discrimination, etc. The most important shared feature was that they tried to return to the order that had existed before the colonial power had arrived. The Senussi rising in Tunisia in 1881 may serve as an instance of a protest at the establishment phase, while the Indian mutiny of 1857 largely broke out in areas that had long been under British control.

Such revolts could represent sources of inspiration for the nationalist movements that later emerged, but ideologically they were quite distinct. The revolts pointed back to a bygone era; the nationalist movements tried to establish a new order. However, the transition between these two phases could be a state of flux. The revolts in some of the African colonies just before and after the turn of the century seem to some extent to have been precursors for those that were to follow. The Saya San revolt in Burma in 1930 was another example of such an intermediate incident.

The Three Stages

The historian Geoffrey Barraclough has divided the struggle for independence into three schematized stages that can be identified in the course of development of many of the colonies. The first stage was dominated by what he calls 'proto-nationalism.' During this period colonial rule was accepted, but new social groups and political movements emerged that strove for reforms within this system. The Congress Party was established in India in 1885, but until 1905 it was largely a debate forum for a narrow upper class. British civilization was considered superior. The most important demands for reform included limited local autonomy and more job opportunities for educated Indians. In Indonesia, this first stage began with the creation of the religious-nationalist movement Sarekat Islam in 1911. Similar movements were established in important African colonies such as the Gold Coast, Nigeria, and Tunisia around 1920.

Barraclough identifies the second stage as 'the rise of a new leadership.' Nationalism began to gain ground in a growing middle class. The demands the new leaders made on the colonial power were expanded substantially, and independence was considered at least a future goal. In India, this second phase can be said to have lasted from 1905 to 1919. Although the social base for the Congress Party was expanded, it was still far from a mass movement. Demands for independence were raised, but this was not a unifying common goal. In Indonesia, Sarekat Islam committed itself to independence as early as in 1917. Even so, the Partai National Indonesia was not established until 1927. Similar turning points can be said to have been reached in Tunisia and Nigeria in 1934 and 1944, respectively.

The third stage was a nationalist movement with 'a mass following' working actively to achieve independence. Nationalist movements grew so strong that the use of force had to be stepped up in order to maintain the colonial system. Whereas the colonial power had formerly been able to play the masses off against the narrow social groups that led these movements, this was now more difficult, although there were still many who were not directly engaged in the political struggle. Again, India serves as the model. Under Gandhi's leadership, from 1920 onwards the Congress Party established clear lines from the political center to India's tens of thousands of rural villages. The objective was now clearly independence. In Indonesia, the PNI under Sukarno's leadership did not manage to launch a comparable mass mobilization until during the Second World War. This stage was initiated in Tunisia as well during the war. In Nigeria, the initiation of the third phase occurred in 1951. In the Gold Coast, the second phase and the beginning of the third phase almost converged during the years 1947–49.

Thus, these stages were not equally distinct everywhere. The process tended to extend over the longest period of time in the British colonies. In the French colonies in Africa south of the Sahara, the entire course of development could take a mere 10 to 20 years. In some instances it went even more quickly. In the Belgian Congo, for instance, there were hardly any demands for independence until 1955. Even then, local leaders thought that it might take 60 to 100 years before the colony would become independent.

Economic and Cultural Development

The three stages were closely linked to economic and cultural developments in the colonies. The establishment of mass parties, which at least to some extent felt that they had ties to the nation, and not primarily to regional, tribal, or upper-class interests, tended to presuppose economic modernization and a certain minimum level of cultural strength based on an educational system.

To a considerable degree, the colonial powers contributed to shaping the reactions against themselves. The leaders of the independence struggles were very often educated in Western countries, most likely in the mother country itself. The central names of the Indian–Pakistani freedom struggle exemplify this fact, although they were highly influenced by non-Western cultures as well. Jinnah, Ali Khan, Nehru, and to some extent Gandhi had all been influenced by British political and judicial ideas during prolonged stays in Britain. Western influence was even stronger in Africa, as illustrated by Nkrumah, Nyerere (Tanganyika), and Kaunda (Northern Rhodesia). If nationalist leaders in the British colonies were influenced by British ideas, the leaders in the French areas were even more characterized by French ideas. Houphouet-Boigny in the Ivory Coast and Senghor in Senegal were two clear, though differing, examples of this French influence.

The national idea as such was frequently a product of Western impulses. This was most evident in Africa. The recently established colonial territories of Africa did not have a common past and a shared cultural tradition to fall back on to the same extent as in Asia. As Nkrumah wrote in 1958, it was Europeans who 'set the pattern of our hopes, and by entering Africa in strength ... forced the pattern upon us.' Likewise it was the colonial powers, through the borders they established, who decided what territory each individual 'country' was to comprise.

This Western influence could have beneficial aspects. But the point is rather that the colonial system had disruptive effects, effects that strengthened the independence movements. Communications were expanded, a factor that contributed to reducing the traditional boundaries within the individual colonial areas. Cities grew rapidly and with them educational institutions and new elites. Lagos, for example, had 75,000 inhabitants in 1914, 230,000 in 1950, and 675,000 in 1962. The corresponding figures for Accra were 20,000, 135,000, and 325,000. In the years just after the Second World War, more than 600,000 children attended school in Nigeria, more than 250,000 in Kenya, and 120,000 in the Gold Coast. Universities were established in the Gold Coast, Nigeria, Uganda, and Sudan. Previously there had been only one university in the British-controlled colonies in Africa south of the Sahara, and that was in Sierra Leone.

In Africa, modernization was largely responsible for the creation of new groups such as clergy, teachers, shop owners, politicians, etc. In Asia, the numbers of people in these groups grew. Racial discrimination, which in many ways was strongest in the British colonies, became intolerable. Those who had gained a little under the colonial system wanted more. Those who had gained nothing, protested, and the protests became steadily better organized.

The native soldiers who had participated in the Second World War did not want to return to the old colonial system after having fought for the triumph of democracy. The large-scale production of persons with primary education created a group that became important supporters for the new elites in the struggle against the colonial powers. Trade regulations of various types often limited the opportunities for the native population. Conflicts arose continuously regarding wages and working conditions. These were circumstances that primarily affected the cities. But the independence movements themselves were largely urban phenomena, especially in Africa south of the Sahara.

Reactions against the colonial powers arose first and most strongly in the areas where there were both highly developed native cultures and a strong, early Western influence. Once again India was the clearest example. The country had thousands of highly educated persons as well as strong religious and cultural traditions. Comprehensive social changes had taken place during the years of British rule. The areas which most resembled India in these respects were Indonesia, Vietnam, and Islamic North Africa.

The independence movements of East and Central Africa were the weakest. Western influence could be too strong. In these areas the opposing forces, most easily measured by the number of local whites, were substantial. Of all the British colonies, those in this area had the least experience in local self-government. Few Africans had higher education. As late as in 1963, there were only eight Africans among the 116 top administrators in Nyasaland (Malawi). In the following year the country became independent.

The Influence of International Events

A number of events in various parts of the world contributed to strengthening the independence movements (or to weakening the mother countries – these two aspects are difficult to keep entirely separate). Among the earliest of these were the black Ethiopians' victory over the white Italians at Adua in 1896; the Boer War, which resulted in independence for South Africa while at the same time strengthening anti-colonial sentiments in Britain; Japan's victory over Russia in 1904–05, which showed that the white man could also be defeated by the yellow man; the First World War, which brought hundreds of thousands of natives from Asia and Africa to Europe as soldiers and workers at a time when radical ideas and slogans flourished; and the Russian Revolution, which created highly conscious Communist groups that would act as a vanguard in many of the independence movements.

However, the Second World War was the most important single factor. This war led to changes on the international level, and it contributed to the creation of new attitudes towards the colonies in their mother countries. At least equally important were the changes the war brought about in the colonies, especially in Asia. The Second World War had many of the same effects there as the Napoleonic wars had had on the Spanish and Portuguese colonies in South and Central America.

Japan occupied all Asian colonial areas up to the Indian border. The European colonial powers had been decisively defeated by Asians. The Japanese occupation would strengthen the independence movements in a number of other ways as well. New governing structures were created and psychological barriers broken down. Partly to gather support against the allies and partly as a step on the way towards Japanization, the Japanese promoted nationalism in several areas. National leaders were given offices and to some extent power that they were certainly not prepared to relinquish when the war was over. National languages were encouraged in Indonesia and Burma, and national armies established. Independence was even proclaimed for the Philippines and Burma in 1943 and for Vietnam, Laos, and Cambodia in 1945, although this was primarily a formality. Those who cooperated with the Japanese, such as Sukarno in Indonesia, Aung San in Burma, and Roxas in the Philippines, were seldom seen in the same light as the Quislings of Europe.

Of course there were conflicts between Japan and the national movements as well. The Japanese concessions were always too limited. Brutal economic exploitation stimulated revolt and opposition.

In the areas Japan did not occupy, the war meant that the colonial powers had to exert themselves to the extreme in order to secure material and political support. As we have seen, such considerations were an important factor behind the India declaration of 1942, which laid the foundation for the country's independence after the war.

Perhaps most important of all was the vacuum that arose when Japan suddenly capitulated in August–September 1945. The Japanese were defeated without the Europeans having advanced into their former areas. Vietnam and Indonesia received, or rather seized, their independence and were not at all willing to relinquish it when the colonial powers were eventually in a position to send in troops. France and the Netherlands never managed to re-establish the control they had had before the war.

The liberation of Asia necessarily had substantial consequences for Africa as well. As the historian D. A. Low has stressed: 'It is not fanciful to assert that many of the critical battles for British colonial Africa were fought, not on the banks of the Volta, the Niger, or the Zambezi, but on the Ganges.' After all, four-fifths of the population of Britain's colonial territories lived in India. The floodgates were opened and the pattern established, not only for the British colonies, but for all colonies.

THE NONALIGNED STATES IN WORLD POLITICS

The vast majority of the new nations that emerged first in Asia and then in Africa were firmly determined to keep at a distance from the two major power blocs. Some form of non-alliance was nearly self-evident. Geographically, many of these new nations were located far from the two blocs. The ideology of independence was strong; independence meant revolt against a Western power, which in itself made alliance with the Western bloc difficult, or even impossible; yet very few of the new nations carried the anti-Western sentiment so far as to tie themselves to the Eastern bloc.

The question of cooperation with other liberated nations became highly relevant. There could hardly be a question of a third 'bloc,' because in the opinion of the nonaligned nations the bloc policy was responsible for much of the tension that existed in the world. Even so, the movement needed a foundation on which to stand. Defining this foundation would prove difficult.

The first meeting among African and Asian countries was held in Bandung, Indonesia, in 1955. All the independent countries from these two parts of the world were represented, with the exception of South Korea and Israel. Western-oriented states such as Turkey, the Philippines and South Vietnam, and Communist nations such as China and North Vietnam all took part. The 29 participants concentrated their efforts on condemning colonialism, emphasizing the need for economic growth in the Third World, and calling for a decrease in international tension based on the principles of cooperation and peaceful coexistence.

Shortly thereafter, two of the conference's leaders – Nasser from Egypt and Nehru from India – travelled to Yugoslavia to have talks with Tito, the most prominent neutral leader who had not participated in Bandung. In a joint statement they expressed their support for the resolutions from the meeting that had been held and moreover sharply attacked the two major power blocs. Thus nonalignment was focused in a much clearer way than at the Afro-Asian meeting, where representatives for the two blocs had participated.

The first summit meeting of the nonaligned nations was held in Belgrade in 1961 with 25 nations participating. The clearly bloc-oriented countries that had been in Bandung were excluded, as were the so-called Brazzaville nations, the most pro-French of the former French colonies. On the other hand, Yugoslavia and Cyprus had been added from the European countries and Cuba from the Latin American countries. The participants in Belgrade placed primary emphasis on the struggle for peace in the world. The meeting was dominated by the belief that nonalignment would be different from traditional neutrality. Nonalignment was to be active and positive, whereas neutrality had been passive and negative.

New conferences were held generally every third year. The fifteenth nonaligned summit took place in Sharm El Sheikh in Egypt in July 2009 and the sixteenth in Teheran in August 2012. The seventeenth meeting in Venezuela in 2016 had few participants due to chaotic economic conditions in Venezuela. The number of participants increased each time, from 25 in 1961 to 120 in 2012. The African and Asian nations consistently composed the core, but Latin American countries also joined the movement in increasing numbers. Such European countries as Sweden, Finland, and Austria took part in some of the conferences as observers or guests. After the collapse of the Soviet Union some of the new states that emerged joined the nonaligned movement.

Defining nonalignment precisely proved impossible. The criterion that was the most important for a long time was that the participants could not grant the major powers military bases, but even this was far from strictly practiced. Cuba and Vietnam have been among the most Soviet-oriented participants, the Philippines, Saudi Arabia, and Pakistan among the most pro-USA. In addition to them there were the many African countries that retained their close ties with France. The level of development was also widely divergent, from the wealthy oil nations of the Middle East to the poorest of the poor in Africa. Nor have conflicts and wars been unusual among the participants, such as between India and Pakistan, Vietnam and Cambodia, Iran and Iraq.

The conferences of the nonaligned nations all concentrated their efforts on decolonization, economic development, and anti-bloc policies. The balance among these themes varied. Decolonization became less relevant as the vast majority of the colonies gained their independence. Even so, the nonaligned nations were highly concerned about the remaining areas, such as Namibia and South Africa. The Palestinian problem was also considered in this light. The same was true of the Falkland Islands (the Malvinas), where Argentina's claim enjoyed support. (In 1982 the islands were seized by Argentina but then retaken by British troops.)

Demands for a new economic world order became increasingly prominent. As early as 1964, the nonaligned countries had been instrumental in bringing about the first United Nations Conference on Trade and Development, UNCTAD (see pp. 000–0). The economic problems of the 1970s reinforced the concentration on these issues. Most of the oil nations and certain others enjoyed strong growth, but the majority suffered from economic stagnation.

The nonaligned nations long tried to distribute the responsibility for the bloc policy fairly equally between East and West, between the Soviet Union and the United States. The emergence of the new nations probably served to strengthen the forces within the two blocs that favored an easing of tensions, as an uncompromising policy could repel the nonaligned nations. However, this was far from a decisive factor, as the worsening of the international climate in the late 1970s and early 1980s demonstrated.

Even so, the verbal attacks on the colonial empires and the demands for a new economic world order almost inevitably meant a focusing of attention on the Western powers. They were the ones that still had colonies, and they were the ones that dominated the international economic system the developing countries protested against. Yet criticism of the West varied somewhat from one summit to another.

Condemnation of the bloc policy faded somewhat into the background during détente in the late 1960s and early 1970s. When relations between East and West became strained once again, this condemnation increased too. At the fifth summit in Colombo in 1976 and the sixth in Havana in 1979, there was a clear tendency to place the primary responsibility for this increased tension on the Western powers in general, and on the United States in particular. To a great extent the nonaligned nations rallied round the Cuban charges against the Western powers and at least indirectly supported the Soviet stance on several important issues. During the 1960s Fidel Castro had represented the most radical wing. Now his stance was shared by increasing numbers of nonaligned nations, despite Cuba's close ties with the Soviet Union.

The meeting in New Delhi in 1983 helped return the nonaligned movement to a more balanced course. Vietnam's policy in Cambodia and that of the Soviet Union in Afghanistan resulted in a sharper tone towards Moscow, but criticism of Washington was still the harshest. In Harare in 1986, and even more so in Belgrade in 1989, the participants tried for the most part to avoid direct attacks on the West in general and the United States in particular. This was also the case in Jakarta in 1992 and Cartagena in 1995, although the United States was still criticized for its policy towards Cuba. Later it was criticized for its actions vis-à-vis Iraq, Iran, and North Korea. At the most recent conferences, reform of the United Nations has been a dominant issue as the nonaligned countries wish to acquire greater influence within the organization. South–South cooperation has also been emphasized. The nonaligned movement is the most extensive organization in the world after the United Nations and its subordinate organizations. Cohesion has proved greater than could be expected in consideration of the large number of members and the many conflicts between various participants. When voting in the UN, these countries have on the whole shown a higher degree of agreement among themselves than was to be found both among the Western-oriented nations and among the neutral nations that do not participate at the nonaligned meetings.

The nonaligned nations have to a great extent managed to determine what issues the UN system is to concentrate its efforts on. The struggle for a new economic world order and against colonialism, racism, the arms race, and related issues have thus been recurrent themes on the international agenda.

However, the results have not been proportional to the time expended on these discussions. With the partial exception of decolonization, the resolutions passed by the UN and other bodies have resulted in very few concrete changes. The possibilities of applying pressure on the major powers have been very limited. Even countries such as South Africa and Israel were largely able to ignore continual condemnation from the nonaligned nations without much consequence. An office of coordination has been established to promote mutual interests, but the attempts at large-scale economic cooperation between developing countries have generally produced small results.

DECOLONIZATION: THE LITERATURE

My presentation has been influenced by the chapter on decolonization in Geoffrey Barraclough, *An Introduction to Contemporary History* (London, 1964). For the grand sweep of history, see D. K. Fieldhouse, *The Colonial Empires: A Comparative Survey from the Eighteenth Century* (London, 1966) and, even grander, John Darwin, *After Tamerlane: The Rise and Fall of Global Empires, 1400–2000* (London, 2007). See also Hedley Bull and Adam Watson (eds), *The Expansion of International Society* (Oxford, 1984).

A wealth of information is to be found in Rudolf von Albertini, *Decolonization: The Administration and the Future of the Colonies, 1919–1960* (New York, 1971); Henri Grimal, *Decolonization: The British, French, Dutch and Belgian Empires 1919–1963* (Boulder, CO, 1978); and Martin Shipway, *Decolonization and its Impact: A Comparative Approach to the End of Colonial Empires* (Malden, 2008). A good anthology is Tony Smith's *The End of the European Empire: Decolonization after World War II* (Lexington, KY, 1975).

With regard to Africa, this presentation is particularly indebted to Prosser Gifford and Wm. Roger Louis (eds), *The Transfer of Power in Africa: Decolonization 1940–1960* (New Haven, CT, 1982) and Jarle Simensen, *Afrikas historie: Nye perspektiver* ('Africa's History: New Perspectives') (Oslo, 1983).

A competent survey of the early nonaligned movement is to be found in William M. LeoGrande, 'Evolution of the Nonaligned Movement,' *Problems of Communism,* January–February 1980, 35–52. Useful information can also be found in Peter Willetts, *The Non-Aligned Movement: The Origins of a Third World Alliance* (London, 1978). There are few, if any, good recent surveys.

Two key accounts of the history of the British Empire, each in its own way, are the massive *Oxford History of the British Empire* in 5 volumes (Oxford, 1998–99) and Bernhard Porter, *The Lion's Share: A Short History of British Imperialism 1850–1995* (London, 1996). John Darwin has produced a succession of important books. The most recent one is *Unfinished Empire: The Global Expansion of Britain* (London, 2012).

ECONOMIC RELATIONS BETWEEN NORTH AND SOUTH, 1945-2016

Political independence for the colonies led to great changes. In terms of foreign policy, most of the new nations chose to avoid the struggle between East and West. Domestically, local leaders now controlled the government. Only a few of the countries followed the conventions of Western democratic government, but socially many of them underwent substantial improvements in such fields as health services and education. During the period from 1960 to 1990, the average overall life expectancy in the developing countries rose from 46 to 62 years. From 1950 to 1985 the number of pupils in primary schools increased sixfold.

Both the nationalist leaders and the population in general expected political independence to produce great results in the economic sphere as well. Kwame Nkrumah's advice to the other African countries was typical in that respect: 'Seek ye first the political kingdom and all else shall be added unto you.' It was not expected that everyone would become exactly wealthy, but the possibilities of material progress were considered extremely good.

In relation to these soaring expectations, the disappointments were tremendous. A few countries achieved substantial results. For many, however, independence seemed to mean little or nothing in the form of concrete economic results. In several countries foreign influence increased, at least in certain areas. Thus, there were approximately 300,000 French citizens residing in Africa in 1983, or more than twice as many as during the colonial era. Radical politicians and social scientists began to question whether independence had actually altered the fundamental ties between the former mother countries and colonies, or between industrial countries and developing countries in general.

AID AND TRADE, 1945-2016

Before undertaking an evaluation of certain aspects of two main theories about economic relations between North and South, it may be useful to outline the course of developments in the North's economic relations with the South. The postwar era can be divided roughly into five main phases: from 1945 to the mid-1950s, a phase in which economic assistance was initiated, but was kept at a relatively modest level and during which the international system of trade showed little concern for the South's interests; from the mid-1950s until the mid-1960s, characterized by an increase in development assistance, considerable optimism, and the gradual emergence of international plans to regulate trade in order to improve conditions for the developing countries; a third period from the mid-1960s to the early 1980s, with stagnation in development assistance from the major industrialized countries, growing tendencies towards pessimism, and a widening gap between the developing countries' demands with regard to the trade policy the industrial countries ought to pursue and the policy they actually pursued; a fourth period from Reagan's inauguration in 1981 to the turn of the century characterized by the West's growing insistence on privatization, deregulation and liberalization, and also applying this in the Third World. This became known as the Washington Consensus – as the only road to success. Accordingly there was less interest in development assistance and less was given. Despite considerable rhetoric to the contrary, trade talks still focused primarily on the needs of the rich countries. Finally, there was a fifth period after 2000 with renewed emphasis on the need for reform both at the international and the local level. The Doha Round on trade was allegedly to focus on the needs of the developing countries. While different national roads to growth and success were again possible, they all now had to be based on good governance. Ambitious new targets were set, in the form of the Millennium Development Goals. Influenced by the rapid economic growth of China and other parts of Asia, the emphasis was nevertheless still on export-led growth. Development assistance increased again, particularly from China, although less than anticipated.

1945–1955

The colonial powers undertook a number of investments in their colonies that could have the effect of promoting development, and after 1945 they launched substantial development programs financed primarily by the colonies' own budgets, but based on transfers as well. However, promoting economic growth in the independent nations was primarily the responsibility of the new nations themselves, supplemented by private capital.

The first meager plans for assistance to the developing countries were laid through the UN Technical Assistance Program (1949), the US Point 4 program (1949), and the British Colombo plan (1950). Point 4 was an attempt to transfer the experience gained from the Marshall Plan to the less developed countries. The tasks ahead were much more extensive than in Europe. The means were much smaller. The Colombo plan provided modest assistance from the wealthier Commonwealth countries (Britain, Canada, Australia, and New Zealand) to the new nations in Asia. After the United States joined the Colombo plan, Asian countries outside the Commonwealth were also included.

The World Bank was not truly a world bank, as its efforts were long concentrated on conditions in the industrial nations. All in all, the Bank granted loans to the developing countries amounting to only 583 million dollars up to 30 July 1952.

The developing countries played a most modest role in terms of international trade policy as well. The charter for the International Trade Organization (ITO) left some room for their interests, but this organization did not materialize. Instead, GATT was established, placing virtually sole emphasis on the needs of the industrialized countries. For that reason, many of the new nations chose not to join GATT.

The industrial countries were eager to trade with the developing countries but did not make any serious attempts to adapt the international system of free trade to their special situation. The developing countries, for their part, were few and weak, and their policies were poorly coordinated. The Depression of the 1930s and developments during the Second World War had stimulated a course of self-sufficiency in Latin America and in many of the colonial areas. This course was now maintained, emphasizing import substitution. The developing countries themselves were to produce many of the industrial goods they had imported previously. To some extent, this policy succeeded. Industrial growth was substantial in several areas.

1955–1964

During the course of the 1950s, changes could be observed in the attitudes of the industrialized nations. The amounts spent on development assistance were stepped up. World Bank loans to the new nations increased. New loan institutions were created: in 1956 the International Finance Corporation, then four years later the even more important International Development Association, which granted cheap, long-term loans to countries in the Third World. Bilateral programs were increased considerably. In the United States, total development assistance increased from 2.0 billion dollars in 1956 to 3.7 billion in 1963. In Britain and France the corresponding figures showed an increase from 205 to 414 million dollars and from 608 to 863 million dollars, respectively.

The change of attitude in the industrial nations arose from at least three considerations. One factor was the many new nations that acted as a pressure group for increased assistance. International organizations were gradually dominated by these countries, and the established powers considered remaining on good terms with them essential. By 1959, the United Nations consisted of 122 member nations, among them 87 Third World nations.

A second important factor was the optimism that prevailed regarding the possibilities of initiating economic growth in the developing countries. Many economists felt that if only a specified investment level was reached, the developing countries could 'take off' and create a self-generating growth. The clearest expression of this growth optimism was W. W. Rostow's book, *The Stages of Economic Growth*, published in 1960. Growth in the developing countries would increase their purchasing power, which in turn would have favorable effects on world trade and the industrial nations' own economies. This optimism was largely based on the course of development that had taken place in North America and in Western Europe, but it fell on fertile soil in the newly independent countries as well.

However, the most important factor, particularly for the US stance, was the increased Soviet interest in the new nations. After Stalin's death, the Kremlin began to pursue much more active policies than previously (see pp. 54–9). Assistance was granted, industrial projects initiated, political declarations of support issued. In the West, the impression spread that Asia and Africa would be the primary arena of the Cold War.

If the Western powers did not take care, the new nations could drift in the direction of the Soviet Union. Especially the United States had to recognize its responsibility, as the country was the leader of the 'free world' and was not compromised in the same way as the former colonial powers.

With regard to trade, the industrial nations concentrated nearly all their attention on trade among themselves. Growth in this trade was very rapid, particularly within Europe. Most of the new nations still pursued the policy of import substitution. The growth in trade among the industrial nations in particular contributed to a fall in the South's share of total world exports from 31.6 per cent in 1950 to 21.4 per cent in 1960.

Even so, new signals could be observed. Import substitution seemed to produce poorer results as time passed. Countries that concentrated on exports, such as Taiwan, South Korea, and Singapore, began to enjoy a considerably more rapid growth in the 1960s than those that concentrated on protecting domestic industry. Actually, Taiwan and South Korea had also experimented with import substitution in the 1950s.

The established trade organizations had shown little willingness to adapt to the developing countries' increasing demands for reforms. With the interest the Soviet Union now showed in the Third World, from 1956 onwards Moscow would promote the creation of an organization separate from GATT, of which the Soviet Union was not a member. The Western powers now tried in earnest to accommodate the wishes of the developing countries within GATT, but in 1964 they finally gave in to pressure for the establishment of a new organization, the United Nations Conference on Trade and Development (UNCTAD).

1964–1981

There was no increase in development assistance during the late 1960s and throughout the 1970s. Instead, the contributions of the large industrial nations tended to taper off. In absolute figures the amounts spent did increase, but because of the high rate of inflation there was an actual decline. This was most pronounced in the United States, where development assistance had represented 0.58 per cent of the national product in 1965 and 0.32 per cent in 1970. By 1981 this figure had dropped to 0.27 per cent. Britain's reduced presence in the Third World countries contributed to a stagnation in British development assistance as well. In 1981 it represented 0.39 per cent of the British national product. A substantial increase in assistance from some of the smaller OECD countries was not always sufficient to compensate for the drop in the larger countries' contributions. Moreover, an increasing share of the assistance was linked to purchases from the donor country, which further reduced its effect.

The Organization of Petroleum Exporting Countries' (OPEC) member countries with their newly acquired wealth contributed far more than the OECD countries if assistance is measured as a percentage of the gross national product. But even OPEC's contributions declined from the end of the 1970s. Moreover, their contributions went primarily from one Islamic country to another. Thus the geographical distribution of this assistance was limited.

The stagnation in development assistance was due to several factors. The slow rate of economic growth in the 1970s was undoubtedly one of them. In many industrialized countries development assistance became less popular. Much of the motivation disappeared when it became evident that economic assistance did not necessarily secure political support. Many began to doubt the economic efficacy of development assistance. There were numerous examples of support that appeared to have been futile. Assistance was only one of a great number of factors influencing development in the various countries.

In the developing countries there was increasing dissatisfaction with the terms of international trade. The first meeting of UNCTAD was held in Geneva in 1964. Here, and at subsequent conferences that were held every three to four years, the developing countries – the G 77 as they were now often called – presented a number of demands: the industrial countries should remove restrictions on imports from developing countries, but the developing countries should not be required to make similar concessions in return. The prices of commodities should be stabilized, loan opportunities improved dramatically, investments by multinational corporations regulated and all forms of economic assistance stepped up. OPEC's success in 1973–74 with rapidly rising oil prices (see pp. 276–7) both gave added force to the developing countries' demands and increased the need for trade and aid. The result was a call for a New International Economic Order (NIEO).

The many demands resulted in few significant changes for the developing countries. New programs of assistance were initiated for the very poorest developing countries. More funds were placed at the disposal of the World Bank and the International Monetary Fund. A commodity fund was established in 1980. The gap between demands and results was illustrated by the fact that whereas the developing countries had proposed a 6 billion dollar fund, the two programs that eventually materialized had 750 million dollars at their disposal. Several of the most important industrialized nations, led by the United States, refused to contribute to one of the programs. A target of 0.7 per cent of GNP in development assistance was established by the UN, but far from met by the developed countries. During the 1970s a system of trade preferences was established in principle, but there were so many and such complicated exceptions for numerous goods of particular interest to the developing countries that the system had little practical significance.

Somewhat better results were achieved through regional agreements, of which the most important were the two Lomé agreements of 1975 and 1979. In these, the members of the EC extended themselves further than most other industrial nations, but only in relation to the 46 – later 58 – developing countries in the Caribbean, Africa, and the Pacific that were associated with the EC. Even here the practical results were limited.

The developing countries' volume of trade expanded, but measured as a percentage of the growing international trade there was no increase during the 1960s and 1970s: their share remained largely constant. At least the decline from the 1950s had been halted. In spite of a growing pessimism with regard to development, a number of countries, particularly in Southeast Asia and among the OPEC members, continued to experience rapid economic growth.

1981–2000

The stagnation in development assistance continued during the 1980s and 1990s. The Reagan administration in the United States and the Thatcher government in Britain placed relatively little emphasis on development assistance, which dropped to 0.20 per cent and 0.30 per cent of the gross national product, respectively, in these two countries in 1988. In 1997 the percentages had declined further, to 0.08 and 0.26 respectively. In this, as in other areas, it was primarily market forces and private interests, such as the multi-national corporations, that were to solve the problems that prevailed. The decline in assistance from the OPEC countries also persisted throughout the 1980s. The level of development assistance was generally maintained in a number of the smaller OECD countries such as the Scandinavian countries and the Netherlands, and for a while it increased so much in Japan that from the end of the 1980s Japan became the largest contributor in absolute terms.

The Washington Consensus of neo-liberal development policies did, however, pro-duce limited economic results. The 1980s were a difficult decade for many developing countries. A combination of a lower growth rate in both developing and industrialized nations, widespread inflation, falling commodity prices, a high interest level, and a somewhat stronger dollar caused great problems, particularly in Latin America. Many developing countries had pursued highly expansive policies during the 1970s, as had many banks in the industrialized countries, and these countries had to accept stringent retrenchment measures in order to be granted new economic assistance from abroad. In 1989, Latin America's foreign debt exceeded 400 billion dollars. The influx of new capital was reduced and the capital outflow showed a substantial increase, resulting in a net capital drain from the developing countries. This was a new situation for the poor countries of the world.

Contrary to what might be expected, this situation did not result in increasingly radical stances, political extremism, and new demands on the part of the developing countries. In fact, in Latin America the debt burden coincided with a strong democra-tization wave in the 1980s, even though the sometimes stringent measures to reduce the level of debt were a strain on the new democracies. On the international level, the demands for a new economic order were more or less abandoned. Long-term reforms had to yield to immediate needs. The negotiating position of the industrialized coun-tries was too strong and that of the developing countries too weak. Moreover, there was a clear tendency for the solidarity among developing countries, which had never been particularly strong, to become further weakened. The interests of oil-producing coun-tries were contrary to the interests of those without oil; likewise, debtor nations had interests in conflict with those of creditor nations, and the interests of the newly indus-trialized countries (NIC) differed from those that were least developed.

There was little doubt that countries that concentrated on export-based growth dur-ing the 1980s and 1990s enjoyed the best economic results. The results were particularly impressive among what have been called Asia's 'four tigers' – South Korea, Taiwan, Singapore, and Hong Kong. Other countries, such as Thailand and Malaysia, also experienced rapid economic growth. The contrast between Latin America and East Asia was striking. For many years growth in Latin America ceased altogether, whereas it continued unabated in East Asia. Almost all of the countries of Latin America had large debts, but the only major debt problem in Asia was in the Philippines. The worst setbacks were in Africa, the area that was already suffering the most.

East Asia's success undoubtedly contributed to undermining the earlier call for a new international economic order. The problem now facing the newly industrialized countries was that their relatively open access to the industrialized countries' markets, which had been such an important factor for their success, was threatened by various more protectionistic measures. The industrialized nations maintained that when developing countries advanced to a more prosperous level, it was reasonable that they should forfeit previous preferential measures.

To stimulate the export-led growth strategy, to combat Western protectionism, and to advance their interests in general, many developing countries now joined GATT. While only 17 developing countries were members of GATT by 1987, 29 new countries joined between 1987 and 1994. They also created many different regional customs unions or free trade areas, one example being Mercosur formed in 1991 by Brazil, Argentina, Uruguay, and Paraguay. Bolivia and Chile became associate members later. The main dividing lines at the GATT negotiations during the Uruguay Round were not primarily between industrialized countries and developing countries, but within these two groups, and particularly among the diverse industrialized countries.

In 1997–98, however, the great success of the East Asian model appeared to come to a very sudden halt. Most of the countries in the region encountered economic problems (see p. 265), but they recovered surprisingly fast. The rate of growth in China in particular was staggering.

The East Asian experience bolstered interest in free trade in nearly all developing countries. Thus they became much more active within GATT/WTO than they had been previously. They were dissatisfied that their interests had not been taken into consideration to a greater extent in the Uruguay Round. The developing countries were particularly irritated that the industrialized countries continued to employ strong protective measures in the agricultural sector when they so ardently advocated free trade in other areas.

2000–2016

The Washington Consensus had simply produced less than expected in the developing countries. Latin America experienced slow growth and major debt problems. East Asia had rapid growth, but the crisis of 1997–98 had still shaken confidence in the system. The world, certainly including the Third World, was simply too diverse to fit within a narrow, neo-liberal Western agenda.

The new framework, often called the Monterrey Consensus, stressed a collective effort by rich and poor countries together. The international system had to be changed, but so had national policies. In 2001 what was dubbed the Doha Development Round was initiated. Its objective was to continue the lowering of trade barriers around the world, but special attention was to be paid to the needs of the countries of the South. Finally, something was to be done to promote agricultural exports from the South; the huge agricultural subsidies of the North were to be reduced. In 2001 the UN member states adopted the Millennium Development Goals, eight ambitious goals to eradicate extreme poverty and hunger, achieve universal primary education, promote gender equality, etc. by the year 2015. No longer was it good enough simply to have growth; growth had to benefit the very poor. Development assistance was again to be substantially increased. The old UN target of 0.7 per cent of GNP was reaffirmed.

Although the amazing success of East Asia meant a continued emphasis on export-led growth, different models were in principle encouraged. Good governance had, however, to unite all the models. One could talk endlessly about all the many factors affecting growth, but without good governance, allegedly, very little was possible.

The diversity of the South was only increasing. East Asia was growing very rapidly. The economies of certain African countries were more or less collapsing. Some countries were actually achieving many of the Millennium Development Goals; a few were not on track to realize any. In the Doha Round there were major differences between developed and developing countries, but also within these two major groups. In 2008 the Round more or less ended, in part because of an agricultural dispute between the United States, on one side, and India and even China, on the other, clearly illustrating the new dimensions that were evolving in international affairs.

After some major promises at the G 8 meeting in Gleneagles in Scotland in 2005, optimism about development assistance, particularly debt retirement, again increased. Aid did reach the highest level ever, but still fell short of promises and expectations. In 2009 the United States gave by far the highest nominal amount, but still only 0.21 per cent of GNP; Japan gave 0.18, but assistance from Japan had now declined by 40 per cent compared to when it was the highest in the world; and Britain gave 0.52. The average for the industrial North was 0.31. Five countries gave around one per cent of GNP: Norway, Sweden, Denmark, the Netherlands, and Luxembourg. Some oil-rich Arab countries offered much more, but with the traditional strings attached. China, once a recipient, was now in the middle rank of donors, often emphasizing aid to countries with useful natural resources. In 2007–09 the world economic crisis threatened to reduce aid dramatically in many countries. Some researchers, even in poor states, argued that assistance was counter-productive. Yet, aid was now increasing again in part because of the strengthened involvement of many different private foundations and because there was an emphasis on combatting poverty since poverty could allegedly stimulate terrorism in 'failed' or 'fragile' states. Reducing terrorism was now often more important than building democracy, as could be seen in relations for instance with Ethiopia and Uganda.

In the history of development assistance there have been many different periods and many different fashions. When, however, we look at the concrete projects around the Third World there is reason to believe that the changes have been much smaller. The challenges in making a project work have been more or less the same; the transfer of learning has been more limited than one would have expected. Often aid projects worked the best where they were least needed, where development was in fact already taking place.

THE SOVIET UNION AND NORTH-SOUTH ISSUES

The Soviet Union and the Eastern bloc had an interesting position in the negotiations related to UNCTAD and a New International Economic Order. As mentioned, Moscow was one of the driving forces behind the UNCTAD process and supported the demands of the developing countries in principle almost without exception. As they were primarily aimed at the Western powers, all proposals for increased development assistance, remission of debt, integrated commodity funds, and reduced tariff restrictions could be supported. Particularly until the mid-1970s, most of the so-called 77 country group considered the Soviet Union an ally on these issues.

However, the negotiations would also represent a number of problems for Moscow. In the first place, the fact that the demands of the developing countries were a matter of reforms within a system dominated by the Western industrial nations had always given grounds for concern. In 1979, trade with the Soviet Union and Eastern Europe accounted for only 3.2 per cent of the exports from and 5.3 per cent of the imports to the countries of the Third World. The proposed reforms would not loosen these ties. On the contrary, they could tend to make them even closer. In the opinion of the Kremlin, a truly new world order could only be established by the developing countries breaking away from the capitalist nations. The New International Economic Order could thus at best be merely a first step on the long road to independence.

In the second place, the developing countries gradually became less willing to accept that the Soviet Union took the stance it did as to the demands they raised. Moscow could deny having any responsibility for the former colonies' poverty, but why shouldn't the Soviet Union, too, increase its development assistance, renegotiate debts, and import more? Soviet development assistance was modest. In 1982 it amounted to only about 20 per cent of US development assistance. Debts were renegotiated only on an individual basis with nations that had proved themselves deserving of it. Even though the volume of trade increased substantially as time passed, it remained small compared with Western trade with the developing countries.

The Soviet Union became increasingly skeptical about the intrinsic authority UNCTAD developed. The political and economic expectations to which the Soviet Union was subject had an unfortunate tendency to rise incessantly. The country's unwillingness to fulfill these expectations meant that the Soviet Union was considered an increasingly less interesting actor within UNCTAD and in the discussions concerning the New International Economic Order.

Under Gorbachev's leadership, the Soviet Union reduced its economic involvement abroad, concentrating on the economic problems within the Soviet Union itself. Ideologically the Soviet development model, once seen as so successful, had largely proved a failure, even before the collapse of the Soviet Union in 1991.

Russia's aid varied with its oil income. Russia also used energy prices and debt forgiveness to reward or punish neighbors.

ECONOMIC RELATIONS BETWEEN NORTH AND SOUTH, 1945-2016: THE LITERATURE

This bibliographic section also includes recommended further reading relevant to Chapter 14. A good starting point for the discussion about why Europe developed more rapidly than the rest of the world is found in E. L. Jones, *The European Miracle: Environments, Economies and Geopolitics in the History of Europe and Asia* (Cambridge, 1987). An anthology containing several important contributions is Andrew Mack, David Plant, and Ursula Doyle, *Imperialism, Intervention and Development* (London, 1979). A fascinating collection of essays is to be found in W. Arthur Lewis, *The Evolution of the International Economic Order* (Princeton, NJ, 1978). The present work is also considerably indebted to David K. Fieldhouse, *Colonialism 1870–1945: An Introduction* (London, 1981); C. Fred Bergsten, Thomas Horst, and Theodore H. Moran, *American Multinationals and American Interests* (Washington, DC, 1978); Malcolm Gillis, Dwight H. Perkins, Michael Roemer, and Donald R. Snodgrass, *Economics of Development* (New York, 1983); Gerald M. Meier, *Emerging from Poverty: The Economics that Really Matters* (Oxford, 1984); and John Ravenhill, *Global Political Economy* (Oxford, 2008).

A successful survey of relations between North and South over a long period of time is found in D. K. Fieldhouse, *The West and the Third World: Trade, Colonialism, Dependence and Development* (Oxford, 1999); see also Tony Smith, *The Pattern of Imperialism: The United States, Great Britain and the Late-Industrializing World since 1815* (Cambridge, 1981).

John Kenneth Galbraith, *The Nature of Mass Poverty* (Cambridge, 1979) provides an early key to understanding how difficult it is to generate economic growth. A more recent ambitious effort to do the same is David Landes, *The Wealth and Poverty of Nations* (New York, 1998).

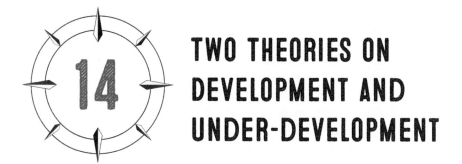

TWO THEORIES ON DEVELOPMENT AND UNDER-DEVELOPMENT

THE LIBERALIST AND THE STRUCTURALIST SCHOOLS

In this book we are interested in the relationship between states and blocs of states. That makes relations between North and South a major theme. A number of theories have been launched to explain these relations and the economic situation in the 'developing countries.' In this field there are nearly as many theories as there are authors. However, we can roughly identify two main schools, which in turn can be subdivided into numerous subgroups. While such diverse views would not normally be grouped together, the primary issue at hand here is economic relations between North and South, and on this subject the degree of concurrence is great enough to defend such a schematic division.

The dominant school in the West has long been the liberalist or traditional school. Despite the great diversity of views within this school, its adherents all believe that in principle rich and poor countries alike benefit from international trade. The second school is called the structuralist, under-development, or dependency school. Instead of accentuating mutual interests between rich and poor countries as the liberalists tend to do, this group emphasizes the conflicts between them.

Within the school of liberalists, we find relatively early development economists (Haberler), neo-classicists with great faith in the growth capacity of market economies (Bauer), stage theorists who are preoccupied with the developing countries' economic 'take-off' (Rostow), researchers who are primarily interested in the multinational corporations and who perceive positive effects from their presence in developing countries (Vernon), and the many who place greatest emphasis on how domestic conditions in the developing countries have impeded their growth, whether these conditions are problems within and among various economic sectors (Lewis), general political-economic weaknesses (Galbraith), or even deeper factors such as culture, social organization, as well as climate (Landes).

Extreme liberalists may be skeptical of government intervention in the economy, but most of them will actually favor not only intervention in the form of establishing the much-needed national infrastructure, but also moderate reform such as land reform, effective taxation, etc.

To the liberalists there is not necessarily anything wrong with a country specializing its production to a considerable degree. According to the principles of comparative advantage countries should indeed focus on the production of goods where they have a natural advantage compared to other countries. To a great extent, such specialization is a necessary condition for international trade. Trade may even be more important for the developing countries than for the industrialized countries, as their domestic markets are smaller. Many liberalists consider export-based growth the most effective in promoting development.

Moreover, contact with industrialized nations can supply capital, technology, and so on. The multinational corporations are often important instruments for transferring resources of this type. Thus, liberalists generally consider these corporations advantageous for the developing countries from an economic perspective.

As one such liberalist study of developments in seven countries (Argentina, Brazil, Mexico, India, Pakistan, the Philippines, and Taiwan) concludes:

> Emphasis should be placed on the development of exports so as to earn the foreign currency required to pay for essential imports, whether of machines, materials, or food, which cannot be economically produced at home. Administrative control should be replaced by better use of the price mechanism; and high cost internal production be replaced by a reorganized agriculture and industry, capable of gradually becoming competitive and assuming their place on the world market.

The liberalists deny that there are nearly absolute divisions between industrialized and developing countries. Industrialization began in Britain and spread from there. New countries have joined and will continue to join the ranks of the industrialized nations. Agriculture too can play an important role in the development process. If a nation has a fairly good resource base and pursues a reasonable economic policy, it will have the possibility of participating in economic prosperity.

In recent years there has been renewed emphasis on the importance of good governance and responsive political systems for economic growth. There would seem to be a close relationship between good governance and innovation, production and job creation. Countries that had been successful for a considerable period of time, such as Thailand and Turkey, could suddenly face domestic challenges that impacted negatively on growth. In Egypt both Mubarak and the Muslim Brotherhood ignored good governance while in Tunisia religious and secular forces were able to cooperate. The Chinese example illustrated that even dictatorships could provide elements of good economic governance. In many African countries, the rule of long-term personal dictatorships showed few signs of good governance and of economic growth.

On the structuralist side, in the 1950s leading leftist scholars such as Gunnar Myrdal, Raul Prebisch, and Hans Singer argued that, in Myrdal's words:

> Market forces will tend cumulatively to accentuate international inequalities, [and] a quite normal result of unhampered trade between two countries, of which one is industrial and the other underdeveloped, is the initiation of a cumulative process toward the impoverishment and stagnation of the latter.

During the 1960s and 1970s a number of writers continued to develop the analysis of 'disequalizing forces' in the international economy. Prominent representatives of the new school of structuralists were André Gunder Frank, Johan Galtung, Samir Amin, and

Walter Rodney. Their theories dominated in the developing countries for a long time, as well as enjoying support among leftist intellectuals in the North. Greatly simplified, this school maintains that the South became under-developed and has remained under-developed as a result of the development of the North.

According to this perspective, many different structures produced this result. The local economies in the colonies were adapted to and made dependent on the needs of the mother country rather than those of the colonies themselves. Thus, agriculture was oriented towards export rather than towards self-sufficiency. Exports were often concentrated on a single product. In return, the colonies imported processed goods from the mother country or from other industrialized countries. The terms of trade between raw materials and industrial goods were biased to the advantage of the latter category. Attempts to initiate industrialization were stopped because of the colonial powers' own interests in this area.

The structuralists maintain further that although with independence the colonies attained greater freedom of action, they were so bound to the international capitalist structure that development was still difficult, if not impossible. They were still producers of raw materials. The terms of trade were just as biased as before. Feeble attempts at industrialization did not improve conditions noticeably. Investments by multinational corporations tended to make things worse, as their net effect was to withdraw more capital from the developing countries than they invested in them.

Thus, the industrial countries continued to occupy the 'center,' while the developing countries remained on the 'periphery.' The power of the center also depended on the ties it established with local elites in the periphery. These elites profited by the international economic system, although the system as a whole worked to the advantage of the North.

How were the masses in the developing countries to be included in economic development? It would not be easy in any case. The industrial countries and the local elites were prepared to use economic, political, and military sanctions to defend their interests. The solution was to be found, according to the structuralists, in severing the links to the prevailing economic world order in some way or other. The individual country or groups of countries must direct their efforts towards increased self-sufficiency. The repressed majority in the developing countries must organize themselves and take control of their lives.

Most Marxists would be willing to accept the main features of the theory of under-development, although there are clear differences between them and other structuralists. For one thing, Marxists place greater importance on rivalry among the industrial countries, which in their opinion certainly do not always have coinciding interests. Marxists also emphasize their conviction that belonging to different classes produces different attitudes within both industrialized and developing nations. Moreover, Marx and even Lenin considered imperialism a progressive factor. At least in the short run it contributed to economic development in the colonies and was a necessary step on the path to socialism and communism.

DISCUSSION OF SOME ISSUES CENTRAL TO ECONOMIC DEVELOPMENT

The theories of the structuralists and the liberalists are far too comprehensive to be discussed in their full scope. Moreover, too little research has been carried out for anyone to give decisive answers to many of the most controversial questions. Further-more, much of the research has had, and to some extent still has, more the form of political pamphleteering than of empirical enquiry.

Much of the remainder of this chapter is relatively speculative compared with the rest of the book. Four central issues in the discussion of economic relations between North and South will be especially considered: to what extent contact with the industrialized nations has contributed or not contributed to economic growth in the developing countries; the role of multinational corporations; the relative prices of raw materials and processed goods, including the significance export agriculture has had in the developing countries; and the question of how dependent North and South are on one another.

The North's Development – The South's Under-development?

The structuralists have emphasized that only by breaking the ties to the capitalist world order can the developing countries achieve development. As an extension of this thesis, they tend to maintain that there were highly developed cultures in many of the areas that were subjugated by the Western colonial powers. They often argue more or less explicitly that if developments had been allowed to continue unimpeded, many countries in the Third World would probably have been industrialized today. They frequently maintain that the growth that has taken place has been in relatively isolated states and usually in periods when the developing countries had little contact with the international economy, such as allegedly during the world wars.

Our knowledge of conditions in Asia and particularly in Africa before colonialism is highly inadequate, allowing for both idealization and the painting of gloomy pictures. An important counterfactual element is the uncertainty that will always remain as to what would have happened if the colonial empires had not arisen.

It is not difficult to find instances in which the colonial powers exploited their colonies economically. They are manifold, and the further we move into the past, the more numerous they were. But the examples of development effects are also numerous. The colonial powers' policies do not seem to be a sufficient or even a primary factor in explaining the developing countries' lack of development. This is particularly true for countries that were not colonies at all. Non-colonies such as Ethiopia, Afghanistan, and, to a lesser extent, Thailand did not have a higher standard of living than their colonial neighbors. Traditional colonialism also seems to have limited validity as an explanation for conditions in Latin America, which became independent after the United States but before Canada.

Nor do the industrialized nations that have had colonies seem to be or even to have been wealthier than others. The United States, Canada, and Australia are all among the world's wealthiest nations. They were colonies themselves at one time, and they were relatively highly developed at that time as well. Likewise, for such countries as Switzerland and the Scandinavian ones it must be unreasonable to maintain that their especially high standard of living is based on exploitation of the developing countries.

The industrialization of India is one of the most controversial themes in this historical perspective. It is dubious to claim, as some structuralists do, that the country could have been an industrialized state today if developments had been allowed to continue along their original course. When growth had really started in Europe in the 1800s, India had fallen technically and economically far behind Europe. At the close of the century, however, a sizeable textile industry developed. Britain was undoubtedly interested in limiting this industry to promote its own. But in the first place it did not carry its policy particularly far. The Indians wanted to grant their industry special favors – that was the source of the controversy – and were allowed to do so from the 1920s onwards. London never tried to stop the process of industrialization, although it could probably have proceeded somewhat more rapidly with tariff barriers, at least in the short run. In the second place, the Indian textile industry grew even when it was subject to British competition.

The problem is more what the British did not do than what they did. Of course they could have done much more to promote economic growth. The responsibilities of government were quite limited during this period of history, especially under British liberalism. The government actually tended to be more active in India than in Britain itself. An era has to be understood in the light of the ideas of the time, not of the postwar period, when it became much more common for governments actively to pursue economic growth.

If we move from traditional colonialism to the more general economic ties between North and South, a comparison of Argentina and Australia is interesting. They both began to grow quickly around 1850; they sold basically the same products; in 1913 they each had a per capita income that was among the ten highest in the world. Thereafter, their paths parted. What may be the explanation? Structuralists have pointed to the strong British and later North American influence to explain why no extensive industrialization took place in Argentina. Comparatively, however, this explanation is problematic because the extent of foreign influence was probably even greater in Australia. Many different local factors were very likely more important than the international factors. The chronic fiscal mismanagement, the rigid social structure and the unstable but still rather undemocratic political culture in Argentina, which limited both the incentive and the possibilities for industrialization and further economic development, were probably of great importance. In the growth years up to 1930 the Argentine economy was also relatively open. The later growing protectionism, emphasizing import substitution, was not successful. Argentina rapidly slid down the economic ladder.

On the other hand, China and India are often compared to prove that sheltering the economy gives better results than openness. Economic growth was probably somewhat higher in the relatively closed China of the 1950s and 1960s, and China certainly did the most of these two countries to provide for the very poorest segments of its population. However, the points of departure were radically different in these two countries, and it is significant that the setbacks were great during China's most sheltered periods: the Great Leap Forward and the Cultural Revolution (see pp. 192–3). Nor has the Indian economy, with its emphasis on import substitution, traditionally been particularly open in an international perspective.

From the end of the 1970s the Chinese economy became steadily more open. This coincided with a nearly explosive economic growth in China. From 1977 to 1987 the production output per inhabitant was doubled, one of the most dramatic examples of growth in economic history, although it began from a relatively low base. Later growth rates have been equally impressive, and China's potential for the future seems great, although there are clearly problems in combining political control and economic liberalism as the Chinese do. Starting in the 1990s, India also experienced rapid economic progress with a more open economy, although not quite at the Chinese pace.

In the course of its long period of economic growth, China's poverty rate (less than one dollar a day) has fallen as low as 10 per cent of the population. In India the percentage was 34. China accounts for by far the largest share in the more than 400 million drop in the number of people living in poverty. In fact, excluding China, poverty long fell only marginally, particularly in sub-Saharan Africa, where it actually increased in the 1990s. The highest number of poor people was still in South Asia, although the fraction of the population that lives in extreme poverty is highest in sub-Saharan Africa.

Since 2000 poverty has been reduced in every region, now definitely including southern Africa. Primary education rates have been increased around the world. Health care has improved dramatically; child mortality has plummeted in many countries. Thus, though achievements varied much from country to country, considerable progress was made in fulfilling the Millennium Development Goals.

The international economic system has not proved to be as rigid as it may appear in the structuralists' theories. The annual increase in total production in the developing countries was 4.9 per cent from 1950 to 1960, 6.0 per cent from 1960 to 1973, 5.5 per cent from 1973 to 1980, and 2.9 per cent from 1980 to 1993. For all of these periods, the figures were actually higher than the corresponding aggregate figures for the Western industrial countries. Even in recent years, growth has been more rapid in the developing countries than in the Western industrial countries (with growth rates of 3.4 per cent and 2.0 per cent, respectively, during the period from 1990 to 2001 and 7.9 and 2.5 per cent for 2002–08). While Africa had very slow growth in the 1990s, after 2000 the continent as a whole has experienced 7 per cent annual growth. Most recently growth has been slower again.

Yet, the very low base of the developing countries has to be taken into account. So does the rapid population growth of most of these countries. Global income continues to be distributed quite unequally, and by some measures the inequality is increasing. The share of world income for the richest 20 per cent of the global population rose from 70 to 85 per cent from 1960 to 1991; the share of the poorest 20 per cent declined from 2.3 per cent to 1.4 per cent during the same period.

Production has increased much more rapidly in some developing countries than in others. Almost all the countries enjoying the strongest growth have also had close contact with the rest of the world. Several of the oil nations are among them, but they are such special cases that it may not be reasonable to place too much emphasis on developments there. Other countries experiencing strong growth have been South Korea (8.6 per cent annually from 1960 to 1970, 10.1 per cent annually from 1970 to 1980 and 9.1 per cent from 1980 to 1993); Taiwan (9.0 and 7.7 per cent for the first two of these periods, respectively) and, measured on a per capita basis from 1985 to 1995, Thailand (8.4 per cent); Indonesia (6.0 per cent), and Malaysia (5.7 per cent). In Malaysia in particular this growth has persisted. Africa was experiencing by far the most difficult situation, but even here growth successes could be found. The most striking example was Botswana (11.5 per cent from 1970 to 1980, 9.6 per cent from 1980 to 1993, and 4.7 per cent from 1995 to 2012). The country went from being a very poor country to becoming a middle income country. In recent years Mozambique has also experienced high growth rates, as have some of Africa's new oil states.

There are also examples of countries that have been relatively isolated from the international economy but that have experienced strong growth. The Soviet Union, especially during the period between the two world wars, is one such example. Several countries in Latin America had at least short-term benefits from the fact that their infant industries were spared from European competition, particularly during the First World War. Certain colonies that were fully or partially isolated from their mother country during the Second World War experienced an upswing. Finally, the highly developed Western industrial nations have not always favored free trade. The United States and Germany pursued protectionist policies vis-à-vis British competition during their build-up phases. Japan has long combined free trade with clearly protectionist elements. A similar policy has been pursued by the East Asian 'tiger' economies, with the exception of Hong Kong, which has consistently employed a liberal policy.

However, a great number of colonies experienced economic growth during the Second World War. Their very inclusion in the international economy, in the form of the enormous wartime demand, contributed strongly to this growth. W. Arthur Lewis has demonstrated that the growth cycles in developing countries and industrial countries have coincided closely. When the industrial countries experience growth, the developing countries enjoy growth. When there is a recession in the North, there is a recession in the South. The examples of the United States and Germany primarily illustrate that protectionism can be advantageous at least in the short term. Japan and the tigers of Asia have largely practiced a more long-term, systematic policy of having it both ways: export-based growth and restricted imports. The remarkable growth in Japan and South Korea in particular shows how a country can be transformed in the course of a few generations from a largely under-developed country to an advanced industrial nation. Something similar applies to the rapid growth in relatively open China since the late 1970s, although China still has far to go before it becomes an advanced industrial country.

The benefits of a long-term protectionist policy alone are considerably more questionable. Most observers today agree that import substitution has not yielded the desired results in the developing countries that have pursued this policy over an extended period. UNCTAD's first Secretary General, the moderate South American structuralist Raul Prebisch, himself emphasized the limitations of import substitution:

> The relative smallness of national markets, in addition to other adverse factors, has often made the cost of industries excessive and necessitated recourse to very high protective tariffs; the latter in turn has had unfavorable effects on the industrial structure because it has encouraged the establishment of small uneconomical plants, weakened the incentive to introduce modern techniques, and slowed down the rise in productivity.

On the other hand, the crisis that developed in the East Asian economies in 1997–98 appeared to question the success of the export-led model. The problems started in Thailand in the summer of 1997 and quickly spread to Indonesia and South Korea, and from there to most other countries in East Asia, although they were not all hit equally hard. (China and Japan were among the least affected, although Japan had been experiencing economic problems since 1992.) Their gross national products plummeted, their currencies depreciated deeply, and unemployment increased dramatically. A total crisis was only averted through the massive intervention of the IMF under American leadership. While economic growth had stimulated democratic reforms in many East Asian countries, the economic crisis now brought an end to the Suharto regime in Indonesia and strengthened democratic rule in Thailand.

However, international and national measures soon stimulated new growth, so that a number of countries had regained their former level by 1999–2000. Yet the crisis could be seen as reflecting deeper questions not only about the East Asian model, but about economic growth in general. This was particularly so as the crisis spread to Russia and began to affect even the Latin American countries. If too many other countries pursued the same export-led strategy, could that not lead to a situation where the exporters out-bid each other and the world market was overburdened? And, on perhaps the most profound level of all, what would happen to the world's environment if all poor countries tried to follow the East Asian model and, more dramatically, actually succeeded in reaching the levels of consumption of the industrialized countries?

The real estate and banking crisis that originated in the United States in 2007–08 soon developed into a global economic crisis and threatened to have serious consequences not only for the world economy, but also for international politics. This was clearly the most serious crisis since the Great Depression in the 1930s. A collapse in the American housing market revealed serious shortcomings in American and world finance and production. To a large extent this was a debt crisis among governments, corporations, and individuals. It may also have been an environmental crisis in the sense that there were indeed limits to the growth that could take place in the world, as the food and energy crises had indicated. The conviction of leading Western economists that they could forever control the growth cycle suddenly disappeared. Internationally coordinated counter-measures had only limited effect, at least initially. Most of the world became affected, Europe and Japan at least as much as the United States. Although China was able to maintain substantial growth, its growth rate fell significantly. The less developed countries were generally less affected. No one could tell what the political consequences would be, but surely debtors would suffer more than creditors. In the past such crises had speeded up the rise of some states and the fall of others. The economies of the world were definitely interconnected. So were economics and politics.

The Multinational Corporations

A corresponding line of reasoning can be applied to the role of the multinational corporations. Once more, there are many examples of them entering into unreasonable agreements, so unreasonable that they must be termed exploitation. When corporations pay little or no tax on huge profits over long periods of time, such as was long the case with the US copper industry in Chile, then that is exploitation. But sweeping generalizations concerning the role of multinational corporations cannot be made on the basis of a few such examples – nor a few to the contrary.

It is often impossible to determine what the alternative to multinational investments may be. The structuralists often take as their point of departure the assumption that the

Table 14.1 Key Indicators of Development

	Population	Gross National Income (GNI)		Life expectancy at birth	
			Gross domestic product per capita		Adult literacy rate % ages
	Millions 2010	$ per capita 2010	% growth 2009–10	Female Years 2009	15 and older 2009–10
Afghanistan	31	..	..	44	..
Albania	3	4,000	3.0	80	96
Algeria	35	4,460	1.5	74	73
Angola	19	3,960	−0.4	50	70
Argentina	41	8,450	8.1	79	98
Armenia	3	3,090	0.7	77	100
Australia	22	43,740	..	84	..
Austria	8	46,710	1.7	83	..
Azerbaijan	9	5,180	3.8	73	100
Bangladesh	164	640	4.4	68	56
Belarus	10	6,030	7.8	76	100
Belgium	11	45,420	1.4	84	..
Benin	9	750	−0.1	63	42
Bolivia	10	1,790	2.5	68	91
Bosnia and Herzegovina	4	4,790	1.0	78	98
Brazil	195	9,390	6.8	76	90
Bulgaria	8	6,240	0.5	77	98
Burkina Faso	16	550	5.7	55	29
Burundi	9	160	1.3	52	67
Cambodia	14	760	5.5	63	78
Cameroon	20	1,160	0.4	52	71
Canada	34	41,950	1.8	84	..
Central African Republic	5	460	1.4	49	55
Chad	12	600	1.6	50	34
Chile	17	9,940	4.2	82	99
China	1,338	4,260	9.7	75	94
Hong Kong SAR, China	7	32,900	6.4	86	..
Colombia	46	5,510	2.9	77	93
Congo, Dem. Rep.	68	180	4.4	49	67
Congo, Rep.	4	2,310	6.6	55	..
Costa Rica	5	6,580	2.1	82	96
Côte d'Ivoire	22	1,070	0.6	59	55

(Continued)

Table 14.1 (Continued)

	Population	Gross National Income (GNI)	Life expectancy at birth		
	Millions 2010	$ per capita 2010	Gross domestic product per capita % growth 2009–10	Female Years 2009	Adult literacy rate % ages 15 and older 2009–10
Croatia	4	13,760	−1.1	80	99
Czech Republic	11	17,870	1.9	80	..
Denmark	6	58,980	1.4	81	..
Dominican Republic	10	4,860	6.3	76	88
Ecuador	14	4,510	2.5	78	84
Egypt, Arab Rep.	84	2,340	3.3	72	66
El Salvador	6	3,360	0.5	76	64
Eritrea	5	340	−0.7	62	67
Ethiopia	85	380	7.3	57	30
Finland	5	47,170	2.7	83	..
France	65	42,390	1.0	85	..
Georgia	4	2,690	5.4	75	100
Germany	82	43,330	3.9	83	..
Ghana	24	1,240	4.4	58	67
Greece	11	27,240	−4.9	83	97
Guatemala	14	2,740	0.1	74	74
Guinea	10	380	−0.6	60	39
Haiti	10	650	−4.3	63	49
Honduras	8	1,880	0.6	75	84
Hungary	10	12,990	1.3	78	99
India	1,171	1,340	8.3	66	63
Indonesia	233	2,580	4.9	73	92
Iran, Islamic Rep.	74	4,530	..	73	85
Iraq	32	2,320	−1.7	72	78
Ireland	4	40,990	−1.1	82	..
Israel	8	27,340	2.8	84	..
Italy	61	35,090	0.7	84	99
Japan	127	42,150	5.3	86	..
Jordan	6	4,350	0.7	75	92
Kazakhstan	16	7,440	4.4	74	100
Kenya	41	780	2.6	55	87
Korea, Rep.	49	19,890	5.9	84	..
Kyrgyz Republic	5	880	−2.2	72	99
Lao PDR	6	1,010	6.5	67	73
Lebanon	4	9,020	6.2	74	90

	Population	Gross National Income (GNI)	Life expectancy at birth		
	Millions 2010	$ per capita 2010	Gross domestic product per capita % growth 2009–10	Female Years 2009	Adult literacy rate % ages 15 and older 2009–10
Liberia	4	190	1.7	60	59
Libya	7	12,020	..	77	89
Lithuania	3	11,400	2.0	79	100
Madagascar	20	440	−1.1	62	64
Malawi	15	330	3.8	55	74
Malaysia	28	7,900	5.4	77	92
Mali	15	600	1.4	50	26
Mauritania	3	1,060	2.7	59	57
Mexico	109	9,330	4.4	78	93
Moldova	4	1,810	7.0	72	98
Morocco	32	2,850	2.0	74	56
Mozambique	23	440	4.9	49	55
Myanmar	50	..	..	64	92
Nepal	30	490	2.7	68	59
Netherlands	17	49,720	1.2	63	..
New Zealand	4	29,050	1.2	62	..
Nicaragua	6	1,080	3.1	77	78
Niger	16	360	4.7	53	29
Nigeria	158	1,180	5.4	49	61
Norway	5	85,380	−0.7	83	..
Pakistan	173	1,050	2.1	67	56
Panama	4	6,990	5.8	79	94
Papua New Guinea	7	1,300	5.6	64	60
Paraguay	6	2,940	13.3	74	95
Peru	29	4,710	7.6	76	90
Philippines	94	2,050	5.8	74	95
Poland	38	12,420	3.7	80	100
Portugal	11	21,860	1.2	82	95
Romania	21	7,840	1.1	77	98
Russian Federation	142	9,910	4.1	75	100
Rwanda	10	540	4.6	52	71
Saudi Arabia	26	17,200	..	74	86
Senegal	13	1,050	1.5	57	50
Serbia	7	5,620	2.2	76	..

(Continued)

Table 14.1   (Continued)

	Population	Gross National Income (GNI)	Gross domestic product per capita	Life expectancy at birth	Adult literacy rate % ages 15 and older
	Millions 2010	$ per capita 2010	% growth 2009–10	Female Years 2009	2009–10
Sierra Leone	6	340	2.4	49	41
Singapore	5	40,920	11.1	84	95
Slovak Republic	5	16,220	0.3	79	..
Somalia	8	..	..	52	..
South Africa	50	6,100	1.5	53	89
Spain	46	31,650	–0.7	85	98
Sri Lanka	20	2,290	7.2	78	91
Sudan	44	1,270	1.9	60	70
Sweden	9	49,930	4.5	83	..
Switzerland	8	70,350	1.8	84	..
Syrian Arab Republic	22	2,640	0.7	76	84
Tajikistan	7	780	2.0	70	100
Tanzania	45	530	3.9	57	73
Thailand	68	4,210	7.2	72	94
Togo	7	440	0.9	65	57
Tunisia	11	4,070	2.7	77	78
Turkey	76	9,500	7.7	75	91
Turkmenistan	5	3,700	6.7	69	100
Uganda	34	490	1.8	54	73
Ukraine	46	3,010	4.8	75	100
United Arab Emirates	5	..	..	79	90
United Kingdom	62	38,540	0.6	82	..
United States	310	47,140	2.0	81	..
Uruguay	3	10,590	8.1	80	98
Uzbekistan	28	1,280	7.0	71	99
Venezuela, RB	29	11,590	–3.4	77	95
Vietnam	88	1,100	5.5	77	93
West Bank and Gaza	4	..	..	75	95
Yemen, Rep.	24	1,060	..	65	62
Zambia	13	1,070	5.9	47	71
Zimbabwe	13	460	8.0	46	92
World	6,055	9,097	3.0	71	84
Low income	817	510	3.6	59	61
Middle income	4,915	3,764	6.5	71	83

	Population	Gross National Income (GNI)	Life expectancy at birth		Adult literacy
			Gross domestic product per capita		Adult literacy rate % ages
	Millions 2010	$ per capita 2010	% growth 2009–10	Female Years 2009	15 and older 2009–10
Lower middle income	2,467	1,658	5.7	67	71
Upper middle income	2,449	5,884	7.0	75	93
Low and middle income	5,732	3,304	6.3	69	80
East Asia & Pacific	1,957	3,691	8.8	74	94
Europe & Central Asia	408	7,214	5.2	75	98
Latin America & the Caribbean	578	7,802	5.1	77	91
Middle East & North Africa	337	3,839	..	73	74
South Asia	1,591	1,213	7.3	66	61
Sub-Saharan Africa	862	1,165	2.3	54	62
High income	1,123	38,658	2.5	83	98

Source: World Development Report 2012.

alternative is government-owned businesses with the same efficiency as the foreign firms. Many liberalists go to the opposite extreme and assume that the alternative is no investment at all.

Empirical investigations seem to indicate that the multinational corporations normally have a positive effect on a country's national income and even on government revenue. However, it appears that their effect is more questionable with regard to the balance of payments. The corporations export much of their profits, whereas the original investments often originate in the local market. Moreover, they often obtain their production equipment and capital goods from abroad, so that the spill-over effect of such new industry is less than in developed economies.

It is misleading to consider the capital flows in and out of a country in a certain year in isolation as many structuralists do. For instance, when a company manages to take out more than it has contributed, an important reason may be the increase in value which has taken place in the meantime and which may also have expressed itself in terms of employment, taxes, etc.

Many multinational corporations have contributed to an uneven distribution of income because their employees have been relatively well paid in relation to the vast majority. Such investments can also result in a reduction in the number of jobs because new technology tends to require fewer workers than the old processes did. Here as elsewhere, the differences can be great from one country to another and from one sector to another.

The structuralists claim that the ties between multinational corporations and local elites are often so close that they make colonial control obsolete. Why send in troops when the local elite can do the job? Once more there are many examples of such coinciding interests. Many elites lack both the will and the capacity to control foreign firms. The number of corrupt and/or incompetent regimes in the South is substantial.

But governments of varying political persuasions have shown great ingenuity in terms of regulating the activities of such firms. A much discussed phenomenon in this connection is the so-called 'host country's learning curve.' Governments are willing to provide favorable conditions in order to attract a firm. When it has established itself and committed its activity, the time is ripe to impose stiffer conditions. When one country has struck out on this course, others will follow.

The oil companies (often considered the strongest of the strong among the multinationals) and their course of development may be instructive. From having controlled the entire process, from exploration and exploitation to distribution and sales, and from having paid merely symbolic taxes, in many countries they have now been reduced primarily to the role of distributors who pay large, increasing percentages of their profits in taxes.

Not only radical regimes have precipitated changes. A breakthrough was achieved in the oil sector when Aramco agreed to share the profits with Saudi Arabia on a fifty–fifty basis in 1950. Even in Chile, the Christian Democrat Eduardo Frei was in the process of nationalizing the North American copper companies before Allende took over in 1970. After an interval, conservative leaders have often continued where the radical leaders left off. In Iran, Mossadeq was deposed in 1953; the new Western-oriented government under the leadership of the Shah increased the country's share of the oil companies' profits from 68 per cent in 1954 to 80 per cent in 1970. In Venezuela, the dictator Jimenez and reform-minded elements such as Betancourt saw to it that the same share increased from 51 per cent in 1950 to 70 per cent in the 1960s.

The historian David Fieldhouse has shown in his analysis of the British–Dutch Unilever group's activities in Africa that strong governments have been able to influence a company's local policies to a great extent. Where this will or capacity was not to be found, the results naturally failed to appear. There has also been a clear tendency for governments to impose the condition that foreign capital cooperate with local capital. Before 1951, only 17 per cent of the US companies in the Third World were subject to such limitations. During the years 1971–75, 38 per cent of new US ventures abroad fell into this category. The corresponding figures for European firms were 15 and 49 per cent, respectively, and for Japanese firms 29 and 82 per cent. The attractiveness of multinational corporations even in leftist countries under certain conditions is best illustrated by the fact that in the course of the 1970s even most of the communist countries, led by the Soviet Union, began to show an interest in such investments. China would soon go much further yet to attract foreign investors. Now virtually all developing countries work hard to tempt investment from the North.

Raw Materials and Processed Goods

The relative prices of raw materials and processed goods have been another central issue in the debate between structuralists and liberalists. Is it true that the price trend has been unilaterally in disfavor of raw materials and thus the developing countries? Prebisch was among those who first and most strongly claimed that this was the case. In 1950 he published a study based on Britain's terms of trade during the period 1870–1936. Later, several similar investigations have been carried out. The conclusions of these later studies are not as unambiguous as those of Prebisch.

A number of methodological objections have been raised against Prebisch's study. He has largely ignored quality improvements and thus given a distorted impression of the increase in prices for processed goods. Transport costs have not been 'correctly' calculated. Even so, the most important result of these studies is that much seems to depend on what goods and what time periods are considered. The relationship between commodity prices and the prices of processed goods has often, but certainly not always, been to the advantage of the latter. Another element is the fact that fluctuations have normally been greatest for raw materials, with the obviously unfortunate consequences that entails. Overall, while in the early 1970s non-fuel commodity prices were high, in the 1980s and 1990s they were, in relative terms, low. After 2000 they increased again, until the collapse of 2007–09.

It should be borne in mind that developing countries do not solely export raw materials and industrial countries solely processed goods. In 1965, 16 per cent of exports from developing countries consisted of processed goods. By 1992 that figure had risen to 53 per cent. Many developed countries, such as Australia, New Zealand, and Denmark, have joined the ranks of the richest nations of the world precisely by exporting agricultural products. The United States long remained the world's largest exporter of raw materials.

The structuralists have claimed that the colonial powers placed sole priority on exports of agricultural products, and that this took place at the expense of production for the local market, to some extent at the expense of the local population's ability to survive. There is little doubt that exports of agricultural products were an important aspect of the colonial powers' policies. The controversy concerns primarily the effect of this policy on the colonies.

Again it is difficult to make a generally applicable decisive assessment. Local variation was considerable. India seems to illustrate the advantages of such a policy. Export agriculture was clearly the most dynamic. Exports paid for the import of other goods. Moreover, in many countries local sales were insufficient to satisfy basic needs. With rapid population growth, this would probably have become even more pronounced. Finally, for the most part agriculture for domestic use remained more important than agriculture for export. But it is a valid criticism of the colonial powers that they promoted export interests virtually everywhere, even in areas where there was little to be gained and perhaps more to be lost by such a policy, such as in Mali and Niger.

The Question of Dependence

It is one thing to claim that the industrialized nations' development has caused the developing countries' under-development and that the latter group is trapped in the existing structure. However, the structuralists have enjoyed greater support when they emphasize the fact that the developing countries are highly dependent on the industrialized countries and that this dependence can have a series of unfortunate consequences for them, both politically and economically.

Whereas the vast majority of the poor countries are dependent on income from a single or a few export goods, the import of these goods represents only a small fraction of the industrialized countries' imports. Several developing countries often compete with one another, with the consequences this entails for both price and general bargaining position. An economic recession in the center has great effects in the periphery, whereas a crisis in the periphery need not have great effects in the center. This imbalance in trade is accompanied by an even greater asymmetry with regard to investments.

Thus in 1982, trade with the Third World accounted for 25.2 per cent of the Western industrialized nations' exports and 27.2 per cent of their imports, while those same countries were the purchasers of 66.5 per cent of the exports from the South and the source of 61.2 per cent of their imports. Whereas 51.8 per cent of all trade by EC members was with other EC countries, the poor countries' trade with one another accounted for only 27.5 per cent of their total trade. The tendency in recent years has been for the South to become somewhat less dependent on the North, but the lack of balance is still striking.

Many developing countries became increasingly dependent even in relation to foodstuffs, especially grain. Whereas several of the large Asian countries became self-sufficient, the situation was extremely grave in Africa. Africa's imports of grain increased from an average of 1.2 million metric tons in 1960–63 to 8 million in 1980. But this could not prevent as many as 200 million people – 60 per cent of the population of Africa – from having a daily calorie intake that was less than what the UN considered the subsistence level. The situation was most acute in Ethiopia in 1983–85 and then (and also later) in Sudan, as well as in Somalia in 1992. The agricultural crisis had many causes, as did the debt crisis. The tragedies in Sudan and Somalia, and to some extent also in Ethiopia, were related to the wars going on there. More generally, the colonial countries had placed priority on exports; Africa was hit by serious droughts; and the various governments pursued policies that in many different ways favored urban and consumer interests over rural and producer interests, despite the fact that approximately 60 per cent of all Africans were still engaged in agriculture.

In certain areas, however, the dependency is primarily in the other direction. The North is most vulnerable in relation to the South in terms of certain strategic goods such as oil, chromium, copper, manganese, nickel, tin, phosphates, etc. In general terms, Japan is more dependent on importing such goods than Western Europe is, although Western Europe is in turn more vulnerable than the United States.

Population, Gender, Environment

The rapid increase in population was a key factor in international relations, affecting the political, economic, and social situation both inside countries and among countries. In 1850 the world's population had reached 1 billion, in 1930 it reached 2 billion, in 1975 4 billion, and in 2012 it reached 7 billion. The growth rate peaked at 2.2 per cent in 1963 and had declined to 1.1 per cent by 2011. Estimates of world population in 2050 vary from 7.5 to 10.5 billion; longer-term estimates are highly uncertain and differ from further growth to overall decline.

The rise of China and India was in part related to their population size, with India likely to overtake China in the next decade. Population growth in the United States is fairly balanced, based on a combination of a higher fertility rate and larger immigration than in most of Europe and in Japan where the population was already declining. Since 1970 life expectancy has increased dramatically almost all over the world. The exceptions are some countries in southern Africa (AIDS) and Russia (alcohol-related problems).

At birth, boys outnumber girls everywhere in the world by much the same proportion, 105 male children for 100 female children. Still, since women in all parts of the world live longer than men there are substantially more women than men in the developed countries. The situation is very different in most of Asia and North Africa. A total of more than 100 million women are 'missing' in these countries, primarily in India and China, due to the treatment they receive not only through abortions but also after they are born. In these countries the death rate for women is considerably higher than for men in all age groups until the late 30s.

Still, in historical perspective the treatment of women has improved considerably. In 1893 New Zealand became the first country to give women the right to vote at the national level; now only a few countries in the Middle East limit women's right to vote. Women's representation in politics is increasing dramatically, less so at the highest levels of business. Women's property rights have improved, as have earnings, although they are both still limited in many countries compared to those of men. Education for girls is improving in all regions of the world. Among developing countries, girls now outnumber boys in secondary schools in 45 countries and there are more young women than men in universities in 60 countries. However, female illiteracy is still a major problem in some sub-Saharan countries and in parts of South Asia.

The question of the world's population had major bearings on the world's environment. In 1798 the economist Thomas Malthus had predicted that continued population growth would exhaust the global food supply by the mid-nineteenth century. Others have later issued similar predictions. The reality is that so far food production has kept pace with population growth. Food production has increased dramatically. Starting in the 1950s the Green Revolution in agriculture transformed production. The easing of population growth should help in this context; on the other hand, rising living standards could create resource shortages.

Environmental problems were long considered local in nature. Often they were the result of the Industrial Revolution. Air pollution became a major concern. In 1952 thousands were killed in the Great London Smog. This led to the first Clean Air Act in the United Kingdom. In the United States much of the focus was on the protection of natural resources in the West. The National Park Service had been formed as early as 1916. The publication of Rachel Carson's *Silent Spring* in 1963 was important for the modern environmental movement with its attack on the indiscriminate use of pesticides and weed-killers. Environmental organizations, such as Greenpeace, were formed. In the 1970s many environmental reforms were passed in the United States and in other countries.

With growing awareness many of these local problems, such as the pollution of cities, lakes, and rivers, were alleviated especially in developed countries. Yet, it was becoming increasingly clear that the most important challenges were global in nature. They could only be addressed by the countries of the world joining forces. The first major environmental conference was held in Stockholm in 1972 and here the UN Environmental Program (UNEP) was created. In 1987 the World Commission on the Environment and Development published its report *Our Common Future* (the Brundtland report).

In 1988 the Intergovernmental Panel on Climate Change was founded. The panel consisted of scientists from all over the world who were increasingly concerned about global warming. Calculations had been made even in the late 1800s about the existence of global warming, but for decades the debate had raged about whether the planet was warming or cooling. In the 1980s a consensus started to develop: the planet was indeed warming and the consequences could be quite serious. The ice on the poles and elsewhere was melting, the deserts were spreading and the ocean was rising. The 'deniers' were slowly losing out in this big scientific debate.

In 1997 in Kyoto delegates from 159 countries formulated an agreement on binding targets for cutting the emission of six greenhouse gases. In practice, nearly all the measures were to be implemented by the developed countries, and hardly any by the developing countries. And the United States chose to remain on the sidelines. After 2000 the reports on global warming became increasingly concerned in tone. Stronger action was definitely needed on a worldwide basis. Yet, a succession of conferences produced few results of a binding nature. For the United States, China, India and several others economic growth was still the over-riding priority. 2016 was the warmest year ever recorded, virtually every month was the warmest of its kind since contemporary records began in 1880 and with the exception of 1998 all the ten warmest years have been after 2000.

Expectations for the environmental summit in Paris in November–December 2015 were relatively modest, but the actual outcome was better than many had feared. The agreed target among the more than 190 countries participating in Paris was to limit global warming to 1.5–2.0 degrees centigrade. Five-year review conferences were to be held in an effort to push the member countries to ever more ambitious targets. It was left up to the individual countries to reach the more specific targets they themselves had spelled out in advance. It was, however, far from clear that this would be sufficient to reach the 2.0 degree goal. The United States and even China were limiting their use of coal, which would help the global climate. The developing countries, with India in the lead, were insisting on the need for further economic growth and continued to ask for increased funds from the rich countries to undertake their respective national measures. India even foresaw a substantial increase in the use of coal. With Donald Trump coming to power, the United States again lost interest in the issue of global warming.

Thus, the development of new technology could not, at least not yet, prevent a slow, but steady rise in the global temperature. Indeed, it appears that the close link between economic growth and greenhouse gas emissions needs to be severed for human development to become truly sustainable.

PRODUCTION OF CRUDE OIL

Particularly with regard to oil, altered power relationships have had dramatic manifestations. The producers among the developing countries organized themselves in 1960 in the Organization of Petroleum Exporting Countries (OPEC). Oil consumption increased incessantly in the Western industrialized nations. The dependence on imports rose correspondingly as the industrialized nations' own production far from managed to keep up with consumption. The reversal was particularly great in the United States, which had long been self-sufficient, but which in 1977 imported almost half of the oil the country needed. That share has now gone up even further.

These long-term trends, combined with the solidarity the Middle East crisis of 1973 created among the Arab nations, provided the background for the major price rises OPEC was able to introduce in 1973–74, when prices were approximately quadrupled. In 1978–79, they were doubled once more. This time the trigger was the fall of the Shah and a sharp decline in Iran's oil exports.

The oil shocks had sweeping effects in the industrialized countries. Among other things, they contributed to increasing further the rate of inflation that had been accelerating for some years already. US oil imports, and the exports to the oil nations that these nations' large incomes now enabled them to afford, were an important explanation as to why US dependence on foreign countries also increased sharply. As late as 1970, exports and imports together accounted for only 8.7 per cent of the US gross national product. By 1992 this figure had risen to 21.9 per cent.

The oil nations' success in determining prices in 1973–74 created high expectations among other commodity producers as well. Producers' cartels were established or renewed for such products as copper, bauxite, iron ore, bananas, and coffee. The developing countries applied pressure for a new economic world order.

However, it soon became evident that no one could copy OPEC. The other cartels did not manage to maintain high prices, especially when the effects of the economic recession of 1974–75 appeared in the West in earnest. Disagreement among producers could be substantial. With regard to bauxite, for instance, Jamaica, Surinam, and Guyana reduced production in order to stimulate price rises, whereas Australia and Guinea increased their production. The demand for copper proved smaller than anticipated. Other cartels had additional difficulties because of their products' perishability and the possibilities of using substitutes in the industrialized countries.

During the 1980s, oil prices dropped off sharply from the peak they had reached in 1980. This was due to many factors: demand fell because of high prices and increased environmental awareness; solidarity within OPEC began to disintegrate; the supply of oil was greater than anticipated; oil production in countries outside OPEC increased significantly, etc.

The fluctuations in the price of oil made many industrialized countries feel the problems related to price dependency, but the industrial countries' dependence on oil was modest compared with some of the developing countries' virtually total dependence on the price of the single or few commodities they exported.

Oil prices have fluctuated dramatically. A recent low point was reached in September 1999 of 16 dollars per barrel. Then, the price reached 147 dollars per barrel in 2008 before falling to 40 dollars a barrel after the collapse of 2007–08. It was obvious that this had to do not only with supply and demand, but also with world events, the state of the world economy and, even, with psychology.

In 2012–13 the most dramatic new development was the production of shale oil and gas made possible by new drilling techniques. These new resources were developed first in the United States, but other countries were expected to follow quickly. It was

Table 14.2 Production of Crude Oil

	1950	1960	1970	1980	1988	1999	2005	% 2011
				1,000 tonnes				
World	538,470	1,090,680	2,350,700	3,081,900	3,030,800	3,452,200	3,867,100	100
Western Europe	1,980	15,300	21,900	121,400	198,000	329,400	331,500	–
United Kingdom	40	90	100	80,500	114,200	137,100	95,400	1.8
Norway				25,800	56,000	149,100	149,900	2.8
Middle East	86,050	260,705	688,100	927,400	739,300	1,052,000	1,186,600	–
Saudi Arabia	26,620	61,090	176,200	493,000	257,100	411,800	565,900	12.0
Iran	32,260	52,065	191,300	73,700	113,200	174,200	202,600	4.8
Iraq	6,650	47,480	76,900	130,200	127,700	125,500	99,700	3.8
Kuwait	17,290	81,860	137,500	71,500	66,800	99,300	119,800	3.0
Africa	2,550	14,720	299,900	301,701	262,500	355,000	441,100	–
Nigeria		800	52,900	102,300	67,600	99,900	122,200	2.6
Libya			159,800	88,400	50,600	68,000	75,800	2.6
Algeria	80	8,630	48,500	52,200	46,000	56,500	83,000	2.5
North America	289,080	411,560	609,000	565,800	545,900	475,000	477,400	–
USA	285,200	384,080	537,500	484,100	462,500	354,700	329,800	8.9
Canada	3,380	27,480	71,500	81,700	83,400	120,300	147,600	3.9
Latin America	102,500	194,555	272,700	298,500	341,000	506,200	532,700	–
Mexico	10,490	13,940	23,900	107,300	141,000	166,100	190,700	3.6
Venezuela	78,140	148,690	192,200	125,400	96,400	160,500	153,500	2.9
Far East and Australia	11,830	27,090	59,400	135,300	162,800	205,200	205,000	–
Indonesia	6,450	20,560	42,200	78,300	63,300	68,200	55,100	1.7
China	110	5,500	20,000	105,800	136,100	159,300	179,500	4.6
Soviet Union/Russia	37,500	148,000	353,000	603,000	624,000	370,000	458,700	11.0
OPEC share				1,357,600	1,030,500	1,409,900	1,588,200	44.0

Source: Kunnskapsforlaget, 2001, Store norske leksikon, 2009, CIA World Factbook, 2012.

predicted that as early as 2015 the United States would surpass Russia as the leading producer of natural gas; in 2017 the US would overtake Saudi Arabia as the biggest oil producer. In two decades the United States would be self-sufficient in meeting its energy needs, a most striking reversal of trends that had developed over several decades. This would also cut the emission of greenhouse gases in the US dramatically.

WHY POVERTY?

The debate on development has naturally not only dealt with relations between North and South. A number of other factors exert decisive influence on the situation in the South. In the first place it may be valid to ask what it is that actually requires explanation, and what is normal. Is it development or poverty? In a long-term historical perspective, rapid growth is the exception. Poverty and a lack of development have been the norm. This fact in itself is significant in order to understand the poverty of the developing countries.

In the second place, although breaking loose from centuries of accommodation to poverty has always been a difficult task, not least in terms of attitudes, the difficulties related to initiating economic development are in some ways greater now than previously. Population pressure is substantial; death rates have sunk dramatically while birth rates in some countries have remained high. The number of industrialized countries is already high; the world is more closely-knit than before; the entrance ticket to industrialization in the form of advanced technology and investments is often more expensive. Moreover, the results of industrialization are sometimes less significant than previously. In the 1970s it was estimated that Brazil needed only 8,000 workers to produce a million tons of steel. When Britain, as the first country in the world, reached that level of production, 370,000 workers were required.

On the other hand, developing countries today do have certain advantages. Most forms of technology are more readily available now than formerly. Insight into how economic growth is created and controlled is much greater than previously. Trade barriers have been reduced and assistance from abroad is available, in the form of grants, loans, and other resources. The balance between advantages and disadvantages can vary considerably from one sector to another and from one country to another.

In the third place, it is important to emphasize the diversity and the local variation in what is still often called the Third World. The term 'the Third World' is obviously more poorly suited in 2016 than previously, in part because this world is so complex and in part because of the collapse of the second world (the communist world). The economist John Kenneth Galbraith distinguished between three main models to explain why economic development has not taken place. They are extremely schematic, but these models may nevertheless establish a point of departure for a discussion of this local dimension.

First is the model from Africa south of the Sahara. Most of the barriers to economic growth are to be found here, including a majority of those that will be mentioned in connection with the other two models. However, Galbraith placed particular emphasis on the insufficient 'cultural base.' As late as in 1958, only about 10,000 Africans were studying at universities, more than half of them in Ghana and Nigeria. The situation in Congo was the most extreme, where only 16 Africans had completed a university education before independence was achieved in 1960. Although the new states on the whole placed greater emphasis on education than the colonial powers had done, the countries south of the Sahara are still in a weak position in this regard. It is difficult to imagine development without education, including everything from university studies to many different types of practical training.

A number of other problems are more or less unique to much of Africa. The soil is often poorly suited for agriculture; rainfall is uncertain in large parts of the continent; deserts and jungles complicate transportation; the basic infrastructure is lacking (power, roads, ports, etc.); diseases have flourished; illiteracy has deep roots; regional disputes and tribal conflicts are still highly significant. It is true that there were highly adapted cultures in parts of Africa before the colonial powers arrived. On the other hand, in this period sleeping sickness ruled out the use of draft animals and meant that important conditions for economic growth, such as the wheel and the plow, were not to be found south of the Sahara. A feature many African countries share with various other developing countries is the fact that their regimes are so weak, corrupt and incompetent that they represent a very significant obstacle to development in themselves; so, most definitely, do the many civil wars. Property rights are often not clear, regulations abound, and local or regional markets are small. In recent years HIV/AIDS has become a vast problem on many levels, including in economic terms, particularly in southern Africa.

The second model is the South-Asian model (which can also be applied to certain other countries, particularly in the Middle East). Here the primary obstacles seemed to be population growth and capital shortage. Population growth was so rapid that it often swallowed up any progress that was made. Capital shortage still makes investment difficult both within agriculture and more 'modern' sectors. The differences between the countries in this model and the African countries can be striking. A country such as India has an educational system that is clearly insufficient but it still has a surplus in several types of highly educated manpower, a surplus that is part of the background for the export of such personnel to industrialized countries such as the United States and Britain.

However, capital shortage and overpopulation are features that characterize other developing countries as well. Several countries in Africa have had considerably higher population growth than e.g. India, Pakistan, and Egypt. When such great attention was focused on precisely these two factors, the explanation was in part that it was difficult to identify other basic obstacles to development. However, a number of major and minor obstacles are to be found here as well: a hierarchic social structure; the skewed pattern of ownership, particularly in agriculture; a paralyzing bureaucracy; widespread corruption; relatively closed economies, etc.

The third main model is the Latin American model (which is appropriate for a few nations in other regions as well). These countries, too, enjoy a high level of education. To some extent they even have relatively substantial capital resources. On the other hand, the population pressure was great – often very great – although it has been substantially reduced in recent years. Nevertheless, this has not prevented some of the countries from achieving an impressive economic growth, measured in terms of gross national product. Thus Brazil and Mexico were among the growth successes of the 1960s and 1970s and they have also done well in recent decades, although they are now again experiencing problems.

Their growth was of a type that has figured prominently in structuralist arguments. Several structuralists practically define development in such a way that it cannot take place in a capitalist society. 'Development' is largely reserved for countries that emphasize self-sufficiency. Such a definition does not seem particularly fruitful. However, a different point they make is of greater interest in this context: the significance of the internal distribution of growth. Growth that does not benefit the vast majority of the population has obvious drawbacks, both morally and politically. Even from an economic point of view, growth is retarded by the majority being largely excluded from taking part in it. What is more, many of the countries in this group have not experienced much growth at all, in part because the purchasing power is limited to a small minority.

In few places is the social structure more inequitable than in many Latin American countries. Land distribution is one example. Most of the small peasants find few opportunities for increasing production. If they manage to do so, others often make off with the profit for their extra effort. In the rapidly growing cities, a rather extensive industrialization may be taking place, but the profit here is often shared among three main groups, in a complicated mixture of cooperation and competition: the multinational corporations, the government, and the local economic elite. Corruption is rampant. Society must also provide for other local elites: the military, the clergy, and the politicians. As there is seldom enough for everyone while making certain minimum concessions to the rest of the population, more and more money is printed. The result is that many of the highest inflation rates in the world used to be found here. They in themselves constitute an obstacle to further growth.

Latin America provides many examples of economic growth that has primarily benefited a minority, although in recent years social differences have been somewhat reduced because democratic governments have emphasized education and social reform. In Africa, Kenya and the Ivory Coast are countries that earlier experienced growth but inequitable distribution. But other countries, such as South Korea and Taiwan, have combined growth with an income distribution that is fairly even according to most estimates. It is more so even than in China, although the validity of comparing two such relatively small countries with the world's most populous nation may be questioned.

Industrialization and growth have taken place under various conditions. No single model has brought the industrialized nations to where they are today. Some scholars employ five main models: the English, the German, the French, the Japanese, and the Soviet model. A corresponding view applies to the developing countries. Even in the global economy of today, various paths lead to growth, just as various paths sustain poverty.

However, it appears as though the later industrialization has got underway, the more important the role of the state has been in the process. In most of the developing countries, too, strong government will probably be necessary to provide the required infrastructure (education, communications, etc.), to stimulate capital formation and moderate population growth, encourage, but also control foreign investment, implement tax and many other reforms, etc.

TWO THEORIES ON DEVELOPMENT AND UNDER-DEVELOPMENT: THE LITERATURE

For further reading suggestions on the topics discussed in this chapter, see the bibliographic section of Chapter 13 (p. 258).

GLOBALIZATION AND FRAGMENTATION

GLOBALIZATION

Globalization was certainly not a new phenomenon after 1945. Throughout the centuries cultures all around the world had established contact with other cultures. The world religions illustrated how this happened. Judaism, Christianity, and Islam all originated in the Middle East and they then spread to the most distant corners of the world. Pests and plagues illustrated the same basic development, as did economic transfers, in the form of technological inventions and economic cycles. The world of pre-1914 was in some ways more integrated than the world of today. Workers could travel much more freely from country to country, practically all around the world, than they can today. The Great Depression after 1929 clearly illustrates the economic interdependence of the world; as such it had great influence on the way in which policy-makers after 1945 thought about these issues.

What was new after 1945 was the rapid improvement in communications of all types. Soon we could fly to practically anywhere in the world, and many of us did travel to ever more distant destinations. On television we could take part in major events almost anywhere, as they happened. Only very gradually did exports and imports exceed the relative levels before the First World War. For centuries there had been multinational companies, such as the British, French, Dutch and even other East India Companies, although they had – as their names indicated – a firm national basis. The number of multinational companies exploded from 3,500 in 1960 to 40,000 in 1995. The increase in global currency turnover grew exponentially. Globalization helped bring rapid economic growth to most countries of the world. The emergence of first Japan, then China, and to some extent even India illustrated this – or rather their re-emergence, since China and India had a few centuries ago been leading economies and cultures. On the other hand, the housing and banking crisis that originated in the United States in 2007–08 and then turned into a global economic crisis showed the more problematic side of globalization.

Ideologies and religions of all possible kinds spread quickly; democratic or totalitarian, violent or non-violent. In the interwar years totalitarian regimes had been on the offensive. Democracy was found largely in North America and most of Western Europe. In 2000 almost 60 per cent of the world's population lived under democratic rule. The primary holdouts were China and large parts of the Muslim world. We could all cross borders as salesmen and tourists, but so could terrorists; goods and, to a lesser extent, labor could also travel relatively freely, but so could pollution.

After the creation of the railroads in the nineteenth century it was said that the small German states had lost their relevance since you could pass through some of them in half an hour. Germany simply had to be united. With modern aircraft we can fly across entire countries in that time. Although there has not developed one overall government, many global institutions have evolved. The United Nations became a stronger and geographically much more comprehensive organization than the interwar League of Nations. GATT has developed into the more effective World Trade Organization. A whole series of transnational nongovernmental organizations have become influential (Amnesty International, Greenpeace, the International Campaign to Ban Landmines, etc.). These applied pressures on governments around the world; they were even able to work out international treaties, such as a ban on landmines. Some observers even started referring to the development of a 'global society' or a 'global consciousness,' even the 'global village.'

Technological improvements are constantly being made which will improve communication across the world. This part of globalization may well be close to being inevitable and irreversible. Other parts of the process are clearly more politically driven. Thus, in the 1930s, under the influence of the Great Depression and totalitarian ideologies, globalization slowed down very considerably. Today, with rising economic problems, there are signs that the pace might be slowing again. The nation state is still very much alive today, as we see also in the EU.

REGIONALISM

The nation state was also being challenged by developments at the regional level. Sometimes the goal of global cooperation was too ambitious or impractical. Regional cooperation then became a relevant alternative. The European Union was the most successful and comprehensive of these regional institutions. The EU came to include a rapidly increasing number of new members; the integration spread to ever new areas. Similar, if not quite so strong institutions were evolving in many regions of the world.

The most significant among these other regional organizations were the Organization of African Unity (OAU, founded in 1963 and renamed the African Union in 2002) and the much older Organization of American States (OAS, founded in 1948). Asia was too big and complex to have one overall organization, but here, as on the other continents, a host of regional organizations developed. Among these were the Association of South-East Asian Nations (ASEAN, founded in 1967) and many different organizations around the world formed to promote freer trade among the members. With the end of the Cold War and also improved cooperation between North and South on economic issues (see pp. 254–5), new organizations encompassing both allied and nonaligned, rich and poor countries were established. Perhaps the most important of these was Asia-Pacific Economic Cooperation (APEC, founded in 1989).

To a large extent countries such as China and Russia were participating in the general international framework of the UN, the IMF, and the World Bank. As their position was becoming stronger they also took an increasing interest in developing an alternative international structure. The first summit of the BRIC countries (Brazil, Russia, India, and China) was held in 2009. With the inclusion of South Africa in 2010 the group became known as BRICS. The group aimed to strengthen the member countries against a Western American-dominated world and to promote political, commercial, and cultural cooperation among the member countries. Yet, there were obvious differences among the five, such as the border dispute between China and India, which limited the practical results of their cooperation. All of them were also strong believers in national self-determination, not really in supranational cooperation.

The Shanghai Cooperation Organisation was formed in 1996 and reformed in 2001. The members were China, Russia, Kazakhstan, Kyrgyzstan, Tajikistan, and Uzbekistan. In 2015 India and Pakistan joined the organization. The members had a common focus on the dangers of terrorism, separatism, and extremism and opposed Western attempts to intervene in other countries' internal affairs on the pretexts of humanitarianism or human rights. Cooperation between China and Russia was definitely increasing, but there was also a certain rivalry for influence between the two in the –stan countries. There have been a number of joint military exercises and many joint economic projects have been established.

FRAGMENTATION

If we look more closely, we see that that the world has in some respects become larger, and more fragmented than it used to be, rather than smaller and more globalized.

In 1945 the UN had 51 members, fewer than the number of countries in Africa today; now it has 193 members. Then there is the small number of states that do not want or are not financially able to join the United Nations. So, somewhat depending on the definition used, today there are at least 200 states. The fate of modern empires and other large territorial units illustrates the point. The colonial empires were amazingly quickly dissolved after the Second World War. In 1945 virtually no one, including most colonial leaders, had really any idea about the dramatic developments that would take place in the ensuing decades. What the British started in India spread with amazing speed to the distant colonies of France, the Netherlands, Belgium, and Portugal. The Soviet Union was anti-colonial, but this did not prevent it from having its own 'colonies.' In 1989 the Soviet empire in Central and Eastern Europe disappeared in the course of a half year, from the elections in Poland in June to the fall of Ceauşescu in Romania in December. In 1990–91 even the Soviet Union itself was dissolved into its 15 constituent republics.

In Europe we have seen not only the break-up of the Soviet Union; the not-so-large Yugoslavia broke into seven parts (so far) and Czechoslovakia broke into two. In Africa the creation of Eritrea represents the first break with the arbitrary borders so strongly protected also by the new rulers; once the dam breaks, no one can be sure where the water will flow. In China more than 90 per cent of the population are Han Chinese, but the status of Xinkian and Tibet (not to mention Taiwan) are still matters of contention. East Timor has broken away from Indonesia; Bangladesh has split from Pakistan and many questions still remain about Pakistan's future. India has been threatened by separatism ever since its creation. Even in liberal-democratic Canada, the Quebec question has remained a festering sore. And, most paradoxically, the old colonial powers that spread from their small territories to encompass huge swathes of land are now themselves threatened by division. Belgium is in great trouble. Spain has its rebellious provinces. In Britain, Scotland's independence is hotly discussed. France has its Corsica. The United States had its own civil war that almost broke the union apart. Today the US is virtually alone among the big powers in that virtually nobody questions its territorial unity.

Nobody knows how many 'nations' there are in the world since it is up to the various individuals to decide how they want to define their identity. It has been estimated that there are at least 3,500 'nations.' In only half of the world's states is there a single ethnic group that comprises at least 75 per cent of the population. If, eventually, most 'nations' are to have their own states, then the process has just started. In the early nineteenth century, many thought Belgium and Greece too small to become independent; in the early twentieth century many thought Iceland and Malta too small. Today there are at least 87 countries with a population of under 5 million; 35 have fewer than 500,000. Some of the most populous states of the world, such as China, India, Indonesia, Pakistan, Nigeria, are poorer than the microstates of Nauru, St Kitts and Nevis (which might split up), Antigua and Barbuda, Dominica, Seychelles, and Grenada.

WHY BOTH GLOBALIZATION AND FRAGMENTATION?

When we are to explain the simultaneous globalization and fragmentation of the world, it should be noted that to a large extent the two processes take place in different spheres. Although examples of political globalization and technological-economic fragmentation can certainly be found, it is still true that globalization is overwhelmingly a technological and economic process while the fragmentation is primarily political. It is often assumed that there is a close relationship between the two spheres – and of course there often is – but sometimes this is less true than we think.

Both Marxists and economic liberalists have argued that national boundaries would break down. Both Marx and Cobden were largely wrong, however. The outbreak of the First World War showed that the workers of Europe did not unite; nor did free trade necessarily lead to peace. To a large extent the Industrial Revolution, in fact, coincided with the rise of the nation state. As Ernest Gellner and others have argued, the Industrial Revolution in many respects created nationalism (improved communications brought the country together; the creation of a national school system did the same, as did the introduction of conscription).

In fact, in several ways technological-economic globalization probably stimulates political fragmentation. The stronger the globalization, the stronger the fragmentation. The explanations may be found at four different levels: political-psychological; ideological-cultural; technological; and economic.

The psychological-political explanation should be easily grasped by anyone who has done even the slightest traveling abroad. When we travel we find many interesting things to see, and we may even become great admirers of the country we visit. At the same time, however, we often discover that we become quite patriotic. Abroad we realize who we are and what our identity means to us. This can be noted not only among tourists travelling abroad, but also in so-called long distance nationalism (the Irish in the United States, Third World students in the West) and in the blossoming of all kinds of local cultures in the face of increased pressure from the outside.

Globalization frequently means that white, Christian, rich, Western culture is exported to other parts of the world, the implication often being that there must be something wrong with these local cultures. It should not be difficult to understand that this might cause a reaction in many circles. The entire process of decolonization might be seen in this perspective, although it certainly also meant turning Western ideals against the Westerners themselves. Modernization was frequently welcomed; Westernization was more controversial. The striking rise in religious fundamentalism, which we see in virtually all religions, may at least in part be a response to Western culture spreading throughout the world. In Western Europe religion is declining in significance; in most of the rest of the world religion is becoming increasingly important. Obviously we cannot talk about the challenge of globalization as the only explanation for fundamentalism and nationalism, but it may well be an important part of the explanation.

On the ideological-cultural level, it is true that ideologies cross borders much more easily than before. Thus, the rise of democracy in one part of the world often stimulates democracy in other parts as well. One of the ideologies that spread most easily, however, was nationalism. In the old days ethnic groups simply disappeared as separate cultures or they were amalgamated into larger groups. This is what happened to Angles, Saxons, Picts, Vandals, and Visigoths. This process continues today. Groups are still merged into other groups and languages disappear on a large scale. (There may still be about 6,000 languages in the world, although 2,500 of them may be in danger of disappearing.) Yet, for many large groups nationalism, not assimilation, has become the preferred alternative. In modern times, there have always been historians around who can help create the necessary 'invented traditions' or 'imagined communities,' that is, to inform their people and the rest of the world that the 'nation' in question has had a long and distinguished history.

Technologically, to take television as an example, we can now watch all kinds of events 'live' on a huge number of available channels. However, both indirectly and directly, technological advances stimulate not only globalization but also fragmentation. Often technology becomes so simple that even small groups can exploit it for their own purposes. Thus, the Welsh language in Wales and the Sami language in Norway are now doing much better than they did only a few decades ago. This probably has to do with a combination of the establishment of television and radio stations and educational reforms benefitting these languages. Somewhat more surprisingly, there is also a clear trend that in the 'global village' international news is losing out to national and local news. In a global world many would rather learn more about 'us' than about 'the others.' The Internet and the social media are another illustration of how technology can strengthen globalization and fragmentation at the same time. We can all communicate instantly with each other across the globe. This, however, also goes for the very small groups that could otherwise have faced extinction.

Finally, there is the economic level. Often globalization will have a negative effect; the groups so affected will work to modify or reverse the globalizing policies of the respective governments. This we see almost every day in many countries of the world. Brexit in Britain and the election of Donald Trump in the United States in 2016 provided dramatic examples of this phenomenon. The driving forces were the same: slower economic growth, immigration, and terrorism. There is also the effect, already referred to, whereby the economy has become so globalized that virtually any region, however small, can break out and form its own country without suffering significant negative economic consequences. Globalization has made the size of a country almost irrelevant for the success of its economy.

EAST, WEST, NORTH, SOUTH

The effects of both globalization, or perhaps in this case rather integration, and fragmentation can be noticed also in the four geographical units used in this book to analyze international relations after 1945. The four units are all very comprehensive and thus illustrate the effects of integration in global politics. The countries and peoples within each unit are obviously influenced by the fact that they belong to this unit. Still, flexibility exists. Countries can move from one unit to another. The countries within one unit can pursue quite different policies, despite the overall common framework.

One crucial phenomenon in this period was clearly the Cold War. In this struggle there were two definite blocs, East and West, with two clearly recognized leaders, the Soviet Union and the United States. The East, in the sense of the Soviet-led bloc, was the most strictly defined. It was made up of the Soviet Union itself and the countries in Central and Eastern Europe that it came to dominate after 1945. Then, certain countries in Asia – Outer Mongolia, China, North Korea, and North Vietnam – definitely associated themselves with this bloc; from the 1960s Cuba also did. Certain African countries developed close relations with Moscow. What had been 'Socialism in one country' (actually two since Soviet-inspired communism also prevailed in Outer Mongolia in the interwar years) became a worldwide ideology that dominated large parts of the world. Yet, movement was clearly taking place. Yugoslavia moved from the East to a leader of the nonaligned movement in the South; China split with the Soviet Union, as did Albania. North Korea developed its own course.

In 1989–91 the entire East quickly disintegrated. The Central and Eastern European countries that had been set free in that miraculous half-year from June to December 1989 quickly came to make it clear that they virtually all wanted to belong to the West. Within the next two decades most of them were indeed able to join both NATO and the EU. The Soviet Union itself collapsed into its 15 constituent republics; even some of them joined NATO and the EU. Communism was dropped in virtually all countries; in China its characteristics were very Chinese indeed.

Traditionally, 'the East' had of course referred to Asia, and particularly to East Asia. Just at the time the Communist East was losing its cohesion, even its meaning, the old East was beginning to re-emerge as the most vibrant part of the international economy. Based on their economic strength, first Japan and then China came to play increasingly important roles economically, and also politically and even militarily. Most other economies in the region were also booming. A new East was indeed rising. This transformation of 'the East' is one of the stories focused on in this book.

The West had existed as a concept for centuries, but then normally in opposition to the East of China, Japan and India. The West that arose after 1945 was something new. On the security side, but certainly not on the economic and the cultural side, the United States had returned to 'isolationism' after its brief intervention in the First World War. After 1945 it redefined its role. The Second World War changed the United States much more dramatically than did the First. The United States had been attacked; it had fought all over the world for almost four years as opposed to only a year and a half in Western Europe at the end of the First World War; it now had to take on basic occupational duties. It was also 'invited,' by the governments and to a large extent even by the peoples of Western Europe, to play a major role in the reconstruction and defense of Western Europe.

The United States cooperated closely with Western Europe. It also cooperated closely with Australia and New Zealand, Japan, South Korea, Taiwan and other countries in Asia, although it proved impossible to set up one coordinated defense organization like NATO in the Pacific and Asia. In the definition of the Cold War, although not more generally, these Asian countries clearly all belonged to the West. Defense organizations were built up all around the Soviet Union and its allies.

It was something new that the United States cooperated so closely with all these countries. It was also something new that the Western Europeans cooperated so closely with each other. European, even international, Great Power politics had for centuries focused on the rivalries between Great Britain, France, Germany/Prussia and Austria, with Russia in the wings. Now France and Germany went from rivals to partners in integration; Britain gradually realized that its future lay more in Europe than with the Empire/Commonwealth. Europe was becoming more integrated. And through a complicated set of alliances and organizations the West as a whole became more integrated. The OECD was probably the single organization that best expressed the membership of the West.

Yet, recent proposals, especially found in the United States, to create a league of democracies, where membership would supposedly coincide with the countries of the West, have not met with much support. In most potential member countries there is a strong interest in dialogue and cooperation with the countries that would be left out, whether Russia, China, or many of the countries of the South. Some democracies, such as India – the largest one – felt it belonged to a different group entirely.

For a long time the North to a large extent coincided with the West. The members of the West were with few exceptions also rich Northern countries. Some of these countries had had colonies; most had not. Some of the Asian countries that were part of the West were also perceived as part of the North (Japan, South Korea, Taiwan), although some that had alliance membership with the West but were culturally more ambivalent took part in the meetings of the South (for instance the Philippines, Thailand, Pakistan). The former group was also on the whole among the richest countries in Asia. With the dissolution of the Communist East in 1989–91 most of the Central and Eastern European countries became members of the West. While during the Cold War the communist countries were geographically positioned in the North, they had staunchly refused to be included in a Northern grouping against the South.

The South was by far the most complex of these four units. The countries of the South were indeed located in the South, although some very Southern countries, such as Australia and New Zealand, definitely belonged to the North. On the other hand, the South came to include some rather Northern countries, such as certain former parts of the Soviet Union.

The South was best defined by its political institutions, primarily the nonaligned movement and the Group of 77 at the UN. These units primarily contained the rapidly growing number of independent countries in Asia and Africa. In the first meeting of the nonaligned movement in 1955, all the independent countries of these two continents had taken part, with the exception of South Korea and Israel.

The greatest confusion concerned the Latin American countries. They were clearly Western in their cultural orientation; through the Rio pact they belonged to a security system dominated by the United States. Still, they had been colonies and clearly felt an association with other ex-colonies. Some of the Latin American countries, such as Argentina, had in the interwar years been among the richest countries of the world. After 1945 they had been on a downward slide, at least relatively. All approaches were represented in Latin America vis-à-vis the nonaligned movement. Some countries, such as Cuba, Colombia, and Venezuela, came to participate in this movement; others, such as Brazil and Mexico, were generally observers; some, primarily Argentina, stayed out. With the exception of Mexico, they were generally all members of the Group of 77 in the UN. This group coordinated the matters of the South in the UN and also acted to promote the economic interests of these countries in various multilateral contexts. Today the Group of 77 actually has 130 members, the vast majority of the UN's 192 member countries.

Sometimes the term Third World was used about the countries of the South. This concept came into being first in French in 1952 and then in English in 1961. It gained some prominence after the nonaligned summit in Bandung in 1955. The term had a clear reference to the 'third estate' (tiers état) of the French Revolution. There were definite resemblances: both groups represented the great masses, respectively in the world and in France, and they did not in any way have an influence that corresponded with their numbers. The concepts 'First World' and 'Second World' were thus not directly related to the 'Third World' and only appeared in 1966.

The First World was then the countries of the West; the Second World was the countries of the Communist East. With the collapse of the Second World the Third World has become a still frequently used, but somewhat awkward term. It is awkward also because some of the countries of the South have become among the richest countries in the world. This applied particularly to the rich oil-producing countries of the Middle and Near East and to Singapore. The few European countries that had been members of the institutions of the South dropped out. Malta and Cyprus left because they joined the EU. While Yugoslavia had been a key member of the nonaligned movement of the South, the republics that came out of its collapse decided to reorient themselves to the West and North.

East, West, North, South are all useful geographical and political expressions. Yet, all four of the units illustrate the complexities of the world and the limits of international organizations. Although the main categories were clear, it was frequently difficult to know exactly what countries belonged where. None of the categories developed any really effective overall organizations. The Communist East collapsed entirely; the new

East was quite diverse and key members China and Japan were traditional rivals; the North and particularly the West were in many ways more effectively organized, but any effort to establish a truly effective overall organization was bound to fail; the South was the most complex of all units. Since it was so complex it was also nearly impossible to achieve any truly operative organization.

SUPERPOWERS, STATES, AND INDIVIDUALS

The distance might seem huge from the level of the big units, East, West, North, South, and the superpowers down to the nation states, not to mention all the way down to the single individuals of the world. Yet, these individuals make up all these states, superpowers, and overall units. It is the sum of the actions of all the world's individuals that leads to economic, political, military, and cultural change at all these levels. From one day to the next we do not recognize the changes, but over time they lead to big units collapsing, like the Communist East did, to superpowers rising and falling, to some states and individuals getting richer and some getting poorer.

Empires have come and gone. Superpowers have come and gone. The Roman and Hapsburg empires have risen and fallen, so have the Chinese and Mogul empires, the British and the French empires. No country can forever remain the leading power of the world. This will be further discussed in the Conclusion.

The international political and economic systems certainly produced structures and policies that had an impact on virtually all the countries of the world. The leading powers of the world definitely influenced the policy choices of others, particularly the smaller states. Yet, there was no shortage of evidence that the world was constantly changing and that states and individuals could respond to these changes in many different ways.

Although the United States remained the leading power throughout the years analyzed in this book, the balance between its strengths and weaknesses changed. Other powers moved up and down in the hierarchy. In 1945, when the UN was established, the United States, the Soviet Union and Great Britain were the obvious leading powers. They were the three 'superpowers' when the term was first used towards the very end of the Second World War. China was included on the Security Council because the United States insisted it should be and because its potential was considerable. France was included because Britain pressed for its inclusion and because the world had not taken fully into account the nature of its collapse in 1940.

The Great Powers of today are different. Britain and France have much weaker claims than they had in 1945. Germany is now the leading economic power in Europe. The EU has become increasingly important. The Soviet Union has been replaced by Russia. China has solidified its claim to Great Power status. The obvious omissions on the Security Council are Japan, with the world's third largest economy; India, with its rising economy and status; and regional Great Powers such as Brazil, perhaps Mexico, South Africa and possibly Nigeria.

Still, globalization in many ways made the constant talk of the rise and fall of superpowers somewhat less relevant than it had been in the past. All countries, even the largest, were now finding that their freedom of action was circumscribed by global forces that were only very partially under their control. The economic crisis after 2007 illustrated the world's economic interdependence. The environmental interdependence was also becoming increasingly evident; so was the global village culturally.

This did not mean that the nation state was in any way disappearing. In Europe, where this view was most frequently expressed, the nation state was being modified by the EU, but even here it still remained strong. Even people in Europe identified primarily with their countries, not with the EU. National identities were still very strong, as was evidenced by Britain's decision in 2016 to leave the EU after more than 40 years of membership. The nation state is still the primary unit even in Europe's economic affairs. The national government's share of the gross national product remains very high, in some cases 40–50 per cent. In the United States neither Reagan nor George W. Bush was able to reduce that percentage, although it remained lower than in Western Europe. Even more surprisingly, 60–90 per cent of the production of goods and services in the most important industrial countries still goes to the home market.

Japan, China, South Korea, and several other countries in East Asia provide evidence of how quickly states can move up economically. The Soviet Union provides the grand example of how powers can collapse; Zimbabwe and even Argentina show how quickly a state can slide down the economic ladder. In 1960 South Korea and Ghana were at the same economic level; so were Indonesia and Nigeria. On a per capita basis, in 2013 South Korea was at the level of Greece and Portugal and twenty times richer than Ghana; Indonesia was more than three times richer than Nigeria.

Most countries behaved in fairly normal ways compared to the rest of the world, but those that insisted on going their own very separate ways certainly had the opportunity to do so. Poor Portugal kept its colonies longer than virtually anyone else; Cuba, although a neighbor of the world's most powerful country, could challenge the United States decade after decade; North Korea, bordering on China and Russia, pursued its own fiercely nationalistic course, more or less immune to advice from any outsider; South Africa defied the world's basic norms, until in 1990 it decided to change its course; Burma and Zimbabwe went their own very separate ways; Rwanda and Cambodia killed off large parts of their populations without the world doing anything of significance in response.

Why did the Soviet Union collapse? Why did the countries of East Asia enjoy more rapid growth than most other countries? And, when we reach the individual level where the various decisions are made that together constitute 'development,' what makes one person change whereas another remains in the traditional pattern? With regard to great power politics, development and poverty, as in most North–South and East–West issues, comprehensive explanations must always be supplemented by a knowledge of local conditions. Such conditions tend to modify nearly any generalization. Local diversity is difficult to grasp and virtually impossible to handle in any book surveying the world situation after 1945; it is easily neglected or even entirely forgotten in the stream of top-level international events. Yet, despite the growing significance of political, economic, and cultural globalization, the many different local factors will always remain crucial. In other words, we can all make a difference.

GLOBALIZATION AND FRAGMENTATION: THE LITERATURE

The literature on globalization and fragmentation is huge and rapidly growing. My own views on this are found in 'Why does globalization encourage fragmentation?' in *International Politics*, 2004: 41, pp. 265–76. I have found the following books particularly useful: John Baylis, Steve Smith and Patricia Owens (eds), *The Globalization of World Politics* (Oxford, 2008); John Ravenhill (ed.), *Global Political Economy* (Oxford, 2008); Ian Clark, *Globalization and Fragmentation: International relations in the twentieth century* (Oxford, 1997); and Benjamin B. Barber, *Jihad vs. McWorld* (New York, 1995). Regular reading through the years of *The Economist* has also provided me with much useful information about globalization and fragmentation.

CONCLUSION: THE FUTURE

Making predictions about the future is risky business. No sooner is the prediction made than it is proven wrong. Statements about the permanent nature of the Berlin Wall, the Cold War, and the Soviet Union come to mind. Those few who got it right often got the reasons wrong. Thus, the Soviet Union did not collapse either because of war with China (Andrej Amalrik) or because of the dissatisfaction of the Soviet Muslim republics (Hélène Carrère d'Encausse). Even more recently, we have discovered that there is no permanent economic boom. The downturns may still be considerable indeed. Hardly anybody predicted the Arab Spring of 2010–11. That the self-immolation of the fruit-seller Mohamed Bouazizi in Tunis in December 2010 would have the consequences it did was apparently foreseen by nobody. So academics, or other people for that matter, have time and again fallen rather short in predicting concrete events. The great weakness of historians and historically inclined political scientists may well be that while we are not good at making predictions, we are very quick to pronounce something historically inevitable once it has happened. Few things in history are really inevitable.

We may have fared slightly better in outlining broad historical processes than in predicting specific events. Thus, many came to understand that the Soviet Communist system was facing increasing difficulties. It was just beyond our imagination that the outcome of these difficulties would be the total collapse of a system, an ideology, and a country. Similarly, few had doubts about the problems in the Arab world. The Arab Human Development Report of 2002 had outlined all the shortcomings of these countries in great detail. The assumption was clearly that sooner or later they would have to reform or fall. Yet, the problems had been developing for decades. No one could say exactly when the moment of truth would come.

OLD AND NEW SUPERPOWERS

Predictions about the transfer of power have often proved to be wrong. We missed not only on the collapse of the Soviet Union, but the fall of the United States as the leading power has also been predicted time and again. Nikita Khrushchev was not in any way alone in his statements in the 1950s and 1960s that the Soviet Union would come to surpass the United States. The growth curves were clearly pointing in that direction.

Then there were all the predictions in the 1970s and 1980s about Japan becoming Number One. Again, it seemed so obvious. If you extended Japan's and America's economic curves into the future, at some point Japan would have the biggest economy. And once you had the biggest economy, the rest would presumably follow. Then at the turn of the millennium the European Union had its years in the sun. There was much to admire in the European experiment. The unification process was moving briskly ahead. EU membership was constantly being enlarged; the content was forever being deepened. And did not the EU already have a combined GDP that was larger than that of the United States? We all know what the situation is today: the Soviet Union has disappeared; Japan has been at a political and economic standstill for 20 years; the EU is in a prolonged political and economic crisis.

But now there is China. The fact that something has not happened in the past does not mean that it will not be happening in the future. China has much that is going in its favor. Since the reform policy was launched in 1978 the economic results have been spectacular. No major power in history has grown as rapidly over such a long period as has China. After the West was hit by economic recession in 2008 and has had slow (US) or no (gradually EU) growth after that, China coughed briefly at 6 per cent growth, and then resumed its growth not at the normal 10 per cent, but at roughly 7 per cent. Although there may be questions about Chinese statistics, there is no doubt about the overall direction. In recent years China's production first surpassed that of Germany, then that of Japan. China had the world's second largest GDP. From 1990 to today the ratio of China's economy as a share of the American one moved from 15:1 to 2:1. If China continues to grow at the rate it has grown over the last ten years and the United States does the same, China will surpass the United States some time between 2019 and 2022, if not even earlier. If the gross national product is estimated according to PPP (purchasing power parity), China has already surpassed the United States as estimated by recent statistics from the World Bank and IMF.

Economically China is already a global actor. It is the world's leading exporter and the second largest importer. It is investing more and more in ever new regions and countries of the world. China's foreign exchange reserves have risen from relatively insignificant to by far the largest of any country. Based on its strong economy, China is expanding also militarily. Its ability to project power is increasing, particularly in the East Asian region. Its policy in the South China Sea and in other waters near its coast is becoming increasingly ambitious. The ratio in defense spending between the United States and China has moved from 25:1 to 5:1 from 1990 to a few years ago or even to 3:1 today. With the cuts in American defense spending to reduce the overall debt, this ratio moved more quickly than it would otherwise have done. Yet, in 2011 China for the first time spent more on domestic security than on defense.

Naturally, the world is impressed with the Chinese model. Books and articles are written about the inevitable rise of China and how it will ultimately overtake the United States as the world's leading power. In other words, China will revert to the leading position it had for centuries. Some have called this 'the post-American world' or even the 'Beijing Consensus.'

Yet, there is reason for doubt. As David Shambaugh has recently argued in his *China Goes Global: The partial power,* 'China's global presence is more broad than deep while its international influence is considerably limited.' Not only are there the many predictions of the past about the Soviet Union, Japan, and the EU surpassing the United States. Time and again we have seen that growth curves could not be extended indefinitely into the future. The US share of world production declined steadily from almost 50 per cent in 1945 to 40 per cent in 1950, 30 per cent in 1960 and 25 per cent in 1975. The assumption was of course that the slide would continue. It did not. The US percentage of world production has held at close to 22 per cent. China and East Asia have clearly risen, but primarily at the expense of Western Europe, not the United States.

Soon, however, Asia is likely to produce more than Europe and America added together. If China's production were to surpass that of the United States around 2020 – which could well happen – this would be an historic event since the US has had the largest production since around 1870. China would still be a relatively poor country on a per capita basis since it has a population four times larger than that of the United States. Yet, economic power is not normally measured on a per capita basis. Nobody sees Oman, Luxembourg, and Norway as the economic leaders of the world. Still, the estimates about China's economic success are bound to be influenced by the personal wealth of its citizens.

While it is true that America's many military problems in Iraq and Afghanistan have shown the limits of its military power and the huge damage asymmetrical warfare can inflict on the United States, in terms of alliance politics and so much else, military power is still important. Again, although the rate of growth is higher in China than the US, with the long-term consequences that might have, the United States still spends three times more on defense than does China. While the United States has 11 carrier groups, China is working to master the intricacies of its first carrier, bought from Ukraine in 1998 and rehabilitated recently. The United States has allies all over the world. Contrary to the expectations of political science realists, NATO has not disappeared with the end of the Cold War. It now has 28 members and the United States is still the definite leader, although its role is much more complicated than during the Cold War. The rise of China has created renewed interest in much of East Asia and the Pacific in maintaining the United States as a counterweight, far away, but still projecting its power even here. Barack Obama certainly has his difficulties in the United States. Yet, even more important in this context, his standing as a world leader is still in a league of its own compared to that of the rather faceless Chinese leadership.

There is a reason that growth rates cannot be extended indefinitely. In China the supply of labor is beginning to be limited, wages are rising, and competition from new entry-level countries is becoming a challenge. The state sector is still huge and heavily subsidized with many problems; many banks are shaky; bubbles are beginning to develop. The high growth rates have already begun to decline.

There are, moreover, two even deeper reasons for doubt about the long-term preeminence of China. First, although China has also made tremendous progress in innovation and research and has become a leader even in modern sectors such as solar energy and high-speed trains, the question remains of whether it will have the ingenuity to become the leading power scientifically as well. Multinational companies account for over two-thirds of China's high-technology output and over 90 per cent of its high-technology exports. Science is the basis of much modern economic growth and so far China has definitely been lagging far behind the United States in this category. The Chinese educational system is still characterized by rote learning. Creativity is lacking.

The extensive Chinese copying of Western innovation and science can take the country only so far. It is no coincidence that at least until now China has not won a single Nobel prize in the sciences.

The Dalai Lama and dissident Liu Xiaobo have received the Nobel Peace Prize, but for this they have received absolutely no compliments from Chinese authorities. Instead they have both been severely criticized and punished in different ways by the government. The second and the ultimate question relates to China's political system. The rise of China has frequently been predicted, but something always happened in the past that blocked the process, whether under the Nationalists after 1911 or under the Communists after 1949. The twists and turns under the Great Leap Forward and the Cultural Revolution were disastrous. The most ambitious efforts to overtake the West ended in ruin.

In the last decades the political system has been remarkably stable with transfers of power from one generation to the next. Still: Can the domination of the CCP be maintained indefinitely? In history huge changes at the economic level are normally sooner or later accompanied by political changes. The Communist party has broadened its membership and is intent on having a dialogue with the new economic elites. As long as the economy continues to improve at a rapid pace, political loyalties may well be maintained. Pride in China's achievements has also strengthened a nationalism that benefits the party. Yet, in a longer-term perspective the party has a mixed record indeed. As many as 40 million people may have lost their lives during the recklessness of the Great Leap Forward. Tens of thousands of 'mass incidents' are taking place in China every year. The number is apparently increasing rapidly.

Human rights and various forms of democracy have been spreading throughout the world. In recent decades there appeared to be two geographical exceptions to this development, the Muslim world and China. Now democracy has made great strides in Turkey, although its status was again more uncertain in 2016, in Indonesia, and even in Malaysia as well. In 2011 the situation in the recalcitrant Arab world also appeared to be changing rapidly. The regimes in Tunisia, Egypt, Libya, and Yemen fell. Syria could well be next. Soon, however, the old regimes were fighting back and only in Tunisia did democracy survive. Can China hold out more or less on its own against this wave? China has been opening up in so many different ways. It is a much freer country now than some decades ago. Still, the party maintains its privilege of alone determining the answers to the most central political questions. Will it be able to continue doing so in the future? I have my doubts. In some way the Chinese people will probably insist that its voice be heard more strongly than today.

The United States has many things going for it. It has a strong economic basis. In recent decades the most innovative companies in the world have almost without exception been American (Microsoft, Apple, Google, Facebook). The United States has a growing population with a better balance between young and old than virtually any other major power, except India. America stood for and still stands for important economic and political values. Through immigration it is still able to draw in many of the most talented people from virtually the entire world, despite the restrictions imposed after September 11. Its elite universities remain the leaders of the world.

America's problems are, however, also substantial. They are largely twofold. First, the economy is in trouble. Growth has been slow or even non-existent in recent years.

Debts have been piling up. Unemployment is higher than the 5 per cent still reported in official statistics, since many have more or less given up looking for jobs. Inequality has risen sharply with the top percentages earning extraordinary amounts of money and paying limited taxes. Virtually all Americans take it for granted that social mobility always has been and still is higher in the US than anywhere else. This is definitely no longer true; several countries, particularly in northern Europe, have higher social mobility. Most Americans appear to have forgotten how important the government in Washington was for America's growth and welfare. For decades the United States lectured the world on the importance of balancing its budgets. Yet, it did not do so itself, except briefly at the end of the Clinton presidency. Under George W. Bush, taxes were substantially cut while expenses increased dramatically. The wars in Iraq and Afghanistan were expensive. Costly social programs were added, also under Bush, in the form of the drug prescription program. On top of all this came the huge expenses in fighting the economic recession in 2008–09. True, the debt has already been substantially reduced, particularly the yearly federal deficit (from more than 10 to around 3 per cent of GDP), but it still limits America's economic freedom of action.

Second, while most Americans are incredibly proud of their political system as such, the politicians have been performing at a disappointingly low level in recent years. The system of checks and balances meant that powers were shared. The President may be the most powerful individual in the world, but domestically his authority is clearly limited. Many hurdles have to be overcome before anything really significant can actually be accomplished. Traditionally reform came only in brief spurts, when the political powers were properly aligned. Obama's situation was difficult. Gridlock existed in the form of a center-liberal president facing Republicans who continued to try to do almost everything they can to oppose the President. The outcome was clearly detrimental also to the position of the United States in the world. When the President is unable to really lead the United States, he definitely cannot lead the world. The election of Donald Trump in 2016 could change this since the Republicans were able to maintain control also in the Senate and the House of Representatives. Yet, Donald Trump was quite controversial both in the United States and in the rest of the world and it remained to be seen what kind of leadership he would able to exert in the years ahead.

No power can expect to remain forever Number One in the world. This would definitely appear to be against the laws of history, to the extent that such laws exist. The United States may still be the world's only fully global power, but its influence is being checked by a whole series of regional powers. In Europe, the United States is doing less than it did during the Cold War. Despite its many problems, the EU is doing more. No one could write off a union that has a much larger population than that of the United States and a somewhat larger total production. Yet, after a referendum in 2016 Britain decided to leave the EU after more than 40 years of membership and the political situation was quite complex even in France and in several southern and eastern European EU countries. Japan too faces serious problems, but it does after all have the third largest economy in the world. In the Asian balance of power Japan should definitely not be overlooked. With Japan on America's side China will not be able to dominate entirely even in East Asia. Russia has been facing great problems, but its renewed military base and those of its natural resources that remain provided some basis for its international role.

Then, there are the new and rising powers. India is developing quickly. There are those who argue that with its democracy and creativity India may in the long run come to rival China. It has, however, a long distance to do. Its production is still only between one-third and one-fourth that of China; its infrastructure is far inferior to that of China. Brazil has clearly emerged as a regional leader and is eager to play a larger role, not only in the Western hemisphere but also in other parts of the world. Its growth has already slowed a great deal, however. In Africa, particularly in the southern part, South Africa is the crucial actor, despite its huge problems. Indonesia is emerging as an important country. So is Turkey. In short, it is becoming increasingly difficult for anyone, much less for a struggling United States, to be the world's predominant power in the way it used to be for decades.

In its report from December 2012 the US National Intelligence Council predicted about the period until 2030 that 'There will not be any hegemonic power. Power will shift to networks and coalitions in a multipolar world.' The direction is most likely correct, but it may well be that the report somewhat underestimates the position of the United States. The exploitation of shale oil and gas in the United States is a most important factor in this context. Thus, the International Energy Agency has recently predicted that by 2030 the United States will be 'all but self-sufficient' in meeting its energy needs. So, at least in the energy field the United States might go back to the dominant position it had in the 1950s and 1960s.

Yet, things happen every day that affect the position of the Great Powers, militarily, politically, economically, technologically, organizationally, and in terms of their soft power. The relative strengths of the leading powers never remain constant. The picture drawn up today may look terribly outdated within a decade or two, most definitely in 50 years.

WHAT WILL HAPPEN TO THE INTERNATIONAL SYSTEM?

Following Charles Kindleberger, some observers have argued that the international system requires a hegemon. Before the First World War Britain was that leader. After the Second World War the United States was. In the interwar years there was no leader. Britain no longer had the resources to lead, the US did not have the will. Today, while the United States is still the preeminent power, it is not able to lead in the way it did in earlier decades. Its position has been relatively weakened; the American president also faces greater leadership challenges at home.

Still, the wider international system that was established after the Second World War has in many ways remained remarkably stable. On the political side, the United Nations remains a key instrument for coordination and legitimation. After the end of the Cold War this role has actually increased in importance, despite the lack of reform of the Security Council. On the economic side, the International Monetary Fund and the World Bank, despite periods of drift and uncertainty, have taken on new life with the West's economic problems, particularly the international debt situation. On the trade side, GATT has been replaced by the stronger World Trade Organization. The current Doha Round has not been completed, at least in part a reflection of America's reduced role, but the WTO dispute mechanism has proved of considerable consequence. Yet, in 2016 the free trade ideology was definitely on the defensive both in the United States and in

Table 16.1

Per the International Monetary Fund (Estimates for 2016)

Rank	Country	GDP (millions of US$)
	World	75,212,696
1	United States	18,561,934
—	European Union	17,110,523
2	China	11,391,619
3	Japan	4,730,300
4	Germany	3,494,900
5	United Kingdom	2,649,893
6	France	2,488,280
7	India	2,250,990
8	Italy	1,852,500
9	Brazil	1,769,601
10	Canada	1,532,343
11	South Korea	1,404,380
12	Russia	1,267,750
13	Australia	1,256,640
14	Spain	1,252,160
15	Mexico	1,063,610

Per the World Bank (2015)

Rank	Country	GDP (millions of US$)
	World	73,891,889
1	United States	18,036,648
—	European Union	16,229,464
2	China	11,007,721
3	Japan	4,123,258
4	Germany	3,363,447
5	United Kingdom	2,858,003
6	France	2,418,836
7	India	2,095,398
8	Italy	1,821,497
9	Brazil	1,774,725
10	Canada	1,550,537
11	South Korea	1,377,873
12	Australia	1,339,539
13	Russia	1,326,015
14	Spain	1,199,057
15	Mexico	1,144,331

Per the United Nations (2015)

Rank	Country	GDP (millions of US$)
	World	74,196,404
1	European Union	18,518,430
—	United States	18,036,648
2	China	11,158,457
3	Japan	4,383,076
4	Germany	3,363,600
5	United Kingdom	2,858,003
6	France	2,418,945
7	India	2,116,239
8	Italy	1,821,580
9	Brazil	1,772,591
10	Canada	1,552,807
11	South Korea	1,377,873
12	Russia	1,326,016
13	Australia	1,230,859
14	Spain	1,192,955
15	Mexico	1,140,724

Europe. In fact, large groups now favored protectionism. A similar lack of leadership is seen in the international environmental field, although a significant new agreement was worked out in Paris in late 2015. Traditional regional organizations such as NATO, the EU, and the Organization of Economic Cooperation and Development (OECD) have been replicated in weaker form in many different regions of the world, such as in the Association of South-East Asian nations (ASEAN) from 1967, the African Union (AU) that in 2002 replaced the Organization of African Unity, Asia-Pacific Economic Cooperation (APEC) from 1989, and many others.

Prominent scholars have suggested that even China will be incorporated into this wider Western-dominated international system. To some extent this has already happened through China's membership in the UN, APEC, and in WTO. China's emphasis on rapid economic growth is bound to make it interested in rules and regulations that facilitate continued growth, although it is now showing stronger interest in building China-led banks and free trade areas. In political matters the Chinese record is even more ambiguous. On the whole Beijing insists on the importance of national sovereignty. No one should interfere in the internal affairs of China, or any other state for that matter. It should be added that several of the BRIC states (Brazil, Russia, India, China) have similarly insisted on the priority of national sovereignty, although not quite as unwaveringly as China. As we know, even the United States has refused to ratify some important international agreements, such as the Kyoto protocol and the International Criminal Court.

The alternative scenario is that the rise of China is bound to create conflict and possibly even war. Since Thucydides, political science realists have insisted that the rise of one state and the fall of another is bound to produce such an outcome. The story seems to have been repeated over and over again in European history. China's rise implies that it should be the preeminent power at least in its own East Asian region. China's objective is allegedly to 'win without fighting.' When this role is not favored either by most of the regional countries or by the United States, conflict is likely to follow, although this may not necessarily be in the form of war. Even political science liberals, who tend to favor more optimistic scenarios, will have to admit that the differences between China and the West in their approaches to democracy and human rights are bound to produce tension.

No one can be certain how the rise of China will work itself out. The rise of one state and the fall of another do not have to lead to war, as evidenced by the rise of the United States and the fall of the United Kingdom since the late nineteenth century. China does have an obvious interest in peace as a precondition for its continued economic rise. China has given up its revolutionary political ideology and has adjusted to the international regime in many economic ways. The United States and China are also much further apart geographically than were the various European powers whose wars provide so much of the basis for realism.

It is becoming increasingly clear that while China is taking a stronger interest in the Western-dominated international system, Beijing is also insisting that the system be reformed: China should be given stronger influence; human rights should not be part of the international regime, etc. The outcome seems to be that while there is broad support for the basic principles of international economic exchange, anything that more politically transcends the sovereignty of the nation state is much more difficult to agree on.

Yet, as long as Taiwan does not openly secede from China, war would seem to be a very unlikely outcome, although the situation particularly in the South and the East China Sea is increasingly worrisome. Through the huge American market for Chinese goods and China's investments in the United States the two countries, one the leading creditor, the other the biggest debtor, are bound together in a state of mutual dependence.

History does not really repeat itself. And if it does, it is virtually impossible to find out what, among the hundreds of possible parallels, it is that repeats itself. Normally one simply picks the example in history most convenient for making whatever point one wants to make. Historians repeat themselves. That is less remarkable and underlines the need to end the present book.

CONCLUSION: THE LITERATURE

The conclusion is in part based on my edited volume, *International Relations Since the End of the Cold War: New and Old Dimensions* (Oxford, 2013).

INDEX

Brezhnev, Leonid, 70, 71, 85, 88, 89, 94, 99, 103, 104, 139, 166, 192, 205
Brezhnev Doctrine, 105, 194, 199, 203, 220
BRIC states, 285, 301
Britain *see* United Kingdom
Brown, Archie, 102
Brown, Harold, 142
Brzezinski, Zbigniew, 95
Bulganin, Nikolaj, 55, 66
Bulgaria, 20tab, 22, 23, 24, 26, 184, 187, 197, 203, 204, 211
Burma, 42, 224, 240, 243, 292
Burundi, 115
Bush, George H.W., 102, 103–4, 146, 173
Bush, George W., 114, 117, 118, 120, 147–8, 149, 177, 180, 299
Byrnes, James, 17, 28, 127

Cambodia, 51, 83fig, 84, 91, 104, 105, 114, 201, 220, 243, 292
Cameron, David, 180
Camp David, 66, 95
Canada, 161, 232, 240, 250, 262, 286, 300fig
capitalism, 11, 13, 33, 66, 88
cartels, 277
Carter, Jimmy, 94–5, 96–7, 98, 103, 142, 143, 144, 171
Carter Doctrine, 96
Castro, Fidel, 60, 61, 75–6, 201, 246
Ceaușescu, Nikolae, 105, 197, 203, 204, 285
Central Intelligence Agency (CIA), 60
Central Treaty Organization (CENTO), 52, 77
Chad, 115
Chechnya, 110, 118, 209, 210
chemical weapons, 104, 151
Chernenko, Konstantin, 99, 103
Chiang Kai-shek, 22, 37, 38, 39, 40, 47–8, 49, 50, 55, 163, 189, 194
Chile, 76, 272
China
  Algeria, 58
  civil war, 21, 37–41, 43, 54
  Communist Party, 298
  defense, 225, 296, 297
  democracy, 221, 298
  economy, 111, 183, 190, 213, 214, 221–4, 226–7, 250, 255, 260, 263–4, 265, 266, 283, 292, 296–8, 300fig, 301–2
  India, 225
  Japan, 37, 43, 217, 218, 219
  Korean War, 47–9
  nuclear weapons, 68, 74, 148, 150, 190, 191, 193–4, 224, 225
  population, 223
  Soviet Union/Russia, 5, 21–2, 39–40, 43, 45, 73–4, 81, 183, 186, 188–95, 219–20, 222, 223, 285
  as superpower, 1–2, 297–8, 301–2
  terrorism, 118
  United States, 21, 38–9, 73–4, 217, 219, 220, 222–3, 224–5
  Vietnam, 82, 91
China Act (1948), 38
Chirac, Jacques, 176

Chou En-Lai, 194
Christian Democrats, 69, 157, 174, 176, 179
Churchill, Winston, 7, 16, 20tab, 22, 27, 33, 149, 154, 162, 232–3
CIA (Central Intelligence Agency), 60
Clay, Lucius, 19, 27
climate change, 117, 224, 276
Clinton, Bill, 110–11, 114, 116, 117, 147, 175–7, 222
Clinton, Hillary, 123, 225
Coal and Steel Community, 156, 158
Cold War
  (1945-1949) in Europe, 5, 9–35
  (1945-1962) global, 37–63
  (1975-1984) renewed tension, 87–100
  (1984-1990) end of, 101–8, 146
  Africa, 13
  Soviet Union, 11–12, 13–15, 21–6, 33–4
  United Kingdom, 12
  United States, 11–12, 13–14, 15–21, 30–3, 289
Colombo plan, 250
COMECON, 185, 188, 196, 197, 200, 201
COMINFORM, 185, 187
Commonwealth (British), 159, 233, 234
Commonwealth of Independent States, 109–10, 208
communism, 5, 11, 13, 18, 21, 26, 41, 42, 45, 48, 50, 52, 57, 66, 73, 81, 88, 160, 185, 202, 204, 205, 206, 208, 209, 288, 298
confederalism, 156, 157
Conference on Security and Cooperation in Europe (CSCE), 70, 102, 145, 146, 169
Congo, 58–9, 67, 89, 115, 120, 202, 238
  see also Zaire
containment policy, 101
Crimea, 109, 123, 210–11
Croatia, 112, 211
cruise missiles, 142, 144, 145
Cuba, 58, 60–1, 62, 65, 67, 68, 70, 75–6, 82, 87, 88, 90, 92, 105, 135–6, 139, 183–4, 194, 201, 246, 292
cultural base, 279–80
Cultural Revolution, 74, 192–3, 214, 263, 298
Cyprus, 170, 179, 290
Czech Republic, 179, 211
Czechoslovakia, 18, 19, 23, 24, 26, 30, 69, 76, 87, 109, 154, 184, 185, 187, 194, 197–9, 201, 203, 204–5, 211, 285

Darwin, John, 1
de Gaulle, Charles, 58, 73, 81, 102, 106, 137, 150, 153, 157, 158–9, 164, 237, 239
decolonization
  Belgium, 238
  colonial power attitudes, 238–40, 287
  France, 233, 235–7, 239
  health and education, 249
  independence movements, 240–4
  India, 41
  League of Nations, 231
  nonaligned states, 244–6
  Portugal, 233, 238
  rapidity of, 285
  Soviet Union, 230

Things to brush up on

- Marshall Plan
- Truman's Points (us?) 4
- Potsdam Conference
- Yalta Conference
- Atlantic Charter
- Truman Doctrine

WWII 1 Sep. 1939
—
2 Sep. 1945

Korean War 25 Jun. 1950
27 Jul. 1953

Vietnam war 1 Nov. 1955
30 Apr. 1975

Marshall Plan (European Recovery Program) - Economic assistance to Western Europe from the US following WWII

Four Point Program - Technical assistance program for developing countries announced during Harry Truman's inaugural speech Jan 20, 1949.

Potsdam Conference - last of the WWII meetings held by "The Big Three" heads of State (Truman, Churchill and Stalin) to discuss what would happen to Germany following the war in terms of economy, war criminals, land boundaries, and reparations. Also established a Council of Foreign Ministers and a central Allied Control Council. (July 17 - Aug 2, 1945)

Yalta Conference (Feb. 1945) — 2nd wartime meeting of Churchill, Stalin, and Roosevelt. Agreed to demand Germany's unconditional surrender & occupation zones

The Atlantic Charter (1941) - Joint charter released by Roosevelt & Churchill to provide broad statement of U.S. and U.K. war aims

Truman Doctrine - U.S. Foreign policy to counter Soviet expansion. Announced Mar. 12 1947 and developed July 12 1948. Would provide political, military, and economic assistance to nations under threat from authoritarian forces